First Edition

SKIER'S DIGEST

Edited by Larry Sheehan
former Editor
SkiWeek and Snow Country magazines

FOLLETT PUBLISH
Chicago/New York
T-0096

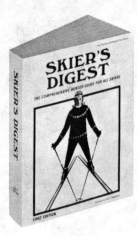

OUR COVER

When she's not schussing midwest slopes, our cover girl, Jutta Hogan, manages to find time to commute between Chicago and New York as a fashion model. Jutta's ski equipment, as pictured here, includes: Fischer Superglass skis, Marker bindings, Humanic Coverite boots, Allsop poles and Uvex goggles—all by Garcia.

Graphics Director, Richard M. Ference. Assistant Editor, Carolyn Meyer

Material published in this volume has been prepared in cooperation with Golf Digest, Inc., Norwalk, Connecticut. Right to reprint any material appearing in this volume without the written permission of the persons and/or organizations owning the original copyrights to the individual articles is prohibited.

Article starting on page 7 is reprinted from *How Did Sports Begin?* by R. Brasch. Copyright© 1970 by R. Brasch. Reprinted by permission of the publisher, David McKay Company, Inc. Article starting on page 16 is reprinted from the book, *Skier's Exercise Manual* through courtesy and by permission of the copyright owner, A. S. Barnes and Co., Inc., Cranbury, N. J. Article starting on page 26 is from *Let's Learn To Ski.* Copyright© 1969 by Gene and Barbara Tinker. Reprinted by permission of Walker & Co., New York.

Article starting on page 68 is reprinted from *Travel & Camera* Magazine with permission. Article starting on page 81 is reprinted through courtesy and by permission of the copyright owner, *Eastern Skiing* Magazine.

Article starting on page 90 is from the book, *The Fall Line* by John C. Tobin. Copyright© 1969 by John C. Tobin. Price $7.95. Published by Hawthorn Books, Inc., 70 Fifth Ave., N. Y. Article starting on page 110 is reprinted from *Let's Go II, The Student Guide To Adventure,* through courtesy and by permission of the copyright owner, Harvard Student Agencies, 993A Massachusetts Ave., Cambridge, Mass. 02138.

Article starting on page 116 is reprinted from *Ford Times* Magazine with permission of the copyright owner, Bill Thomas.

Article starting on page 121 is reprinted from the book *Ski With Toni Sailer* by permission of Cornerstone Library. Copyright© 1964 Wide World Photos, Inc.

Article starting on page 128 is reprinted by permission of the editors. From the April 7, 1970 issue of *Look* Magazine. Copyright© 1970 by Cowles Communications, Inc.

Article starting on page 135 is reprinted from *The Skier's Bible* by Morten Lund. Copyright© 1968 by Morten Lund. Reprinted by permission of Doubleday & Company, Inc.

Articles starting on page 198 and page 210 are reprinted by permission of *The New York Times.* Copyright© 1969 by The New York Times Company.

Article starting on page 216 is from the book, *The Kandahar Story* by Sir Arnold Lunn and is reprinted through courtesy of and by permission of the copyright owner, George Allen & Unwin Ltd., Great Britain.

Article starting on page 227 is from *The Apres Ski Book* by Eileen Holm Matthew and reprinted through courtesy and by permission of the copyright owner, A. S. Barnes & Co., Inc., Cranbury, N. J.

Article starting on page 286 is reprinted through courtesy and by permission of the copyright owner, *Snow* Magazine.

Article starting on page 292 is reprinted from *Skier's Gazette* through courtesy and by permission of the copyright owner, Bob Chamberlain.

Article starting on page 298 is reprinted from *Western Ski Time* Magazine through courtesy and by permission of the copyright owner, Midge Stapleton.

Library of Congress Catalog Card Number 72-118934   ISBN 0695-80096-5

Printed in U.S.A.

TABLE OF CONTENTS
by subject categories

INSTRUCTION

SKI THE AMERICAN WAY

by Paul Valar, Dr. Richard Voorhees and Edward Wyman. The 14 stages of skiing from the simple traverse to the short swing on the steep, as taught by the American Ski Technique. **31**

1. Straight Running
2. Snowplow
3. Snowplow Turns
4. Traversing
5. Stem Turns
6. Sideslipping
7. Christie Uphill
8. Snowplow Christie
9. Stem Christie
10. Advanced Stem Christie
11. Parallel Turns
12. Check in the Parallel Turn
13. Short Swing
14. Short Swing on the Steep

THE CHALLENGE OF ICE

by Stu Campbell. How to negotiate that frequent visitor to Eastern ski slopes. **81**

REACH THE TOP

by Toni Sailer. Perhaps the world's all-time greatest natural skier explains how intermediate skiers can look like experts. **121**

TIPS FROM GREAT INSTRUCTORS

Key pointers that directors of the country's leading ski schools give during their private lessons. **182**

Paul Valar: Shape Up With Shortswing Jump. *Roger Staub:* Use Your Hips For Control. *Neil Robinson:* Make the Hop to Skidded Turns. *Alf Engen:* Watch Shoulder Position in A Turn. *Bob Gratton:* Ski Moguls To Improve Technique. *Luggi Foeger:* Aim For Good Forward Balance. *Ernie Blake:* Check Position Of Inside Ski. *Egon & Penny Pitou Zimmermann:* Practice Check Hop Garland For Edge Control. *Fred Iselin:* 'Float' Through Your Turns. *Jack Nagel:* 'Talk' Yourself Into Parallel.

SKIING THE DEEP AND STEEP

by Bob Chamberlain. Tips on maneuvering your tips in deep, dense, delicious powder. **292**

GUIDES & ANALYSES

CONDITIONING COUNTDOWN FOR SKIERS

by Paul Davidson and Robert Fuller. Special exercises to put yourself in top skiing shape. **16**

HOW TO SKI MORE SAFELY

by Dr. James G. Garrick. Timely tips from an expert in the accident-analysis field. **22**

NINE RULES FOR BEING NICE

How much do you really know about etiquette on the slopes? **24**

GOING UP: HOW TO RIDE LIFTS

by Gene and Barbara Tinker. Proper procedures for mounting, riding and dismounting all basic forms of uphill transportation. **26**

SOMEDAY ALL THIS SNOW WILL BE MINE

A review of the opportunities for profit available in your favorite winter pastime. **62**

START YOUR CHILDREN RIGHT

by Ruedi Wyrsch. The famed children's instructor reveals his basic Do's and Don'ts. **66**

HOW TO TAKE HOME SKI MOVIES

Tips from one of the world's leading ski filmmakers—John Jay. **74**

COMMON SENSE GUIDE TO BUYING EQUIPMENT

by Morten Lund. Tips on what to look for in skis, boots, poles, bindings—and even underwear. **135**

SKIER'S DIGEST OF NEW EQUIPMENT

Catalog of the latest in skis, boots, poles, bindings, with prices and product descriptions. **143**

RAISE HIGH THE WINTER-HOME ROOFBEAMS, CARPENTER

by Marilyn Levin and Jess Maxwell. Key thoughts to have in mind when considering the second-home gambit. **286**

TRAVEL

HOW TO MASTER WINTER DRIVING

by Denise McCluggage. Half the challenge of skiing, sometimes, is getting there. **68**

HOW TO ENTERTAIN OTHER SKIERS

by Eileen Holm Matthew. What to serve for food or drink when you're partying. **227**

HOW TO ENTERTAIN YOURSELF

by Peter Miller. If you have a few extra bucks, here's how you'd spend them. **232**

FIFTY RECOMMENDED MOUNTAINS

Ski resorts where you are apt to find as much as you hoped. **235**

FOR STUDENTS

AMERICA'S SKI COLLEGES

by Carolyn Meyer. The country's 100 leading institutes of higher skiing, and the competitive and recreational ski programs offered at each. **102**

SKIING ON A STUDENT BUDGET: MIND OVER MONEY

by Kim Chaffee and Dave Lyman. A limited income requires taking greater care with the outgo. **107**

HOW TO SKI IN EUROPE FOR FEWER FRANCS, LIRA OR MARKS THAN YOU THINK
Special cost-cutting guide to the Alps prepared by Harvard Student Agencies. **110**

GENERAL FEATURES

SKIING'S SURPRISING FUTURE
by *Michael Strauss*. The decade of the '70s may be as exciting as the '60s. **12**

WHO WOULD WIN—ERIKSEN, SAILER OR KILLY?
by *John C. Tobin*. A provocative comparison of the racing styles of the three greatest figures in Alpine skiing. **90**

HANDS OFF MY SNURFER
A mongrelized surfboard is used in this latest rage on the slopes. **116**

COME TOUR WITH ME
Photo-essay tantalizingly tells of a typical ski-touring weekend. **160**

SKI TOURING IS A GROWING WINTER WORLD
by *Karin Eversen*. Tips on how to get it all together. **166**

I'D WALK A MILE FOR A...
by *Louise A. Colby*. At Tuckerman Ravine, you combine the solitude of touring with the thrills of downhill—if you're lucky. **169**

LET'S CALL IT A SKIBILL, OR A SKIBEN
No, let's call it a skibob, and explain how this trike-on-skis works. **173**

SKIING AMONG THE STARS
by *Walt Roessing*. How stars of stage, screen and television fare on the slopes. **176**

IT'S A BIRD, IT'S A PLANE, IT'S A...
by *Frank Elkins*. It's a ski jumper, engaging in what may well be the most exciting spectator sport winter can offer. **179**

HIGHLY SPIRITED SKIS
Still another craze on the slopes, it features skis peeled from wine barrels. **196**

STATUS REPORT ON SNOWMOBILES
by *Seth King*. The pros and cons of this wildly growing winter activity. **198**

NEW WINTER BREED: THE SNOWMOBILE RACER
by *John Sherman*. One view is that they are the old motorcycle packers grown up. **203**

ANYBODY FOR SNOWSHOEING?
by *Nelson Bryant*. What it is, and what it ain't. **210**

THE MAN-MADE BEASTS THAT BEAUTIFY THE HILLS
by *Michael Strauss*. Some intriguing information on snow-making machinery. **212**

SKIING AGAINST PAR

by Gloria Chadwick. How Nastar, the competitive program for the recreational skier, works. **224**

LOOK AT THEM LEAP

Show me a man who can *gelandesprung* with equanimity, and I'll show you a 5¢ cigar. **290**

HUMOR

HOW TO GET HONEST SNOW REPORTS

by Leonard Bernstein. An amusing—and effective—way to find out about snow conditions straight from the horse's mouth. **60**

THE BEST WAY TO FLUNK OUT OF SKI SCHOOL IN TWO DAYS

by Peter S. Prescott. **128**

WHAT AM I AND MY WATER BOTTLE DOING TONIGHT?

by Lora Heller. Amusing advice to the ski-lorn, straight from Women's Lip. **194**

CARTOONISTS ON SKIS **209**

HOW TO SHARE A SKI CABIN

Sample of the kind of rules that communal ski living leads to. **298**

HISTORY & ORGANIZATION

HOW IT ALL BEGAN

by Dr. R. Brasch. A scholar speculates on the origin and early development of skiing. **7**

WHAT SMOKEY THE BEAR DOES FOR WINTER

by Kip Hinton. The U.S. Forest Service—an important figure in the winter sports scene. **76**

UNDERSTANDING THE USSA

Inside the 100,000-member bastion of amateur skiing in America. **118**

WINTER OLYMPIC RECORDBOOK

The Gold Medalists, 1924-1968. **130**

WHAT THE SKI PATROL IS ALL ABOUT

by Harry G. Pollard. Head of this vital national service group speaks out on the role of the Ski Patrol. **132**

HOW TO BE AN EXPERT AT 13

The Little League of skiing is called the Buddy Werner League. **206**

ENGLISH ACCENT IN THE ALPS

by Sir Arnold Lunn. How the Anglo-Saxons gave skiing a French accent. **216**

IN HONOR OF GREATNESS

Word and picture sketches of the 107 members of the Ski Hall of Fame. **300**

HOW IT ALL BEGAN

*Skiing started, actually, early one morning back in the
Neolithic Age. The goddess Skadi awoke to find white powder on the ground
outside her cave. She pursed her lips, and then . . . .*

by Dr. R. Brasch

What made man first think of skis? No doubt, it was his wish to improve his foot grip on the snow. To achieve this he must have thought initially merely of enlarging the soles of his boots with some crude contraption made from material near at hand. A chance experience might then have led him to the next important discovery: that it was so much easier and swifter to glide along the snowy surface than to traverse it step by step. But to enable him to glide, his novel platform had to be lengthened and narrowed down. That is how, looking back, it can be imagined the earliest skis came into existence.

The word "ski" has a northern European linguistic root describing a splinter cut from a log. It became the Scandinavian term for a shoe and was pronounced *shee*.

All evidence shows that men have been skiing from before the dawn of history, in the northern parts of Europe and Asia. Skis, thought to be more than 5,000 years old—the oldest known pair in the world—are displayed in the Djurgarden Museum in Stockholm. Hundreds of ancient "snow shoes" have been dug up, most of them in Finnish and Swedish bogs. Illustrations of skiing were found in the form of rock engravings on the shores of the White Sea and Lake Onega in Russia. Oldest of all—dating back 4,000 years—is a stone carving discovered in a Norwegian cave.

The northern countries of Europe worshipped a goddess of skiing. She was Skadi who, while moving about on her snowshoes across vast stretches of snow and ice-covered land, was shooting wild creatures with her bow and arrows. Icicles were the jewelry that adorned her hair and her clothes. The god Ullr was her male counterpart. He excelled so much as a snow runner—on skis with turned-up tips—that none ever attempted to out-distance him, and his speed was so great that at times he became invisible. A giant in size, he was thought to travel across the snowfields with ships on his feet, though philologists still doubt whether this descriptive phrase really refers to skis and not to a shield. Believing in his protective care, many skiers used to carry with them a medal embossed with the god's image.

The Finnish national epic, *Kalevale* (compiled of numerous songs actually existing among the people), vividly recalls how one of its heroes chased the elk of the mountain ghost Hiisi, on skis:

> *On his back he bound his*
> *quiver,*
> *And his new bow on his*
> *shoulder,*
> *In his hands his pole grasped*
> *firmly,*
> *On the left shoe glided*
> *forward,*
> *And pushed onward with the*
> *right one . . .*
> *Chased the elk upon his snow*
> *shoes,*
> *Glided o'er the land and*
> *marshes,*
> *O'er the open wastes he*
> *glided.*
> *Fire was crackling from his*
> *snow shoes,*
> *From his staff's end smoke*
> *ascending . . .*
> *Once again he speeded*
> *onward,*
> *And they could no longer hear*
> *him,*
> *But the third time he rushed*
> *onward,*
> *Then he reached the elk of*
> *Hiisi.*

Greek authors described primitive skis that travelers had seen in foreign lands as wooden horses. This gave rise to the myth of the existence of people with horses' hoofs. Pliny, the famous Roman historian, quotes an ancient authority who had claimed that when accompanying Alexander the Great on his conquest of the East, he had met horse-footed men there. Similar reports stem from the first pre-Christian century from China. Turks also are known to have had skis in most far-off days.

Skis helped man in earliest times to move about freely and swiftly across the snow-clad or frozen ground. They served him in his search for food, in hunting reindeer and elk. It is not surprising that eventually skis were used in war. However, historical records in this regard go back only to the battle of Ilsen (near Oslo) in A.D. 1200, during which King Sverre of Sweden equipped his reconnaissance troops with skis. It is told how six years later, two skiers (referred to as "birch legs") who were loyal supporters of the king, prevented the capture of his two-year-old son by the enemy by carrying the child to safety across vast snow-covered mountain ranges. To recall in perpetuity their valiant and daring achievement, the "Birch Leg" Race was introduced, a sporting event demanding utmost exertion and agility on the part of the skiers, who have to negotiate most difficult and mountainous country over a distance of 35 miles.

During their rebellion against Danish rule in 1521, Swedish soldiers used skis to rescue an injured comrade from the battlefield. They improvised a stretcher, possibly the first of its kind, by *stretching* animal skins between two skis!

Certainly, skis became an established feature in the Scandinavian armies of the sixteenth and seventeenth centuries. Four thousand soldiers, mounted on skis, were employed in the campaign of 1610, ranging as far as Moscow.

It is strange that for a long time no one thought of making use of skiing for recreation and competition. Skiing as a sport was first practiced as late as the eighteenth century, and then only very spasmodically. Norwegians created the modern pastime.

The sport began as such as part of a military competition that also included a contest in the fast firing of rifles. This was held in Oslo (then known as Christiania) in 1767. Soldiers were invited to vie with each other in skiing down a steep slope "without riding or leaning on their sticks." Another feature anticipated the modern slalom. Those taking part had to descend "a moderately steep slope," but had to do so "between bushes without falling or breaking their skis."

An early chronicler tells of Austrian peasant skiers crossing the countryside on skis of a mere five-foot length: "No mountain is too steep, or too overgrown with big trees to prevent them skiing down it; they wind and twist about like a snake. But if the terrain is open they run straight, leaning back on their sticks, firmly and stiffly as if they had no limbs or joints in their bodies."

However, the real start of skiing as an independent competitive sport dates only from the late 1850s, in

Norway, when in the valley of Telemark farmers inaugurated an annual "meet."

The first ski jump took place at Huseby Hill, near Christiania, in 1879. A description, given by Crichton Somerville, recalls the occasion:

The Huseby slope was one which, only a few years previously, had been described as highly dangerous and impossible to descend when snow was fast and in good condition. The leaping competition proved most highly interesting, though in some respects quite comical. Every man, except the Telemarkings, carried a long, stout staff, and on that, so they thought, their lives depended. Starting from the summit, riding their poles, as in former times, like witches on broomsticks, checking the speed with frantic efforts, they slipped downwards to the dreaded platform or "hop," from which they were supposed to leap, but over which they but trickled, as it were, and landing softly beneath, finally reached the bottom somehow, thankful for their safe escape from the dreaded slide.

But then came the Telemark boys, erect at starting, pliant, confident, without anything but a fir branch in their hands, swooping downwards with ever-increasing impetus, until, with a bound, they were in the air, and seventy-six feet of space was cleared ere, with a resounding smack, their ski touched the slippery slope beneath and they shot onwards to the plain, where suddenly they turned, stopped in a smother of snow-dust and faced the hill they had just descended! That was a sight worth seeing, and one never to be forgotten, even if in after years such performances have been, in a way, totally eclipsed.

No individual has done more to foster the sport than Fridtjof Nansen, the Polar explorer. His feat of crossing the frozen wastes of Greenland on skis in 1888 and its description in a book he published subsequently (in 1890) thrilled the world and popularized skiing far and wide. He wrote: "Nothing hardens the muscles and makes the body so strong and elastic; nothing steels the willpower and freshens the mind as skiing. This is something that develops not only the body but also the soul . . . ."

The patronage of the Norwegian Royal Family gave further impetus to the sport and led, in 1892, to the inauguration of the world's most famous skiing "Derby"—an annual tournament at Holmenkollen, a site distinguished by its exquisite ski run. A small museum just below the ski jump-off treasures some 500 historic pairs of skis.

All through the decades, Norwegians spread the new and exciting sport into almost every country where it could be practiced. Small wonder that its best-known terms are in their language.

The *Christiania* (a swing used to turn or stop short) perpetuates the former name of Norway's capital city. The *telemark* recalls that region of Norway in which the earliest competitive ski games took place. The word denotes an expert maneuver in changing direction or stopping short.

Although, like many other ski features, the slalom was greatly developed by the British (its modern type is the invention of Arnold Lunn), its name is Scandinavian. It was adopted from the Telemarken dialect into the Norwegian tongue about 1890 and is a combination of two words: *sla*, meaning "a little slope" and *lom*, describing the track left by something that has been dragged.

Throughout the ages, skis have differed in many ways. The world's first skis were probably of bones from large animals. There are remnants of Neolithic, Bronze Age, and Iron Age skis. To begin with, the woods most favored were pine and spruce. The ski itself was cut from the outer curve of a tree.

It took a long time for skis to become standardized. In the eleventh century skiers considered that their speed would be greatly increased if the length of the two snow shoes was not the same. They thus made the "kicking ski," worn on the right foot, much shorter than the "running ski," on the left foot. However, this differentiation, with a few exceptions, was eventually abandoned.

From early times man's artistic instinct led him to decorate his skis. Carved ornaments on the upper surface of skis proved of great value to the modern researcher in dating their origin.

Generally the ski was strapped on with leather thongs. Primitive types had a footrest, hollowed out of the wood, with two wooden tongues holding the foot in position from either side. The thong itself was threaded through holes in those side pieces. Other skis employed a contraption held to the board by a thong fastened through holes bored vertically into the ski. Yet a third kind had those holes driven horizontally through the footrest, which, for the purpose, was raised.

The earliest skis were made smooth on the running surface. But here, too, necessity was the mother of invention. Soft snow got stuck to these "wooden runners," which greatly impeded the skier's progress. They, therefore, began to cover the boards with skin from the elk, reindeer, and seal. This gave the ski the necessary grip.

Toward the end of the Bronze Age, grooves (approximately two inches wide) were made in the snowshoe, and filled with hairy skin. This was then secured by wooden borders. When skiers realized that this arrangement greatly assisted them in keeping a straight course, many abandoned the inlaid skin but retained the raised borders.

Skiers learned the advantage of using a stick that, for many centuries, was simply a sturdy branch. Bone points were then fixed to its lower end and a hoop to its top. It was only in 1615 that mention (from northern Finland) was made of the use of two sticks. But there were skiers who never adopted any. They secured themselves by a rope that they tied to the point of each of the skis.

All this demonstrates the great variety of experimentation that took place and how experience continually taught skiers to improve their "wooden horses." In modern days, Germans and Americans introduced special alloys and plastics to take the place of the hard woods, such as ash and hickory, that, centuries earlier, had been substituted for spruce and pine.

Few people realize that Australia introduced skiing as a sport long before it was taken up by Switzerland and Austria. Its birthplace was Kiandra, in the Australian Alps, where the snowfields, in extent, equal those of Switzerland. It was started early in the 1680s by Norwegian gold miners, who, no doubt, had brought their skis with them from their homeland.

Waxes were homemade and known as *moko,* a typical Australian abbreviation derived from the expressive "more go." The word was adopted in other countries and is Australia's contribution, in the form of a word, to the world of skiing.

Photos accompanying article show scenes of early skiing in the European countries. Note, on this page, the gondolier-like one-pole technique.

SKIING'S
SURPRISING FUTURE
by Michael Strauss

The day of the bubble-dome-protected slope, the extinction of the chairlift, and the comfort of battery-warmed ski clothes is closer than you think. Remember, a dozen years ago snow-making machinery was still rather avant-garde . . .

The Revolution! Has it arrived?

Now that big corporations usually associated with ticker tapes are conglomerating their interest in the direction of ski areas, liquid state urethane elastomer is being injected into ski boots to provide the perfect fit and ski clothes are being made in such way-out colors as moss rose and funky silver green, the natural question that arises is—what next?

For me, it's almost a frightening question. Less than a decade ago when I was asked to write a tongue-in-cheek piece of what skiing in the future would be like, I took all kinds of liberties.

"Jet planes wil carry schussboomers from New York to, let's say Stowe, in seven minutes," I wrote. "Upon arrival over the Vermont resort, skiers will be deposited into auxiliary, self-propelled modules which will convey them from the jet plane to the top of Mount Mansfield. They will then schuss to the base on disposable, collapsible skis made of wafer-thin titanium magnesium alloys carried by the planes as a courtesy."

Sounds way out, doesn't it? Still within that year airborne

Opposite page: a startling view of Sandia Peak (N.M.) aerial tramway against the face of the moon.

paratroopers with skis were landing at Stowe. As a result of my reverie at that time, I also envisioned and wrote about the inevitability of taped television for ski school classes so that students could be shown their mistakes in the comfort of heated base lodges. I went into depth about the built-in improvements in ski equipment that automatically would make enthusiasts keep their confidence as well as their balance. As a clincher, I prophesied the day would soon come when making artificial snow would present no greater problem than making pudding. Remember, I thought I was kidding!

But today these dreams are realities. Taped television for ski schools is here to stay. Skis, custom-built to fit boots and vice-versa are now said to be the greatest aid for balance in skiing since the discovery of gravity while a snow-making machine, 10 times easier to handle and many times less expensive than the present compressor-powered models, is about to be marketed.

Of course the Revolution is here! But when hasn't it been? Skiing's aspects have been changing ever since Scandinavian soldiers, two centuries ago, began using one long ski and one short one to improve their maneuverability. Only a few decades ago, recreational skiers started substituting light parkas for heavy loggers' jackets. And only in recent years have wooden skis made way for light and sleekly metallic and fiberglass substitutes.

Naturally, the changes will keep changing in the years to come. In what direction? In every direction. Lifts, skis, bindings, boots, transportation, lodging and even ski poles seem certain to take on a newer "new look" within a decade. And, as for ski area management, it seems des-

tined to go Madison Avenue at many of the major ski centers.

One of the chief reasons for the probable transition in management is that huge corporations are slowly but surely moving into the ski business. Examples are Weyerhauser (Jay Peak), Ling Temco Vought (Steamboat Springs) and Playboy (Lake Geneva) among others. Eager to find avenues along which to conglomerate, the winter resort business is becoming increasingly attractive to ticker-tape tycoons. One of the magnets has been the increasing amount of money spent in recent years on recreation. Another is the manner in which values of land around ski areas seem to mushroom.

A big change seems certain in the lift phases. This business of sitting out a mile-long ride in an open chair while frigid winds are blasting right at you undoubtedly will become a memory at the major ski areas. In their places will come gondolas and more tramways. The trams will be capable of accommodating as many as 200 skiers in one uphill trip. And as for the gondolas, they probably will soon be handling eight or more skiers apiece. And, there's no reason not to expect that the new trams and gondolas will be heated. The old fashioned chair lift? It will either be relegated to the woodpile or remain at the smaller areas where freezing wind on the shorter rides is not too great an ordeal for skiers and where inexpensive lift tickets make retaining the chairs an economic necessity.

"In northern New England, the chairs at big areas probably will be gone with the wind," a veteran Vermont expert told me recently. "It is more taxing on those bone-chilling days for skiers to ride up than to ski down.

Many skiers, after being blown blue by the blasts, just call it quits. In gondolas and tramways, the problems are minimized."

"The big trend in the future will be to devise lifts capable of carrying many more people than they do now and at faster rates of speed," says Channing Murdock, the operator of Butternut Basin in the southern Berkshires of Massachusetts. "I think the monorail may become popular among ski people. It has the advantages of providing high capacity transportation and cars capable of accommodating scores at one time. And, the cars can be loaded quickly. It will take little longer than it does now to pack a subway train at Times Square in New York."

Bill Norton, the manager of the state-owned Cannon Mountain in New Hampshire, the first center in the United States to introduce a tramway for skiers (1938) maintains, however, that the chair lifts are destined to remain on the scene for many years to come.

"They still are ideal for the smaller ski centers," he insists. "In fact I can see the day when they will be replacing many of the present-day surface lifts such as the T-bar and the Poma. To cope with the wind and cold, I believe engineers will start thinking in terms of installing chair-lifts closer to the ground whenever possible.

"But a big item at ski areas, I feel, will be the installation of more intermediate unloading stations at lifts whether they be chairs—or gondolas. These will enable all skiers—whether they be little more than beginners or experts to ride the bigger Alpine lifts and disembark at points that service terrain in keeping with their respective abilities. We tried this scheme on one of our lifts and found that traffic on it multiplied many times as a result of this idea."

Norton also believes that come, say 1980, that areas will find it extremely necessary to offer more beginners' terrain to their patrons.

"Interest in skiing has barely scratched the surface," he says. "It · has been increasing rapidly in recent years and is certain to keep doing so. Propaganda that skiing is only a little less dangerous than igniting sticks of T.N.T. with inch-long matches is on the wane. Few ski centers today have enough novice terrain."

To get some impressions on what the future might have in store for winter-time ski slope preservation, Paul Bousquet was sought out. Bousquet, who has returned to Pittsfield, Mass., to operate the pioneer Bousquet ski center, has been a student of snow maintenance ever since he was a six-year-old. At that time, back in the rope tow era's whirling thirties, his father Clarence was the major domo of the primitive Berkshire Mountain ski center that bore his name.

"But primitive or not," says Paul Bousquet proudly, "we did a land-office business. There were days when we had as many as 6,000 skiers come by snow train and automobile to use our creaky rope tows. We charged $1 per day and kept wondering where all the people came from. Then as is the case now, our major worry on the Wednesday or Thursday night before a week-end was whether we were going to have snow fit to ski on when the mobs arrived."

As a result, Bousquet, who until a few years ago was in charge of maintenance at the major Killington, Vermont, resort, always has watched the development of manicuring machines for snow surfaces attentively. Among his duties at Killington was the supervision of snow-making.

"Snow maintenance means just that," Bousquet explains. "If you get snow, the trick is to try and learn how to keep it, and I've been trying to learn. Last winter, for example, New England had only one major snowstorm— around Christmas time. Yet almost all of the areas in that part of the United States were able to stay in business through March because their maintenance crews had mastered the technique of preserving, moving and grooming snow."

Bousquet, however, insists that almost everything being done now to preserve snow is primitive compared to the white cover's handling in years to come.

"I can foresee the day," he maintains, "when preserving snow at a ski area will be little more difficult than blowing soap bubbles. In this case, the theme probably will be controlled environment geared around enclosures that simply will be inflated by air. A present-day example is the now popular day use of inflated nylon-like material over swimming pools. When that day comes, a ski operator won't have to spend a few days before each week-end worrying about the possibility of rain. If that prospect rears its ugly head, he merely will push a button that will start the inflation of a big bubble or any number of small ones to provide roofs for his surfaces. If he has an immense ski area and such bubble installation is not feasible, then he probably will only service a part of his terrain in this manner."

Bousquet maintains that the snowmaking problem will be just as easy to handle.

"There will be no more of this putting your finger out the window to see from which direction the wind is blowing," he says with a smile. "It's all going to be automatic. As soon as the thermometer goes below the freezing point and the humidity makes snowmaking feasible, thermostats will immediately set the snow machines into operation. It will be the same system we use right now in our homes to make sure that room temperatures remain comfortable."

Since clothing always has been a major factor in skiing's growth, John Clair, Jr., the former manager of the United States Olympic Team, who always has helped set the pace in fashion on the slopes, was asked about his impressions about the future.

"There's no doubt that ski clothing is going to be much lighter than it is even now," he said. "Parkas and heavy sweaters will become outmoded and the chances are that we'll be seeing people skiing in the same light clothes that they now wear while lolling around at their ski lodges. When they get ready to ski, all they'll do is dig out their ski boots and a pair of light coveralls designed to resist cold, wind and rain. Once in them they'll be ready for the slopes.

Clair also believes the day will soon come when a beginner will remain in that unhappy state for little more than a day or so. He is convinced that bindings are certain to become an integral part of the ski and the boot. Boots, he avers, will have wedges in them that combined with the bindings will help put skiers in a stance that will make turning almost automatic. This convenience, he concludes, will enable the novice to progress into the intermediate ranks in little longer than it now takes a desperate neophyte to learn the proper emphasis to give to the term "track."

So far as skis and boots go, it

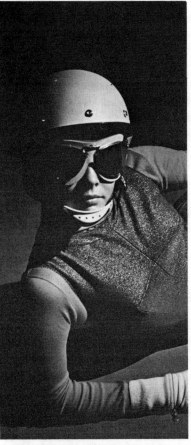

Fake slopes, as above (Scotland), and the Space Age, slightly zombified, look in ski fashions, are dubious factors in skiing's future.

seems inevitable that lessons learned from the space program are certain to make an impact. Skis are certain to be stronger but lighter—and probably less expensive if someone discovers a way to do away with fillers and returns the ski to the one piece item it was three decades ago. The chances are that even racers won't need different skis for the slalom, giant slalom and downhill events. Aerodynamic engineering probably will be able to produce a ski for all three types of plunges. Plastic will undoubtedly do away with the need of leather in boots in view of the fact that the former will provide the stronger material, one capable of shaking off water even on rainy days. One buckle is all that will be needed on the boots. As for ski poles, they will become even lighter than they are now while becoming virtually unbreakable.

Almost all need for uphill climbing for downhill skiing will be eliminated. The major areas probably will introduce some type of moving platform that will even enable enthusiasts to strap on their boards and ride the moving escalator platform from the base lodge to the lift.

Keeping warm even on days when the weather turns unexpectedly frigid?

"No problem," maintains John Clair who, on a volunteer basis, has spent most of his recent winters comforting and encouraging ski touring novices. "That will be easy. Thanks to what we've learned from the astronauts, skiers will be wired for warmth. Two tiny batteries connected to wires running through the clothes will provide the heat necessary to ward off the rigors of an 'Arctic Anguisher.'"

Anyone have any questions about skiing's future?

Conditioning Countdown for Skiers

by Paul Davidson
and Robert Fuller

Think back to the beginning of last season. Remember what the *second* day on the slopes was like?

The first day wasn't so bad—you were probably surprised at how smoothly you got back into the swing of things, not nearly as rusty as you had thought.

But that second day was a different story, when all those muscles, unused since last season, were screaming for relief. Promise yourself that never again will you start the season without the conditioning exercises—and keep that promise. Prevention is always easier than cure. In addition to not hurting, you'll ski better, you'll be able to ski longer without tiring, and you'll reduce the risk of injury.

Authors Paul Davidson, physician, and Robert Fuller, physical therapist, and both avid skiers, have developed a balanced program of exercises for the recreational skier. The program consists of 14 exercises that can be done in 30 minutes a day. Allow five weeks for conditioning. For the first week repeat each exercise only the number of times specified for each—and then work up gradually to the maximum number recommended over the five-week period.

Exercise 1. HAMSTRING STRETCH

Sit on one chair and put your right foot on another chair, with the leg fully extended and the knee straight. Keep your left foot on

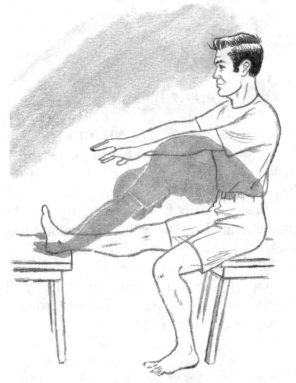

the floor. Point toes of right foot straight up.

Bend forward and try to touch the right knee with your forehead. Sit up. Repeat 8 times, working up to 12. Do the same exercise with the left leg.

Exercise 2. PARALLEL KNEE BENDS

If you are a snowplow skier, stand with your hands on your hips and your heels 2 feet apart. Point your toes *in*. Sink into a deep knee bend until your thighs are parallel to the floor. Straighten up.

If you are a more advanced skier, stand with your hands on your hips and your heels 2 feet apart and point your toes *out*. Sink into a deep knee bend until your thighs are par-

allel to the floor. Straighten up. Repeat 5 times, increasing to 12.

Exercise 3. RUNNING IN PLACE

Stand with your hands and run in place, lifting your knees above your waist. In this exercise it's important to lift your knees high. Count each time the right leg hits the ground. The rate will vary from 60 to 90 times per minute, depending upon your physical condition. Start off with a half minute, increasing to 2 minutes.

Exercise 4. ANKLE RANGE OF MOTION WITH TOWEL

Sit on one chair and put your right foot on another chair, with the leg fully extended and the knee straight. Wrap a towel around the

ball of your foot. Then do these three separate exercises:

Pull on the towel, stretching the heel cord as far as you can. Then push the foot down while you keep pulling on the towel.

Pull on the towel while you describe a wide counter-clockwise circle with your foot.

Pull on the towel while you describe a wide clockwise circle with your foot.

Do each exercise 8 times, increasing to 12, before you go on to the next in that series.

Exercise 5. TRUNK CURL

Lie on your back with your knees bent, feet flat on the floor, and hands behind the head. Press the hollow of your back at the waistline close to the floor and tighten the buttock muscles. This will raise the buttocks slightly.

Curl up to a sitting position. Don't hook or support your feet. If you can't make it all the way up, curl as high as you can. Repeat 8 times, increasing to 15.

Exercise 6. HEEL WALKING

Wear tennis shoes or do this exercise on a carpet. Put your hands on your hips and stand on your heels with the toes pulled up as high as possible. Walk on your heels without letting your toes down. Start off with 1 minute, increasing to 2 minutes.

Exercise 7. TRUNK ROTATION AND SIDE BENDING

Sit on a chair holding a broomstick across your shoulders, behind your neck. Twist from the waist as far as you can to the right, then as far as you can to the left, stopping momen-

Exercise 8. LOW BACK STRETCH

Lie on your back with the hollow of your back at the waistline close to the floor. Pull up your knees and hold on to them with your hands. Keep your head on the floor and pull your knees as close to your chest as you can. Release. Repeat 8 times, increasing to 10.

tarily at the midpoint. Repeat 6 times, increasing to 12.

From the same position with the broomstick, bend as far as you can to the right, then as far as you can to the left, stopping momentarily at the midpoint. Repeat 6 times, increasing to 12.

Exercise 9. JUMPING JACKS

Stand with your feet together and your hands at your sides. Jump up in the air, clapping your hands over your head and spreading your feet. Then jump up and return to the starting position. Try to do about 60 per minute, starting at ½ minute and increasing to 2½ minutes.

Exercise 10. TOE RAISE

Stand with the balls of your feet on a block of wood or a book 2 inches thick, placed near a wall. Leave your heels touching the floor. Put your hands against the wall for

knee straight and raise your leg as high as possible—at least as high as your waistline.

Drop your right leg and shift your weight onto it. Then begin the swing with the left leg. Repeat 5 times, increasing to 12.

support. Rise up on your toes as high as possible and sink down again. Repeat 10 times, increasing to 25.

Exercise 11. CROSS-OVER HIP SWING

Stand with your hands on your hips and your right leg crossed over the left with the right knee straight. Swing your right leg up and out to the right side. Keep your right

Exercise 12. CHINS — MEN

Stand grasping the chinning bar with the palms of your hands toward you at shoulder's width. Bend the knees to raise the feet from the floor, so that your body hangs from the bar. Pull yourself up and let yourself down again to the hanging position.

If you have trouble starting from the hanging position, start from a standing position. If no chinning bar is available, try the Women's Chins or the Alternate Chins.

CHINS — WOMEN

Place the chinning bar in the doorway about 30 inches from the floor. Lie under the bar, grasping it with the palms of your hands toward you at shoulder's width. Pull your whole body up and let yourself down again.

ALTERNATE CHINS

If you don't have a chinning bar, lie under a table, grasping an edge. Pull your whole body up and let yourself down again. For all of these repeat 5 times, increasing to 12.

Exercise 13. DIPS — MEN

Place the palms of your hands on two chairs that are slightly farther apart than shoulder's width and put both feet on a third chair, couch, or bed. Bend your elbows and lower your body, then return to the starting

position. (Make sure the chairs are not on a slippery surface.)

DIPS — WOMEN

Stand and lean backward against a table with your knees straight and your feet from 2 to 3 feet from the base of the table. Bend your elbows and lower your body, then push back up to the starting position. Repeat 5 times, increasing to 12.

Exercise 14. LUNGES

Stand with your hands on your hips and your feet several inches apart. Lunge forward onto your right leg with your right knee bent and the left leg kept straight. Keep your trunk curled over your thigh, and make sure that you don't arch your lower back. Hold the position momentarily.

Then flex the left knee by bending the leg back, balancing on the right leg. Return to the lunging position and then to the standing position. Repeat 5 times, increasing to 10. Then lunge on the left leg.

SKI MORE SAFELY

*Advice for novice and inter-
mediate skiers, based on an
investigation of more than
4000 slopeside accidents*

by
Dr. James G. Garrick

DIRECTOR, NATIONAL SKI SAFETY RESEARCH
HEAD, DIVISION OF SPORTS MEDICINE,
UNIVERSITY OF WASHINGTON

In most sports being a beginner is grim. Usually, whether the competition is fierce or non-existent or between teams or individuals, the newcomer gets very little special consideration. He or she must play by the same rules and on the same ground as the experts. Not so with skiing.

The novice skier need not face the entire 3,000 vertical feet of the mountain nor need he face the shoulder-deep moguls or the steeper slopes—which appear to him as snow covered cliffs. This is one reason why there are beginning skiers of all ages. Strangely enough, the beginning skier might well negotiate these circumstances of geography quite safely but in so doing he might have little opportunity to improve his technical skills which are based on his ability to turn and not on his ability to survive. Gradients of expertise in skiing are determined by the skier's ability to execute certain maneuvers, usually variations of turns. To progress from novice or beginner to expert generally requires the following sequence: snowplow, snowplow turns, stem turns, stem christie turns, parallel turns, and finally advanced forms.

As the skier becomes able to execute the more advanced maneuvers his skiing ability increases and the likelihood of his being injured decreases. But the skier need not become an expert to enjoy this added degree of safety. Indeed, the greatest decrease in injury rates (i.e., his likelihood of being injured) occurs in the earliest stages of his skiing.

By merely advancing from the ability of snowplow (A Class) to the ability to execute a snowplow turn and traverse (B class) the likelihood of injury decreases by 37 per cent. A further increase

in ability allowing stem turns (C class) reduces injury rates by an additional 33 per cent. Thus the skier need only barely qualify as an intermediate or C class skier to enjoy reduction in injury potential by nearly ¾ (70 per cent).

The individual's progress up the ladder of expertise is, no doubt, enhanced by the fact that there are slopes at nearly every ski area commensurate with the various ability classes. Thus more challenging slopes are available for practicing more expert maneuvers.

Regardless of the terrain skied on, there are two other important factors influencing the advancement of abilities—lessons, and experience. Nearly ¼ (23 per cent) of the skiers who have skied one year or less will have achieved at least intermediate abilities during that year by virtue of the fact that they just skied. By the second year of skiing over ⅔ (69 per cent) of the skiers will have advanced out of the novice or A and B class category. These ability increases are based only on the time skied because the skiers considered here have not taken lessons.

Thus, a skier can decrease his likelihood of being injured by merely skiing. Of course if, in the process, he increases his abilities, all the better, for while injury rates decrease with experience, they decrease more with the attainment of higher abilities.

The goal of the safety-conscious beginning skier is, then, to ski, and, while skiing, to improve his technique as rapidly as possible. Ability increase during the first two years of skiing is markedly influenced by taking lessons.

During the first year, over half (52 per cent) of tutored skiers (i.e., those taking lessons) will

have graduated from the novice or A and B class ranks as opposed to only 33 per cent of the untutored group. Indeed with lessons, 10 per cent of the first-year skiers state that they have achieved expert abilities during that year, whereas only 2 per cent of the untutored made this same claim. The same general findings are true for the second year of skiing.

Equipment may also play some role in injury prevention for less-than-expert skiers. There is a paucity of research data regarding the influence of equipment on injury rates or increases in abilities. However, the consensus among many professional skiers is that novice skiers are ill-advised to begin their skiing career using skis or boots designed for the competitor and/or expert skier. Large, well-known equipment manufacturers and distributors usually have a line of skis and boots which are not only more suitable for the novice but less expensive as well.

The material presented above is a small part of the results compiled over seven years, inquiring into the causes of ski injuries. These studies were carried out at 11 ski areas across the United States and involved interviewing 4,032 injured and 5,355 uninjured skiers. Much of the work was funded by a United States Public Health Service Grant.

These studies did not yield clear-cut answers to many of the ski injury problems. They did however, focus attention on the highest risk group—novices, females, etc.—as well as provide some mechanisms by which these groups might be protected. Ski lessons aimed at the skier's rapid progression out of the lower-ability categories is among the most important mechanisms.

NINE RULES FOR BEING NICE

Observing this Skier's Courtesy Code, prepared by the National Ski Areas Ass'n, will lighten everyone's day on the hill

1. All skiers shall ski under control. Control shall mean in such manner that a skier can stop in time to avoid other skiers or objects.

2. When skiing downhill, the overtaking skier shall avoid the skier below him.

3. Skiers approaching each other on opposite traverses pass to the right.

4. Skiers shall not stop in a location in which they will obstruct a trail, where they are not visible from above, or where they will impede the normal passage of other skiers during loading or unloading of a lift.

7. When a person is walking or climbing on a ski slope or trail, he shall wear skis and keep to the side of the trail or slope.

5. A skier shall check for approaching downhill skiers before entering a trail or slope from an intersecting trail.

8. All skiers wearing release bindings shall also wear safety straps or other devices to prevent runaway skis.

6. A standing skier shall check for approaching downhill skiers before starting.

9. Skiers shall keep off closed trails and posted areas and shall observe all traffic signs and other regulations of the ski area.

GOING UP!
HOW TO RIDE LIFTS

For beginners of any age, going up the hill is often as much of a challenge as going down. Here, to help your children learn to use all types of ski lifts safely, are practical hints from which grown-up beginners can pick up pointers and confidence, too.

by Gene
and Barbara Tinker

Uphill lifts help make skiing easy. They take all the work out of getting up a slope. They should be used only by skiers who can stop when they want to and steer themselves where they want to go. If a skier cannot do this, he is probably going to get hurt, and he may hurt another skier at the same time.

LIFT LINE MANNERS: Many ski areas are crowded on weekends and holidays when most of us can get away from school and jobs to go skiing. There is often a long line at the bottom of the lift. This is one of the times when good manners show on the ski area. Stay in line when waiting your turn to use the lift. Don't try to sneak in ahead of others. Stay off other skiers' skis. If you shove and fuss because you have to wait your turn, you will not have much fun and neither will your fellow skiers. When it is your turn to use the lift, move quickly. If you are not sure about how to use it, ask the operator. That is one of the reasons he is there. If an operator or attendant asks you to do something, do it. He is there to make sure that the lift runs smoothly and he is an expert at his job.

At the top of the lift, get away from the unloading area as soon as you can so the skiers behind you won't find you in their way. If you use a rope tow, a poma lift, a J-bar, or a T-bar and fall off, get out of the way quickly so you don't get in the way of the skiers behind you. Snowplow back down to the bottom again and get back in line.

SKI AREA MAPS: Every ski area has a map showing all the trails, open slopes, lifts, and lodges. The map might be a signboard, outside, with the trails,

etc., painted on it or it might be a printed paper map, much like a road map, which is given to skiers.

Take a little time to study the area map. You will notice that the steepness of each trail is shown. Pick a novice lift for your first trips. A novice lift lets you off at the top of a gentle slope. It would be a mistake to take the wrong lift and end up at the top of a steep slope.

GONDOLA, CABLE CARS: These are the luxury uphill lifts. In these, you are out of the wind and arrive at the top nice and warm. Cable cars are found mostly in Europe; however, they are now found in some areas in this country and are more and more popular. With cable cars and with some gondolas, you will have to take your skis off before you go in. The attendant puts skis and poles in a special rack, and you either stand or sit inside the car. Some gondolas are built so that you can keep your skis on — they rest on a bar outside of you. Attendants at the top of the mountain open the door for you.

These uphill lifts are used for carrying skiers to the very top of the mountain. When you are a more skillful skier and can handle long trails from the top, you can use them.

CHAIR LIFTS: Chair lifts are found at almost every ski area of any size. They have chairs hanging at regular intervals from a steel cable. Powerful engines move this cable around giant wheels at the top and bottom of the mountain and over rollers at the top of towers going up the mountain. The chair usually holds two skiers. A safety bar is used after the skiers are seated in the chair.

Some chair lifts are hung from the overhead steel cable by one steel bar, which fastens to the center of the chair. Other chair lifts have two vertical bars that attach to each side of the chair. Here is how to get on a double chair lift:

1. As soon as the two skiers ahead of you and your partner are seated in their chair and move uphill, move quickly to the loading spot. There may be arrows or some other sign or the attendant will tell you where to stand.
2. Hold your poles together in your outside hand, the one away from your partner.
3. Stand with your skis a comfortable distance apart, pointing uphill, and turn your upper body toward the inside (toward your partner), and look back toward the chair as it comes toward you. (If the chair lift you use has two vertical bars, one on each side of the seats, you can turn to the outside.)
4. When the chair comes close, reach your inside hand back and use it to steady yourself on the vertical bar when the chair arrives.
5. Sit down quickly with your back against the chair back. Do not wave your poles around—you could hurt someone.
6. As you start to move forward, remember to keep your ski tips up to avoid catching a ski tip in the snow.

Chair Lift: *These pictures show you the steps in getting onto a chair lift:*

Move to the ready position when the skiers ahead of you move toward the loading spot. As soon as the chair ahead of you is loaded, move quickly to the loading spot.

Hold your poles together in your outside hand. Point your skis uphill and twist around to face the oncoming chair.

When the chair comes, sit down and enjoy the ride to the top.

(Top) *To get off a chair lift, raise the safety bar, raise your ski tips so they don't catch on the unloading ramp, and hold your poles in your outside hand (the one away from your partner). When your skis touch the surface, shift your weight evenly to both skis.*

(Center) *Slide forward and away from the chair. Some unloading ramps are much steeper than this one. If you unload on a steep ramp, lean well forward and snowplow down the ramp.*

(Bottom) *Move away from the unloading area right away so you're not in the way of the skiers coming in behind you.*

7. Pull the safety gate across in front of you and sit quietly. Rest your skis on the support bar if your chair has one.

8. Either hold your poles in your hand or hook the straps in the pole hooks if the chair has them. Do not let your poles hang below the chair. They could catch on a tree or something below you. Hold them firmly to keep them from slipping away and falling to the snow below where they might hit and injure another skier.

Riding uphill is enjoyable. You can admire lovely scenery on the way up and can think how lucky you are that you don't have to do a lot of climbing. If you have buckle boots, you can loosen them and wiggle your toes to warm your feet.

When you near the top, here's what you do:

1. Open the safety gate and footrest. There is often a sign that tells you when to do this.

2. Hold your poles the same way you did when you got on. Keep them in front of you to make sure they don't catch on the chair when you get off at the top.

3. Keep your ski tips up as you approach the unloading ramp.

4. When your skis touch the surface, shift your weight evenly to both skis, lean forward, and ski off the ramp.

5. Move away from the unloading area to make sure you won't be in the way of the skiers behind you.

If you are unloading on one side of the chair lift and want to cross to the other side, watch the oncoming chairs and skiers carefully. You wouldn't want to get hit by them. If the unloading area does not have a sloping unloading ramp and is flat, step or skate off to the side to be sure you're out of the way.

T-BARS, J-BARS: While chair lifts give you a ride to the top, the T-bars and J-bars pull you to the top. T-bars pull two skiers at a time and look like an upside down T. Each skier places the crossbar of the T against his bottom and is pulled uphill. The J-bars do the same thing except that they pull one skier, instead of two. They look something like the letter J — or L. There are attendants at the loading place for both kinds of lifts. Here's the recommended way to use a J-bar.

1. When the skier ahead of you has started to move uphill, move quickly to the loading spot. It will either be marked or shown to you by the lift attendant.

2. Hold your poles together about halfway down the shafts. Keep them in your outside hand (the one away from the upright part of the J-bar).

3. Keep your skis a comfortable distance apart, parallel, and pointed uphill.

4. Twist around at your waist so you can look back and see the oncoming J-bar.

5. The attendant will hold the crossbar so you can place it properly under your bottom.

6. Reach back with your inside hand and hold the straight-up part of the J-bar.

7. Let the J-bar pull you uphill. Keep your knees bent and your weight evenly divided between both skis. Do not try to sit on the bar. It is made for pulling, not lifting.

8. Keep your skis parallel and in the tracks made by other skiers. If you ski off to the side, you might fall, and you might make it hard for other skiers behind you to stay in line.

If you should fall while going uphill, roll off to one side, out of the way of the skiers behind you. Snowplow down the hill and

J-bar: *When the person ahead of you starts to move uphill, move quickly to the loading spot. Point your skis uphill and hold your poles in your outside hand (the one away from the J-bar). Twist around to face the oncoming J-bar. As the J-bar approaches, reach back with your inside hand to steady it when it gets near.*

The attendant will place the crosspiece under your bottom. Let it pull you uphill.

Keep your skis in the tracks and your poles in your outside hand. Do not try to sit on the J-bar — let it pull you up the hill.

Rope Tow: *Here's how you use the rope tow: Loop the straps of your poles around your outside wrist, the one away from the rope. (Top left) Stand with your skis in the tracks, parallel, pointed up the slope. Put your inside hand around the rope and slowly tighten up to get moving. Bring your outside hand behind to hold the rope. Your inside hand will be ahead and the outside hand behind you. Bend your knees. (Bottom left) Lean back and let yourself be pulled uphill.*

get back in line for another ride up.

When you arrive at the top, ski or skate away from the unloading area.

T-bars are used in much the same way as J-bars, except that they are used by two people.

1. Get onto the loading spot the same as described in the J-bar instructions. Hold your poles in your outside hand, the one away from your partner. Your boots and your partner's should be in line.

2. Twist around from your waist (toward your partner) and watch the oncoming T-bar. When it arrives, the attendant will hold the crossbar so you and your partner can place it properly under your bottoms.

3. Keep your knees bent, your skis in the tracks, and let the bar pull you up the slope. Do not sit on the crossbar.

When you arrive at the top, here's what to do:

1. The person on the side which is away from the T-bar returning downhill can ski off first, out away from the loading area.

2. The other skier moves out when the first one is out of the way. If there is a downhill unloading ramp, you can snowplow downhill. If it is flat, you can step away or skate out of the way of the skiers behind you.

Riding a T-bar is easier if you ride with someone about your same height.

When you use a T- or J-bar, watch the returning bars carefully when crossing through them. They are the ones that have gone around the big wheel at the top and are returning downhill. You could get hit by one if you aren't careful.

POMA LIFT: The poma lift (sometimes called a platter pull) is something like a J-bar. The difference is that the steel bar that pulls you up the hill is not attached to the cable. It is hooked onto it by the attendant after you are in place and ready for your uphill trip. There is a curve at the end of the steel bar, and at the end of it is a round "platter." Here's how you use it:

1. Stand on the loading spot with your skis in the tracks, parallel, pointing uphill. Hold both ski poles in one hand.

2. Place the platter between your legs and put it under your seat.

3. Hold the bar tightly and let the attendant know you're ready.

4. He will put the bar on the moving overhead cable and you will start up the slope. Many poma lifts start with a jerk, so be ready, with knees bent.

5. Riding uphill is much like using the J-bar. Don't try to sit. Let the platter pull you. Be sure to keep your skis in the tracks.

6. To get off, slide your hand down the bar, spread your legs, and take out the platter. Let it go and ski out of the way.

ROPE TOW: A rope tow is a moving rope which you hold tightly to go uphill. The rope goes around two large wheels, one at the top of the slope, the other at the bottom. Powerful engines turn the top wheel, which keeps the rope moving.

Be careful that loose clothing doesn't get caught in the rope. It is best to wear a pair of old gloves or mittens, or gloves with tough palms. The sliding of the rope through your hands can wear out a pair of soft leather or wool gloves.

When you near the top:

1. Let the rope go with the outside hand, the one behind you.

2. When you are at the spot for unloading, let go with the other hand and ski away from the unloading area.

Advanced Pointer

HOW TO FALL SAFELY

Any person who claims that he's never taken a fall is: 1) not telling the truth, 2) not really putting any challenge into his skiing. Bear in mind that spills happen to every skier from the novice to the expert. They are just as embarrassing to the great as they are to the rest of us — and they can be just as dangerous.

One thing is different: pros and highly conditioned racers are physically stronger and therefore more responsive than the recreational skiers. So, the answer is that when you know you are going to fall—fall. Don't fight it when you have begun to lose your balance. Melt into the snow as softly and compactly as you can. By resisting, you exert muscle effort to overcome the impending disaster. Your body becomes contorted to regain balance. If the fall comes at this point, you are in no condition to prepare yourself for the impact and you risk one of those falls called "egg-beaters" or "cartwheels." In short, you may wish you had gone down at the first opportunity, rather than prolong, and possibly intensify the agony.

An appropriate axiom is "Those best able to recover from trouble are seldom in it." A time proven method of falling is to collect yourself into a compact ball. Tuck in elbows, hands and draw your knees up close. Be sure that knees, boots and skis are as close together as possible. Never sit back on the tails of your skis, for they will keep running after you fall. In unity there is sometimes another chance.

SKI THE AMERICAN WAY

*Complete, step-by-step introduction to the American Ski Technique,
as taught by members of the Professional Ski Instructors of America, and interpreted
on the next pages by three keen analysts of the sport:*

PAUL VALAR Former member of the Swiss Olympic ski team, director of ski schools at Franconia, Sunapee and Mittersill, all in New Hampshire, and a co-author of the official American Ski Technique manual. Valar has served as a director of PSIA and chairman of its technical committee and is presently devoting his time and energy — and his fluency in four languages — to directing the PSIA foreign relations committee. He was one of the organizers of the 8th Interski Congress in Aspen in 1968. Last year he chaired a meeting in Italy to study the possibility of creating an international uniform ski technique.

DR. RICHARD L. VOORHEES Certified ski instructor in the Pacific Northwest as well as a practicing physician who specializes in the treatment of disease and surgery of the ear. He is a member of the PSIA technical committee and a contributor to the official American Ski Technique manual. In 1969 he was a delegate to the ski teaching committee at the International Ski Federation (FIS) convention in Barcelona.

EDWARD L. WYMAN Harvard graduate and a longtime instructor in physics, he is now employed in private industry. He has served on the PSIA technical committee and has contributed to the official American Ski Technique manual. He was an official U.S. delegate to 8th Interski in 1968.

STRAIGHT RUNNING

SKI THE AMERICAN WAY

STAGE 1

0° FALL LINE

If your straight-running form isn't perfect, it's occasionally going to throw you. Proper straight running is just as important as any of the other more complex maneuvers in skiing. And don't be deceived by how easy it looks or sounds. It's a finished form frequently overlooked by beginners and forgotten even by experts. And it's on the easy slopes that loss of form can be most embarrassing. Standing up straight and abandoning correct body position on the run-out is the best way to catch an edge and lose your balance — and bruise your pride.

WHAT Straight running refers to skiing in the fall line. Skis are parallel and equally weighted. You stand naturally erect and relaxed, ankles and knees slightly flexed. Your arms are freely forward, elbows away from your body, hands about hip high, and poles straight back. Keep your body at least at right angles to the surface. Lean forward or backward as snow structure or slope changes.

Straight running means learning to "ride" your skis properly, attuning to the sliding sensation. To maintain balance and control on moving skis, you must be able to freely move parts of your body to meet the demands of speed and terrain, while the base you are standing on glides constantly out from under you.

If you don't master this, you will be ill-prepared for more complex maneuvers; you will tend to "work" your skis by muscle power alone and will be on the defensive forever.

HOW In straight running, lateral balance is best maintained by a moderate skis-apart position. Ski instructors debate just how far apart they should be, but in general it is where they feel most comfortable. An individual with wider hips may be more comfortable with skis about 8 to 10 inches apart.

Too wide a stance, however, changes the axis of body alignment. Then weight bearing be-

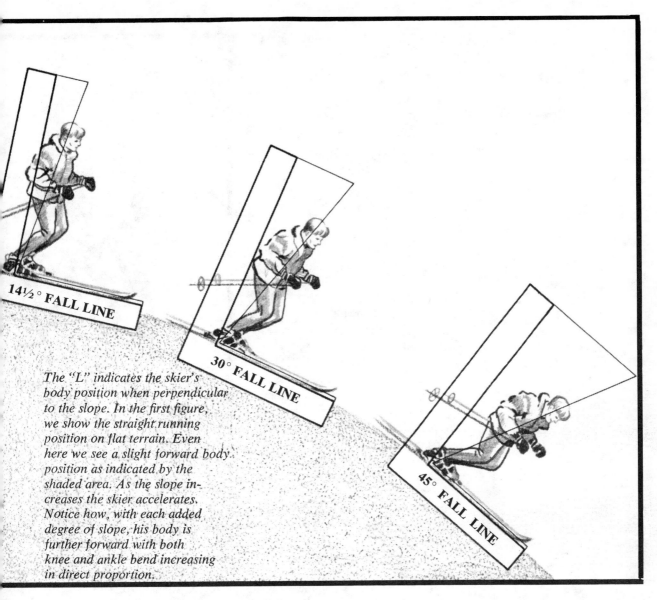

14½° FALL LINE

30° FALL LINE

45° FALL LINE

The "L" indicates the skier's body position when perpendicular to the slope. In the first figure, we show the straight running position on flat terrain. Even here we see a slight forward body position as indicated by the shaded area. As the slope increases the skier accelerates. Notice how, with each added degree of slope, his body is further forward with both knee and ankle bend increasing in direct proportion.

comes a function of the muscles rather than the skeleton and fatigue results. Too wide a stance also promotes unequal weight distribution and edging.

As you pick up speed in straight running, you bend your knees and lean forward more and more, at the same time exerting more pressure downward with your toes against the tips of the skis and more pressure upward with your boot heels against the downhold on your ski bindings. A good rule of thumb for knee position is to have them bent forward until you can't see the tips of your boots.

With practice and experience,

a skier learns when and how to adjust to maintain balance. "Informer sources" in the body detect speed and contour changes. The eyes are an early warning system for both. Once the muscles learn to react reflexively to messages from the receptor sources, balance can be maintained.

WHY If your skis were nailed to the floor, and the floor was tilted forward, you would lean back in order to keep your body in line with the gravitational "pull" and thus avoid falling forward.

On the slopes, however, be-

cause your skis are constantly sliding out from under you, you lean forward to counteract this. The faster you go, the more you have to lean.

In straight running, at least half of your body weight should be applied to the front half of the skis. This "tip pressure" makes your skis hold better and provides control. Sitting back causes pressure on the tails of the skis and the tips will "wander" or "flutter."

Thus, in straight running, the body is essentially perpendicular to the surface (see diagrams) — or even somewhat forward of this position.

The snowplow, many instructors agree, is one of the most utilitarian, and valuable maneuvers in the average skier's handbook, even though it's the one most novices-on-the-way-to-intermediates want to forget. This basic slowing device can mean the difference between success and failure in many situations — not just on the beginner's slopes but on the race course, too.

WHAT The snowplow may be accomplished either from a standing start or from the straight-running position.

From a standstill on a down slope do this: plant your poles downhill for support. Point your skis straight down the fall line. Now, using heel pressure, push the tails of your skis out so they form a wedge — each ski an equal distance from the straight (or parallel) position.

Press your knees forward until you can't see the tips of your boots and then move them together slightly so that your skis are edged. Assume the straight-running position with your upper body, pull your poles out and you're off.

Going into a snowplow from the straight-running position merely requires a slight "down" motion with the knees and ankles, often called "sinking," followed by an upward and forward motion, "unweighting," to permit an easy spreading of your ski tails as you settle back down.

While the primary function of the snowplow is speed control, it is basically a *slow speed* maneuver. Don't try it at high speeds until you're thoroughly familiar with it and are prepared to execute it under all conditions; otherwise it may lead to a spill.

HOW The source of both control and motion in the straight snowplow is the same — body weight. But body *position* can make the weight work either *for* or *against* you. When more than half of the weight acts on the rear of your skis, the skis and hill rule you.

Viewed from the side, the correct position for the snowplow is essentially the same as for straight running — body leaning forward, with weight applied to the tips of the skis by pressure from your toes. The more weight so applied, the greater the braking effect of the snowplow, *if* the skis are edged.

Also, the wider the angle between your skis, the more effec-

SKI THE AMERICAN WAY

STAGE 2

THE SNOW PLOW

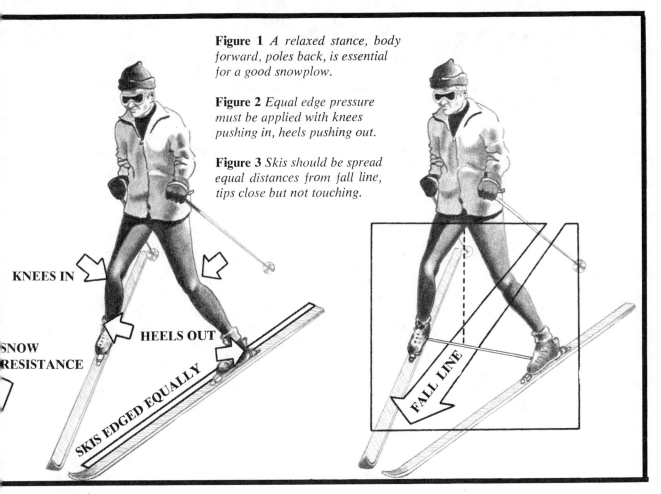

Figure 1 *A relaxed stance, body forward, poles back, is essential for a good snowplow.*

Figure 2 *Equal edge pressure must be applied with knees pushing in, heels pushing out.*

Figure 3 *Skis should be spread equal distances from fall line, tips close but not touching.*

KNEES IN

SNOW RESISTANCE

HEELS OUT

SKIS EDGED EQUALLY

FALL LINE

tive the snowplow will be in controlling speed. But relaxation and proper position of all parts of your body are the keynotes. Let your weight do the work and spare the muscles.

It is important for you to acquire a feeling of equal weight distribution and symmetrical knee and ankle bend. As these are applied against an edged ski, increased strength is required of the leg and thigh muscles to maintain proper body position during the maneuver.

In straight running you are largely at the mercy of gravity, whereas in the snowplow you acquire a degree of control. This adds a measure of safety to all maneuvers in skiing.

WHY The forces in the snowplow are the same ones that concern us in straight running, though to the majority they may seem altogether different.

In the straight snowplow, the thrust of the legs and skis is oblique to the surface. On each side the lateral resistance of the snow has a component opposing the forward motion. The horizontal push of the snow on one side, is offset by that on the other side, assuming equal weight, spread and edging on each of your skis.

The key to control with a minimum of effort is a relaxed stance with the body positioned (Fig. 3) so that a line drawn perpendicular to the surface from

the skier's center of weight bisects a line connecting the insteps of both feet.

Then, the leg muscles have only to sustain the body weight and a few extra pounds. For a 120-pound skier on a 10-degree slope, this is about 80 pounds per leg — not as much effort as is required to climb a flight of stairs.

The most common error in snowplowing is a position with the weight too far back — applied to the rear half of the skis — combined with, or resulting in, a determined push with the legs. The cure is a forward position and a relaxed stance with the weight divided equally between both feet.

SNOW PLOW TURNS

SKI THE AMERICAN WAY

STAGE 3

The snowplow turn is a positive step to parallel skiing, and for those who are already "there," it continues to be a useful warm-up for wedeln. A relatively simple maneuver, it requires movement of the upper body to provide weighting. This weighting changes from one ski to the other to produce the connected series of turns.

WHAT In straight-running and straight snowplow, one acquires confidence, control and a feeling for movement on the snow. In them you maintain a fairly fixed body position. But, to turn, you must "create" movement.

From a good snowplow position, it is easy to turn. It requires only a slight change of lower body position and angling of your upper body over one ski on the side *opposite* the direction of turn. The weighted ski will turn in the direction it is headed. For increased turning effect, edge this outside (downhill) ski by increasing knee and ankle pressure into the hill.

Be sure to keep your body slightly forward and away from the slope. No matter what happens, don't straighten either leg or your skis will not "flow" properly over the snow.

To turn in the other direction (connect your turns), rise gently and shift your weight to the other ski, at the same time bending your other knee and ankle slightly forward and into the slope. Avoid a static position and you should not become fatigued. Develop rhythm by coordinating your movements between turns. Choose a course and decide in advance how many linked turns you will make. When you've done it, are your tracks symmetrical and smooth?

The key things to avoid in the snowplow turn are "sitting back" (keeping weight on tails of skis which causes your tips to cross), stiff knees and rotation.

HOW The essential ingredient in the snowplow turn is proper weight transfer. Since both skis are slightly edged in the snowplow, it is only necessary to increase the body lean to one side to cause them to turn.

What happens in the muscles to create this turning power is unique and subtle. Too often, skiers try to overdo the weight shift and the result is stiff body muscles which act as an impediment to the turning action. When properly executed, weight shift should be obvious only in the upper body. The lower body — hips, knees and ankles — all change during the process of weight shifting, but not to a perceptible degree.

The best way to practice this maneuver is at low speed, thus using a minimum of "muscle power." With confidence at the lower speed, the skier may gradually increase his speed. While doing so, he should also increase the forward pressure on the downhill knee and, at the same time, push it harder into the hill. With this increased "edging," the ski will "carve" a sharper, more precise turn. The snowplow turn can be used in many situations and as the skier develops the strength and "feel" for this maneuver, he will be able to use it more often and with greater success.

The snowplow turn is one of a progression of American Ski

HEAD MOVES OVER SKI BOOT

SHOULDER MOVES DOWN AND BACK

KNEE AND ANKLE PUSH FORWARD

The most important ingredient in the snowplow turn is a proper shift of weight. In the straight snowplow, weight is equally distributed, as in the silhouette. To initiate the turn, the majority of the weight is transferred to the downhill ski (the outside one in the turn) and, with the knee and ankle pressing forward and toward the center of the turn, the ski will "carve" an arc. The outside shoulder must also be lowered and remain in the fall line.

Technique "forms" designed to bring a skier step-by-step to more difficult maneuvers.

WHY Snowplow maneuvers are to skiing, what the multiplication tables are to math: You can get along without them, but there is no substitute for their many benefits.

No turn can be accomplished without the action of a force external to the skier and skis. Gravity and resistance are the only such forces. Gravity urges the skier into the fall line and only increased resistance from one side can get him out of it.

In most turns, the skier uses gravity (weight) on an edged ski to bring the forces of resistance into play. To increase the effect of this lateral force, the skier applies forward lean with his body.

For the greatest stability and most effective results in turning control, the inside ski should bear only enough weight to maintain balance. Avoid thrusting out either leg in an attempt to improve control or turning results. Remember in this, as in all downhill skiing maneuvers, your forward projection or "lean," must be sufficient to keep at least half of your weight on the front half of your skis.

The snowplow turn embodies, in slow motion, all of the fundamentals of short-radius turning except side-slipping, which itself can be learned from an exercise in the snowplow position.

Unweighting, in the language of the American Ski Technique, is an "aid" to a turn, not a "requirement." It is done by an upward extension, followed by a sinking to diffuse weight.

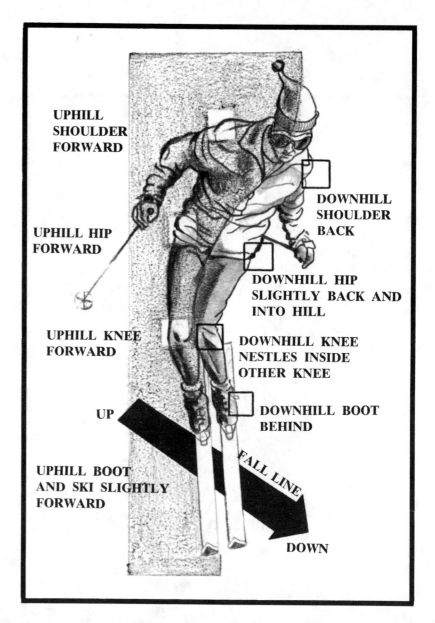

UPHILL SHOULDER FORWARD

DOWNHILL SHOULDER BACK

UPHILL HIP FORWARD

DOWNHILL HIP SLIGHTLY BACK AND INTO HILL

UPHILL KNEE FORWARD

DOWNHILL KNEE NESTLES INSIDE OTHER KNEE

UP

DOWNHILL BOOT BEHIND

UPHILL BOOT AND SKI SLIGHTLY FORWARD

FALL LINE

DOWN

SKI THE AMERICAN WAY

STAGE 4

Nearly every major skiing maneuver begins from the deceptively easy-looking traverse position. Practice on your living room carpet before the first snowfall can prepare you for correct position on the hill and condition the right muscles. Put your boots on, if it's convenient, and assume the position. Flex the knees and ankles and angle the upper body more over the "downhill" ski.

Do this a few times, then get into the opposite traversing position.

WHAT Straight running and traversing are the two basic positions in skiing, but few would argue against the traverse being far more important. Every major skiing maneuver (except parallel from the fall line) begins from the traverse position.

TRAVERSING

The traverse, like straight running, can be considered a static position. That is, once the basic position is assumed by the skier, there is very little obvious motion necessary to complete the form. Don't be fooled by this, however, because the terrain on which we ski is constantly changing, so it's necessary to be ready to make adjustments at any time.

Just as in straight running, the leg joints must remain flexed at all times to assist us in "feeling" the motion created by our skis on the snow. We must be certain that we remain comfortable and at ease. Advance the uphill ski slightly. Knees and boots are nestled together and the inside (uphill) hip is forward.

Angulation of the upper body is similar to that in the snow-plow turn. It keeps our weight on the downhill ski. Shoulders are turned to face downhill and the downhill shoulder is slightly back.

When you have a good position you are ready to give it a try with motion. Aim your skis across the slope toward a land mark. Be careful not to aim too close to the fall line for you will surely gain too much speed.

Now push off with your poles. When you have reached your predetermined stopping point, look back. Did your skis make two distinct tracks? Or did they make a blurred line that indicates your edges are not holding? Perhaps you notice a tendency for your skis to run slightly uphill. This is the result of side camber built into the skis at the time of manufacture. When properly corrected for by you, this represents an additional means of control in more advanced parallel skiing.

But remember, in traverse we are seeking a straight line across the slope. To successfully achieve this it may be necessary for you to lean further forward, or possibly even slightly backward. This is what professionals refer to as "leverage." Skiers who have mastered it find it even more useful in parallel turns.

HOW The bone and muscle structure of the body dictates the requirements for a good traverse. However it does not always occur and, even when it does, it **may** not be easy for the individual skier.

To be at all comfortable on the slope, the uphill ski must be advanced approximately half-a-boot length. This brings the inside or uphill hip forward. To this point there is little effort or difficulty.

However, angulation is necessary to get body weight over the lower (downhill) ski. As we do this we must lean toward the valley and actually tilt the upper body out and over the downhill ski. By twisting the upper body at this point, so that the shoulders face the valley, we can keep the muscles on the uphill side of our body from becoming uncomfortably stretched.

Obviously we cannot continue to lean out over the downhill ski without compensating by applying some weight to the uphill side for counter balance. This is done with the lower body. The action is most apparent in the knees, but the prime source of motion is in the hip joints. Of course it is still important to maintain knee and ankle flexion for forward lean.

You may ask "Is this really a natural position?" We maintain that it is because it is dictated by the physical principles governing skiing and the bio-mechanical principles inherent in the skier's body.

WHY In straight running we have the opposing forces of weight and snow resistance. Then, in snow plows and snow plow turns we use these forces to first slow our forward motion and then help create a turn. In traversing, we utilize these same forces, but apply them to both skis, side by side, and that is the essence of parallel skiing.

Here is what the traverse position does for you. At the outset it should allow you the necessary freedom of action and economy of movement necessary to facilitate useful application of natural forces.

The American Ski Technique stresses the importance of traversing as a means of control that provides a stable platform from which to begin your next maneuver. It helps to ingrain a basic body position which allows a means for edge control.

With the ability to create adequate edging under any slope conditions, the traverse effectively reduces the pitch of the slope to the angle made between the ski tracks and the horizontal plane. Thus the traverse is capable of controlling how fast the skier descends.

Finally, but by no means lastly, a good traverse can help the skier prevent fatigue caused by inefficient use of muscles which may actually be working against the natural forces.

SKI THE AMERICAN WAY

STAGE 5

THE STEM TURN

The whole world of knees-together skiing unfolds for the skier who has really mastered the stem turn. But there are two kinds of stem turns: the kind that push you forward into parallel skiing and the kind that hold you back.

By employing the quick-close technique to the stem turn, you can learn faster the sensations of parallel skiing. Pick a slight bump and stem on your approach to it. At the very top of it, shift weight to the stemmed ski and immediately "close." That is, place your unweighted ski beside your downhill ski. If you find that you are in a forward sideslip, so much the better. Hold the slide and keep enough forward pressure on so that the tips of your skis will be leading the turn. As your skis cross the fall line, increase angulation and traverse.

If this is too difficult at first, begin more gradually by quick closing from a straight snowplow. Begin by weighting the downhill ski as you would for a snowplow turn. While still straight in the fall line, close the skis as suggested. Straighten up and then return to a flexed-knees position.

WHAT The key that unlocks the mysteries of the stem turn is a good traverse position. In that position, you will achieve proper body balance to hold a straight line across the slope. This is possible because you have learned to "hold an edge" with your inside (downhill) ski by proper upper body angulation and knee action (fig. 1).

Before practicing the stem turn, it is wise to test your traverse. To do this, raise the tail of your uphill ski leaving the tip touching for stability. If your downhill ski continues to track straight, you have a good traverse. But if it slips down the hill, you must increase your body angulation

over the downhill ski and create more edging by increasing your knee and hip pressure into the slope.

To go into a stem turn from the traverse position, you begin by sliding the unweighted uphill ski away from the downhill one and into the stem position (fig. 2). Notice both tips stay close together but not touching, just as in the snowplow. Now you transfer your weight to the stemmed or uphill ski, keeping your knees flexed and your body forward in the straight running position. (fig. 3).

This starting phase is simple as it requires the skier simply to lean into the hill. As the turn progresses, especially after you cross the fall line, you will be leaning away from the hill toward the valley, though your body position relative to the skis remains the same (figs. 3 and 4).

As you continue around, you will find your skis beginning to come together in a new traverse, if your weight transfer has been complete.

If, however, your skis do not come together in another traverse, it means your traverse position is not correct and some of your weight has remained on or transferred to the uphill ski.

HOW The principle of the stem is very similar to that of the snowplow turn — weight shift to the ski which has been placed in the direction of the turn.

Actually, in stem turns we are creating a half snowplow and physically placing our unweighted ski in a direction closer to the fall line. To move the uphill ski it is absolutely essential to have almost all of your body weight on the downhill ski. It is unlikely that anyone could lift the ski he was standing on without shifting to the other foot.

From a traverse position it is good practice to try the stemming motion while standing still on the hill. When you feel that you have mastered it, try it while traversing across the slope but do not complete the weight transfer to the stem ski. Control in holding the inside edge of the downhill ski in a straight line can be developed by practicing this several times in both directions on the slope.

When you have developed confidence in your ability to stem properly, make the weight shift and turn.

WHY In a correct stem turn we make a complete transfer of weight from one ski to the other, not unlike the more advanced christy turns. In traversing, both before and after turning, we essentially assume the appearance of a parallel skier.

Our skis, boots and knees are together. Our upper body is angulated over the downhill ski and shoulders are facing the valley.

The complete transfer of weight, combined with forward lean and angulation, assures the continuation of lateral resistance to accomplish the desired change of direction and the return to the next traverse.

The advantage of the stem turn is that it permits the basic parts of each turn to be executed very *slooooowly*. Many skiers tend to make their movements too rapidly, losing the fluidity and smoothness of control which they so earnestly seek.

From one traverse to the other, the stem turning action can be performed as deliberately as you choose, provided that it is continuous. There should be nothing hurried nor strained about a stem turn. It is the embodiment of total and continuous motion.

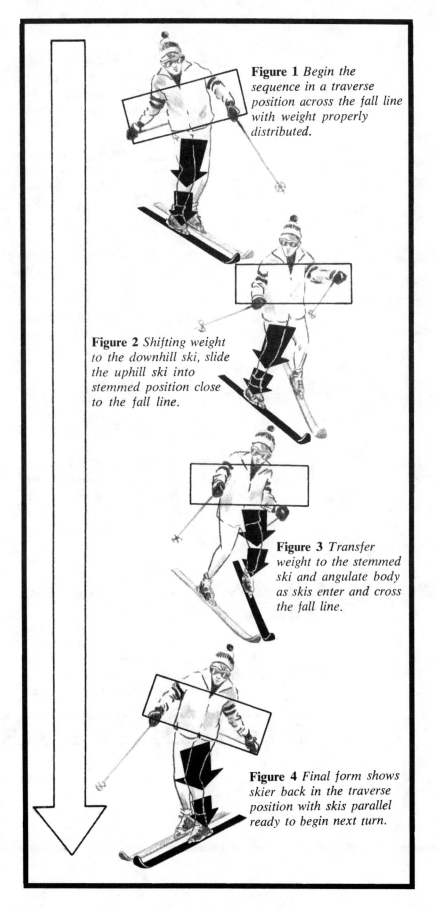

Figure 1 *Begin the sequence in a traverse position across the fall line with weight properly distributed.*

Figure 2 *Shifting weight to the downhill ski, slide the uphill ski into stemmed position close to the fall line.*

Figure 3 *Transfer weight to the stemmed ski and angulate body as skis enter and cross the fall line.*

Figure 4 *Final form shows skier back in the traverse position with skis parallel ready to begin next turn.*

Every skier sometimes encounters a situation in which the terrain or the conditions are just too tough to handle — a sheer drop-off, so steep that the snow won't even mogul, or a more gentle slope, glassed with frozen sleet. The solution is to sideslip. More skiers than will ever admit it have been helped out of uncomfortable situations simply by sideslipping through, over, or around the problem. In addition to being a safety device, it is also a basic skiing form.

WHAT For modern alpine skiers, sideslipping (lateral and forward) is a most important exercise on skis.

A controlled sideslip from a true parallel position is the secret ingredient in short swings and wedeln. To begin with, *both* skis must move sideways down the slope. When traversing, we hold our edges and run straight but now we must release our edges to create controlled skidding. This means flattening our skis.

Start a shallow traverse across the fall line with normal body angulation over the downhill ski. To release edges, simply stand up straight and then slowly sink down again. Your skis will slide on the up motion and hold on the down. The key to controlled sideslipping is in the knees, an-

kles and skis — they must be together and work as one unit. Use hips to maintain balance. For more support, use your poles, particularly when starting to sideslip from a standstill.

Common problems encountered at this stage may be: separating skis, sliding forward or backward erratically, catching outside (downhill) edges and skiing over ski pole. All can be corrected by one or more of the following: keeping the ankles, knees and hips forward; leaning out over the downhill ski; avoid flattening the downhill ski too much; using the downhill pole properly.

HOW The importance of the ankles in sideslipping becomes apparent when you try to maintain a constant sliding motion. To understand how the ankles function we must know more about them.

Basically, the ankle is a hinge-type of joint. A mortise is formed by the small bone on the outside of the leg — the fibula, and the larger bone, the tibia, on the inner surface. They join over the top of the ankle joint which is called the talus. The mortise of the ankle joint prevents it from lateral movement or rotation. Ski boots, tightly laced (or buckled), further limit movement. The inability to flex

**SKI THE
AMERICAN
WAY

STAGE 6**

SIDESLIPPING

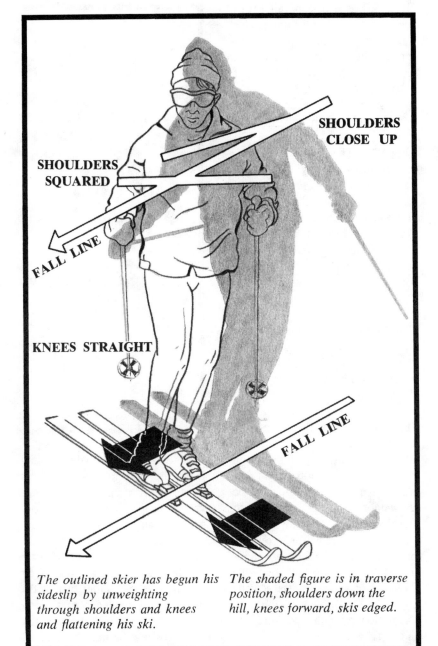

SHOULDERS CLOSE UP

SHOULDERS SQUARED

FALL LINE

KNEES STRAIGHT

FALL LINE

The outlined skier has begun his sideslip by unweighting through shoulders and knees and flattening his ski.

The shaded figure is in traverse position, shoulders down the hill, knees forward, skis edged.

the ankle sideways assures maximum control of edging. The ankle does flex forward along a longitudinal axis of the "Big Toe" and the heel but the outer two-thirds of the foot is largely for balance. For this reason the term "flatten the ankles" is not a part of the American Ski Technique — it doesn't work and furthermore it is not necessary to control skis.

WHY The up-motion of the body in sideslipping will reduce the weight on the skis. It also moves the center of mass to the downhill side, causing a flattening of the edges. In other words, the skier's center of mass must be moved before his skis can move.

Gravity does the rest and the skier simply rides the gently moving skis, controlling resistance to motion with angulation and body position. When the weighted ski is nearly flat (complete flattening can be disastrous), the end bearing the greater weight seeks the fall line. As the skis are edged gently, resistance from the side increases and the end bearing the greater weight feels more resistance, and therefore is less able to slide than the lighter end.

Sideslipping requires good use and knowledge of weight placement and edge control; gravity will do the rest.

Regarded as a true parallel turn, the christie uphill is the perfect "one turn" device to test the skiing conditions and to give you a "feel" for how you must react. It is also a safe way to make a fast stop when a snow plow would send you flying.

WHAT The parallel christie can be broken down into three basic forms: the christie uphill, christie from the fall line and the completed parallel turn. Because these maneuvers are basically the same, American Ski Technique suggests that they all be performed in the same way.

In its most simple form, the uphill christie is merely a slight sideslip from the traverse. While you are moving, direction change is caused by releasing the edges of both skis and re-setting them.

Start from shallow traverse (fig. 1) and flex the knees and ankles with a down motion (fig. 2), follow immediately with an up-weighting motion and forward lean (fig. 3). During the up-weighting it is possible to steer your ski tips toward the slope. In other words, you not only start a sideslip up-weighting, but you also change the direction of your skis. Reset your edges with a down-motion and angulation over the downhill ski (fig. 3).

Finish the turn by once more going into the traverse position.

This is the most simple *correct* way to do the christie uphill. There are many more, but whichever you use, be sure first that it

will work for you when skiing from the fall line. Many skiers try to learn a particular maneuver using a too difficult method, which results in slow progress.

HOW In substance, the christie uphill teaches us all the body actions of the parallel turn without the real challenge of turning through the steepest part of the hill (crossing the fall line). Thus, at the slow speeds which instill confidence and a secure feeling for the balance necessary to maintain the parallel position, we are able to execute the turn in a relaxed and natural position.

SKI THE AMERICAN WAY

STAGE 7

THE CHRISTIE UPHILL

*The christie uphill begins with the skier in shallow traverse (away from the fall line) as shown in **figure 1.** Note proper traverse position, knees forward and shoulders downhill. In **figure 2,** the skier rises, and with an up-motion, releases his edges. Then, as in **figure 3,** the edges are reset with a down-motion; knees are bent, body properly angulated. In **figure 4,** skier has now assumed a new traverse, however the direction is now up the hill. Notice that in the release period the skier's body is distinctly forward; in other phases, it is more erect. This relationship of stance to edge is of extreme importance.*

Having learned the basic maneuver and becoming acquainted with the weight positioning, executing the turn from closer to the fall line will present no serious problem. Each "element" of the maneuver must simply be intensified as you near the fall line.

The importance of the natural position is to provide economy of motion and to let the body weight be carried by the skeleton rather than the muscles and ligaments. Notice too, that in the figures, the body is held fairly erect and that the flection to create the turn is not extreme at any point in the maneuver. Relax, and let your body's balance mechanism direct your forward lean in order to anticipate forward motion. In this way, you will not be opposing the forces of gravity and friction.

WHY In the American Ski Technique, the christie uphill is regarded as a true parallel turn. Once a parallel turn is begun, it is nothing more than a narrow sideslip the direction of which is continually changing. To terminate the slipping action requires creating some lateral resistance by angulation just as in the traverse position.

To increase the effectiveness of the christie uphill, use counter-rotation by twisting upper body in opposite direction of skis.

The function is the same as that of stemming one ski. When the ski is unweighted it is placed in a position that will encounter lateral resistance when it is weighted once again. In a parallel maneuver, counter-rotation occurs on the up-weighting motion (fig. 3). It ceases when the weight returns to the skis.

Counter-rotation is particularly important when doing a christie uphill from the fall line.

THE SNOWPLOW CHRISTIE

SKI THE AMERICAN WAY

STAGE 8

The snowplow is a confidence-inspiring position that is a natural bridge into stem turns. If every skier, trying to master his stem christie, would first spend an hour performing the snowplow christie as a preparatory maneuver, he'd find himself well on his way to perfect stem turns, probably in half the time.

WHAT It is best to start the snowplow christie from a very shallow snowplow position in the fall line and on a gentle slope. As you begin to move forward, sink down on both skis without changing their angle (fig. 1). Then, with an up-motion (unweighting), push off on one ski transferring all your weight to the other (fig. 2). As you have increased the "push" on the weighted ski, it will begin to carve an arc. Now quickly move the unweighted ski parallel and slightly ahead of the other (fig. 3). The up-motion will release, to some degree, the "edge" on the weighted ski resulting in a sharper turn. Sinking (unweighting down) will result in more release. When you've cut as much of an arc as you wanted, stand up slowly. This will equalize the weight, reestablish direction to your skis and you will find yourself in a new traverse.

To link your snowplow christies first begin in the standard snowplow turn position and start to turn from your traverse into the fall line. As you cross it, instead of continuing to let the weighted skis "track" together again, transfer your weight — as described above — and carry on with the method for the snowplow christie.

The next maneuver — the one which "grows" out of the snowplow christie — is the stem christie from the fall line. This, in turn, will lead to the beginning stem christie, then to the final form of the stem christie, and so forth.

To perform a stem christie from the fall line, instead of stemming both skis, stem only one. You will find that having a tracking (straight-running) ski will make the weight transfer much more simple. The rest of the form is the same as for the snowplow christie.

Always try to keep your body in motion during this maneuver and be sure your weight transfer is total.

HOW The snowplow christie is an excellent maneuver in which to observe knee and ankle bend in its more dynamic phases. It is true, however, that at this stage we often tend to focus more on the obvious manipulations and movements of the joints and forget the application of "total motion" at seen in knee and ankle bend.

Remember, the knees and ankles are the control centers for transmitting and effecting proper edging on your skis. For example, though all your weight may be on your downhill ski (as it's supposed to be), you will not be able to edge effectively unless both your knees and ankles are flexed. You can stand on one ski all day and unless you're down and forward, you won't even approach positive edging. Without flexing there can be no lateral movement, hence, no edge control. Stiff, straight, knees and ankles also make it impossible for the "shock-absorbing" mechanisms in your legs to do their jobs.

FALL LINE

Shaded ski is the weighted ski. Starting from a snowplow position, as in **figure 1,** *the skier unweights his uphill ski and stems it. In* **figure 2,** *he shifts his weight back to stemmed ski and arcs through the fall line. In* **figure 3,** *he has brought his skis parallel again, weight on the new downhill ski. He is now in his new traverse, body angulated.*

When knees and ankles are "in motion," they sense changes in your balance as well as in the terrain.

A simple test to check for proper flexing is to stand upright and flex your knees forward as if you were trying to kneel while standing. Rock your knees to the left, then to the right. Now, stand up straight and try it. It doesn't work. Therefore, if you want to ski limber, you must have those knees and ankles working all the time.

WHY You will notice that from a simple snowplow, at low speeds and on a gentle grade, you can simply "step" into a parallel turn. It's as simple as that. But what you're really doing is using all the forces of weight control and edging (or lack of it), to overcome the resistance of your skis on the snow and their affinity for going in a straight line.

From experience — and common sense — we know that a ski in the fall line is encountering less resistance on its path than one moving at right angles to the fall line (as in edging or sideslipping). Hence, by stepping off one ski and onto the other, it will begin to move freely in the direction it has been pointed. Once again, we can feel the platform we have created as our skis glide out from under us.

With practice, the snowplow christie — and the all-important knee and ankle bends, can be done on steep and varied terrain and, ultimately, even over moguls. But always remember that the body must move ahead of the feet when entering the fall line. And the only way to do this is through flexing the knees and ankles.

The most basic stem christie is performed at the lowest speed and becomes more **difficult** as speed increases. The easiest of all, the snowplow christie, lets the ski arc through the fall line before it is closed again to parallel. But in the beginning form of the stem christie, you learn how to close to parallel while the outside ski is in the fall line — and come one step closer to parallel skiing.

WHAT The stem christie is nothing more than a combination of the stem turn and the snowplow christie. But, because more advanced turns require the skier to perform them at higher speeds, the timing, coordination of elements, and "total motion" become of increasing importance.

Starting from a good traverse position, stem but don't change your body position. Stay high and initiate the turning power with weight and forward lean. Now, as you approach the fall line, begin your motion. This should be immediately followed by the up-and-forward motion and the closing of the skis for the christie phase. This, of course, assumes complete weight transfer to the outside ski. In the beginning, it might be well to hold the stem longer than we have suggested to gain balance and confidence but work toward a short period. If you are unable to do the maneuver, check your weight transfer and then practice christies uphill and snowplow christies.

HOW The mark of the expert skier is the seemingly effortless performance of high-speed maneuvers. He seems to glide through turns, edges cutting over the boilerplate. The lesson here is that confidence and relaxation can make for better skiing; muscles strong but not inflexible, joints ready to respond to changing conditions.

Stem turns are confidence-building maneuvers, basically. The stem that is right for you will allow you to develop the confidence to ski limber. Most skiers can understand — from a verbal standpoint — the elements of a stem turn or, for that matter, of a royal christie. But doing them is something else. We must ski at our level, not above it. Pushing ahead too far or too fast will result in slow progress.

Keep yourself limber throughout this turn. After you have it down, try increasing and decreasing your edge and the speed of your closing. Practice will give you a "lighter" feel on the snow.

WHY Now is the time to master weight placement. When starting the turn, the downhill ski must provide a solid platform from which to launch your un-

SKI THE AMERICAN WAY

STAGE 9

THE STEM CHRISTIE

From a shallow traverse (figure 1), square your shoulders forward, sink and stem your uphill ski (figure 2). Be sure downhill edge is holding. As you drift into the fall line, shift weight to the outside ski with up-motion and angulation (figure 3). Begin to close to parallel position (figure 4) as you pass through the fall line and assume new traverse (figure 5). Arrows and shaded area indicate weight during each phase.

weighting. The outside ski must be a satisfactory base on which to stand. A common failing is to let your lower ski skid out from under you. This will happen only if you are not exerting the force into the ground to make the platform which, after all, is only the product of resistance. The force of the edged ski piles up snow beneath it. In the same way, it would be futile to try pushing an automobile if you were wearing roller skates during the attempt.

While you're making a turn, always be thinking about your position relative to the next one. If your body position is right — and you are creating the proper frictional resistances — the "built-in" characteristics of your skis will do the rest. That's the beginning of real skiing.

ADVANCED STEM CHRISTIE

SKI THE AMERICAN WAY

STAGE 10

This last of the stem christies scarcely involves a stem at all—just enough to steer the skier into the turn. The outside ski is closed *before* you get to the fall line.

WHAT We are now on the brink of making truly parallel turns, for the advanced stem christie is hardly a stem at all. In fact, "step-over christie" might almost be a better title since the stem is held for but an instant and is so slight as to barely allow a change of edging from one ski to the other while changing direction. However, complete weight transfer and forward lean remain vital in making this turn result in a true arc. During the turning motion and weight shift, the body position should not be referred to as "counter-rotation." What it really is, is "counter-motion" and it serves simply to maintain the skier's balance. It should occur at the same time as the turn and not prior to it. How far you displace your ski will depend on your positive edging and balance. As far as learning goes, the less you stem it, the better.

Regardless of how slight the stem, this is still considered a "steered" turn. Therefore, stemming the outside ski must be accompanied by a quick and positive down, up and forward motion. In all christie turns, the

skier's body must move before the skis can be displaced. Don't ever rely on last-minute attempts to regain control that should have come from proper weight shift.

However graceful and beautiful parallel turns may appear, the stem christie is still the mainstay of alpine skiing. In extreme conditions, or when the visibility is poor, even expert skiers use the stem to some degree or other. Without a good solid stem, you are not a really expert skier.

HOW Watch an accomplished diver sometime. Perhaps 90 per cent of his excellence depends on how well he uses the springboard to make himself airborne. This is true with a skier too, particularly during the stem-turn phase. Few people notice the launch mechanism, they concentrate on the finished product. Yet, the launch is a most important ingredient in the effective weight transfer from ski to ski.

While the diver gets his spring from the board, the skier must use his leg muscles and the platform his skis have formed. During the stem, the strong leg, thigh and calf muscles stretch in the down-motion. When the weight is shifted to the outside ski, the muscles of the downhill leg contract vigorously. The propulsion created is an up-and-forward one and the body mass quickly trans-

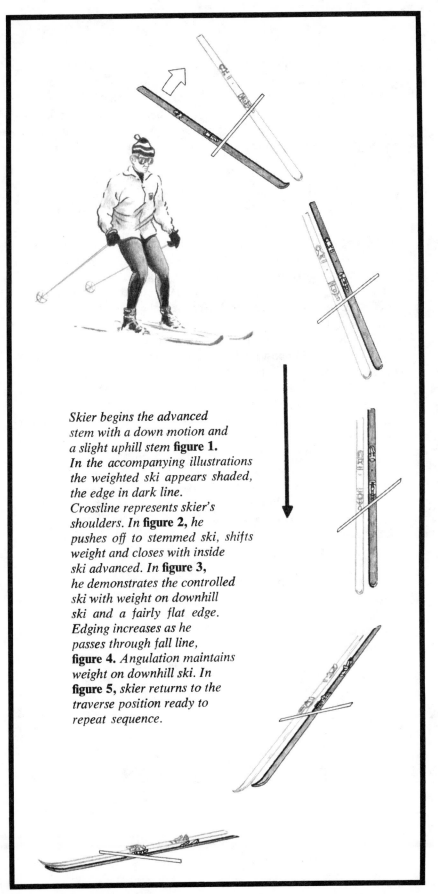

Skier begins the advanced stem with a down motion and a slight uphill stem **figure 1.** *In the accompanying illustrations the weighted ski appears shaded, the edge in dark line. Crossline represents skier's shoulders. In* **figure 2,** *he pushes off to stemmed ski, shifts weight and closes with inside ski advanced. In* **figure 3,** *he demonstrates the controlled ski with weight on downhill ski and a fairly flat edge. Edging increases as he passes through fall line,* **figure 4.** *Angulation maintains weight on downhill ski. In* **figure 5,** *skier returns to the traverse position ready to repeat sequence.*

fers to the outside ski. The power of this released energy is enough to carry the thrusting leg in the direction of the stemmed ski until it comes to rest neatly alongside the other in a completely parallel position.

WHY The key action to remember in the advanced stem christie is a smooth, continuous, vertical displacement of the body: sinking, rising, sinking deeper and rising again. Since we are still maneuvering at relatively low speeds, it is possible to steer the turn. Because the inside ski carries virtually no weight, it is relatively passive to the turning function. The weighted ski meets all the resistance on its inside, or uphill edge. The way in which this weight is applied, can mean a long arcing turn, or a short skid; thus, the types of turn can be varied by the skier.

Rarely does a skier change his weight from one ski to another without a reason. He knows he must maintain his up-and-forward control position with knees flexed and supple. Above all, he must keep his knees moving while his upper body continues to anticipate forward motion.

Here again, weight is the main control of the turning force. Used effectively, it will make for great control.

Together at last! But *keeping* the skis together in the turns is a technique to be mastered through practice. Remember that the faster you're going, the more you have to lean into the turn to remain stable.

WHAT The parallel turn, and its elements, are among the most important basics in all really good skiing. They must be thoroughly learned and understood before genuine progress may be made.

Begin from a normal traverse. When you start the unweighting portion, however, do not change your upper body positioning. Think of skiing on one ski at a time, using the other as a stabilizer. Then, as you sink, you will maintain or even increase your edge.

Planting the pole, transfer all your weight to the downhill ski. Rise forward, as in small figure 1, on your upper ski; change your lead and begin to counter-rotate. The amount of rotation will depend on the snow conditions and your ability to completely unweight. Come up straight forward, as opposed to the direction in which you're moving. You cannot begin your angulation until your edges have been set in their new line and the side resistance is brought to bear on the skis.

As soon as your skis have swung through to their new course, as in small figure 2, initiate a slow sinking motion and angulation to the outside, as in small figure 3. Avoid a static position throughout this turn and the subsequent traverse. Continuous "total motion," together with proper forward lean, will enable you to get sufficiently unweighted for this turn. These positions will also keep your weight distributed properly and your skis cutting a firm arc as you execute each turn.

HOW Starting from the traverse, the initial down-motion prepares the leg and thigh muscles for action by increasing intra-muscular tension on them — like winding the mainspring of a watch. The following up-motion brings the hips (center of skier's gravity) forward to "lead the turn." When the body is up and unweighted, the ski is now free of the resistance created by the body weight and is able to be acted upon by the counter-rotation. Motion of the upper body (shoulders), in the opposite direction of the turn results in a deflection of the ski into the turn. The degree of the ski's turn will not be equal to the degree of counter-rotation because a certain amount of power is lost within the muscles.

The hardest part of the turn— the beginning — is now achieved. As the skier comes down on the outside ski, the weight is reapplied and the force continues to deflect

SKI THE AMERICAN WAY

STAGE 11

PARALLEL TURNS

The center of the skier's body mass lies along a straight line from the ball of the outside foot; through the same knee and up through the inside shoulder to form a triangle with the fall line (dotted line) and the slope (horizontal line). The inside edge of the downhill ski controls the degree of skid (curved line).

the ski in the direction of the turn.

This description of the bio-mechanical aspects will help you turn if you think about it and understand it before beginning the maneuver.

WHY The body position relative to the skis is of extreme importance in any turn. When speed is of no concern, you can slow down and analyze the various stages of the parallel turn that you are making.

Most important, you must always know where you are over your skis, and you must be there for a reason. We call this "body mass," and in the parallel turn it is a vital function without which a good turn is impossible.

Actually, this is two positions in one: *weight forward,* with the body at right angles to the slope; and *lean,* with angulation to the inside of the arc of the turn.

Notice in the drawing how the knee and ankle of the outside leg apply weight to the edge through the ball of the foot. In this two-dimensional view of his position we see that the skier's center of mass is along a line to the apex of the triangle. But, because he must maintain balance over his skis, he uses angulation to counteract the body's tendency to go in the direction of travel. The forward lean guides the arc of the turn. Faster and sharper turns require more lean.

THE CHECK IN THE PARALLEL TURN

SKI THE AMERICAN WAY

STAGE 12

Learning to set your edges precisely is important in parallel skiing for complete control on all surface and all terrain. Knowing how much edge is required — and how much is available — allows the skier a measure of confidence, especially under adverse conditions. The check in the parallel turn will give more precision and more authority to your skiing.

WHAT The check — or setting of edges prior to the parallel turn — rates as one of the most difficult exercises on skis. This abrupt edging or braking requires complete coordination of skis and body movement.

The American Technique accepts two basic methods: a quick drop from the traverse position deflecting the ski tips slightly uphill with a distinct increase in angulation and pole plant or the christie uphill into a check with pole plant. To many observers, the difference between the two methods may be unnoticeable. However, the effectiveness of the check is what really counts.

First, your body weight must come down hard and precisely on the inside edge of your lower ski. At the exact instant your skis stop skidding, you must push off and up for the next turn. Since you can not compensate for the sudden stopping of the skis, you must absorb the shock with the lower pole.

Additionally, you cannot sit back to compensate for the braking effect of the check, or you will be off balance for your next turn. So, you must learn to slow down the skis without slowing the body.

This is what the check can do for you; it bounces you up as if on a springboard and at the same time throws your weight forward. It is this quick un-weighting and forward lean that are vital to short radius turns on steep terrain.

HOW Now that we are up to "operating temperature," we find that muscle rhythm has been established which has a desirable effect on neuro-muscular activities within the body. We find it natural to continue rhythmic, up-and-down motions from turn to turn. Unweighting begins to come "automatically" and the resulting counter-rotation becomes a more effective turning force. In short, motion conditions both our minds and our bodies. Operating together they complement each other to the point that maximum turning power is achieved with minimum muscle exertion.

WHY The parallel turn with check manifests the full potential of counter-rotation. As the skier rises to unweight, his body straightens. The untwisting away from the old weighted ski becomes a twist in the opposite direction, achieving counter-rotation over the newly weighted ski.

The check at the beginning has two distinct uses: it can control speed as well as provide a solid base from which the skier can unweight. While the check may be achieved through either of the methods suggested above, its proper execution will be a boon when skiing terrain with pitch as steep as 30 to 40 degrees.

With proper counter-rotation and reasonable skid, your skis will change direction from 30 to 40 degrees before they are again weighted. By combining this motion simultaneously with forward lean, the turning effect can be magnified, causing an even broader deflection before the edges begin to bite.

The "check" in a parallel turn is the culmination of one turn and the beginning of another. Skis are edged abruptly **(figure 1)** by a quick sinking from the traverse position, increased angulation and pole plant. From the platform created by the check, skier springs upward and forward, transfers weight to outside ski, and begins controlled skid across the fall line **(figure 2).** With uphill ski advanced, skier completes counter-rotation, increases angulation and sinks to control tracking **(figure 3)** before rising into a new traverse.

Nothing in the history of modern skiing has caught the fancy of beginners and experts alike quite so much as the wedel turn. While the American Ski Technique calls the maneuver "short swings," this turn embodies all the grace, fluidity, and seemingly effortless coordination which makes the sport so pleasing to skier and watcher. The short swing often resembles a double-jointed metronome as the skier swings from side to side through the turn and, at the completion, swings in the angulation phase. Short swings are valuable as a functional maneuver and as a harmonious coordination of weight, skis, and motion.

WHAT When we speak of short swings, we really refer to "linked parallel turns in the fall line." They are closely linked in the sense that there is no distinct turn-traverse-turn phase as in, for example, the stem turns.

Practice on a moderately gentle slope with few moguls. Skiing in the fall line, set your edges with a down-motion, then un-weight upwards. Follow this with counter-rotation, weight transfer and, finally, forward lean. As your skidding skis cross the fall line, angulate to finish the turn and begin the next. On the gentle slope, you may use your poles or not.

Developing the steady, rhythmic flow of turns is the most crucial aspect of the short swing. Turn must follow turn in an un-broken chain. When practicing, should you bobble a turn, don't stop the series; continue on until you've mastered it.

Initially, you may want to give yourself a little help with the aid of a slight "hop" to unweight. Once you have the rhythm down, decrease the hop until just the unweighting is carrying you across the fall line. Keep your speed down by increasing your edges at the conclusion of each turn.

Gradually try the short swing on more difficult terrain. Once you do, you will quickly see that in order to keep speed and motion under control, it will be necessary to apply both edge and angulation. But, by this time, the movements will not be strange to you and it will simply be a question of increasing them.

HOW The response of body muscles in the short swing must be rapid for there is so much different muscle activity going on simultaneously. With each turn, the knee and ankle joints are extended during the down, up and forward movement. The hips are twisting with the counter rotation and the upper body is bending to maintain angulation.

As you enter the lower arc of the turn, total motion reaches its full effect on the body. When you sink to set edges, leg, thigh and trunk muscles are compressed like a coiled spring.

It becomes easier to overcome

SKI THE AMERICAN WAY

STAGE 13

THE SHORT SWING

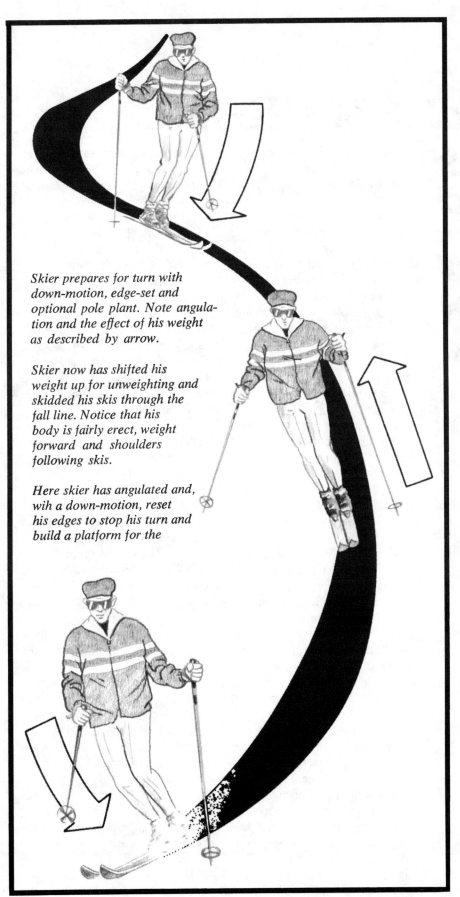

Skier prepares for turn with down-motion, edge-set and optional pole plant. Note angulation and the effect of his weight as described by arrow.

Skier now has shifted his weight up for unweighting and skidded his skis through the fall line. Notice that his body is fairly erect, weight forward and shoulders following skis.

Here skier has angulated and, wih a down-motion, reset his edges to stop his turn and build a platform for the

inertia when making a long series of turns than just a few short ones. Therefore, plan your turn pattern to allow for at least two in each direction, hopefully more. Be sure to predetermine start and finish points. This is an aid in that it gives you definite points at which to make both left and right-hand turns.

You will find that, as your speed increases, the muscles and rhythm will settle into a pattern. The maintenance of this regular pattern aids in both practice and performance.

WHY There is an almost infinite variety to the short swing. At one extreme is the series of fan-shaped sideslips in which the skis appear to turn about a point near the binding, while at the other, the skis carve clean, connected curves in the snow—lovely to watch.

It is characteristic of the short swing from the fall line that the counter-rotary movements of the upper body are not apparent. What one sees is the lower body twisting against the relatively stable mass of the trunk. During all phases, the angular momentum of the legs and trunk remains nearly equal in magnitude.

If trouble is encountered in the turn, it is most likely due to problems in the release stage. In this case you are not sufficiently reducing the mass of your body and the frictional resistance of your skis to the turn and must "get off" them more.

SHORT SWING ON THE STEEP

SKI THE AMERICAN WAY

STAGE 14

The short swing on a steep slope is the key maneuver in any good skier's bag of tricks. If he can depend on it, no slope is too difficult, for this series of turns gives the skier a positive, reliable way to control both his speed and his course. To use the short swing as a braking action, the edge set can simply be increased. But the skier who aspires to short swings on steep terrain needs confidence, precision, and an aggressive nature—in addition to good, strong parallel skiing. Unlike the fluid "wedeln" turns on a gentle slope, these rapid turns are sharp and almost violent in their power and are the mark of the truly expert skier.

WHAT There is little room for mistakes when doing the short swing on steep terrain, for each turn must follow closely on the heels of its predecessor, if the skier is to have maximum speed control and maneuverability.

To start, find a small mogul, check against it and make your first turn. As your skis are skidding through the turn, stop them with a quick edge set, rise forward, skid them back through the fall line and sink to a third reset phase. The pole plant occurs just as the edges are set.

The chief problem is that on steep terrain a lack of positive edging will find the skier going too fast with a loss of maneuverability. If you have that problem, try bringing your weight still farther forward. If your weight is back, the tips of your skis will be "light," and unable to give you the needed carving power.

The back-and-forth rhythm of this maneuver can be varied depending on the requirements of prudent speed. It is wise to note, however, that the more frequent the turns, the less the upper body and shoulders will have to "counter" the effect of the turns.

In soft or deep snow, the down-up motion will have to be more pronounced as the resistance of the snow will tend to throw the skier's weight back. Always keep rhythm in your turns as repetition has a favorable cumulative effect which will help you through successive turns.

HOW Proper body positioning is of critical importance when doing these turns from steep terrain. The basic principles of forward lean, angulation and total motion are never more prominent than here. Recall that in "angulation" your shoulders and your **hips tend to face the valley. This** distributes the body weight properly on the inside edge of the downhill ski.

Prepare for the turn with a slight sinking motion to flex the knee and ankle joints. Follow it with an up motion to unweight. In this way, the degree of angulation is reduced (for less counter) and the weight is quickly transferred to the outside ski. Then follows the sinking which triggers the next turn.

To maintain good forward position, and proper center of gravity location, the hips must always be forward of the boot heel.

As the finish of one turn is the beginning of the next, the rhythmical pattern which evolves re-

In the short swing on steep terrain, the critical phase is the one shown above. Note that the skier's body is "cocked," ready to spring up and forward to unweight, knees pressing hard to build the platform, body properly angulated and pole planted far forward to finish the previous turn and begin this one.

sults in muscles acting at maximum efficiency.

WHY The chief attribute of this turn, or series of turns, is its ability to control speed. While it is basically true that the degree and duration of the edge set phase control the speed, this is not always the case.

Most often, the braking effect depends on the time the ski is in the speed-decreasing sideslip before the edge is set. This reduces the angle between the fall line and the component of resistance, which is parallel to the slope surface and maximizes the magnitude of breaking.

The same ultimate effect, however, can be achieved by a skier, even though he may use more physical effort, simply by employing a shorter radius of skid. A good skier can easily demonstrate that a shorter, sharper skid will achieve the same end with less muscle power.

HOW TO GET
HONEST-TO-GOODNESS
HONEST
SNOW REPORTS

A new method that is practically as foolproof as the snow dance.

by Leonard S. Bernstein

Right now I am going to tell you the most important thing any skier has to know. A guaranteed, absolutely foolproof system for finding out about ski conditions on any mountain in America BEFORE, not after, you drive six hours to get there.

Don't say it. I know. You don't believe me. You've tried everything. You don't call Vermont Ski Reports—you call the mountain directly. Or maybe you don't call the mountain—you call the cook at the ski lodge. No matter how you do it, you lose. Every place quotes better ski conditions than exist. Every mountain competes for the weekend ski crowd and every mountain assumes that the others are going to exaggerate snow conditions. And what else can they do to stay in business but a little of the same thing?

So what do you do on Friday evening after getting a report of a 23-inch base and 12 inches of fresh powder? You take off. And what sustains you? I'll tell you what. This 12 beautiful inches of new powder.

But what do you find when you get there?

It's killing me to think that I'm about to give out this secret that is going to benefit the entire ski world. I have the feeling that someone should be bringing me a big bundle of cash. Perhaps I should start a Ski Advisory Service with paid members who call every Friday for the word.

Everyone knows I have the word. They return from Vermont on Sunday and tell me how bad conditions were. And I say, "I know. It started raining there on Friday at three in the afternoon." And they say, "How did you know? There were no announcements."

This is how I know.

One Friday afternoon with my boots packed, I called my favorite mountain direct for a last minute report. I knew that the report was suspect but it was the best I could do.

"Hello. Is this Mount Jefferson? Could you tell me what the ski conditions are on the mountain?"

"Sorry, this isn't Mount Jefferson. This is McCarthy's Drug Store."

(Damn it. Wrong number. And long distance no less.)

"I'm very sorry. I'm calling from New York City. I dialed Mount Jefferson to get a ski report and I must have gotten a wrong number."

"Well, we're only a mile and a half away from the mountain and it's raining like hell here. All the skiers who have stopped by this afternoon say it's a washout for the weekend. I wouldn't drive up from New York if I were you."

Now, that's a ski report!

That was four years ago, and if anyone does not know what I have been doing for the past four years, they do not deserve good skiing conditions.

The first thing is, you get the name of a drug store in every town that has a ski mountain that you like. Other stores will do, but the drug stores are the best. First, a lot of skiers stop by at drug stores after skiing and talk about the conditions. The druggist is usually a knowledgeable guy and quite agreeable. He will appreciate your "wrong number" dilemma. And finally, he will tell you the truth. Your arrival in town the following day is just not financially important to him.

O.K., you get a list of drug stores. From phone books when you are in ski towns. From the library. You can use a Dun & Bradstreet book which lists the businesses in every town in America. You can even get the name from the long distance operator.

"Operator, in the town of Waterville, Vermont, the phone number of McCarthy's Drug Store."

"I'm sorry, there is no McCarthy's Drug Store. Does it go under a different name?"

"Well, yes, it might. Do you have anything close?"

(Silence, as she fingers the list of 17 businesses in the town.)

"I'm sorry, sir, the only drug store in Waterville is Waterville Drug."

"Yes. That's it. Of course. Can I have the number?"

"Hello, Mount Jefferson Ski Information? I'm calling from New York City . . .

"Waterville Drug Store?

"I'm terribly sorry. I've been trying to get Mount Jefferson for half an hour to find out how conditions are up there and I must have gotten the wrong number. Say, as long as I have you . . ."

Let me report that in four years of drug store calls I have never been turned down and I have never received less than an absolutely accurate report. Sometimes I even get the weather report for the following day.

"It's poor today, but they promise snow for tonight, and it's already starting to fall."

There's no telling what you can find out.

"Yes, it's great. Come on up. How are you driving? No, don't take Route 95, they're backed up for miles. They just opened up a new 26-mile stretch of the thruway. It's empty."

Alas, the truth is that the idea will never work again because McCarthy's is going to get 247 phone calls next Friday.

But think about it. There are lots of variations.

And happy skiing.

"SOMEDAY ALL THIS SNOW WILL BE MINE"

*Or so goes the daydream of the skier
wondering what his favorite sport can do for his
favorite bank account. What can it do?*

No skier worth his bindings has failed to consider, at least once in a while, the possibility of getting involved in his favorite sport as a business proposition. If the skier happens to be disgruntled by his present job and/or wife, he will dream of chucking it all and going skibumming, ultimately to find a comfortable social and economic niche somewhere in the ski industry. Or, if the skier happens to have an extra $5,000 in his bank account, and has been wondering about which mutual fund to plow it in, it may come to him in a burst of sentiment that he sort of owes the money to skiing—for all the satisfaction the sport has given him—and he may seek out a place in that world to make the money work, hopefully as effectively as the mutual funds of legend, but if not, at least to help spur on the progress of winter's only sensible alternative to Drink. Finally, there is the skier, happily employed and/or married this time, who also has extra coins rattling around his pocket but who, though also sentimentally attached to the sport, considers poking into the ski world in a businesslike manner, with a view toward putting his money to work there—provided it will return some measure of profit or, at the least, pleasure.

That roughly describes the occasional daydream of a ski bum *manqué,* a well-off good sport, and a smart business type. The daydream surfaces in many other personalities, too, of course, but one thing that is common to all of them is a need for orientation. What are the various possibilities for investment?

Let's consider some of the general categories in which you could operate as an investor. First, ski areas themselves.

AREAS. Recently the Forest Service invited private investors to help develop ski areas at Skyline Basin in Washington and at Trail Peak in California. Since such start-from-scratch ventures require mil-

lions of dollars, they have limited appeal for the small investor, but their existence at least proves that the growing sport is seeking investment. Actually, you could eventually jump into an operation of this type, even with limited funds, if you kept track of developments, contacted major parties interested in the venture, and perhaps combined your resources with those of friends or business associates. The example also points up a continuing source for information in this field, since so much skiable terrain in the country is under the jurisdiction of either state or national forest authorities. Information on state forest matters is available from the particular state's commissioner of land or natural resources. Information on national forest matters is available from any of nine regional offices of the Forest Service, which is a part of the Department of Agriculture and carried as such in the U.S. Government listings of the phonebook.

A more realistic possibility for small investors may be found in the stock offerings made by existing ski areas from time to time to develop capital for expansion and improvement efforts. Such investments are often limited to residents of the particular state in which the corporation is licensed to operate. Most states protect potential investors by requiring that the corporation disclose background facts of the proposed enterprise. Interstate offerings—at least those involving more than 10 shareholders—call for registration with the Securities and Exchange Commission, so again you would have access to a full disclosure of all aspects of the enterprise.

In the past decade, nearly 50 ski resorts have

Ski area ownership requires such capital investments as clearing trails (top photo, opposite page, at Breckinridge, Colo.), installing gondola platforms (below, left, at Mammoth, Calif.), laying snowmaking equipment (bottom, at Jay Peak, Vt.), and hoisting lift towers (far right, at Alta, Utah).

SKIER POPULATION & SALES

YEAR	HARD CORE SKIERS who ski an average of 12 days per year	OCCASIONAL SKIERS who ski fewer than 12 days per year	RETAIL SALES of clothing, equipment, footwear, accessories	TOTAL SALES including Retail Sales plus lift tickets, travel, food, lodging, etc.
1960-61	1,083,750	490,500	$ 58 million	$282.9 million
1961-62	1,275,000	577,000	$ 75 million	$332.9 million
1962-63	1,500,000	679,000	$101 million	$391.5 million
1963-64	1,650,000	798,400	$115 million	$460.5 million
1964-65	1,815,000	939,250	$135 million	$542.0 million
1965-66	1,996,000	1,105,000	$150 million	$637.5 million
1966-67	2,196,000	1,300,000	$175 million	$750.0 million
1967-68	2,416,000	1,495,000	$201 million	$862.5 million
1968-69	2,657,000	1,720,000	$231 million	$992.0 million
1969-70	2,923,000	1,977,000	$266 million	$1.14 billion

Personal Estimates of R. A. Des Roches, Executive Director, Ski Industries America

DISTRIBUTION OF SHOPS & AREAS

NEW ENGLAND	SHOPS	AREAS
Connecticut	200	8
Maine	77	45
Massachusetts	343	39
New Hampshire	140	46
Rhode Island	35	—
Vermont	180	41
	975	179

MIDDLE ATLANTIC STATES	SHOPS	AREAS
Delaware	6	—
District of Columbia	22	—
Maryland	30	5
New Jersey	265	10
New York	1,343	129
Pennsylvania	270	50
Virginia	20	4
West Virginia	15	6
	1,971	204

SOUTHERN STATES	SHOPS	AREAS
Alabama	1	—
Florida	5	—
Georgia	4	—
Kentucky	3	—
Louisiana	1	—
North Carolina	13	8
South Carolina	1	—
Tennessee	9	1
	37	8

SOUTHWESTERN STATES	SHOPS	AREAS
Arkansas	1	—
Oklahoma	2	—
Texas	24	—
	27	0

MIDWESTERN STATES	SHOPS	AREAS
Illinois	77	7
Indiana	13	3
Iowa	6	8
Kansas	4	2
Michigan	200	85
Minnesota	55	34
Missouri	13	2
Nebraska	6	
North Dakota	6	5
Ohio	65	9
South Dakota	8	2
Wisconsin	97	54
	550	211

ROCKY MOUNTAIN STATES	SHOPS	AREAS
Colorado	272	45
Idaho	98	28
Montana	87	26
New Mexico	52	10
Utah	97	51
Wyoming	42	11
	658	172

FAR WESTERN STATES	SHOPS	AREAS
Alaska	34	10
Arizona	16	5
California	626	50
Nevada	33	7
Oregon	107	19
Washington	207	21
	1,023	112
CANADA	165	191
TOTALS	5,561	1,075

"gone public" in this manner. Perhaps the greatest reward for this kind of investment is the vicarious pleasure obtained "owning a piece of the action" at Bilious Bowl, and skiing at "your own" area. Often, however, there is a fringe monetary benefit when a securities offering has free skiing rights tied to it. For the regular skier, the lift ticket credit becomes a very real dividend indeed. Aside from this definite plus, however, you must look upon your subordinated debentures from Bilious Bowl as a long-term investment. Too few ski areas are able to stay in the black even after a good winter to permit any larger optimism about immediate income or capital gains.

AREA SERVICES. In and around ski areas are the many satellite activities that skiers need and are willing to pay for. These include motels, lodges and inns, restaurants, and various retail establishments —ski shops, gift shops, arts-and-crafts shops, boutiques. You don't have to be an experienced hotelier, restaurateur or retailer to get started here, but you better surround yourself with qualified personnel in the field you select. Careful research is essential in spotting the need for a particular service. Most established areas have quite enough of these satellite activities already, so if you are going to invest in some conventional service, you might be better off doing so in the neighborhood of a new area. For example, a group of Minneapolis investors recently bought a 70-unit lodge in the heart of West Village at Snowmass-at-Aspen. They're banking on the success of the new area to insure a market for their conventional service—accommodations. On the other hand, you may have a new service to offer— a different kind of aprés-ski entertainment, for instance—in which case your competitive position will be as good as your product if you move into an existing area.

LAND SPECULATION. As Will Rogers once said, "Buy land—they ain't making any more." Presently, however, particularly in the Northeast and around major existing areas elsewhere, they're not only not making it any more—they're not selling it cheap, either. People who converted to skiing 10 years ago with the idea of saving up to buy a view of the mountain someday, are returning from real estate searches in snow country with the depressing realization that land prices have skyrocketed *there,* too. Today your basic choice is still between a fairly costly piece of land near a ski area, and a cheaper parcel somewhat more removed from civilization. In any event, you can still buy land. Offbeat ways to find the land include moseying over hinterland byways yourself, shopping the United Farm Agencies catalog, and attending Foreclosure Land Bureau auctions. Conventional means to find land still exist, too, and are perhaps more reliable in the long run, and at the least, place less strain on you.

There are plenty of realtors with listings covering virtually any requirement. Two such people are Wendy Morse, chief entrepreneur of Aspen's Mason & Morse, and Harry Ames of Woodstock, Vt., mentioned here, incidentally, because neither was involved in real estate until emigrating to snow country. Ames' Vermont Real Estate Clearing House uses a computer to identify and match real estate parcels to the specific needs of prospective buyers. Another good listings source has been Sam and Peter Miller's *Vermont Real Estate,* a magazine that lists hundreds of properties by county location. Local newspapers and local chambers of commerce are also good sources for the names of realtors and for general leads on land possibilities in the specific areas.

BUYING A SECOND HOME. Every year more and more skiers are sold on the "vacation home" concept, and more and more developers are creating second-home villages in and around ski resorts to answer the demand. If you have bought your own land to start with, of course, you are going to try to be your own developer and erect a suitable chalet. But, assuming you haven't been able to find land near a paved road, you will certainly consider the pre-arranged vacation home investment, including the increasingly popular condominium in which you own a portion of an apartment-type building. Certainly pleasure and not income should be the ultimate purpose of this kind of investment, but selecting your second home wisely will permit you to maximize the pleasure—by seeing to it that you can take advantage of the home during more than one season—and minimize the cost—by providing for rental of your unit when you are not using it. Here, as with purchasing land, realtors and local newspapers can be of considerable help in exposing you to the varieties of investment available. Similarly, the real estate sections of the major metropolitan newspapers often carry features and advertising on vacation homes.

SOURCES. Like the newspaperman whose stories are only as good as his sources, you can't hope to succeed in investing in any phase of the ski business without being well-informed. Besides the sources already mentioned, there are the two important ski industry trade associations: Ski Industries America, 432 Park Ave. South, New York, N.Y. 10016, and National Ski Areas Ass'n, 369 Lexington Ave., New York, N.Y. 10017. Also well worth consulting are the various trade journals in the field which, on the area side, treat in detail the news and problems in area operations, and, on the industry side, deal with all aspects of equipment, from manufacturing through importing and distributing to retail sales. Also, their classified advertising and special sections list employment and acquisition opportunities.

For economic feasibility studies, site and facilities planning, and operations planning, you can go to one of the qualified resort specialists in the field, such as Sno-Engineering, headquartered in Franconia, N.H., or Resort Counseling Associates in Seattle, Wash. Specializing in food and lodging services are such national accounting firms as Harris, Kerr, Forster & Company, and Horwath & Horwath.

Finally, and most importantly, are the people already in the ski world. While you could easily run into one of them in a subway in Manhattan or on a cable-car in San Francisco, you're more likely to make more significant contacts and learn a great deal besides, at such perennial gatherings as the ski trade shows (in the spring) and the ski consumer shows (in the fall) which make a tour of most major cities.

GUIDELINES. Wherever your interest lies, you have options to consider. On a limited financial basis, you can become *directly* involved via some corollary endeavor: real estate or vacation home purchase, equipment and specialty sales, lodging and food services.

Another option is the amount of time you are willing or able to put where your money is. Unless you're the ski bum type, you're not going to chuck it all for the full-time option—at least certainly not at first—and unless you have a Wall Street whiz to manage your finances, you're not going to be an absentee investor, either. But even as a part-time operative, you would do well to follow these general guidelines in attempting to get a piece of the action:

1. Define your objectives in relation to your resources.
2. Don't burn your bridges until the feasibility of your project has been confirmed.
3. Obtain the opinions of qualified professionals.
4. Don't rely too much on national growth statistics; they are probably invalid or misleading when applied to your specific project or locale.
5. Remember that the ski industries have some unique problems, including single-season business and the vagaries of weather. Unless identified and coped with, they can be disastrous.

START YOUR CHILDREN RIGHT!

*Ruedi Wyrsch is well
known for his dazzling acrobatic
performances on skis, but he
also has a fine reputation as a
children's skiing instructor.
Here are the key elements he stresses
to parents who are introducing
small fry to the sport*

GET THE RIGHT EQUIPMENT What should
you look for in buying equipment for children?
The big problem parents face is the high cost of the
equipment compared with the relatively short
period during which fast-growing children can
use it. Parents have come up with various
solutions — of varying merit — to this problem.
One is to buy the cheapest of everything. Very little
money is wasted here, obviously, and such
equipment will usually last until the child
outgrows it. Cheap goods are not well-
designed or
well-made,
however, and can
diminish skiing pleasure and
impede progress. Another
is to buy everything too big.
Out-sized equipment will last one, maybe two seasons
longer, but it really won't perform properly until that
time when it does fit the child. In the meantime, there's
a good chance that the kid, in frustration, has given
up on the sport altogether. A third solution is to rent
the equipment. Many ski areas and other rental
outlets quickly run out of children's gear on weekends
and particularly during school holidays, but, aside
from this drawback, the rental approach does give the
child a decent opportunity to begin skiing.
Finally, you could find a shop with a trade-in program
especially designed for children. This makes it
possible to buy good equipment that fits well, and to
trade it in for good-quality gear next
season, without making another large cash outlay.

START CHILD UNDER GOOD CONDITIONS

Don't introduce a child to the sport on a very cold, windy or stormy day, or bring him where there is so much skiing traffic that it is frightening and even dangerous. The presence of a few other children on skis will be helpful, but make sure the newcomer has plenty of space to move around comfortably and freely. A short, gentle slope with a flat run-out is ideal, and you may be lucky enough to have exactly what you need in your backyard. You can start a child on skis as soon as he or she actually enjoys playing in snow. Snow is like water to a child: some kids like playing in water at the beach at the age of two, while others hate it until the age of six or seven. I started skiing at two. The early experience probably didn't help my style much but it deepened my basic liking for snow play.

FIND A GOOD SKI SCHOOL A child can learn quickly and effectively in the right ski school. For one thing, children tend to learn from other children, and an inspired school will inject an element of friendly competition into the learning process. At the same time, the teacher of the class will represent an impartial force whose presence encourages the child to act respectfully and with a desire to please. Parents who stick around to watch a ski school can have a disruptive influence, however. What is missing for the child in this circumstance is the feeling of, "Now I am on my own and I am going to show those other kids." It doesn't hurt to check the class from a distance, of course, and if it's the first time your child is enrolled, it is even desirable, just in case a problem develops that the instructor can't cope with. Once you have seen that the child has adjusted to the class all right, everyone is better off if you head for the hills.

MAKE SKIING FUN, NOT WORK Avoid turning skiing into just another lesson-to-be-learned. Children very definitely don't like to be taught, but they do like to be exposed to the challenge of a sport. A question like, "I wonder if you can walk on your skis from here to there?" will work better than a statement like, "And now I am going to teach you the straight running position." Before learning to snowplow, kids have to get used to skis. Walking, climbing, straight running and side-stepping (while in motion) are all good exercises — provided they are presented as games or challenges. Small children especially don't like to climb, but they should do enough of it to learn edge control. Make it easy for the child by frequently carrying or pushing him up the hill. Children also like to be picked up and set right after they fall. Don't be surprised if a child learns to make parallel turns before the snowplow. Let him do so, but teach him the snowplow, a very useful emergency brake for kids, afterwards.

HOW TO MASTER WINTER DRIVING

All you need to do is stab at your brakes as fast as a woodpecker pecks, and have the right spray-cans in your glove compartment

by Denise McCluggage

Snow is indiscriminate stuff — it falls on the just and unjust, the winter sports fan and the average motorist. So even if you are not a ski enthusiast, you will have to cope with it this winter. And as a skier, you must face the fact that the best ski conditions often mean poor driving conditions. The choice is simple: give up good skiing, or learn to be a good winter-sports driver.

To drive well under trying circumstances, you will have to learn to trust your instinct — your re-educated instinct, that is — while driving. But first, some background information.

So you think your brakes stop your car? Have your instinct file this: they do not. Brakes stop the wheels of a car from rolling, and that is all they are meant to

do. What stops the car from moving is the friction between the tires and the ground. If there is too little friction, the tires of the car can be perfectly still and your car can still be moving at an alarming speed. That's because it is sliding. Brakes can't stop a slide; indeed, they can induce one. Your instinct has neatly grasped that, since brakes stop a rolling motion only, and you are now sliding (also called skidding), the logic is to apply the brakes in a gentle pumping manner — on, then off — to avoid changing the rolling motion into a slide.

So you think your steering wheel turns your car? It does not. Please instruct your instinct that the steering wheel is merely aiming the front wheels of the

car. What makes the car go in the proper direction is the rolling of the front wheels; if your front wheels are not rolling, your car is not turning. If you put the brakes on, thus stopping the wheels from rolling, the car cannot respond to the steering wheel no matter which way or how much you turn it. Again the on-off-on pumping technique on the brake comes into its own, and you can be slowing down and at the same time maintaining steerage.

How to start off on a slippery surface? In a word, gently. Start in the highest gear possible, apply gas as slowly as possible, and as soon as you break traction, stop and start again. Before you dig yourself in deep with spinning wheels, do something about im-proving the traction directly in front of your drive wheels. Check the other wheels, too, to see if a chunk of ice or packed snow is creating an obstacle. Drape a passenger or two over the trunk or have someone bounce on the bumper.

How to climb a hill? Keeping in motion is the game, and if you break traction you've lost, so plan your attack before you start. Get as good a run as possible be-cause you will need all the mo-mentum you can get. As you climb, you actually come slowly off the accelerator, giving less and less gas, keeping the power you ask from the engine to just under the breaking traction point. It is something you must learn to feel. Know where your tires are on the road and which ones are the driven wheels, so that you can steer them (or it) over the few clear spots, sanded spots, or roughened spots you pick out as you go. As the car starts to drop off headway, then really start fighting. Try everything. Notice the tracks of preceding cars. If they are straight, chances are traction is good there. If they scribble about, look out. Hang a wheel over the side of the road in untracked snow. Maybe there is crusted ice or an accumulation of sand. Try going from side to side, changing your angle of at-tack. Don't stop. Don't break traction. But if you do start to spin and you are very near the top and the choice is try any-thing or lose, try this: break all the rules and tromp on the gas pedal and let the wheels spin like mad. You may salvage enough forward motion from a lot of sliding back and forth to put you over the top. But this is a desperation move only and is only good for a few feet at best.

If you don't make the hill, back down and try again. Simply said, but actually backing down can be very scary, particularly when the hill is icy. Now you have to put the manual override on instinct and force yourself to go against nature. Backing is unnatural — for one thing, the steering is backward. And you are given a lovely dilemma: if you don't brake, you will gain a frightening amount of speed, and if you do brake you lose your steering. So consider that you must brake and steer in rapid alternate intervals to maintain your directional stability. All you need to do is stab at your brakes as fast as a woodpecker pecks, and fight down the fervent desire to keep your foot on the brake for an extra beat. Sometimes it is even necessary to actually accelerate going downhill in order to maintain steerage. This can happen when you are going forward down a steep, glare-iced road and your car is now really a sled.

How to get started in cold weather? This is usually a matter of preparation, so be prepared. Batteries lose about half their power in sub-freezing temperatures, so it is wise to start out a ski season with either a fresh battery or one in top condition. And be sure the terminals are firmly connected. Use the lightest-weight oil possible to make the engine easier to turn over. Keep your spark plugs cleaned and properly gapped. You might also clean up your ignition wires and be sure there is

no spark leaking off before it reaches the plugs. I use a spray stuff called "WD-40" that does all sorts of marvelous tricks like freeing rusted bolts, but it also displaces moisture and thus dries out wet ignition systems. If you have consistent trouble starting, it may be worthwhile converting to a transistorized ignition system. Such a system consistently delivers a hotter spark. Antifreeze should test to 40° or 50° below zero for the east, at least 20° below for the west. Windshield washers should be kept full of the special anti-freeze made for them.

When you try to start your car in the cold, be sure everything using juice is off — radio, lights, etc. Give the gas pedal a few healthy pumps unless experience has taught you otherwise, and hit the starter. If the car does not start right off, don't keep grinding away. Turn it off and try again. You can usually tell very shortly whether it is just a matter of nursing it along until life finally bursts, or whether the battery is being weakened. If the latter is the case, leave it. Let the car sit a half-hour or so, and it might well resuscitate itself enough to start, particularly if it is in the sun. (A good idea: park your car so that it will be facing the morning sun; this helps clear the windshield of frost, too. Another good idea: don't put on your handbrake; it might freeze on.) People who live in cold climates equip their cars with either bolt-on engine-oil warmers or, more commonly, plug-in dipstick heaters. If electricity is not available to you, try wrapping your already warm engine in a fiberglass blanket made for that purpose. It might retain enough heat over-

night to make starting easier in the morning. All cars have their starting peculiarities. Learn yours and act accordingly. And remember — not only is it expensive to have a tow car give you a push or a jump start, but on busy weekends the local garages are overwhelmed with car-starting gigs and you may miss a skiing day waiting for help. Preventive mechanics is a good idea.

How to correct for a skid? I left this to the very last, because it is the classic of all winter driving problems and the constant advice is this: Turn your wheels in the direction of the skid. The trouble is that half the skidders don't know what that means, so their skids go uncorrected. My advice is simpler, and if you feed it to your instinct on top of the earlier stuff about how a car steers and how it stops, your instinct might come up with the instantly proper response. It is this: keep your front end in front of your back end. That, after all, is the essence of all driving.

What cars to take skiing? The best snow-country cars are ones that have good traction. This generally means a large proportion of the weight of the car should be over the drive wheels, which automatically favors rear-engine cars and front-wheel drive cars, since the engine is the heaviest part of a car. If your car has front-wheel drive, then you are being pulled down the highway. If your car has rear-wheel drive, then you are being pushed. Don't think that just because the engine is up front where the horses were that your front-mounted engine is pulling you. Most front-engine cars still drive the rear wheels — in actual fact really drive one rear wheel, as you may

have noticed when your car had one wheel still and useless on dry pavement and the other wheel spinning and useless on an icy patch. (The next time you buy a car, specify a limited-slip differential. It will help correct that particular helpless feeling.)

A front-wheel drive is clearly superior on winding roads. through slush, on icy turns, on roads with crosswinds blowing, or in gusts. But front-wheel drive loses its superiority on extremely steep hills that are slippery (the weight of the car is shifted to the rear wheels just when you need it for traction on the front drive wheels.) Possible exceptions are front - wheel - driven Oldsmobile Toronado and Cadillac El Dorado.

I borrowed a Toronado to give it the supreme test. Could it make my Vermont driveway that had already defied my Lancia, my Mini-Cooper, and once even the

rally champion Erik Carlsson himself, Saab-mounted. Illustrious front-wheel-drive cars all. The Toronado had the advantage of being able to muster a more powerful drag-type start from the right-angled highway at the foot of the drive, and enough weight to keep power on the ground in the steepest part of the hill.

Trumpet fanfare! The Toronado made my driveway through six inches of heavy, unplowed spring snow with a mud base beneath. Four-wheeled Scouts and Land Rovers were the only other vehicles to make it that day. Not that many others tried. But still, the Toronado was impressive.

Rear-engine cars that are also rear-wheel drive also benefit from a weight distribution ratio that is favorable to excellent traction. And traction — that bite a car gets on the road — is the critical factor in the snow country. Rear-

engine cars like Fiats, Renaults, Porsches and an occasional Volkswagen often have good luck. And the Volvo, even though conventionally front-engine and rear-wheel driven, sometimes comes perking up the driveway through all sorts of adversity.

The weight consideration also eliminates many of the "muscle" cars from being ideal ski-trip companions, because the super-engines are generally heavier than the milder engine options and further distort the already unfavorable weight - distribution ratio found in most Detroit cars. Powerful engines are not much use in slippery conditions anyway; they generally spin wheels too easily and are more likely to induce power skids. (The Corvette is a pleasantly surprising exception because it carries much of its bulk rearward even though the engine is up front.) Station wagons are familiar favorites for ski trips because the kids can flake out in the back on the way home. If you order a station wagon with the lightest engine and put your heaviest kids to sleep farthest to the back, you might end up with a decent weight ratio over the rear wheels.

What options on your snow car? I've already insisted on a limited-slip differential for you. I also like the heavy-duty suspension and stiffer shocks and power steering (only because you can get a lower steering ratio). I dislike the super-touchy power brakes on most American cars, but like a slight power assist. I have preferred manual transmission in the past, but some of the automatics are getting so good I might change my mind. The main disadvantage of an automatic transmission in cold weather is that if your car should fail to start, it is next to impossible to start an automatic by pushing it. Another drawback — when you are slightly stuck and want to choose the highest gear possible to drive off the slippery spot, there is no clutch to slip, and it is also impossible to select high gear for starting since the automatics start in low automatically.

Another handy snow-country accessory is the heat-wired windshield and rear window. Don't leave them on in the parking lot, though, in anticipation of a snow storm. I tried it and that must have been what flattened the car's battery. I haven't tried one of the Chevrolets with the cockpit-controlled gadget that dumps a traction-improving chemical in front of the rear wheels much the way locomotives dump sand on the rails. The James Bond in me loves the idea of it, though, and

I have tried a spray can of the stuff they use — it's called Liquid Tire Chain — and it's absolute magic! Invest a dollar in a little can of it and just try it. Other spray-can aids include a de-icer, not only valuable for cutting through the heavy ice on a windshield, but indispensable for thawing out frozen door locks. Also, most winter gasolines now come with an anti-condensation additive, but carry a can of Dry Gas or an equivalent. It keeps the moisture in the gas from freezing and blocking carburetor jets or fuel lines.

What to take? As for other handy items that fit in relatively small spaces and can save you time and towing charges, you'll like an electric dipstick (plus a long outdoor-type extension cord) to keep the engine oil from turning to Jello and to make it easier for a chilled battery to start your car. A small army surplus shovel, the kind with a head that can be turned to make it sort of a hoe, too, is useful, as is a tow cable. Jumper cables for helping thy neighbor and for being prepared when your groaning battery needs thy neighbor's help are a good idea, and so is a large plastic sheet (can save you from direct contact with muck and slush as you search under a car for some firm holds for a tow chain). Include some expendable traction aids such as window screening or an old section of carpet. A hatchet can come in handy for collecting pine boughs to put under your slipping wheels, too. And a small zipper bag that is specially made for carrying sand; the latter you can commandeer from the highway department's stock piles.

One of the handiest tools for

getting unstuck is already in your tool kit — your jack. But carry a sturdy square of heavy plywood along with it to use as a base and to keep the jack from sinking out of sight in the snow. It may seem a drastic measure to jack up a car to prepare a bed of traction under the wheels, but it may actually take less time than all the pushing and heaving. If you are really a long-range planner type, you might have a little pre-season body work done on your car. Have a sturdy piece of plate steel with a hole in it to take a tow-hook anchored firmly to the frame or whatever passes for rigidity in your car, and extended to a point where it is easily accessible — it needn't be visible. Do this both fore and aft, because it is a general rule that a car is best pulled out of a stuck situation the way it went in, and you *can* go in backward. Such forethought might save untold numbers of bumpers from being bent, or even gas tanks from being torn askew.

I seem to have omitted a plastic scraper, but to me that's like saying don't forget the steering wheel. If you should be caught without one, however, be advised that your plastic credit card is a fine substitute for the lighter glazings.

What tires to wear? Finally, radial-ply tires, long common in Europe, have gained ground in the United States. Radial-ply tires are so constructed that the part of the tread that touches the ground, called the footprint, distorts less than other tires and thus maintains a firmer grip on the road. Radial-ply tires are clearly superior in the wet and on ice as well. (Their drawback: they ride a little rougher than other tires on cars with suspension systems not designed especially for them.) Snow tires are tires with what is called an aggressive tread, offering lots of sharp edges that can get a grip on snow with less chance of slipping. They are at their best in untracked unpacked snow. As snow packs down and becomes more akin to ice, snow tires lose their advantage and a good radial-ply summer tire can actually be more secure, particularly against the side forces that produce skids.

Studs are also being used more in this country after a long history in Europe; they are at their best on ice. Chains are the devil's own invention — hard to get on and get off and prone to breaking links and slapping under your fender. Still, a good reinforced chain is the most reliable way to plow through snow-bandaged roads and up clogged hills. Again, however, they are at their best in straight-ahead heavy going.

So what to use? It is all a compromise; there is no best way. If I lived in the city and drove long distances to ski country over mostly dry roads, I would use a radial-ply tire with a mildly aggressive tread. If I lived in the land of heavy snows and used lots of back roads, I'd use studded snow-tires and carry chains. If I drove on high-speed highways that are often slippery, I'd use a radial-ply tire lightly studded. No matter what, I'd use the best tire available. No bargain racks. Remember, it's the tires that stop your car, the tires that turn your car — that everything you do as a driver has to be transmitted to the ground through your tires.

ABOUT THE AUTHOR The reporter's art of living out his story did not begin with George Plimpton. While that "professional amateur" was still in short pants. Denise McCluggage was on assignment skiing against Penny Pitou and Betsy Snite, to the delight of her *New York Herald Tribune* sports page readers. "I wrote *as* a woman, not *for* women," she says now from Vermont. "Most sports writers are either frustrated participants or hero worshippers — that limits them terribly." When ladies weren't allowed in the Yankee Stadium World Series press box she covered the contest from the grandstand. "It gave me a new approach." She founded, then sold AutoWeek, a journal of sport car racing, in favor of free-lancing and publishing a Mad River Glen newspaper called, with her typical directness, "The Newspaper." She drives a Yamaha Trailmaster and a Land Rover with Vermont plate DOG: "I've always wanted a Rover named dog," she says. Her driveway is unpaved: "Only friends with four-wheel drive can visit me in winter."

HOW TO MAKE HOME SKI MOVIES

*A SKIER'S
DIGEST interview with
John Jay, one of
the leading filmmakers
in skiing*

What's the biggest problem most would-be photographers have in making ski movies?

They can't resist the urge to pan. They spray their shots around like a garden hose and usually succeed in giving the viewer an acute case of mal de mer, or the feeling that the photographer was shivering when he shot the film.

How do you avoid that kind of wobbly effect when taking pictures?

The best way is to use a tripod. There is also a gadget available which can be inserted into the top of one ski pole and then screwed into the camera base to make a unipod. With no support at all, you should take pains to brace the camera against your eye with both hands. Eight millimeter cameras are quite light and tend to jiggle around a lot.

How about taking pictures while you are skiing yourself?

Avoid it whenever possible. It requires experience and steady skiing. But if you're going to do it, I'd suggest holding the camera maybe half-an-inch from one eye with both hands, keeping your other eye open at the same time. That way you can get a kind of "split-vision" by seeing through your viewfinder and your other eye as well. It's also advisable to be aware of the possibility of skiing into a tree that you thought was still 100 yards away.

What types of film are best for shooting skiing pictures?

There are several. My favorite is Ektachrome Commercial which, unfortunately, is not available in smaller than 35-mm size. For 8-mm, I'd suggest either Kodachrome II or Dynachrome by Afga. Both have fairly wide margins for error and nice bright tones.

How do you determine exposure?

I use a meter. Anyone who plans to take even a halfway serious approach to ski movies should have one. It's more accurate than the built-in meters on some cameras and a heck of a lot better than none at all.

How do you take a reading for a skier some distance away?

The best way is to hold your hand so that the light falls on it in the same way it falls on the subject you want to shoot. Hold the meter in your other hand, perhaps a foot away, and take your reading. If you're shooting a "back-lit" situation—one where the sun is behind your subject rather than the camera—make your reading and open up one stop—say from f/16 to f/11.

How do you determine which "f-stop" to use?

Generally the light is so strong on ski slopes that you're forced to use either f/16, or f/22 if you have it. This is desirable because lenses are generally sharper at these smaller openings. Even more important, if you're shooting at these stops, your subject will be in pretty sharp focus from about six feet to infinity, with a normal lens.

How many frames per second should you shoot at?

An amateur with an acceptable 8-mm camera would shoot at a normal 16 frames per second. Most professionals who shoot 35-mm use 24 frames per second. This gives us greater stability and freedom from camera motion. Besides, sound track is always put on at 24 frames per second, what we call "half-speed," then screening it at the normal speed. This is very interesting for graceful shots and technique stuff. Or you can go all the way to 64 frames per second for true slow motion. I even have a camera that shoots 128 frames per second and the film roars through there like a machine gun.

Should an amateur follow some kind of script in his movies?

He doesn't have to, of course, but the results will be much better if he does. I approach photography in a kind of journalistic fashion. I tell a story from start to finish and there's no reason an amateur can't do the same.

Could you give an example?

Well, say you're going on a weekend trip. Before you leave, take a shot at 8 frames per second of someone packing a suitcase and dumping in clothes helter-skelter. When you play it back you'll get that speeded-up Chaplin effect. Then, maybe, take a little shot of skis being put on the car rack, or some road signs pointing to an area. The next morning take a shot of the exhaust with the sun behind it and, if you can find one, a thermometer with a real low reading. Boots being laced, skis strapped on—scenes like this set a mood. Use plenty of close-ups of your subjects because it'll be much harder to get these once you're on the hill.

Once you get on the hill, what should you remember?

First, if you have a choice between shooting up a hill or across and down it, always pick the latter. Shooting up flattens out the slope. Shooting across or down makes it look steeper. Then you must realize that your camera's "eye" goes out in a 'V', such that you have a wide range far away and a narrow one up close. Explain to your subjects that they must make long turns as they approach you, gradually shortening them until they ski past. When they get too close for a whole body shot, swing your camera down to show just their legs and skis.

A second approach is to stand on the side of the slope or trail with the sun over your shoulder. Tell your subject to visualize a cord tied between himself and the camera. Have him ski in a large radial arc so that he remains equidistant from the camera.

People are always interested in "technique" shots of how they really ski. You can also learn a lot about your faults if you watch even a short sequence of your own skiing on film. As far as the photographer is concerned, technique shots should be made with as clear a background as possible so as not to interfere with the skier himself. Make an effort to have your subject fill as much of the frame as possible when you're shooting this kind of footage.

How about "zoom" lenses?

They're useful, only their effects shouldn't be overdone. Use them for a purpose and don't just go shot-gunning all over the hill. For instance, you have a guy skiing toward you. Zoom to your most powerful setting so your subject almost fills the frame. Then, as he comes nearer, back off with your lens until, as he sweeps by you, you're using your wide-angle setting.

When is the best time of the day for making ski movies?

Unquestionably the early morning, as early as you've got any sun on your trail or slope. In the early morning and late afternoon, the sun has a soft, warm, yellow feel to it which produces some beautiful shots.

Later, when the sun gets higher and stronger, it casts a "hot" light that washes everything out and makes your skier look like he's plowing through a field of mashed potatoes. Besides, if you do your shooting early, that will leave plenty of time for skiing.

Is there any other equipment you'd recommend?

Yes, a couple of things. One, a black silk cloth about four or five feet square. When you have to change film on the slope, just bend down and throw the cloth over your shoulders. Now you have a heavily-shaded area in which to change film. Otherwise you'll end up with red 'fog' patches on the edges of your film. A second item which can be very useful is an ultraviolet filter. A filter cuts through the haze often found at high altitudes without requiring exposure compensation. If you have a turret lens camera, look into the cost of having this filter mounted behind the lens opening so you don't have to keep fooling with it when you change lenses. A UV filter is also useful—if you want to justify its costs—if you do some shooting at the beach in the summer.

How about editing your film?

Well, if a person tries it once he'll never stop. It improves the quality of your film immensely and allows you to rearrange sequences and chop out the bad parts and boring stuff that sneak into everybody's film. I think that editing is about a third of the movie-making battle. An 8 or 16 mm editor is inexpensive and its something you can have a lot of fun with.

Would you advise the amateur to buy an editor?

I'd advise it for anyone. I know if I ever showed my audiences the raw footage before it was edited they'd probably all walk out on me.

WHAT SMOKEY THE BEAR DOES FOR THE WINTER

The lively role of the Forest Service, and its "snow rangers," in skiing

by Kip Hinton

A dark green parka, highlighted by a golden patch on the left shoulder, marks the Forest Service snow ranger now on duty at more than 200 ski and winter-sports area developments in the National Forests. A product of today's schuss-booming winter-sports industry, the snow ranger is the personal representative of 1½ million skièrs. His job is to assure safe management at ski areas operating under special-use permit of the Forest Service.

It is a matter of conjecture as to exactly when the first official snow ranger was appointed. Many early-day forest rangers, while not bearing the romantic title, deserved it. Skis and snow-shoes were a standard mode of winter travel to the early ranger. One forerunner, certainly, was the late Graeme McGowan, Mc-Gowan was hired by the Service in 1936 to study the potential of skiing on the Arapahoe National Forest in Colorado. He was considered an expert in this field, having operated a private ski lodge in the area. McGowan viewed the weekend skier with frosty dismay, incidentally: "Sunday skiers generally are a detriment to the ski business," he once opined. "They not only make few purchases but also use up space in the inn which might otherwise be used by freer-spending guests.

"I speak on this matter with definite knowledge. These Sunday indigents, or cheapskates, are

In all manners of weather, Snow Rangers conduct safety and feasibility studies of new and existing areas. All lifts operating on Forest Service land must be okayed on a yearly basis.

a real drawback to any business an inn can generate in winter."

Having delivered this Sunday punch to the weekend skier, McGowan grudgingly admitted, "There is actual need of some sort of shelter for these people." Ever since, the ski industry and the Forest Service have been working to provide that shelter. Today, for example, there are seven ski areas on Arapahoe National Forest. Last year those areas accommodated over 700,-000 of the McGowan-maligned "Sunday skiers." Millions have been spent not only to shelter them but to lure them to the slopes. Skiers have grown in the hostel-keeper's respect as rapidly as in numbers.

Entering the era of "to ski is to live and not to ski is unthinkable," the Forest Service, as land-manager host to ever-growing numbers, recognized the need for a program of intensive winter-sports management. Development of high-mountain ski resorts in the west was dependent, above all, upon controlling avalanche danger. If the Sunday skier was to survive — literally survive — he needed protection. It was the threat of snowy torrents that firmly decided the Forest Service's need for the snow ranger. The new breed first started on avalanche control work in the winter of 1937-38 at Alta, Utah, in the Wasatch National Forest.

A snow ranger skiing across the fracture line of a potential avalanche and triggering its mighty power conjures thoughts of derring-do. While his predecessors did just that, today's snow ranger brings down avalanches by remote control, through use of a 75-millimeter recoilless rifle, or the "Avalauncher," a service-devised gun powered by compressed air. With the weapon, explosive charges are dropped into unstable snow from a safe distance.

Less romantically, our snow ranger finds himself confronted with such mundane matters as spot-checking to make certain the ski area operators are performing to standard, in terms of engineering, administration, medical aid, training, and transportation. There are meetings with the National Ski Patrol to assure safe ski slopes and there are safety education sessions for the skiing public. There are meetings with ski area operators on future expansion plans and daily weather data records to be maintained. A snow ranger's winter-sports checklist has no less than 60 individual entries — all directly or indirectly reflecting safety for the skiing public.

One new breed of snow worshipper is the over-the-snow machine fancier. The average snowmobiler is unfamiliar with the complex makeup of avalanches. On developed ski slopes, the snow ranger has things pretty much under control. When conditions arise he can post his warning of avalanche danger. Skiers stick to designated slopes having learned that to deviate can mean discomfort and danger.

But the man on a snowmobile often sees a world of snow-capped mountains to conquer. Alone, or in groups, he takes off. Unless he sticks to designated trails or checks with the ranger before leaving, he is unprotected. It is physically impossible to post every avalanche path in the mountains.

Many hours of off-duty time are now being consumed by the snow ranger in reaching various snowmobile clubs and individual operators. Somehow the message of danger must be transmitted if the ranger is to prevent an icy death.

There is, finally, no simple definition of the snow ranger. He's a complex individual, diversified in duties and training. For his own survival he must maintain top physical condition. He takes his skiing seriously. As a man in uniform, he knows he's being watched by the critical public eye. There's a touch of the mountaineer, as well as of the angel of mercy for those chilling moments of disaster when immediate rescue and first aid must be performed.

He must enjoy working with people. It takes a good public relations man to convince some skiers that safety is the best policy. His public runs the gamut from ski bum to jet set, and he

must mix well with all. And, probably as important as any of the above, the snow ranger is a practicing environmentalist, a man deeply involved with nature but who can look at his environment objectively. The typical snow ranger, as with his non-snow counterpart, does not need to get "psyched up" to appreciate the beautiful land around him. Appreciation is instilled within him, and has come naturally. Or he would have indulged in a higher-paying vocation.

An immediate question arises. What does he do in summer? Does the snow ranger ski off into the sunset with the last snow? In today's complex society, with ever-growing demands on the environment, the snow ranger must be a man for all seasons. Skiing's "other season" keeps him busy at the task of protecting the environment which has made the sport so attractive to the public.

The sport has generated many new developments on National Forest lands. Expansion at ski areas appears never-ending in an effort to keep up with the demand. New runs, increased lift capacity, and complex new resort developments are being installed as quickly as contracts can be negotiated. In winter, public

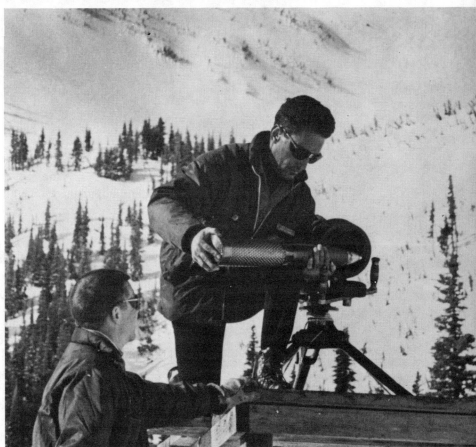

One of the prime functions of the Service is avalanche control, for which 75mm recoilless rifles, or dynamite charges, are indispensable.

Guiding ski tours (top) and working with local Ski Patrols are two additional in-season functions of Forest Service personnel.

safety is foremost to the ranger. In summer he must protect the land and its resources. Ski area developments can have an enormous impact, for good or for ill, on the environment.

Only after the skier and his season of snow have vanished from the scene does the range of this impact become evident. Immediate concerns at this time include erosion, aesthetics, and design. Skiing, glamour sport of the '60's, if not carefully planned for and managed, can produce some very unglamorous results. That 60-inch base winter veneer is easily rubbed off with a few days of warm weather. Most National Forest based ski areas are at high elevations, ranging from a low of 7,000 feet to above 11,000. Soils at this elevation are highly susceptible to erosion when disturbed by construction. Research and planning are necessary to prevent winter's holiday turning into summer's horror.

That old construction standby, the bulldozer, is an essential piece of equipment in ski area development. Improperly used, however, it becomes a dangerous weapon against the environment. On one mountain, bulldozer clearance may be an acceptable method of construction. Here the soils are deep, rich, and highly organic. Grasses spring up overnight. In contrast, on another mountain, the same type of activity can cause massive erosion, silt-filled beaver ponds, and ex-

tensive stream pollution.

In designing and planning National Forest ski area expansion or new development, the snow ranger works closely with the area managers. He calls on expert assistance to serve both public interest and the operator. Forest Service landscape architects assist in aesthetically blending structures with the forest environment. Soil scientists analyze soil types and outline erosion potentials. Hydrologists determine methods of controlling surface runoff to prevent "gullying." Foresters recommend grasses for the best mixture of species to grow rapidly at high elevations.

Ski area operators have given their full support in these efforts to turn barren ski slopes into grassy mountainsides. Today's ski trail planning and development, in fact, is almost revolutionary, when compared with early-day crash construction ventures.

As the ski industry has grown, so has awareness that proper utilization of natural resources is essential in maintaining a desirable environment. Preventing water pollution and soil erosion are of vital importance. Equally as important is the over-all protection of the landscape for the enjoyment of millions of summer visitors to the National Forests. Skiing and snow know-how may head the list in his job description, but today's Forest Service snow ranger is a man for all seasons.

by Stu Campbell

THE CHALLENGE ON ICE

Skiers, particularly those in the East and Midwest, often face descents over conditions familiar to Admiral Perry. Here is guidance on how to handle such conditions both in selecting and caring for your equipment and in making your moves on the hill

Racers thrive on hardpack and ice — the very conditions that "psyche out" many good skiers. Professional instructors don't seem to have much trouble on ice either; they look pretty much the same on all kinds of snow. So what's the closely-guarded secret? Skiing technique manuals and "How to Ski" books spend pages discussing how to maneuver over variations in terrain. But why do they assume that all snow conditions and surfaces are uniform and the same everywhere? Is there a difference between the way a pro skis on a "good" day and the way he skis on an icy day?

Erratic weather patterns over Eastern ski areas particularly can produce some of the most unpredictable, difficult, and varied skiing conditions to be found anywhere in the world. Only rarely does the eastern skier find dry fluffy powder covering his favorite trails. A little more frequently he skis on that more dense, heavier, wetter "powder" so often found in our Northwestern states, in the Cascades. And more times than he likes to, he skis on ice.

Ice seems to come roughly in three grades: *blue ice* (sometimes called "black ice"); *gray ice;* and what the ski reports call *granular* or *frozen granular.*

Blue ice is the type with a very high water content — something like what hockey teams play on. Even the pros steer clear of this. If you have to ski over blue ice, spread your feet apart, relax, and hope for a safe place to stop on the other side. Don't try any fancy stuff.

Gray ice and *frozen granular* are skiable. In fact there's some very GOOD skiing to be had on this type of snow. *Gray ice* is harder, more solid and more slippery than granular. "Granular" tends to be crunchy and brittle. It has the least amount of water content. The important thing that they have in common is that you can set an edge in both if you know what you're doing and if your equipment is in good shape.

Artificial ice (a new skiing term) is produced by lots of skiers skiing on manmade snow on a warmish day followed by freezing temperatures. This is awfully hard sometimes, but it rarely gets to the point where it is as impossible as blue ice.

The ice skier's equipment is very important, and this is perhaps what we should talk about first. No matter how many things you are doing right technically, nothing will work really well for you, if your equipment is poorly maintained or purchased without certain standards and specifications in mind. "Checking out" other skiers, seeing what equipment others are using, is one of the skier's biggest pastimes. And it's all part of the game.

BOOTS The first item of equipment observed are skis. Pros look at people's skis too, but a good pro is likely to look at boots first. Any racing coach worth his salt will invariably tell a young racer with a limited amount of Christmas money to spend on ski equipment, "Get good boots first. Good boots on fair skis is a much better combination than soft boots on the finest pair of skis in the world." And he's right.

"Soft" boots — boots that are old and comfortable — cause the

ON ICE

downfall (literal and figurative) of more skiers who try to ski on ice than any other single factor. Remember: boots are your most important and most critical skiing investment. Two important things to look for: FIT, of course, and LATERAL STIFFNESS. A boot that doesn't fit well or that bends sideways is virtually worthless in the east. If you're willing to spend a considerable amount of time and money when you select your boots, you can find boots that are stiff, that fit well (especially around the heel), and that are still reasonably comfortable.

There is no question that the finest leather boots in the world are still manufactured in Europe. Leather boots should be chosen with care, and, if they are maintained well, can last an average weekend skier five or six seasons with moderate use.

On the other hand, some American and European companies are doing some very exciting things with other materials: namely fiberglass and plastic. Plastic boots seem to be solving many of the problems often found in all leather boots: they don't "break down" as leather seems to after a period of time. Plastic and fiberglass boots are the latest thing. They are selling like mad, and it looks as though they're here to stay. Many very fine skiers swear by them, although they admit that the development of new materials and boot designs are creating a whole new set of edging problems. *Many very good skiers who begin using plastic boots, for instance, find that the stiffness of the plastic causes them to edge too much. Changing from one edge to the other during a turn seems jerky and uncoordinated at first, but most fans of the plastic boot claim that adjustment to the unfamiliar stiffness takes only a couple of hours.*

Try a pair in any case, but remember one thing: Be sure they fit well to begin with, if you're going to buy. Don't expect the stretch and give that you're used to in leather boots. A certain amount of adjustment to your foot is possible, but the shape of the boot will never change. If the basic fit is wrong, forget it! You could be very unhappy.

SKIS Now, what about skis? Skiers are perhaps the largest group of brand name seekers in the world. And too few people understand that what Jean Claude and Karl are using is not necessarily what's best for the average intermediate or expert skier. More has been said and written about skis than about anything else in the ski business — obviously. Most of it boils down to four considerations: cost, shape, flex and material.

Ideally everyone should have at least two pairs of skis; a pair for ice and a pair for powder and packed or prepared snow. In many cases this is impractical or impossible because of the cost factor. So if you live in the east, if you foresee that the majority of your skiing is to be done on "eastern powder" (ice), and if it seems feasible for you to own only one pair of skis, knowing a little about what to look for when you buy skis might be helpful.

Racers (who ski on icy courses almost all the time, don't forget) demand a ski that will turn quickly, precisely, and with a minimum of sideslip. Granted, most racers don't have to pay full prices. But too many recreational skiers are afraid of "competition" models because they are expensive and because they're sure these skis will be too hard to turn. Very few pros would advise someone to buy a competition downhill ski

in most cases, that's true. But slalom or giant slalom skis are designed and carefully engineered to do exactly what the recreational skier *and* the racer want them to do, especially on icy terrain.

Almost all G.S. or slalom skis have certain important shape and flex similarities which are helpful to the ice skier. Learn to compare different skis by holding them together bottom to bottom. If you hold a "combi" and a slalom ski together, you should notice several things: For one thing the slalom has more side camber — that means that it is narrower in the *waist* (right under where your foot is going to be), wider in the *shovel* (that's up near the tip), and wider in the *tail*. Width on the "combi," notice, doesn't vary so much at these different points. The slalom or the G.S. will turn better. It's more likely to carve and less likely to skid or sideslip awkwardly.

Now flex the skis. (With a little practice you can get to look very professional doing this.) There's a difference: The combi seems to bend pretty uniformly throughout its length, right? Or maybe it flexes quite a lot in the tip. That's great for powder, lousy for ice. Now the competition — stiff in the tip, stiff in the tail (the G.S. especially) and softer in the middle. The slalom or G.S. will hold better too.

What the ski is made of is still important these days. It's still awfully hard to beat a wooden slalom ski. In fact, many international racers and old professionals still use them when the snow is particularly hard. Engineers are developing excellent fiberglass and epoxi-plastic skis which behave very much like woods. They hold up better too, although not as long as metals. In fact, some of these skis you can buy right now. The major manufacturers of metal skis have their engineers and advisory staffs working very hard to produce a metal ski that is really good on icy days. Some of them are very good, but in general, metals are not as satisfactory for either the racer or the advanced recreational skier as woods or epoxis on this type of snow. And, by the way, ask your ski shop man about edges too. Harder edges stay sharper longer, last longer and require less care.

One last word about equipment: length of skis. What's the formula that the ski magazines talk about — skis should be six inches to a foot above the top of your head? The theory is that shorter skis are easier to turn. Okay, but don't forget to take your own weight and strength into consideration too, and if you're purchasing ice skis, there is very little resistance between the ice and your skis as they turn. (This is not the case on powder or in slush.) For this reason skis to be used on ice can be somewhat longer. After all, the greater the length of edge surface you have on the snow, the easier it will be to control your skidding. With this in mind then, throw out the new ski-length golden rule and buy ice skis which are 5 to 10 cm. longer.

MAINTENANCE If you ski on ice much of the time, your equipment must be well cared-for and, in fact, it must be kept practically in mint condition. Not only is care and maintenance important if you want your equipment to last. Faulty equipment can affect your skiing far more than you maybe realize. A good professional instructor, for instance, spends 10 seconds before he goes out in the morning to check three things: his bottoms, his edges, and his bindings. He does the same thing when he takes his skis off at the end of the day. If anything needs attention, he sees to it right away. Usually it will take only a couple of minutes to fix whatever is

	Height	Width	Camber	Mounting	Characteristics
SLALOM	20-30 cm. over top of the head	generally the narrowest of the three throughout	much "side camber," very narrow in the "waist"—wider in the "shovel" and "tail" sections	toe of boot should be 5-6 mm ahead of "balance point"	"Side camber" allows for short, choppy turns using sharp, aggressive edging. Slalom skis are designed for continuous turning. They turn with relative ease and hold well on icy terrain, but tend to "wander" or not hold a straight line at high speeds. A slalom ski which is a little longer than normal would make a good ice ski in most cases.
GIANT SLALOM	5 cm. longer than slalom	slightly wider than slalom in most cases— narrower than downhill throughout— much variation here	"side camber" is more subtle— not as narrow as slalom in "waist" section	toe of boot should be right at "balance point" of ski, i.e.—½ way between tip and tail	The G.S. is designed to make smooth, longer radius turns at higher speeds than would be used on the slalom. The G.S. will "track" or hold a straight line quite well. Edging ability is not quite as "quick" or precise as on the slalom, but satisfactory on ice. G.S. skis (good ones) make a fine recreational ski for all conditions—including icy ones.
DOWNHILL	10-15 cm. longer than slalom for competition	widest throughout	very little "side camber" relatively wide even in "waist"	toe of boot should be 5-6 mm. behind the "balance point"	Designed to go straight and fast. Very soft "shovel" section "planes" easily over snow like a hydroplane, while very stiff tail section acts as a rudder to keep the ski in a straight course line. Requires slightly different turning technique: Although some pros use D.H.'s with a G.S. binding placement for high speed skiing, this ski is not recommended as an "ice ski."

ON ICE

wrong. And, you know, he doesn't have a lot of secrets about ski care and maintenance. But he does have three helpful friends: A little knowledge about what things to look for and what to do about it, a kofix candle, and an ordinary 8- to 12-inch mill bastard file.

It's somehow ironic that a recreational skier will bitch and curse at the "clod" in the lift line next to him who inadventently steps on his new skis and scratches the finish on the tops. And yet for months or even years this same guy will neglect the scrapes and gouges on the bottoms of these same skis! These blemishes, even the very small ones, on the bottom running surface of the ski, are the *really* important ones and can have a profound effect on your ability to turn on ice.

The ski is obviously designed to slide. It is designed to slide *forward* in as straight a line as possible until some force is applied which will cause it to turn and then slide forward again. On very hard granular snow or ice especially, a nick or hole tends to inhibit the forward sliding motion, and frequently (because the nicks and scratches are often at an angle to the line the ski is supposed to take) the ski wants to wander off course. If there are many nicks (caused by rocks, stumps, and so on) the ski is guided in all sorts of directions other than the one you want it to take, and this becomes especially apparent and irritating when you're trying to make a precise and accurate turn.

The worst type of bottom problem is what is known as the "railed ski." If a ski is "railed" the kofix or P-tex plastic right next to the steel edge has been somewhat scraped off or removed by something foreign in or under

the snow (see diagram). What happens, in effect, is that the ski is virtually running on an outside "runner" like a sled. Sleds and railed skis tend not to turn at all! Even a pro will have a terrible time making a railed ski go exactly where he wants it to go during a turn on ice or **hard pack.**

The remedy for all bottom problems is ridiculously simple and easy, and yet few people really take the time to fix their bottoms. The panacea: a kofix candle. Buy one at any ski shop. It may cost a buck, but it's worth every cent. You can probably even find one that will match the color of your bottoms if that bothers you. Then take your skis home, wipe them clean, and let them dry.

Lay the skis, bottom up, on the floor or workbench. (Better not use the dining room table.)

Light the wick of the plastic candle. (A match might not be hot enough. A propane torch flame or the flame from the burner of a gas stove works very well.)

As the plastic starts to drip from the burning candle, allow the drops to dribble into the holes, scratches, and nicks in the bottoms. (Don't let any of it drip on *you;* it causes nasty burns.)

Allow a lot more plastic to drip into each hole than seems necessary. When you're finished with this step the bottom will be covered with lumps and ridges of kofix where you have "filled."

It will take only a minute or two to dry.

Smooth the lumps and ridges until they are "flush" with the normal running surface. Sandpaper, steel wool, and razor blades are often recommended for this, but there's one device which is really super: Remove the blade from a Stanley "sur-

form." (You can buy one at almost any good hardware store. It's sort of a combination of a wood rasp and a wood planer.) Use this to gently plane away the excess plastic. The result will be astonishingly smooth and flat.

Check the bottoms by holding the skis up to the light to see what you have missed, and repeat the process where you need to.

KEEP EDGES SHARP
Edges are skiing's scapegoat. More often than not, "dull" edges are blamed for the lack of skiing success on an icy day. 90 per cent of the time the problem is not with the edges so much as it is with technique. In fact one of the most embarrassing ironies of the sport is that often people who complain most about their edges, are people who don't use them properly enough to ever get them dull! On the other hand, if the skier has some idea about what he should be doing technically, there is no question that he must have good, hard, sharp edges if he is to ski really well on ice.

There's an easy rule of thumb to remember when you think about your own edges: "Smoothness and Squareness." If your edges are smooth and square, you are in pretty good shape. To maintain a pair of edges properly you must keep after them constantly, checking them each time you take your skis off. And don't be deceived by the "feel" of your edges. Dull edges, like dull razor blades, often "feel" sharper then they really are. You hardly "feel" a new razor blade at all when you shave, but the old one seems scratchy and cuts you more often because it has nicks and imperfections along its cutting surface. By the same token, new edges on new skis don't feel particularly sharp. Try making a com-

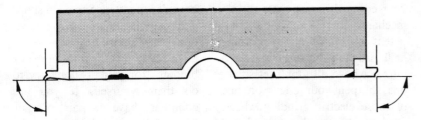

Cross section of a ski shows what can happen to the bottoms. Left to right, edge shows burr which throws ski off course, knicks and gouges in the plastic base, a railed edge and a knicked or poorly filed edge which is ineffective for ice skiing.

parison between new edges and rusty, dull, old ones and see for yourself.

"Squareness," of course, implies that there must be at least two planes or surfaces to be considered in order for them to be "square." Too often skiers seem to forget that the steel edge on a ski is exposed in TWO places — on the side of the ski (everybody know this) *and* on the bottom! It is not enough to merely sharpen the side surface of the edge (as many people do). "Bottom filing" or "flat filing" is just as important. It's also very easy.

Various small sharpening devices which can be carried in your pocket have been developed in the last few years, none of which are anywhere near as effective as a common 8 to 12 inch mill bastard file. Buy yourself one, and replace it when it gets dull. (The longer the file, the coarser the teeth will be.) It won't cost much, and it should be considered a "must" for any eastern skier. Here's how it should be used. Let's start with the bottom first:

Lay the ski flat — bottom up. Rest the ski on something at either end to keep the whole ski from rocking on the binding.

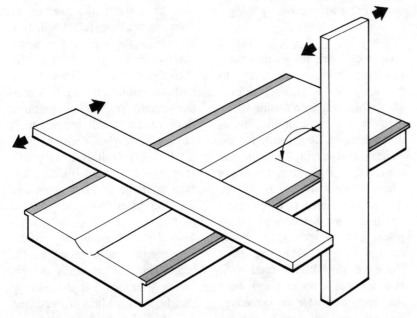

Diagram illustrates the right way to file edges. File must always be held flat on the bottom and the two surfaces of the edge must form a 90° angle. Both surfaces must be smooth and squared. Never file across the line of the edge, make long smooth strokes.

Place the file flat on the bottom of the ski. Hold the file at either end.

Press down gently and evenly at both ends of the file, and push the file forward along the bottom so that you feel the file cutting. You may have to hold the file at an angle, but DO NOT PUSH THE FILE FROM SIDE TO SIDE! You may find that you are smoothing some of the plastic bottom as well as the steel edges. This is fine. Be sure that you are keeping the file flat on the whole bottom running surface at all times.

Repeat until the edges along the entire bottom are shiny. Hold the ski up to light to check this if you need to.

Now the other surface: the side of the edge. This can be a little more tricky. It might be a good idea to practice on an old pair of skis before you work on your good ones.

The first problem is to hold the ski steady. Racers and pros seem to be able to hold the ski between their knees while they push the tip or tail against a wall. This is risky because the ski can move while you work. If you're just starting to file your own edges, put the ski in a workbench vise (you'll want some strips of wood or paper to protect the ski from vise marks or dents), with the side of the edge facing up.

Place the file across the edge holding it at either end.

Push the file gently away from you. You won't need to press down too hard if the file is sharp. Keep the file as level as you can ("square" to the bottom of the edge). Most important: Always file along the edge. NEVER FILE ACROSS THE EDGE WITH A SAWING MOTION!

Keep checking your progress against the light. Where the file has cut the metal will be shiny.

Be sure that you are filing the whole narrow surface of the edge and not just part of it. Make long, smooth strokes.

Once you've completed all four edges (two sides on each), everything should be "square." If both surfaces of all four edges are shiny, everything is probably pretty "smooth" too. But take a minute to check. Look for little scratches or nicks in the metal. Look also for very small protrusions of steel, called "burrs," formed by hitting a rock or hard object while skiing. Sometimes the filing process itself can produce these. These tiny indentations or jagged imperfections in the smoothness of the edge can raise havoc with your skiing on an icy day. So get everything smooth. Lightly file some more if you have to. Some pros even use a small whetstone for this final "touch-up" work on their edges. While you work on your edges, keep checking for "smoothness and squareness" with your fingernail (not by feeling with your finger). Pass your fingernail gently across the edge at any given point. Where the edge is sharp, you should scrape some of your fingernail off onto the edge where you can see it. If the edge is still dull in some places, go back and work on it. It's worth the extra minute or two.

When you are finished and satisfied, wipe off the filings. If you allow them to stay on the edge, they will rust very quickly if exposed to any sort of moisture and stick back onto the metal. A pencil eraser makes a nifty wiper.

Try to keep your edges and bottoms in good shape *all* the time. You probably won't do much damage to your skis on the good days. Don't get caught unprepared on an icy morning and have to rely on somebody in the nearest ski shop to sharpen your edges. In most cases the ski mechanic there can do a competent job, but on an icy morning he'll probably be busy and in a hurry. Above all, don't let someone sharpen your edges on one of those electric grinding wheels used to sharpen large hardened steel tools. Many ski shops, I'm sad to say, have them. In the first place this machine will grind off about three times as much metal as you could remove during several filings. After two or three times on the grinder you won't have any edges left at all. In the second place, although the machine will accomplish the first requirement of the rule of thumb ("squareness"), it will not make the side of the edge at all smooth. Because the edge of the ski is drawn across the circular path of the grinding wheel, rather than *with* it, the effect is the same as filing across the edge with a sawing motion. Instead of really smoothing, this makes a whole series of tiny grinding marks along the whole length of the edge, just like those you have been trying to remove by filing.

GENERAL CARE Just a couple of more things about ski maintenance and care: try to protect your skis as much as possible when you aren't using them. You have a considerable investment in them. Road salt, for instance, makes tiny pits in the metal edges (tape over the edges while the skis are on the top of the car is the answer here), storage in a very hot or very damp place can warp or otherwise change the vitally important shape of the ski. Warped skis, skis without camber, and bent skis are *impossible* to maneuver properly on ice. Don't give up on a bent metal ski though, if the bend is not serious and if the layers of wood, metal and plastic haven't separated. Some ski shops and manufacturers can fix them quite satisfactorily.

And have an expert mount your bindings for you — don't try to do them yourself. If you are going to have a pair of skis which you are going to use exclusively for ice, it might be a good idea to mount the toe piece of the binding so that the front edge of the sole of the boot is slightly ahead (only 5 mm or so) of the giant slalom setting point.

The G.S. point is exactly halfway between the tip and the tail of the ski. If you do have your binding set a little forward, you will find that you will be able to apply more pressure to the front parts of the edges at the "shovel" which will be helpful on ice. Depending on your weight and the length of your skis, this forward binding position may cause the tips of your skis to "hook" at the end of the turn. This means that the tip wants to turn a little too far *up* the hill each time. Sometimes if the skis are "hooking," the tip of the downhill ski (where you have the major portion of your weight, hopefully) will turn up *under* the tip of the uphill ski, so that you wind up with your tips crossed. If this awkward and uncomfortable situation happens often on icy or granular days (when it will happen most obviously, maybe — only maybe) it's the ski's fault and not yours. If you're convinced it's the skis, take your file in hand again and dull the edges from the very tip of the ski back 8 or 10 inches toward your boot, simply by destroying the "squareness" of the edge. This is called, oddly enough, "filing your tips." It should stop the hooking. Many racers and pros feel they have to do it.

So much for the ice skier's major ski maintenance problems, which reveal few great secrets.

ON THE SLOPE If you're really a serious skier — serious about wanting to ski with the experts — go out and ski — whatever the conditions! If you're embarrassed because your skiing looks so lousy on ice, so much the better. Look at it this way: Anyone can look good on those "ideal" days. On packed-powder snow, a skier can get away with technical murder. On ice though, you get away with very little. The nice thing about ice (if anything good can be said for it), is that skiing on it causes your mistakes to become obvious. Learning is impossible when mistakes can't be recognized. Go out and ski on it in spite of the anticipated sore fanny and bruised knuckles.

Successful, controlled, even flashy ice skiing involves just two things: a positive mental attitude, and a deliberate concentration on and application of a few physical principles.

The first is probably the easiest to talk about and the hardest to accomplish. It's one heck of a lot easier to spend your hard-earned weekend in the base-lodge bar, than it is to go out and bounce your bottom down some ice-encrusted mountain. Remember: Those who sit in the base lodge and do the most talking often are poor skiers. Reason? They sit at the bar on icy days! It becomes a cycle. Rid yourself of the comfortable-base-lodge syndrome and come out and ski. You'll become a better skier for it.

Here are a few things to keep in mind when you are out there:

SPEED AND DELIBERATION
Turning a pair of skis involves a series of precise coordinated motions, like swinging a tennis racket. Because in skiing we must turn to both the right and the left, learning to ski well becomes like learning to hit a tennis ball equally well with either hand! This apparent disadvantage becomes an advantage in another sense. In tennis the speed of the motions involved is regulated by the necessity of meeting a ball coming at you from the other court at a speed over which you have little or no control. Not so in skiing. The motions involved in making a turn are regulated *only* by the terrain, the snow's surface, and by the skier's own desire to turn quickly or slowly and deliberately.

Slow down on icy days! Find a relatively flat slope and practice. Concentrate on what you are doing. Make just one turn at a time and come to a stop if you have to. Take time to think about the motions which make it possible to change direction and control speed (mainly unweighting and body position). Make very slow and deliberate turns. As your confidence increases, so can the speed and the steepness of the slope you choose to ski on. Instead of being frustrated by your own awkwardness and lack of courage, take a minute to stop and analyze your mistakes. Keep this in mind too: You *want* the icy conditions to make your mistakes obvious! Besides, you're probably doing most things right! Only by slow, careful deliberate trial and error will you be able to pick out the little things you're doing wrong.

BODY POSITION-ANGULATION
Angulation is a term which is probably most often mentioned in discussions of ski technique and is a concept which is probably least understood. How often have you heard instructors screaming "more angulation!" at an uncomfortable, contorted-looking member of his class?

Angulation is too often confused with the awkward and almost physically impossible *reverse shoulder* and *comma position* of the early 60's. More recent technique manuals now preach *natural position*-body positions that are both feasible and comfortable, but which also provide the balance and weight distribution which the turn and the traverse require. Yet many instructors, unfortunately, persist in teaching exaggerated shoulder delay.

Improvements in ski and boot design have made the *reverse-shoulder-rotation* skier look almost as old-fashioned as an Arlberger. In fact, modern racing coaches have their skiers spreading their feet and hands apart and actually rotating their shoulders to increase speed — a cardinal sin five years ago! At times it almost looks as though the Arlberg technique were coming back. Not quite so: the concept of angulation is still valid—more valid than ever for the average skier on ice.

Angulation as such is very simple. It's really nothing more than making a sideways angle with your body — a leaning away from the hill. This can be more difficult psychologically than it is physically. In your living room it's easy enough:

1. Stand normally with your feet 2 - 3 inches apart.

2. Put your hands on your hips and bend your knees forward.

3. Push your hips as far as you comfortably can to the left and allow your head and shoulders to tilt naturally to the right. (Don't turn your hips or shoulders, or bend forward at the waist.)

4. Holding this angle with your body, allow your hands to fall comfortably to your sides as if you were holding ski poles.

ON ICE

5. Notice that most of your weight naturally seems to be on your right foot. (If you hold this position and try to stand on your left, you will fall over to the left.)

All turns begin and end in a traverse position, and angulation is vital to a good traverse on ice. Exactly the same steps you followed in the living room can be followed in the practice slope while you are standing still. The psychological problem develops as soon as you realize that you *are* standing on a slippery incline rather than on a flat floor. Proper angulation involves leaning your upper body, not toward the comfortable security of the hill above you, but *out* and away from the hill and into space. At first it feels as though you're going to fall off the mountain.

But don't forget: if you lean out (to the right, for example) your weight falls mostly on your right ski (in this case, the downhill ski) making your balance a good deal more stable than if you were leaning *into* the hill with your weight on the uphill ski. If you are moving, if the day is icy, and if you lean toward the hill, your feet (skis and all) slide sideways out from under you and you fall down (as perhaps you have already realized). Angulation, on the other hand, directs the force of your own gravity toward your downhill ski (which is placed on its edge) allowing you later to ski across the slope and turn without sliding sideways. Give it a try. You can't hope to ski well on ice without angulation.

BODY POSITION-KNEE AND ANKLE PRESSURE

"Stand right on 'em" is an expression used by pros and racing coaches alike. It is meant to warn the skier in question that

he is "getting behind his skis" or sitting back. In other words, he doesn't have his weight pressing forward enough to be controlling his skis properly.

"Sitting back," "leaning into the hill," and "standing up too straight," have long been regarded as skiing's three major heresies. Ironically the most successful racers on the international circuit (Jean-Claude Killy included) often flaunt all three rules and usually get away with it. In fact, they've discovered that sometimes, disregard for technical tradition makes them go faster! But for the average skier (you and me) the old principle of "standing right on 'em" as well as the old adage "bend zee knees" is still applicable. To put it more strongly: on icy days especially, if you sit back, stand up too straight, or lean into the hill, you will probably lose control and probably fall down — hard!

To control the skis properly, a skier must have his weight pressing forward against the tips of the skis. When you drive a car, you are concerned primarily with the front wheels. These are the ones you steer with. Similarly in skiing we are concerned more with the tip section of the ski than we are with the tail. To be "standing right on 'em" the knees and ankles must be pressed forward until you can feel pressure against the fronts of the boots. This, in turn, causes the right kind of pressure to be exerted against the skis. This is why ski boots are, after all, so big and stiff and — let's face it — often uncomfortable. If you can't bend your knees and ankles forward, or, if you won't, it will be impossible for you to ski on ice.

When you go out on ice next time, don't hang back. Press forward for control. Exaggerate

at first. Stand right on 'em! If at any time you can't feel that pressure against the fronts of the boots, you are literally out of control and the skis are taking you for a ride. Be aggressive! The steeper the slope and the harder the ice, the more you need to press forward.

CHANGING DIRECTION IN ICE

Changing direction is really the crux of the whole matter of skiing on ice, isn't it? It's terribly difficult to relax and remember everything when you're afraid that you are going to have little or no control over the radius of your turn, or worse, that you are going to lose control entirely and fall painfully on your hip.

Turns are normally used by a skier to control or "check" his speed. On icy days, changing direction, or turning is no problem at all! Because ice is necessarily slippery, turning is very easy, simply because there is no resistance, as there is in powder or wet snow, to the turning action the skis are making. The problem is turning too far and too fast! The skis don't really take you where you want to go. What's even more frightening is the inability to control the skidding action of the skis which you began yourself when you initiated the turn. The skis, instead of running off on an edge at the end of the turn, continue to slide sideways. Frightening and dangerous.

Unweighting is of course essential to any skiing turn. Most ski technicians would agree that the "up-motion" to unweight is an effective and satisfactory way to achieve the lightness needed to release the skis' edges and turn. On icy days this "up" unweighting motion should be kept at the barest minimum! The problem

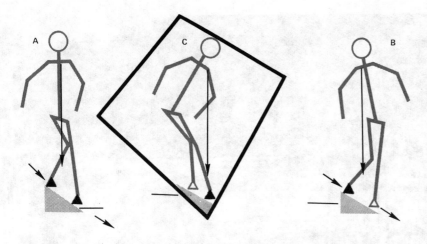

Diagram illustrates the importance and validity of the angulated position, especially on icy days. In figure C, most of the weight is directed at the contact edge of the downhill ski (dark ski in drawing)—a stable position when the skier is in motion. This per- *mits his edges to grip most effectively. In figure A, the skier who stands too straight does not use gravity to his best advantage. In figure B, the skier who is leaning into the hill has most of the weight on his uphill ski and is unable to hold any sort of edge!*

on ice is to *hold* the edge. The unweighting can not be too subtle—unweight *ever* so gently, as though you were skiing on eggs — just enough to allow yourself to change from one edge to the other.

Any "up-motion" must be followed (on any sort of snow) *immediately* by a "down-motion" where the edges are "set" and the upper body assumes an angulated position. On ice this down-motion must be particularly sharp, determined and aggressive to cause the edges to bite into the hard snow or ice. In the down motion the knees are pushed forward and into the hill while the upper body drops out and away from the hill. On ice remember: gently up; aggressively down!

HIP POSITION The position of your hips can and frequently does have a profound effect on your skiing. It is the hip, after all, that controls what the tail section of the ski is doing. If on icy days you seem to be do-

ing everything right (your edges are in good shape, you're unweighting gently, and your angulation is good) and you still feel as though you're overturning or that your downhill ski seems to keep losing its edge and "stem" awkwardly away from the uphill ski, try to determine what you might be doing with your hips.

Hip "rotation" can get you into lots of trouble. There should be as little motion as possible in your hips. If your hips turn with your skis or "rotate," your skis are probably turning farther than you want them to. To keep your hips quiet and always in the right position, remember this: *keep your belly button pointing down the hill at all times.* You'll be amazed at how this will eliminate almost all hip movement (the wrong kind) and make your turns more "carved" and less "skidded."

STRATEGY OF DESCENT
Skiing on ice is tiring: there's no question about it. Certain things can help though, and make

the day a lot more fun. For one thing, the line you choose to take on the way down a given slope can make or break your whole run. Stop often (after every 5 or 6 turns if necessary) and plan how you will attack the next section of terrain.

Avoid "static" positions if you can. On a long traverse you invite trouble and fatigue on an icy day. To traverse a whole practice slope for example, demand that you hold yourself in a given position for the entire length of the traverse. It also means that you must work hard to hold that one edge all the way across. This can be a struggle. Turn as often as you can. See how many times you can cross the fall line. This doesn't require any sort of fancy wedeln or short-swing turns; just keep turning. On ice it's easier to turn than not to turn. Try not to hold one body position or stay on one set of edges too long.

Poling is important too. Use your poles on icy days — they're not just for decoration! *Reach* for your turn — plant your pole as far ahead of you as you can. This will make you press your weight forward more effectively. As soon as you have completed a turn to the left, *reach* for the next turn with your right hand and pole (reach just with your arm though: don't let the shoulder come forward.) Plant your pole as though you mean it! It will help both your body position and your rhythm.

Icy days *are* learning days. Keep your equipment in good shape — ready for ice. We have ice often, and most of the time it's worth skiing on. Don't be proud! If nothing seems to be working for you, get help from a *good* instructor. A lesson is usually cheaper than a full-day lift ticket. Have you noticed?

WHO WOULD WIN, ERIKSEN, SAILER OR KILLY?

The author, by way of explaining the benefit for ordinary recreational skiers in knowing exactly how and why downhill, giant slalom and slalom races are won, compares the styles of three of the greatest figures in the sport

by John C. Tobin

In any sport in which performance can be measured in units, such as time or distance, a participant can compare himself directly with the world's best. In skiing the discrepancy is probably greater between the intermediate and the Olympian than in other sport. In golf, for example, an intermediate player having a good day might shoot a 90 at Pebble Beach, while Jack Nicklaus in a tournament might have a 69. On the famous Stratofana race course at Cortina in Italy, a race might be won by Karl Schranz in under 2 minutes and 40 seconds. To put an intermediate skier on a two-mile course as difficult as this would be sheer folly. To ski it no-stop no-fall he would have to be at the peak of condition. Then, fighting speed all the way, and zigzagging all over the course, he probably could not get down in less than 12 minutes, which would be four times as long as Schranz's run. The intermediate skier, if he could accomplish this, would be extremely proud of himself, and yet he would be nowhere as close to the champion as the intermediate golfer was.

This gap can be narrowed if skiers know more about the racer, his equipment, his conditioning, the way he thinks, and the way he skis. Even the newcomer to the sport should know something about the racer. The novice must concern himself with kick turns, the snowplow, and the correct way to fall and get up, but he will soon leave these basic matters behind. Only by knowing the racer can the average skier set his standards. After all, in golf the par figures for a course give the player something to strive for. There is much in a racer's form which applies to all skiing. For instance, the hotshot on a steep slope, going fast, knows exactly where he is, while the aver-

age skier is lost among the moguls. However, it is of greatest importance to remember that skiing is the most imitative of sports.

A skier should pattern himself not just after an expert on the hill or a graceful instructor, but after the international-class racer.

One of the most marked differences between the recreational skier and the racer is in mental attitude. If the racer has an edge in conditioning he has an even greater advantage in mental toughness. The average skier, worrying too much about the physical challenges of skiing, seems unable to think his way through these challenges. The racer knows that unless he has prepared his mind for the mastery of the mountain, all of his training and practice will have been in vain.

In the end the racer conquers his nervousness, even making it work for him. The loneliest moments in the lonely sport of racing is the pre-race jitters period. This is the part of racing that no one likes and everyone wants to get through as quickly as possible. There is no way for the outsider to reach the racer when he is alone with his thoughts. He is absolutely incommunicado. If he speaks it is only by reflex, for his mind is at work trying to think positively about the race ahead. The skier knows that the only information useful to him would be new revelations about the state of the course. Yet he is leery of revising his plan because of information passed along to him secondhand. Experience tells him that he can rely only on what he has seen for himself. Nor is he in any mood to be molly-coddled by well-meaning friends. He knows that only self-control can keep his nerves calm enough to provide split-second reflexes and skilled judgment. Yet he must never be so relaxed that he loses

the benefit of his fighting spirit.

Perhaps the skier's most important sustenance during his hour of pre-race trial is his ego. It is characteristic of racers to have tremendous inner confidence. The better the racer the more boundless his ego. It is a reflective, somewhat introverted ego rather than a boastful kind, but it can be disdainful of competitors and not above gamesmanship. Sometimes the racer will take great delight in exhibiting to others what he can do best, such as holding a sharp hairpin on a steep icy slope. Or he will talk calmly about an airplane turn on a downhill course that his fellow racers are worried about. He knows too that he must be able to put his competition into perspective, and that his only problem is to ski right up to the outer edge of his ability. If he can truly be master of his own destiny he knows that he can win the race.

To comprehend fully the way the racer must discipline his mind for the contest, one should review each of the three Alpine events. For all three, the racer tries to control his worries and have his equipment in readiness several days ahead. Since the three events are all quite different, some racers ski better in one than in another. Certainly the racer must prepare himself for each event in slightly different ways.

DOWNHILL For the downhill he actually has more than a day to develop his plan in full. In this event the skier is permitted, even required, to run the entire course in a nonstop full-speed fashion. The usual procedure is first to run the course in sections and to get the feel of the slope and the turns, and to adjust to the speed of the course. The objective naturally is for the racer to work out a plan so precise that he can ski as if following a 12-inch-wide painted stripe all the way down the course, leaving it only when airborne.

The downhill, by Olympic standards, must show a vertical drop of 2,468 feet. Often the drop will be more like 3,000 feet over a distance of approximately two miles. The average speed is usually over 50 miles per hour. Strangely enough some of the easiest courses are the fastest.

To win a downhill the racer must be able to concentrate on his profile and try to hold the French egg position throughout. At speeds over 60 miles an hour, a wind check, standing upright with arms outstretched, can reduce speed by one-third within a short distance. Turning at such speeds is no problem; only a slight shift of weight to one ski is sufficient to produce a change of direction. There is no need for pronounced weighting and unweighting, heel thrust, or body angulation. The faster the speed, the easier it is to start the turn, but at high speed the real skill, as with any turn, is to hold it and finish it properly. The racer's problem in the turn, as well as on the straight stretches, is to ride his skis with his weight properly positioned. Even on sharp turns there is no full commitment to the turn, because the skier never knows when a sudden jolt will throw him off balance.

At the top of the course the racer has to make his mind believe in the plan that he has made, and to direct his body to carry it out. The racer does not dare think in terms of a fall, let alone of a crash. He knows that he has already faced all the real challenges of the course in his final practice run, when his mind came to grips with any imagined dangers. Positive think-

ing has now taken over and the skier is ready for speeds of 60 to 70 miles an hour, bumps, pitches, and tricky turns.

From watching the forerunners and the first few skiers on the course the racer can sometimes, for the few seconds that they are in sight, estimate snow conditions on the parts of the course, farther down, which are unseen. Also, after starting he immediately gets a feel of the course which transmits important information about how fast and how icy it is going to be. As he "finds himself," on his first few somewhat deliberate turns, his mind races ahead to what is approaching. His eyes look down the course to a point as far ahead as he can see. He seeks speed, he wants speed, and he feels that his pace is too slow. He wants to be farther down the course, up front where his thoughts are. His muscles are resilient and his legs work with ease over small bumps. Generally, his reflexes take care of what is at hand, while his mind is concerned with what is ahead. He has the poise to hold his egg shape when airborne, reaching for the ground only at the last second. Where a pre-jump is necessary his timing is precise, so as to avoid a long flight curve. In a troublesome section he forgets his egg shape and rides it out, avoiding checking while making a recovery, avoiding it completely if he can. In places where he has planned to check he does it quickly and effectively, rather than gradually and halfheartedly.

He knows above all that most races are won in the flat sections, and he enters such parts of the course with great care from the highest possible line. Attuned to the way his skis are tracking, he keeps them flat and riding easily. He is ready at all

times for trouble, and takes acrobatic recoveries very much in stride. He concentrates more than anything else on keeping low, well over his skis, and avoiding a fall. At such speeds the avoidance of a fall is paramount. He knows, too, that a fall can happen anywhere — often more likely to occur in a safe place than at one of the trail's danger points. His mind never relaxes its grip, and is not blurred by the way the trees go by. He knows precisely where he is and what he is doing every second, even when he is flying off blind drop-offs. He permits his concentration to relax only as he crosses the finish line; he knows then that he has skied a no-fall run. Sometimes, too, he has skied the course so well that he senses he will be the winner.

SLALOM In the slalom it is not very often that the course is set the day before the race. Even when the course is available, the racer looks it over somewhat casually, for his mind is trained to study it the morning of the race. The slalom must, however, be studied with utmost care. If downhill racing requires a dogged concentration, slalom requires a keen concentration. The good slalom runner inevitably knows his course so well that he mentally runs through it several times before the race, and for weeks later he can remember the exact configurations of the gates and the colors of the flags.

The slalom, by Olympic standards, must have a drop of 617 feet and include generally over 60 gates, with the flags set apart by a uniform distance. Of all the three events, the slalom requires the greatest practice and highest proficiency in technique. The racer must ski with rhythm, both as a function of his style and of

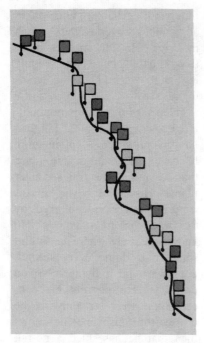

A typical slalom course over 100 yards might look like this. With 13 gates it keeps the competitors constantly turning.

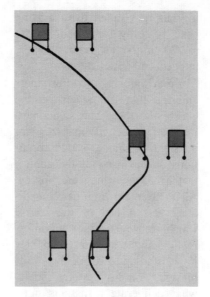

A giant slalom course, however, might have but three gates, inviting sweeping, more accelerated turns.

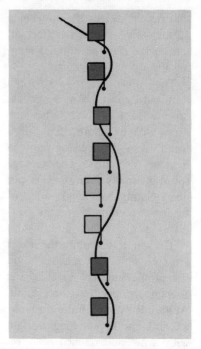

The four-gate flush is one of slalom's most often-encountered patterns and is probably responsible for more wipe-outs than any other single combination. Though this one is set in the fall line, others can be adapted to the terrain while still requiring linked short radius turns.

the way the course has been set. When the racer can watch a forerunner ski most of the course he has an opportunity to adapt his prearranged plan to unanticipated peculiarities of the course. As the racer approaches the starting gate, his nervousness, although different from what it was before the downhill, is just as intense, for in some ways he will need even more judgment than in the downhill, particularly since he will be skiing the course for the first time. Ideally, when the racer is on the course he can sense the rhythm the course setter had in mind. A tight slalom in the fall line can sometimes remind one of the cohesiveness of a Mozart composition. From just skiing the first few gates, the racer can catch the rhythm for the entire run. In the 1960 Olympic slalom at Squaw Valley, Ernst Hinterseer, the Australian gold medal winner, was mentally three or four gates ahead of himself all

the way down the course. Every good slalom runner always knows where he is and completes his turns early.

If a downhill is often won on the flats a slalom is sometimes won in the fairly easy open gates which require sweeping turns and enable the racer to pick up speed. Yet it is the closed gates and hairpins that test precision slalom skiing. In the flush the skier is engaged in disciplined wedeln skiing, generally opening up on speed for the last few gates of the flush. The technique of the slalom racer is very much in evidence in a good run. The speed, the adeptness, the anticipatory work with the poles, with both hands generally ahead in readiness for setting up the turn, are admirable to watch.

Perhaps of all the slalom racer's tools the most effective is the edge check, which allows him at all times to be on the fastest possible line and yet to hold back speed where necessary. But to win slalom races, the racer must ski beyond the point

of control. He has trained himself to do this, and he is skilled in scrambling, always driving forward down the course. His style is that of the modern parallel turn. His feet are apt to be fairly close together, his body position is the comma, his driving knees and feet reflect heel thrust, and as he ducks slalom poles, his shoulders neatly reverse. He works hard every inch of the way, but rarely loses his rhythm. The winner generally has the mark of a champion all the way. Even when he falters he recovers quickly, and he makes the spectators think that no one in the world could have gotten more speed out of the course.

GIANT SLALOM A giant slalom is sometimes erroneously compared to a downhill, being

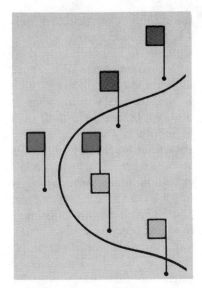

The hairpin is a familiar pattern to all who've watched even one slalom race. The illustrated version shows a fairly open pattern with the racer skiing a "safe" course. This pattern could be made more exacting if the top flag were moved lower on the hill or the bottom one higher up the hill.

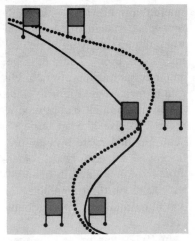

A typical giant slalom pattern might include this configuration of open gates which weave across the course. A prudent racer might pick the dotted line course with its sweeping turns, while a more aggressive one would pick the solid line shorter distance course.

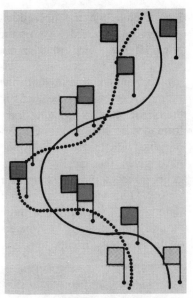

The intricate "Galdhoppigen" figure is one which offers two ways to be negotiated. An early starter would likely choose the conventional course shown by the dotted line while a late starter, who would face a rutted track, might decide the solid line course offered more speed.

thought of as a controlled downhill race. Certainly in its inception it was an attempt to provide a truly safe downhill. Today the giant slalom is as unique as either the downhill or the slalom. However, it does remain safer by far than either the downhill or the slalom. Since in the giant slalom the racer rarely goes over 30 miles per hour, speed in itself is no hazard. In the slalom speed is about 15 miles per hour, but on a relative basis speed is high in proportion to tight intricate holding turns, and racers can get hurt when they "crash and burn" and catch their ski tips on slalom poles in awkward ways.

The giant slalom is laid out in graceful sweeping turns. Unlike the slalom, which gets its rhythm from the course setter, who imposes the order of the flags on the contour of the hill, the giant slalom is laid out in such a way

that it accedes to the contour of the mountain. A good giant slalom course is thus very much an outgrowth of a steep, variable, interesting slope.

The vertical drop, by Olympic requirements, is 1,234 feet, but more often it is something like 1,600 feet over a length of about a mile. There are 30 to 50 gates, most of which are open — that is, laid out at right angles to the fall line rather than parallel to it.

In the giant slalom each turn must be accomplished with a carving action. Merely to ski a smooth race and hold the best line is not enough. The skier must work, poling constantly, sometimes finishing a turn on an inside ski to hold the highest possible line, sometimes skiing for the next gate in the classic manner for a high turn well above the gate, sometimes desperately heading straight for the gate and at the last minute stepping up to the high line and making the turn on one ski. The skier goes from one turn to the next without any

respite, yet occasionally for only a second he will go back into the egg-shaped position. Because of the changes in the contour of the slope each gate must be skied in a slightly different way, and the skier must be adaptable, adjusting his style to each turn. Sometimes on a banked downhill turn, he lets gravity do the work for him.

The giant slalom requires a higher state of conditioning than either of the other two events. It is a long race — in terms of time usually as long as the downhill. There are no breathing spells, for the racer works hard to accelerate his speed each second he is on the course. The giant slalom is a tremendous test of natural ability, and now and then the event will be won by a relative newcomer to the sport, like ex-hockey player Roger Staub, who won a gold medal in 1960 at Squaw Valley. The giant slalom after all is the only completely unrehearsed event, the downhill run being worked out with care and precision by skiing the actual course, and the slalom run being rehearsed in the sense that a winning performance is the result of interminable practice sessions which have given the racer the confidence and skill necessary for victory. The victor in the giant slalom may therefore be a more natural athlete than the winners of the other two events.

STEIN ERIKSEN Stein Eriksen today is known as the great stylist, perhaps the most impressive-looking man on skis. You hear the expression over and over again, "Nobody skis like Stein." He was probably the first man to ski slalom with the reverse-shoulder style. During practices for the 1950 F. I. S. at Aspen his style was a revelation to all racers, including the Austrians. Yet his magnificent form was taken more as a personal idiosyncrasy than as a new style of skiing applicable to racers and recreational skiers. In his own country at one time he was con-

sidered a maverick — actually somewhat ridiculed because he worked incessantly at his "idiotic" style, even skiing at night under lights outside of Oslo. His countrymen wanted him to stand up in races and his new style seemed to give him an unsteadiness. He had more success perfecting his famed forward somersault on skis, as well as his acrobatic feats on the trampoline, for which he attained early recognition.

In 1952 Stein proved the merits of his style when he won a gold medal for Norway in the giant slalom. In the 1954 F.I.S. at Aare, Sweden, he became the undisputed champion of the world by winning the slalom, giant slalom, then nearly taking the downhill, where a quick spill robbed him of victory. The gold medal in this race went to Christian Pravda. Stein won the combined event by a wide margin.

The key aspect of Stein's skiing is the tremendous amount of reserve power he has throughout the turn. His shoulders go to fully reversed position and the hips are the pivotal point, with the upper body in comma position like a poised counterweight. Stein's long sweeping turns are surely the most beautiful sight in skiing. No matter how bumpy or icy the slope, Stein, refusing to accede to difficult conditions, still does the same high-speed sweeping turns. He has been nothing short of inspirational, drawing newcomers to the sport in droves, and spurring veterans on to more graceful efforts.

A spectacularly handsome man, Stein is one of skiing's best-dressed and most glamorous figures. He has been the director of several ski schools, which always have had well-organized, well-balanced classes. As a teacher he manages to be all over

the mountain, so that each person feels he is getting some attention. He is particularly good with children, aware of the thrill they get from talking to him. During the east's meager winter of 1965 before Stein took over at Snowmass, there were two big attractions for Sunday afternoons at Sugarbush. One was Stein's exhibition somersault; the other was a slalom race in which Stein pitted himself against all comers. In the race anyone coming within five seconds of Stein was to be given a medal. The average length of the slalom was 30 seconds, yet no one came very near him. Only one medal was awarded — to one of his ski instructors, a Frenchman who had been trying to beat him all winter. On some runs on the ice prevailing that winter, Stein looked as if he were endowed with supernatural powers.

TONI SAILER Toni Sailer's claim to skiing greatness is well established. This man was nothing short of a genius on skis. His triple win at Cortina in 1956 is what he is rightfully remembered for. Almost forgotten, however, is his double victory in the 1958 F.I.S. at Bad Gastein, where he won the downhill and the giant slalom. He took second in the slalom, and of course won the three-way combined by a big margin. In his last two years of competition he was virtually unbeatable in the giant slalom, his outstanding event.

It is significant that Toni was so good at giant slalom. His fantastic athletic ability and his adaptable style made him an absolute demon in the race. Pictures show him responding to various gates in different ways, but he was always like a tiger, forward on his skis, beautifully balanced, and ready for anything. If there was something striking about the way he stood on his skis, there was something even more notable about the expression on his face. Toni always looked as if he were enjoying himself, almost as if he were playing touch football. Certainly no somber serious champion, he fully understood that to win he must be relaxed enough so that his entire body would react to the skis, the slope, and the speed of the course. Toni's reflexes were always keen, and his ability to recover from a near fall in the downhill often left spectators breathless.

No discussion of Toni Sailer would be complete without reviewing his accomplishment at Cortina. Injuries had prevented Toni from qualifying for the 1954 F.I.S. at Aare, Sweden, but he went into the 1956 winter Olympics at the top of his form. He was already the record holder on the difficult Stratofana downhill, which was to be the course for the Olympic downhill. Fortunately for him, the first race scheduled was the giant slalom, a race he knew to be his best event,

since the previous year he had won five out of the eight that he entered.

Toni raced 18th, and before his turn came, his three other Austrian teammates had preceded him with good times, Molterer and Hinterseer holding first and second best times. So when Toni went down the course, an exceptionally long 60-gate giant slalom, he was able to ski without any special pressure either to take risks or to have a no-fall run. His time was incredible — 3:00.1 — against the great Anderl Molterer in second place at 3:06.3.

In the slalom the conditions could not have been more difficult. The two courses, one set by President Otto Menardi of the F.I.S., and the other by Fred Roessner, involved a total of 178 gates set on a steep slope, the Col Druscie. This slope had been sprayed with water for several days to freeze it, but it had frozen in varying degrees, with the surface in some places consisting of rough lumps of ice. On top of this, the weather was foggy the day of the race, and the racers could only see a few gates ahead. To give some idea of how tough conditions were, the three first Austrians to go down the course, Josl Rieder, Anderl Molterer, and Othmar Schneider, each easily among the best 10 slalom skiers in the world, all fell on their first run. This time the pressure should have been on Toni, but as was his custom he skied according to his plan. He raced magnificently and finished in 1:27.3, the best time — two-tenths of a second ahead of American Brookie Dodge.

Toni studied the second course, a 92-gate slalom, with great care. It was faster than the Menardi slalom, but had several critical spots, including one dangerous

hairpin turn. He had three and a half hours before the second run started, and he used them well. At the start, according to Toni, about 20 people gave him advice, and although he pretended to listen with interest, he had already decided how to ski the second slalom and made no change in his overall plan. He won the second run, too, ending up with 1:47.4, with Chick Igaya, Japanese slalom star, second at 1:48.5. Igaya was also second for the two runs, but he was over four seconds behind Toni.

The downhill, like the slalom, was run under the most adverse conditions. The course was icy and dangerous, strong winds had blown the snow in drifted stretches, and this snow, although dry, had a heavy consistency that was difficult to wax for. The weather was bad, too, with the temperature a few hours before the start between 9 and 18 degrees below zero at various places on the course. And there was a wind storm, with gusts coming from all directions. Toni and his teammate Anderl Molterer decided that the race would be won by skiing with care and that the combination of ice and drifted snow, coupled with fearful moguls on the last quarter-mile corrugated section above the finish, would make it difficult for any racer to ski without falling. This time Toni was slated to be the third Austrian to go down the course, with Rieder wearing number 2 and Schuster number 8. Toni's starting number was 14, and before his turn word reached him that Austria was in trouble again, with both Rieder and Schuster having fallen. Just as number 9 went into the starting gate, Toni broke a strap while getting into his long-thong bindings. There was some scurrying around; the Austrian coach did not have an extra strap, and finally the coach of the Italian team gave him the strap from his own binding. This experience might have upset a lesser man, but again Toni knew how the mountain should be skied that day, and he was prepared for the challenge.

The start of the Stratofana course is on a 45-degree schuss between two mammoth rock towers. Toni skied the entire course with good judgment, getting all the speed he could out of most sections, and skillfully checking at the danger spots. There was a perilous iced path crossing the course, and he checked carefully before this spot. On the final corrugated stretch he was filmed rebounding from one ski to the other, as if fighting for his balance. Incredibly, he never fell. Toni's winning time was 2:52.2 — six seconds more than his 1955 record. Molterer also had an excellent run, turning in 2:56.3 for a bronze medal. Toni's third gold medal was certainly won under the most dangerous and difficult conditions. Out of 90 runners only 17 finished the course without falling, and what was even more staggering, among the top 25 seeded racers, 19 crashed.

So Toni did what no one else had done by winning all three Alpine events in world competition. Since the speed of the slalom has increased to the point where in order to win a racer must go beyond the brink of control, fate plays an increasing role, and the trend in this event is away from dominance by one skier.

I saw Toni ski at Stowe several times. In 1956, a few weeks after Cortina, I was up at the Octagon just before the start of the International Downhill. The faces of the ring of racers around the fire in the center of the room looked as grim as usual before a downhill. Suddenly the twin swinging inner doors burst open and in walked Toni. With all eyes in the room on him, he stamped his feet to shake off the snow with such confidence, such exuberance, that he reminded me of a flamenco dancer. Another year I watched him study a giant slalom course at Stowe, and again I could sense the tremendous assurance of the man.

Surely Toni knew all there is to know about how the mind must master the physical challenges of skiing. He could look at a course and relate it to the way it would be as he skied down. He was not absorbed in technique, either his own or anyone else's. Most racers are so concerned with trying to put themselves in a technique mold, so worried about keeping up with the advancement of the sport, that they never find themselves.

Toni liked being the world's best skier. As a well-tanned handsome idol of the crowd, he enjoyed in every way being Toni Sailer. And he was the first to have a triple Olympic victory.

JEAN-CLAUDE KILLY Of course, at Grenoble, in 1968, Sailer's feat was repeated by Jean-Claude Killy. And what manner of man, or superman is Killy?

Like Sailer, Killy was raised in ski country, where he learned to ski as a toddler off the roof of his house in Val d'Isère. Like Sailer, he became a hero of the whole ski world, but even more than Sailer, Killy is a hero among non-skiers too, especially among young people, who consider him a "cool guy." Large for a racer and certainly for a Frenchman, Killy is almost six feet tall and weighs 170 pounds. His neatly groomed look has helped bring dignity to long hair and sideburns. And Killy, photogenic in a different sense from Sailer, has an expressive face that somewhat resembles David McCallum's, of "U.N.C.L.E." fame. Killy has also contributed a rare stage presence to the ski scene. When talking with reporters, he speaks as though his lines might have been written for a champion by a first-rate scriptwriter. His interest in automobile racing has added to the picture.

If Killy was relaxed both on and off skis, behind the scenes every last detail of his racing career was well taken care of. He was the product of an organization without ever becoming an organization man.

His coach, Honoré Bonnet, took over the French national ski team in 1959, when the Austrians were walking off with all the skiing honors. Bonnet gave the French team a regimentation it needed, and yet as a Frenchman he understood the need for fun and relaxation before races. Bonnet did not believe in year-round skiing, and yet he set high standards for conditioning, placing emphasis on yoga exercises to relax muscles. Killy used the bicycle for muscle and mind tune-up, going on downhill high-speed bike runs as a test of speed with precision.

Bonnet deserves much of the credit for the development of the egg position, and the new technical refinements of racing turns. Also helpful to Bonnet was his ability to organize. In late November training, members of the French team could run as many as 450 slalom gates a day, since up to 20 helpers would be standing by to pick up the gates as they were knocked down by the racers. In nonstop pre-downhill runs the French skiers would be timed along each section of the course. On the morning of a race, snow temperatures were taken with a rectal-type thermometer to remove most of the risk from waxing. During the race, intelligence was transmitted instantly back and forth by means of walkie-talkies. For Killy, there was even a racing stand-in, Michel Arpin, who was a former member of the French team. Michel skied in a style similar to Killy, and used the same length skis and even the same size boots. Killy, who went through boots very quickly, always had Michel breaking in a new pair for him. Michel worked closely with the French ski manufacturers and helped to design and discover skis that were just right for Killy. The great superstar never had to think about any phase of equipment; his well-waxed, edge-honed skis would be ready for him on the morning of the race. In addition to being racing serviceman, Michel was also Killy's friend, confidant, and trusted advisor.

Under Bonnet's organizational genius, the Frenchman started winning right away, taking a gold and two bronze medals at Squaw Valley in 1960, and earning more world championships at Chamonix in 1962 and Innsbruck in 1964. However, it was at Portillo in the summer of 1966 when the Austrians were stopped cold, with the French showing unquestioned supremacy in winning 18 out of 24 medals.

In his early years Jean-Claude Killy was just another expert skier on the French team. Guy Perillat was then the star. Still, in the Olympics at Innsbruck in 1964, Killy came within a second of Bonlieu's gold medal run in the giant slalom, and won several big races in the spring of that year. At the beginning of the 1966 season he won the first couple of races, but then Billy Kidd came over to Europe, and for five weeks was the world's best slalom and giant slalom skier. At Portillo Killy won the downhill, his first big victory in that event, but it was a short course, and extremely fast. He won in 1:344.4, skiing at an average speed of 64 miles an hour. He then set out to win the world's championship in the F.I.S. Alpine combined, and he conservatively settled for a fifth place in the giant slalom and eighth place in the slalom, which was all he needed. On this basis he was now a world champion, but not yet one of the all-time great skiers.

In 1967 a new event was created, the World Cup of skiing. This determined the top skier of the year on the basis of point score in 17 races which covered all three events. In 1967 World Cup competition it was Killy all the way. He accumulated the maximum possible number of World Cup points, winning 12 of the 16 races that he entered, and getting a second, third, fourth and one d.n.f. (did not finish) in the others. No man had ever dominated racing to this extent. He won every downhill he entered, and he actually had eight straight skiing victories in this country when the season ended.

So as the winter Olympics opened in 1968, the big question was, would Killy be able to repeat Toni Sailer's slam. Unlike Sailer, Killy was under pressure to win all three. Victory in just one or two races would be for him a disappointment, yet he was faced with brilliant competition, racing against specialists like the 6-foot 4-inch, 220-pound German, Franz Vogler, in the downhill and the Austrian Herbert Huber in the slalom. And in the slalom there was the trend toward the all-or-nothing type of run.

The Olympic downhill at Grenoble was a short course, just barely in excess of the F.I.S. requirement of an 800-meter vertical drop, with nine radical changes of direction, each one followed by a difficult drop-away which tended to pick up chatter marks. In the practice nonstop run Killy came up with the best time. The next morning, following his custom, he skied a mile or so down the side of the mountain to gain the feel of his skis and break in his wax. He thought he would be skiing in soft snow, but the slope turned out to have an icy surface under a dusting of snow. The result was that he lost most of his wax. He knew then that he would have to go all out on the difficult tight upper stretches of the race. He skied the first few control gates in giant slalom style, aiming at each gate and then at the earliest possible moment cranking in a sharp turn by skating to his inside, uphill ski. He handled the rolling bumps on a section knows as *Les Bosses du Coq* with easy knee action. On one difficult downhill turn his body balance shifted from one ski to another over a surface rough with chatter marks. As he went into the two big rolling bumps of the *Col de la Balme,* where American Moose Barrows made his ill-conceived flight, he wind-checked on the first bump so that he could pre-jump the next and land with perfect timing on the downhill side of the second bump, for the fastest possible outrun. Near the end of the short flat which followed, he was timed at 1.1 seconds faster than anyone else. On the last part of the course he lost most of his margin because he was going over warm moist snow with almost waxless bottoms, yet he beat his teammate Perillat by 0.08 second, to win the first gold medal.

The giant slalom was the first two-run giant slalom ever held in the Olympics. On the first day the hard and icy course, with 70 gates laid out over rolling terrain, glistened in a bright sun. Killy decided to burn up the course for the first heat. He skied in classic giant slalom style, turning high, accelerating, making a technically perfect run, and at the end of the day's competition he had the impressive lead of 1.2 seconds. On the second day conditions were different. Snow during the night had provided a new soft surface, and a heavy fog three hundred yards down from the start restricted visibility to only two or three gates ahead. Killy's job was now to ski carefully and protect his lead. On this run, Billy Kidd posted the best time, but for the two runs Killy's victory was by a comfortable 2.22 seconds, and he had won a second gold medal.

In the slalom fog again was thick. And because the two courses were laid out on not too steep a slope, they were the kind of slaloms where hundredths of a second would be important. The Lord above was kind to Killy, since a break in the fog

occurred as he was waiting in the starting gate. Like a true champion he took full advantage of the clear course to gain a lead of 0.3 second over the Austrian Alfred Matt. Fourteen skiers came within a second of his time. For the second run the fog was thick for everyone. Under the circumstances Killy had a good run, but because of the bad visibility, he held back to some extent and could not be certain that no one would catch him. There were two skiers who did beat Killy's total time: the Norwegian Haakon Mjoen and the great Austrian skier Karl Schranz. The Norwegian sensed that he had missed gates in the fog, and was shortly disqualified. Schranz had missed the same gates, number 17 and 18, but he was given a provisional second run because he had seen the shadow of a spectator crossing between gates 20 and 21. Later the race jury ruled that since Schranz had missed gates earlier than the point of interference, he was not entitled to his second run. Also, pictures of Schranz taken during his short-lived moment of glory show what might be interpreted as a look of concern on his face.

So Jean-Claude Killy, in winning his three gold medals, probably takes the unofficial crown from Sailer as the all-time king of skiing. Killy behind the scenes was a champion too. As a true sportman as well as an interesting personality he was well liked by all the racers, especially the Americans. He and Jim Heuga are great friends, and Penny McCoy told me after the 1968 Olympics, "If it couldn't be an American, there's no one I would rather see win."

Killy as a competitor could be concentrating with mathematical precision, or relaxing, as the situation required. He admitted that

he could fall asleep instantly the night before a race. "I go pouf," he said. At the top of a slalom course, in mentally running the gates, he could imagine the clock ticking away, and almost know where he was going to be every second on the course. Bonnet said of him, "I can tell by his eyes if he will be good. If I see that Killy's eyes are cold and flashing just before the start, I will not have to worry. He will do something wonderful."

And Killy said of himself in a starting gate, "It never occurs to me that I will not be first."

On the course Killy sometimes skied with such dedication to speed that he appeared violently opposed to style. He contrasted vividly with one of the best Austrians of a slightly earlier era, Egon Zimmerman, who during slaloms in the early 1960s would

Photos reflect evolution in equipment as well as varied styles. Opposite: Sailer winning his third gold medal in downhill at Cortina in 1956. Top: Killy duplicating the trick at Grenoble in 1968. Above: Eriksen winning GS gold for Norway in 1952.

make his turn in perfect feet-together angulated wedeln style, as if doing a commercial for the Austrian ski school.

In a slalom Killy seemed to go radically from one type of turn to another, skiing in a wide stance without any apparent rhythm and on the verge of an eggbeater fall all the way down the course. Killy knew more about the outer limits of control than any other racer. Skiing right to the brink but no farther, he always had recovery within his grasp. But Killy, despite not looking pretty on the slalom course, was technically the world's greatest skier. For instance, he mastered two new types of turns, one of which is *avalement,* meaning "swallowing" (of the hill). In the *avalement* the skis are unweighted by being thrust forward, and the turn accomplished by steering with the feet. The racer, like an intermediate skier on fast skis, is left sitting back as if his skis have run out from under him, only he has the power in his muscles to recover. Also, he is ready to push himself forward with both poles if necessary. The other turn is the "jet turn," where an edge set is used as a momentary angulation without any braking, followed by a rebound with a natural unwinding of the body. This produces an almost effortless change of direction, as if the turn after the edge set had been ac-

complished without any technique.

In a downhill Killy skied in a modified egg position, slightly out of the crouch so that his knees could ride the contours softly. Riding the bumps hard would have slowed him down. At 65 miles an hour on a difficult turn Killy could shift his weight quickly by instinct to his uphill inside ski, almost at the exact instant that the downhill ski was about to wander. He could even do this with *avalement,* sitting back on one ski, and thrusting it forward. In one downhill race at the choppy steep finish when he was low in a tuck, his right ski seemed to be going dangerously astray. And he was seen to correct this near-fall situation without even coming out of the tuck.

In a giant slalom Kitty could pole harder and faster at the start than anyone, picking up the good part of a second before reaching the first gate, and then skiing in easy sweeping turns, always taking his gates close, stepping up to his high, fast line.

The objective in any racing turn is to accelerate rather than to skid and lose speed. Killy managed to start his turn early, clip the gates close, and use his wide stance position to push off one ski or the other whenever possible. Whether in a skating step, or stepping uphill to a faster line, usually one ski was in full contact with the snow for perfect sliding action.

Therefore, the answer to Killy versus Sailer is that Sailer may have been the most natural skier of them all, but Killy's commitment to speed was so complete that had the two ever raced against each other under equal conditions, Killy would have found a way to go faster than Sailer.

AMERICA'S SKI COLLEGES

*Here is information on the competitive and recreational programs
at the major institutes of higher skiing in the country*

by Carolyn Meyer

College today isn't all pot and sex and protesting in the dean's office. For many college students, "doing your own thing" means skiing.

A survey of 100 major snow belt schools in 22 states from Maine to Alaska *(see listing on following pages)* reveals the diversity and depth of ski programs for undergraduates.

At most of these schools, team competition is an important part of the ski program. Some 90 colleges field a ski racing team and compete regularly against other schools, and 61 of them also enter cross country and/or jumping meets. Thirty-one of the schools have girls competing. too.

All of these schools—plus many others—also sponsor various programs for recreational skiing. Undergraduates can take skiing as a physical education elective at most of the colleges listed, and at some schools, skiing is actually a required course for freshmen or sophomores. Even when the sport is not officially part of the school's curriculum, it is a big part of winter campus life, thanks to the enthusiastic efforts of local ski clubs.

Although most ski colleges use nearby areas for their programs—a commute that may run from a couple of minutes for the lucky ones to a couple of hours for collegians at "southern" schools like Brown in Rhode Island—an impressive number of schools own and operate their own facilities. These range in size from modest slopes with rope tows to sophisticated developments like the Dartmouth Skiway and the Middlebury Snow Bowl. Colby College in Maine has a snowmaking machine and lighted slopes for night skiing in addition to a T-bar and a 32-meter jump. The University of Alaska, admittedly well-situated for winter sports facilities, maintains 40 miles of cross country trails. Dozens of other schools also have their own set-ups, and many others have plans—or at least hopes—for development of them.

The location and size of the school are important but not overriding factors in determining the enthusiasm skiing generates. Blessed with lots of snow and nearby mountains, Colorado students show their gratitude *en masse*. At the University of Colorado in Boulder, officials estimate that 12,000 of the 16,000-member student body "ski to some extent," and the ski club there numbers a mighty 1,500. At Colorado College the ski club was disbanded because "everyone skis anyway." Nearly half of the 3,300 cadets at the U.S. Air Force Academy in that state belong to the campus ski club, and sometimes as many as 41 buses are chartered on weekends to take the men to surrounding Rocky Mountain slopes.

Johnson State College, conveniently located in the Green Mountains of Vermont, has an enrollment of only 500 students, yet boasts its own ski area and even offers a Phys Ed course in ski coaching techniques. Alaska Methodist University, with the same small enrollment, fields ski racing, cross country and jumping teams, and makes each Wednesday a "free day" so that ski-crazy undergraduates can get on the boards three days a week instead of just weekends. Like so many other colleges, Alaska Methodist arranges reduced-price lift tickets at local areas for student skiers, and furnishes equipment at modest rental rates. Generally, equipment is dispensed free of charge to students enrolled in the various physical education classes. Going one ski step further, the University of Minnesota releases its equipment (100 pairs of boots, 50 pairs of metal or fiberglass skis, 60 pairs of wood skis) to students for unlimited weekend use without charge.

Mackinac College has neither enrollment nor location on its side, yet fosters a skiing spirit that can't be topped anywhere. Located on a six-square-mile island overlooking the strait that separates the upper and lower peninsula of Michigan, the college shares the island with the Grand Hotel, a posh summer re-

An increasing number of colleges in the snow belt offer a wide variety of ski programs, both competitive and recreational, to today's student, as the photos on the opposite page suggest. Students add their own flavor to winter via rock groups and symbolic ice sculpture.

EAST AND MIDWEST School	Enrollment Men/Women	Competitive Program: Alp	X-C	Jump	Participation Men/Women	Recreational Program	Participation Men/Women	Facilities
CONNECTICUT								
Yale University, New Haven	4125/	x	x	x	20/	Ski club (250 members)	250/	Use Vermont ski areas
MAINE								
Bates College, Lewiston	507/ 420	x	x	x	15/	Physical Education course; outing club	125/ 50	Use Lost Valley
Bowdoin College, Brunswick	925/	x	x	x				Use nearby areas
Colby College, Waterville	767/ 609	x	x	x	30/15	PE course, beg. - adv., ski club (30)	75/200	Own slopes, trails, 32m. jump, snow making, rope, T-bar, lights
Nasson College, Springvale	250/ 250	x			10/	PE required course	50	Own slopes, rope tow
U. of Maine, Orono	3550/ 2043	x	x	x	35/	PE course for women; outing club (300)	/250	Use nearby ski areas
MASSACHUSETTS								
American Int'l Coll., Springfield	1200/ 500	x			7/	PE course; ski club (90)	20/ 50	Use Mt. Tom
Amherst College, Amherst	1200/	x			30/	PE course, basic-intermed.	60/	Own ski area (Tinker Hill), rope tow
Babson Institute, Wellesley	750/	x			10/	None		Use nearby ski areas
Bentley College, Boston	1900/ 100	x			15/	Ski club (150)		Use Prospect Hill
Boston College, Chestnut Hill	5600/ 1500	x			25/	Ski club (150)		Use Prospect Hill
Harvard University, Cambridge	4900/	x	x	x	35/	None		Use nearby ski areas
Holy Cross College, Worcester	2300/	x			16/	None		Use Pleasant Mt. & Sugarloaf Mt.
Lowell Tech, Lowell	2264/ 58	x			20/	Alpine club (75)		Use N.H. & Vt. ski areas
MIT, Cambridge	3657/ 200	x	x	x	25/	PE course, basic	65/ 10	Use Blue Hills
U. of Massachusetts, Amherst	7914/ 5443	x			20/20	PE course; Ski club (20)	40/ 50	Use Mt. Tom, Thunder Mt.
Tufts University, Medford	1932/ 1010	x			12/	None		Use nearby ski areas
Williams College, Williamstown	1250/	x	x	x	35/	PE course, beg.-exp.; outing club (290)	200/	Own downhill trail, 1200' drop; slalom slope, 450' drop
Worcester Polytech, Worcester	1570/	x			15/	Ski club (20)	20/	Use Mt. Wachusetts
MICHIGAN								
Lake Superior State Coll., Sault Ste. Marie	650/ 225		x	x	20/	PE course, beginners	40/ 40	Use Mission Hill, Minneapolis areas
Mackinac College, Mackinac Island	150/ 150	x	x		10/10	(See story)		(See story)
Michigan State U., East Lansing	22891/15216	x			10/6	Ski club (200)		Use nearby ski areas
Michigan Tech, Houghton	3675/ 305	x			12/	PE course, beg.-adv. & ski patrol, ski club (200)	380/ 20	T-bar, chair, 2 rope tows, 420' drop
MINNESOTA								
Carleton College, Northfield	800/ 587	x			14/	Women's PE course, men's to start; ski club (200)	6/161	Use nearby areas
Gustavus Adolphus, St. Peter	763/ 823					PE course, basic; ski club (150)		Use nearby areas
Hamline Univ., St. Paul	512/ 594	x			25/5	PE course; ski club (80)	40/ 40	Use nearby areas
U. of Minnesota (Duluth), Duluth	2336/ 1439	x			15/	PE course; ski club (50)	250/250	Own ski hill, rope tow, 225' drop
NEW HAMPSHIRE								
Belknap College, Center Harbor	370/ 80	x	x		14/	None		Use nearby areas
Dartmouth College, Hanover	3065/	x	x	x	60/	PE course, beg.-competition; outing club (1,200)		Dartmouth Skiway - poma, T-bar, chair, 1000' drop.
Hawthorne College, Antrim	400/ 150	x			15/	PE required course; ski club		Own slope, rope tow
Keene State College, Keene	742/ 883	x	x	x	20/16	PE course to intermed; ski club (90)	20/ 60	Use nearby ski areas
New England College, Henniker	450/ 250	x	x	x	25/8	PE course, ski club (300)	200/100	Use Pat's Peak
N.H. College, Manchester	770/ 200	x			12/	Ski club (15)	15	Use Ragged Mt.
U. of New Hampshire, Durham	3587/ 2732	x	x	x	25/10	PE course	100/ 75	Use Gunstock
NEW JERSEY								
Princeton University	3211/	x			20/	Ski club		Use nearby areas
NEW YORK								
Colgate Univ., Hamilton	1800/	x	x	x	25/	PE course for frosh, sophs; outing club (300)	200/	2300' T-bar, snow machine
Cornell Univ., Ithaca	6500/ 2700	x	x	x	35/20	PE course; ski club (60)		Own jumping area; use Great Peak
Cortland State	1045/ 2000	x	x	x	25/	PE course		Use Greek Peak
Le Moyne College	850/ 500	x	x	x	20/	Ski club (120)	120	Use Song Mtn.
Paul Smith's College	700/	x	x	x	12/	None		Use nearby ski areas
Rensselaer Poly. Inst., Troy	3357/ 84	x	x	x	15/	Ski club (25)	25/	Use nearby areas
St. Lawrence Univ., Canton	1050/ 650	x	x	x	20/10	PE course, outing club (145)	86/160	3 slopes, 3 jumps, X-c trail, T-bar, rope tow
Syracuse University	11298/ 6361	x	x	x	25/	PE course; Ski club (100)	75	Own slopes, rope tow, 30m
U.S. Miliary Acad., West Point	3300/	x	x	x	30/	PE course; intramural racing; ski club (200)	800/	20 acres slopes & trails, 500' drop; 25m. jump; 14 km, X-c run, T-bar, poma lift, rope tow
Utica College, Utica	882/ 473	x	x	x	12/	Ski club (20)	20/	Use nearby areas
RHODE ISLAND								
Brown University, Providence	2500/	x			16/10	PE course for Pembroke girls; ski club (20)		Use Vermont and New Hampshire areas
U. of Rhode Island, Kingston						PE course for sophs.	200/	Use nearby ski areas
VERMONT								
Johnson State Coll., Johnson	235/ 240	x			20/5	PE course; ski - coaching techniques course; outing club (40)	50/ 50	Pomalift, 250' drop
Middlebury College, Middlebury	820/ 570	x	x	x	50/25	PE course; mountain club (250)		Own Snow Bowl—3 pomalifts, 1200' drop
Norwich Univ., Northfield	1300/	x	x	x	25/	PE course, sophs; outing club (500)	500/	Own area, 500' drop, pomalift, rope tow
St. Michael's, Winooski	1175/	x	x	x	20/	PE course, beg.-exp.	150/	Building 30m. jump; use Madonna
U. of Vermont, Burlington	2376/ 1771	x	x	x	40/15	PE course, beg.-adv.; club	250/150	Use nearby areas
Windham College, Putney	450/ 250	x	x		16/	PE course, ski club (40)	160	Use Maple Valley
WISCONSIN								
Lawrence Univ., Appleton	725/ 565					PE course	45/ 45	Use Hidden Valley
Northland College, Ashland	475/ 190	x			10/	Basic PE course for frosh; intermed planned; ski club	60/ 50	Use nearby ski areas
Wisconsin State U., Eau Claire	2475/ 2508					PE course; ski club (150)	175/175	Beginners' slope, artificial surface; also use nearby areas

WEST AND ROCKIES School	Enrollment Men/Women	Competitive Program: Alp	X-C	Jump	Participation Men/Women	Recreational Program	Participation Men/Women	Facilities
ALASKA								
Alaska Methodist U., Anchorage	500/	x	x	x	8/3	PE course, Alpine and X-c; free day on Weds. for skiing	100/100	Own 250' hill, ski jump, X-c trails
U. of Alaska, College	1250/ 750		x	x	10/5	PE course, Alpine and X-c	50/ 40	1750' rope tow; 40 mi. X-c trails
ARIZONA								
Northern Arizona U., Flagstaff	3950/ 2900	x	x	x	6/	PE course, ski club (150)	500/400	Use Arizona Snow Bowl
CALIFORNIA								
Chico State College, Chico	2980/ 2808	x	x	x	15/	Ski club (150)	150/150	Use Donner Ski Ranch
San Jose State College, San Jose	12227/ 9573	x	x		12/1	Ski club (400)	400	Use nearby areas
Sierra College, Rocklin	2377	x	x	x	40/20	PE course; ski club (50)	40/ 30	Use nearby areas
Siskiyous, Coll. of, Weed	326/ 220	x	x	x	20/	PE course	75/ 50	Use Mt. Shasta
Tahoe Paradise Coll., Tahoe Paradise		x	x	x	15/5	PE course; ski club	50/ 25	Use Heavenly Valley
COLORADO								
Colorado College, Colorado Springs	800/ 600	x			15/10	PE course for women	/100	Use nearby areas
Colorado School of Mines, Golden	1494/ 7	x			12/	None		Use nearby areas
Colorado State College, Greeley	3073/ 3950					PE course; ski club (400)	80	Use Eldora
Colorado State Univ., Ft. Collins	8768/ 4932	x			14/	PE course; ski club (125)		Use nearby areas
U. of Colorado, Boulder	16000	x	x	x	30/20	PE course, basic; ski club (1,500)		Use nearby areas
University of Denver, Denver	4359/ 2356	x	x	x	30/	PE course; ski club	175	Use Arapahoe Basin
Ft. Lewis College, Durango	900/ 700	x	x	x	40/	PE course; ski club (200)	450/300	Use Purgatory
Regis College, Denver	775/	x			8/	Ski club (100)		Use nearby areas
U.S. Air Force Acad., Colorado Springs	3300/	x	x	x	20/	Buses run to ski areas on weekends; ski club	1500/	Use nearby areas
Western State Coll., Gunnison	1600/ 1100	x	x	x	30/	PE course, beg.-adv.; ski club (150)	150	Use nearby areas
IDAHO								
Idaho State Univ., Pocatello	3200/ 1500	x			6/	PE course, basic; ski club	150/ 78	Use Skyline
Idaho, College of, Caldwell	500/ 335	x	x	x	10/	Intramural program; PE course; ski club (200)	150/100	Use Bogus Basin
Ricks College, Rexburg	3000	x			13/	PE course; ski club (200)	85/ 90	Use Bear Gulch Ski Basin, Sun Valley, Jackson Hole
U. of Idaho, Moscow	4115/ 1845	x	x	x	10/	None		Use Moscow Mt., Brundage Mt.
MONTANA								
Montana State Univ., Bozeman	4267/ 2399	x	x	x	20/	PE course; ski club (200)	1000	Use Bridger Bowl
U. of Montana, Missoula	4043/ 1979	x	x	x	20/5	Certified ski school; ski club (300)	200/200	Use Missoula, Snow Bowl, Marshall Canyon
NEVADA								
U. of Nevada, Reno	2500/ 1500	x	x	x	25/25	PE course; racing club (15)	100/100	Use Mt. Rose, other nearby ski areas
OREGON								
Central Oregon Community College, Bend	900	x	x		10/5	PE course; ski club (30)	100/ 75	Use Mt. Bachelor
Eastern Oregon Coll., LaGrande	850/ 550	x	x		10/5	PE course, beg.-adv.; X-c inst. planned; ski club (60)	80/ 60	Use Spout Springs
Lewis & Clark College, Portland	740/ 740	x			10/	PE course; ski club (40)	120	Use Mt. Hood
Mt. Hood Community College, Gresham		x			10/	PE course; ski club (25)		Use Mt. Hood
Oregon State U., Corvallis	8311/ 4357	x	x		10/8	Ski club (150)	100/ 50	Use nearby areas
U. of Oregon, Eugene	8000/ 5500	x	x	x	25/10	PE course, beg.-adv.; outdoor program (700)	100/100	Use nearby areas
Portland State College, Portland	4132/ 3411	x	x	x	50/	PE training program; ski club		Use Mt. Hood
Southern Oregon Coll., Ashland	2412/ 1726	x	x		12/	PE course; mountain club (25)	150/150	Use Mt. Ashland
Warner Pacific Coll., Portland	175/ 175					PE course through Mt. Hood Ski School	5/ 5	Use Mt. Hood
UTAH								
Brigham Young U., Provo	9931/ 7922	x	x	x	15/5	PE course, basic - racing; ski club (75)	500	Use nearby areas
College of Southern Utah, Cedar City	1000/ 900					PE course	40/ 30	Use Brian Head
U. of Utah, Salt Lake City	17584	x	x	x	20/	PE course; ski club (100)		Use nearby areas
Westminster College, Salt Lake City	400/ 400	x	x	x	12/3	PE course planned; ski club (40)	40	Use nearby areas
Weber State College, Ogden	4014/ 2029	x			6/	PE course; ski club		Use Snow Basin
WASHINGTON								
Pacific Luthern Univ., Tacoma	639/ 564	x	x	x	12/6	PE course for sophs; all levels; ski club (110)	60/ 50	Use nearby areas
U. of Puget Sound, Tacoma	1163/ 1110	x	x		16/12	PE course, beg.-adv.	30/ 30	Use nearby areas
U. of Washington, Seattle	14580/ 8350	x	x	x	10/	PE course; ski club		Use nearby areas
Western Washington State College, Bellingham	2600/ 3500					PE course, beg.-adv.; ski club		Use Mt. Baker
WYOMING								
U. of Wyoming, Laramie	4099/ 2132	x	x	x	30/	PE course, ski club (250)	80/ 80	Use Happy Jack

sort. After the last guests have departed the hotel by boat in September, the 300 Mackinac students take over the island. They learn basic Alpine techniques on the hotel golf course. Their cross country team of 10 men and 10 girls roams the entire island. A steeper downhill area on college property opened last winter, and a 30-meter jump should be ready by next season. Skiing is a required course for the first two years, and no radical frosh or soph marches in protest.

Undoubtedly the spirit of recreational skiing at colleges is captured best in the atmosphere and antics of the winter carnival. One of the oldest of these extravaganzas is the Middlebury College, Vt., carnival which started as a modest jump meet in 1931. Today it is a major winter attraction, bringing in collegians and non-collegians from all over the Northeast. Last year more than 4,000 people showed up for the carnival weekend, usually held late in February, and attended parties, concerts, balls, parties, torchlight parades, ice shows, parties, hockey games, jump meets, ski races and more parties. The pattern is the same for the famous carnival sponsored annually by Middlebury's traditional ski rival, Dartmouth College in Hanover, N.H., where organized skiing in this country is reputed to have begun.

Often the Middlebury carnvial will feature the Eastern Intercollegiate Ski Ass'n championships, the major college-level ski meet in the East, and, until recent years, in the entire country. Today, however, the most competitive of all collegiate ski leagues is the Rocky Mountain Intercollegiate Ski Ass'n, whose teams occupied four of the top five places in the National Collegiate Athletic Ass'n (NCAA) standings last year. The rise of the western league can be attributed largely to the efforts of Willy Schaeffler, Denver University ski coach—and to the efforts of the other coaches to compete with him. Schaeffler came to DU in 1948, began NCAA competition in 1953-54 and his teams have lost only two championships since.

More than anything else, it has been the persistence and ingenuity of coaches like Schaeffler that has made under-graduate skiing, both competitive and recreational, grow to its present level. Sven Wilk, another outstanding Colorado ski coach who retired this year after 19 seasons at Western State College, is responsible for the state's most complete physical education program in skiing. Almost 20 years ago, Ralph Townsend, Williams College, Mass., coach, began to build a "participation" program alongside his varsity ski program, and in recent winters he has engaged student instructors to teach the sport's fun-

damentals to 8 underclassmen at nearby Brodie Mountain. "The new skiers — especially southerners — went wild," says one instructor. "They wanted to ski every day."

A college's potential for introducing the sport in such a way to new people is greatly underestimated, according to another fine coach, Fred Lonsdorf of Michigan Tech.

"Area operators, instructors, equipment manufacturers and the ski association itself have overlooked the possibilities for expanding college skiing," says Lonsdorf. "The skiers are there, the interest is very high and I am certain the sport could be as big at all snow belt schools as it is at our campus." (Six hundred of 4,000 Michigan Tech students buy season lift tickets to the school's facility.)

Lonsdorf believes that more ski coaches at the college and high school level would greatly improve America's long-range potential on the world ski scene, but he points out that it is hard to find a place in which to receive training as a coach.

An ardent proponent of more high school ski programs is John Cress, who coached last season's NCAA championship ski team at the University of Wyoming, but he is not optimistic about it.

One hopeful sign for college skiing is the recent formation of the Collegiate Ski Coaches' Ass'n of America, which may channel the diverse energies of coaches like Cress, Lonsdorf, Wilk, Schaeffler, Si Dunklee of Colby College, Al Merrill of Dartmouth and many others, into something like an orderly march on the problems at hand. While the immediate objectives of the fledgling organization are primarily concerned with the development of inter-college policies and procedures and with coaching per se, ultimately the group may help to define more clearly the relation of college ski activities to the national ski program of the U.S. Ski Ass'n. Unlike athletes in practically every other sport in the country, the best competitive skiers, particularly the ski racers, progress in their skills through what is essentially a non-educational structure—the national ski team program—though most belong to a college ski team as well.

For the vast majority of undergraduate skiers, however, ski competition has only a spectator interest—and a slight one at that. Eventually the most purposeful function of groups like the organization of coaches may well be to create a meaningful national program to serve the growing number of recreational types on campus. One thing's for sure: undergraduates today prefer ski-downs to sit-ins 10 to 1.

SKIING ON A STUDENT BUDGET: MIND OVER MONEY

by Kim Chaffee and David Lyman

In case you haven't already noticed, skiing is getting more expensive every year. Unless your father just left you half his estate, the cost of a $200 pair of skis, $125 pair of boots, $45 bindings, $30 poles, $75 parka, and a $10 lift ticket etc., etc., may make you think twice before venturing out onto the slopes. Yet, with a modest amount of planning, you can have an unforgettable ski season and still remain solvent.

The secret to inexpensive skiing is research—checking into

equipment, transportation, lodging, food, lift tickets and lesson costs *before* you blow a bundle. Let's assume you are a young person (high school, college, or graduate school student or a worker with a modest income) who either wants to learn to ski or wants to ski more, for less money. Let's consider each item of expense separately:

EQUIPMENT: If you are a beginning skier, the array of different brands may bewilder you. The general rule is that you get what you pay for. While ski equipment improves every year, you can save money by buying your skis and perhaps boots and poles second-hand. Good metal skis will usually last for at least five years, fiberglass somewhat less. Wood skis have often had it after a season. Likewise, plastic boots (be careful to get a good fit) will hold up for many years, whereas leather boots become soft in about four seasons.

Keep your eyes open for "ski swaps." They are great opportunities to buy quality used equipment at very reasonable prices. Most ski swaps are in the fall and are run by ski clubs, church and other fellowship groups, ski shows, and ski shops. Other good places to look are college, company, and ski area bulletin boards and classified newspaper ads. Most ski shops that rent equipment have left-over rentals from the previous season. By paying close attention to the condition of the articles, you can often buy excellent one-year old skis, boots, and poles for one-third to one-half the new price.

Like cars, ski equipment models and clothing change every year. You can take advantage of this by waiting until the last week in February to lay out cash for equipment or clothing. During these sales prices are cut from 20 percent to 50 percent and more, but get there early for the best selection.

If you don't already have ski equipment, consider renting until you are sure what kind you want. Renting equipment at a ski shop in the city is almost always less expensive than renting at the area. (We will discuss a notable exception later). Prices range from $5 to $10 for skis, boots, and poles for a weekend, depending on the quality of the equipment.

A word on ski clothing. The only requirement is that you be warm and dry while on the slopes. Eastern winters can be fierce, so if you frequent this region don't sacrifice your body to look chic. The top lines of ski clothing are out of the range of most students' budgets, but anyone can buy a good-looking parka, sweater, stretch pants, gloves, and hat for under $100. If this is still too much, your own sweater, winter coat, Levi's over a pair of long underwear will suffice, provided they are warm and waterproof enough. Don't forget that a parka can be worn practically anywhere during the fall, winter, and spring.

TRANSPORTATION: If you already have a car you're not only in good shape, you're probably also very popular. From the point of view of cost and flexibility, the auto is still the best way to travel. One of the biggest advantages of a car is that it allows you to stay at lodges farther from the ski area, where costs are lower. Be sure that yours has snow tires or chains and a shovel. Towing can be very expensive.

Whether you are looking for a ride or providing one, the car pool is a money saver. With four people chipping in for gas, tolls, and overhead on the car, the 350 mile round trip from, say, Boston to a central Vermont ski area would cost $3 apiece. The best places to find rides and riders is through friends, and school or office bulletin boards.

If a car is out of the question and you are still bent on that weekend of skiing, consider the bus. Most of the larger cities have organized ski charter trips, that also include lift tickets, lessons, rentals, and sometimes lodging (many are day trips). Prices for a weekend range between $35 and $70. Check the Yellow Pages of the phone book under "Ski Tours."

The regularly scheduled bus lines from major cities usually have special coaches leaving Friday evening, arriving late that night, to popular ski areas in Vermont, New Hampshire, Massachusetts, New York, Maine, and New Jersey. The price varies from $10 to $26 round trip; what you lose in mobility at the area you make up for in the friends made and fun had on the trip.

The cheapest way of getting to ski country is, of course, hitchhiking. While standing on a highway with skis, boots, poles, rucksack, and a cold thumb may make you doubt your convictions and dedication to the sport, it will get you there—eventually. Hitchhiking is not recommended, simply because of the uncertainty and hardship as compared to the money saved.

If you are under 22 years old an airline Youth Fare Card will let you fly practically anywhere in the U.S. for 60 percent or two-thirds of the regular rate, depending on whether you are going standby or reserved seat. Getting from the airport to the ski area is the next problem. Some car rental companies have special rates for ski vacations, but many will not rent to anyone under 21. Avis and National do, however.

LIFT TICKETS & LESSONS:
The one indispensable and increasingly costly item that young people have little control over is lift tickets. Although there are still many smaller ski areas where you can buy an all-day lift ticket for $5 or less, most people like to go to the larger areas "where the action is." If you insist on skiing these larger resorts on weekends and holidays, you had better resign yourself to a $7 to $11 lift ticket and long waits in lines.

Fanatics, who ski more than 30 days a season, will probably come out ahead by purchasing a season ticket before Thanksgiving. Prices generally range between $100 and $300.

One national organization that is bringing down the cost of skiing for college and graduate school students, is the Student Ski Ass'n. With the purchase of a $3.50 *Student Ski Card*, a collegian can save at least $1 on every weekend or holiday all-day lift ticket and a whopping *50 per cent* on most weekday lift tickets, ski lessons, and equipment rentals. The card is honored at prominent ski areas throughout the U.S. and Canada and can be purchased by writing to Student Ski Ass'n, Rutland, Vermont 05701. Many lodges also give discounts to Student Ski Card holders.

Whether you are in college or not, weekday skiing, with its lack of crowds and often lower prices has much to recommend it. Five day "Ski Weeks," which include lift tickets, lessons, food and lodging, are generally good buys, and can do wonderful things for your skiing.

Don't overlook night skiing.

Many ski areas close to population centers offer evening (and sometimes twilight) lift tickets at $1 to $5. Night skiing is a unique and very sociable experience, and fits itself easily into a busy schedule.

FOOD & LODGING:
A little initiative can save many dollars on food. It doesn't take a Ralph Nader to figure out that most ski area lunch counter food is expensive. So, before you leave the big city, pack up some high protein non-perishable victuals, such as dried fruits, cold cuts, bread, cheese, raisins, yogurt, and your favorite beverage. Chances are you'll have saved money before you even arrive at the ski area, by not having to stop at a restaurant or coffee shop along the way. Caution: Don't flash your lunch bag around the lodge and don't litter the trails with your refuse, if you decide to have a picnic.

There are still a few hardy souls, who can survive a bitter cold night in a sleeping bag huddled over the emergency brake of their VW or in a tent pitched in a snow-covered field. But the frostbite and lack of comfort and conveniences rarely make it worthwhile. Most major ski areas have at least one inexpensive ($5 per night) dormitory style lodge. Some dorms are even less expensive if you bring your own sleeping bag. Plan on two or three dollars a day extra if you want breakfast and dinner. A letter or phone call to the ski area lodging bureau or inquiring from a local ski shop clerk will usually net you a list of inexpensive lodges. Be sure to find out how far the lodge is from the ski area, unless you don't mind a half hour drive each way. The general rule is that the closer the lodge is to the area the more expensive it is.

(However, even the expensive nearby lodges often have dormitories with reasonable prices).

SKI BUMMING:
The cheapest way to ski is to ski bum. Jobs like being a chambermaid, waiter or waitress, dishwasher, or ticket stapler are plentiful at the beginning of the season. Many positions open up on weekends to accommodate the crowds. This menial work is rewarded with a bed, two meals, and a free lift pass. When ski races are being held, ask to pack the course or gate keep. You'll be given a lift ticket for every so many hours you work.

For the student who can afford to take off a semester, and who is a decent skier, there are jobs available as ski patrolmen or instructors. Such positions are in high demand though, and you should apply during the fall.

ABOUT THE AUTHORS
George "Kim" Chaffee is a member of the skiing Chaffee clan of Rutland, Vt., whose sister, Suzy, and brother, Rick, have been stalwarts on the U.S. Ski Team. Kim, an expert skier himself, is a Harvard graduate and holds a degree in mechanical engineering from the University of California at Berkeley. It was while pursuing a Ph. D. at Berkeley that he became interested in the practical problems of being a college skier. Subsequently he created and organized the Student Ski Ass'n, a nationwide program designed to promote the sport of skiing on college and graduate school campuses.

Dave Lyman, former ski instructor and ski retailer, is an accomplished skier, flyer, sailor and photo-journalist. He is editor and publisher of the Goose City Gazette, a newspaper serving southern Vermont, and the Cape Resorter, a newspaper serving summer visitors to Cape Cod.

HOW TO SKI IN EUROPE FOR FEWER FRANCS, LIRA OR MARKS THAN YOU THINK

A guide to the bargains abroad, prepared especially for young skiers by Harvard Student Agencies

Parachuting down on the Pyrenees or getting away from it all in the Polish Tatras is possible, but when most Americans think of skiing in Europe, they mean the Alps. The Alps are mountains in the true sense, soaring to 15,000-foot peaks, laced with giant glaciers, and blanketed by year-round snow. Glorious runs of 10 and 20 kilometers over wide, treeless bowls in spectacular settings are commonplace throughout the region. New England skiers especially, weaned on granite and ice, and from ski country where news of a two-inch snowfall triggers a human avalanche, are naturally delighted by the prospects of snow reports in meters, hip-deep powder, and uncrowded slopes.

A week skiing in Europe can cost less than a weekend in the States. In exclusive St. Moritz, Zermatt, and Megève, commercial hotel prices are lower than rates at Vail and Stowe. Without a clue to the European skiing scene, however, you might blindly book two weeks at a snowy cure-center for tubercular elders. Special student programs exist which can greatly reduce the cost of any Alpine ski week and which guarantee a groovy holiday. These we shall cover below. First, however, an outline of when and where to go and what equipment to take. (Rates and costs, of course, subject to change, as they say.)

WHEN TO GO The guaranteed season is December through March, and often lasts two months longer. At high-altitude centers, such as Chamonix and St. Moritz, skiing continues year-round. Lifts are efficient and modern, and waiting lines mercifully brief. The only real crowding is at Christmas and Easter.

The 10 days after Christmas and the week of Easter are to European skiers what Memorial Day is to American picnickers. Then, prices, lift lines, and après-ski life reach their zeniths. The rest of January finds many areas half-deserted, with reductions on everything. February is ideal: good weather, lots of students out skiing, and moderate prices. At centers having lifts to 3,000 meters you can ski year-round; lower altitude centers close near the end of April. If you're considering winter skiing in northern Norway, remember that the top of Scandinavia has a month of near-darkness in December-January.

WHERE TO GO Austria has the most skiing centers and is, hands-down, the cheapest. Low-keyed, *gemütlich* evenings of wine and Tyrolean music make for a simple and relaxed nightlife. Four hours a day of group lessons for a week cost $10, a private lesson $2 an hour, both with multilingual, licensed instructors. **Kitzbuhel,** with the fastest downhill in Europe, is a nice town in which to get snowed in. **Innsbruck** offers the diversions of a city plus Olympic trails at nearby Igls and Axams. And **St. Anton** on the Arlberg is another beloved international ski area.

France boasts the highest peak in Europe, 15,771-foot Mont Blanc. At the base of Mont Blanc is spectacular **Chamonix,** the best equipped ski valley in the world. The skiing is sensational and most appreciated by intermediate and expert skiers. The têlêpherique cable which goes to 12,800 feet has been cut three times in 10 years by passing jets but opens up many beautiful trails, one a day long, and leading into Italy, another through a glittering valley of blue glaciers, brilliant snow, and jagged peaks. Chamonix is sophisticated and if your French is good, it swings. The cuisine rivals Paris and is priced similarly. One hour away is cosmopolitan Geneva. Going farther south, there is **Val d'Isère,** a thoroughly French village where Jean-Claude Killy learned to snowplow. Val d'Isère is a picturesque, comfortable Alpine village with lots of young skiers and a friendly, all skiing atmosphere. Near **Grenoble,** site of the 1968 Winter Olympics, the full spectrum of skiing is available. **Alpe d'Huez** has glamorous après-ski life and good bobsledding. **Chamrousse** and **Les Deux Alps** are more student-oriented, most of the skiers come from the University of Grenoble, and prices are lower than in the Chamonix valley. Skiing is a big sport in France. There are beginners' slopes and steep trails tricky enough to test anyone's *sang froid.*

Italians ski like they drive — fast and with zest. Some centers actually station police at trail junctions to flag down flagrantly reckless skiers. (Rumor says battery-powered turn signals may soon be required in ski poles.) This zest carries over to the nightlife, which is chic yet friendly. Smart clothes and an undentable pocketbook are helpful. **Cortina d'Ampezzo** (1956 Olympics) and **Madonna di Campiglio** are two exciting, fashionable centers nestled deep in the Alps. **St. Ulrich-Ortisei** and **Canazei** have equally good skiing and a more moderately priced *dolce vita*. **Courmayer,** on the French border and at the Italian entrance to the wondrous 10-mile tunnel through Mont Blanc, opens up a whole valley of choice skiing.

Switzerland caters to the socially and financially eminent. Lucky for you, many of them don't ski at all. The atmosphere tends to be international, elegant, and subdued; the clientele older and well-heeled. Some of the most beautiful skiing in Europe is here. **St. Moritz, Davos,** and **Zermatt** (the Matterhorn!) are all tremendous places to go with your parents. **Grindelwald** and **Flims** are less celebrated but are still very good. Real budgeteers are advised to ski in another country.

An indispensable guide covering everything in capsule form from the cost of drinks in night clubs to the length of lifts and their altitudes for almost every slope in Europe is Egon Ronay's AA SKI EUROPE, a $3.50, 695-page paperback, the *guide bleu* of the serious skier. It's available through the Automobile Association, Fanum House, London W.C.2 or at any AA office in England.

BUYING EQUIPMENT
Americans not blessed with unusually large feet will really be tempted to buy new skis and boots abroad. European equipment is not necessarily any better than American, but it is certainly much cheaper. For example, competition Kneissel White Stars

have sold in Austria for $125 in recent years, compared with $200 in the U.S. And Koflach buckle boots were $40, not $85. If you are a student in Austria or know someone who is, subtract another 15 per cent. Similar remarks apply for other skis and boots and other countries. It's best to buy in the country of origin and well before the Christmas rush.

Even lower-priced are "seconds." Sometimes there'll just be a paint chip or a skewed decal, but always check for warping or sub-standard elasticity. If you expect to be seen with your skis more often in town than on the trails, then "seconds" are a very good buy. The condition of used skis, like used sports cars, depends on their previous owner. Killy "wears out" new skis in 10 days. A fussy type, on the other hand, may keep his skis unblemished season after season, then pass them on to you when they're about as springy as frozen fondue.

Metal skis rent for about $1.50 a day, but boots are not always rentable. Fortunately, Europe is the best place in the world to buy boots. The ultimate ploy in acquiring equipment is convincing a ski teacher to order for you at his 60 per cent discount. Girls

AUSTRIA

FRANCE

seem to have more luck at this than young men. However, some fatherly advice: in winter the instructor is king of the mountain, but try to imagine what he does the other eight months.

Despite the best of boots, bind-ings, and intentions, you might *schuss* yourself right into a Euro-pean hospital. Whereas European hospitals are in one sense a rel-ative bargain, you can still run up a pretty amazing bill in a month. If neither Blue Cross or your parents' policies cover you in Europe, pick up some cheap ski accident insurance. It's a good buy. With a leg in traction and your clothes taken away, you're pretty much in the power of the doctor, whose fluent Italian and year of college Spanish you match with frantic English and a C- in first-year German. In situations like this, the sub-vice-consul from the nearest American consulate can be of great assistance.

HOW TO GO CHEAPLY
Skiing in Europe, if you still want to go, can be done for an all-inclusive $7-$9 a day, either in a group or privately. European universities arrange dirt-cheap skiing packages during school holidays and right in the middle of the semester, too! You do not always have to be a student to get in on them.

France has a special attraction for young people because of a myriad of skiing discounts un-available in the United States. The French government, through the *Secretariat d'Etat à la Jeu-nesse et aux Sports* actually sub-sidizes skiing for 16- to 30-year olds! Readers should keep in mind that these accommodations are not first-class hotels. The cen-ters are comfortable, however, and have central heating and hot showers. Beds are usually five or more to a room, dormitory-style. The lack of luxury is more than made up for in atmosphere. The centers are nearly all coed. Friendships come easy. The at-mosphere is *sportif,* and the eve-nings are devoted to dancing, soirées, and high mountain tales. These subsidized ski centers are extremely popular. It's advisable to reserve early in October for Christmas. The month of January is naturally much less crowded and lodging is easier to find. When writing for information be sure to enclose sufficient in-ternational reply coupons for an airmail reply.

UCPA, 62 rue de la Glacière, Paris XIII. Only one adjective will suffice to describe UCPA.

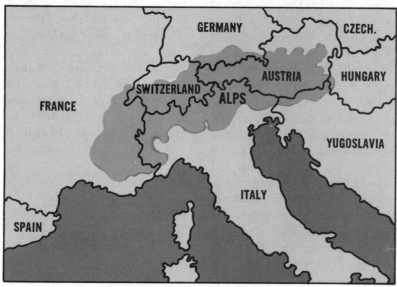

Fantastic! For example, a full week of skiing at Val d'Isère or Chamonix costs about $45. All lifts, metal skis, boots, insurance, excellent daily lessons, room and board included. Unbelievable? Summers, the UCPA offers sailing, skin-diving, canoeing, mountain climbing, and July-August skiing at similar bargain prices.

Havas Jeunes, 26 ave. de l'Opèra, Paris. For 18- to 25-year-olds, a two-week ski vacation at Chamonix, Zermatt, or in Poland, Yugoslavia, or Austria for $100-$120. This price includes round-trip train from Paris, insurance, room and board, discothèques and cinema après-ski.

OTU, 137 Blvd. St. Michel, Paris V. Ski vacations during school holidays to famed resorts in both Western and Eastern Europe. UCPA prices.

Club Mèditerranèe, 516 Fifth Avenue, New York 10036 and 8 rue de la Bourse, Paris 11, plus additional offices everywhere in France and in major European capitals. The Club is open to all ages, but attracts mainly people who think young. No dormitory living here; the Club rents entire hotels of excellent quality. Centers in St. Moritz, France, and Italy. Eight-day holidays for about $100 include very comfortable lodging, good food and wine, insurance, unlimited use of lifts, lessons, use of club library, and free tickets to evening concerts. Inexpensive transportation available from Paris. Head skis rent for an extra $7 a week. The Club is never dull.

Club Vagabond, Box 57, 1854 Leysin, Switzerland. A very international group of ski bums keeps the Club's two large chalets jumping. Bargain rates, prime ski country.

For all their economy and security, a group remains a group. Many will want the freedom and flexibility of going privately. A car offers the greatest mobility, allows you to get to out-of-the-way places, leave when the conditions are bad, and find cheap hotels on the outskirts of town. Snow, however welcome it may be on the slopes, can be a real bother to the driver. Roads that served handsomely as two-laned in the summer look much narrower in the winter with two meters of frozen slush piled on each side and a swaying "semi" dead ahead. Newish snow tires are an absolute minimum requirement even for a car full of good pushers. Preferable are spike tires (legal in Europe in winter) supplemented with chains. Many passes will be closed to traffic in the winter, sometimes for as long as November to April (e.g., the *Grossglocknerstrasse*), sometimes for a few days after a heavy snowfall. Even in spring, when the swans are out in Zurich, nearby passes can be closed because of avalanche danger. Motor clubs have specific and up-to-date information; so do local gas station attendants. Ask beforehand and plan flexibly. Hitchhiking with skis is just about as crazy as it sounds, though it has been done successfully. Remember, though, your driver may not have read these tips about snow tires and blocked passes! Trains are the worry-free solution, as they are re-routed to meet any situation. Beware of arriving at Christmas and Easter without some sort of reservation. The cheap places are the first to go, and with a suitcase, skis and boots, you won't want to do much searching around.

A word about the cost of lift tickets, which come in a bewildering array of prices. Few areas have day tickets, good for all lifts. Instead, each lift has its own price (with reductions for prepaid ticket books) and must be paid for separately each time you go up, a real bother when your hand are cold and your ticket's zipped up somewhere. Left-over tickets end up as expensive souvenirs. The point system, often in use simultaneously, provides you with, say, 100 points for $4 where all gondolas cost 25 points, chair lifts 10, and T-bars 5. Again, there are no refunds. One- or two-week all-purpose tickets are sometimes available. They can cut daily lift costs down to $3 and even less. (Incidentally, be certain to bring some small photos of yourself along for identification on lift passes.)

A peculiarity of European skiing is the invariable one long expensive cable car ride from the village to the mountain top. From here a wealth of trails begins, ending at chair lifts halfway down the mountain. If you pack a lunch and just buy something to drink at a mountain lodge, there is no need to come down until dark and no need to pay for the cable car again.

A European normally takes his meals at his hotel. There are generally *menus,* with beverages in addition to the *prix fixe* meal. The desperate have breakfast in

a local coffee shop, pack a picnic lunch, then eat dinner in a restaurant. The youth hostels that happen to be open in winter and not booked up months ahead offer their usual cheap beds and dull meals of gruel and potatoes. The hostel curfew can be skirted by the older or sugary.

If you're with friends, a final possibility is renting a chalet somewhere on the mountainside. This is the most fun of all and not necessarily expensive or inconvenient. Bring lots of warming liquids.

Hals — und Beinbruch! Bon Ski!

HANDS
OFF MY SNURFER

*But if it suits your taste, you can put your feet on it — that's
all this new winter activity requires*

by Bill Thomas

Snurfing is what it's called — and it's the latest fad to hit the snowbelt. In simplest terms, it's the art of sliding down a snowy hill on a single board — called a snurfboard or snurfer — which makes it a close cousin to skiing, skateboarding and surfing. The challenge of this new sport appeals to a multitude of people, but particularly to those from five to 30 — the young who are constantly seeking something different.

The word snurfer was coined from "snow" and "surfer." In appearance, the snurfer resembles a water ski more than anything else, but it also has other features which make it something of a hybrid. It is four feet long and seven inches wide and is made of laminated wood. The user rides it standing free without benefit of foot bindings. A hand tether at the front end and a shaped keel at the stern are keys to direction control and balance. To turn, you need only to lift the snurfer with the tether and apply foot pressure at the stern.

Snurfing was born less than five years ago, but despite a paucity of promotion it has grown steadily in popularity and already has achieved a national standing. Last winter, at Muskegon, Michigan, more than 150 young people took part in the third annual national snurfing championships.

National competition, however, is only a small part of the total picture. Approximately 500,000 snurfboards have been sold across the country to date and sales are still booming. "We never dreamed that snurfing would become so popular," says Sherman Poppen, the Muskegon businessman who created the first snurfboard.

One reason for its quick acceptance is probably its simplicity. "It's easy to learn to use," Poppen says. "I had one of my little girls on a snurfer when she was only six years old. Any kid who can use roller skates can ride a snurfer."

But one doesn't master the art of snurfing without taking a few falls. It's the kind of sport, Poppen admits, that takes something away from one's ego at the very outset. But once you've learned to negotiate your first hillside — standing up all the way down — the sense of accomplishment makes up for the time spent sprawling.

A few days after the second annual national snurfing championships, I joined some of the pros and the inventor to try out what they enthusiastically claimed to be the "greatest of all winter sports."

The area was ideally suited to snurfing. Sand dunes, built up through the ages by winds from Lake Michigan, still held a two- to four-inch snow cover. A great many trees dotted the landscape — too many, I decided, for a novice.

Poppen took me through the paces, teaching me all the basics of good snurfing. When you stand on the snurfer, you must face 30 to 45 degrees away from the direction in which the bow is pointed. One foot should be approximately in the middle of the snurfer, the other on the extreme rear. You hold the tether in one hand and by the time you get in place, you find you've already on your way somewhere — either downhill standing up or flying through the air prior to sprawling headlong into the snow.

You maneuver the snurfer by leaning from one side to the other, and since it doesn't come equipped with brakes, you stop it merely by pointing it back up-grade and reducing its momentum.

Sounds simple, doesn't it? And it is. To my surprise, I managed the snurfer with only a few tumbles.

Although no ski resorts are offering snurfing on the slopes yet, it could conceivably gain enough popularity, as skibobs have, to obtain limited acceptance at areas.

The snurfboard was invented more by accident than design. It all started on Christmas Day, 1965, at the Poppen home on the shores of Muskegon Bay. A 10-inch cover of snow had fallen and Poppen was looking for a way to entertain his young daughters in backyard play. He's always been handy in the workshop, so he came up with the idea of lashing a pair of 36-inch wooden skis side by side. The little Poppen girls learned they could stand on the improvised platform and coast, slide and skid down their backyard slopes.

Neighborhood youngsters soon joined them; Poppen, an accomplished skier himself, tried it, too. He found it great fun.

Back he went to the workshop, experimenting with other designs. Finally he began trying a number of patterns based on water skis, for greater width and more stability in the snow. After a dozen efforts, he came up with the snurfer.

That spring Poppen took his board to Brunswick Corporation in Muskegon. They were delighted with the idea and agreed to manufacture and market the product. The models, available in most sporting goods stores throughout the country today, sell from $5 to $10 each.

Snurfing didn't start off like a fad, but now it's going great guns — something that may be around to delight us as long as there is snow to slide on.

UNDERSTANDING THE USSA

An explanation of the functions of the chief organization for amateur skiing in this country

A lean attorney of 37 leaves his cluttered desk to address a small California ski club in behalf of the proposed Mineral King ski area. A thousand miles to the east the president of a large corporation phones an associate to thank him for his recent contribution to the ski team. At a small New England ski area a young New York school teacher watches the seven youngsters he has been coaching throughout the winter go through their warm-up routine. Across the Atlantic in a small French ski resort a group of young American men and women put a final check on their slalom skis in preparation for an important international competition.

In spite of the geographic distance that separates these events, all of the people involved were working toward a common goal — a stronger, better U. S. Ski Ass'n. And, at the very same time literally thousands of other volunteers were hard at work all over the country in behalf of the association. Why? Because, regardless of their vocations, their first love is skiing. What's more, each is bound by the keen interest in seeing to it that the U.S. Ski Ass'n properly represents its

117,000 recreational skiers, ski racers and winter sports lovers who are members.

But it wasn't always that way. In 1904, a decade after ski jumping—then the only form of skiing indulged in with any regularity—had become dormant, officials from several ski clubs gathered to create a national organization. Their goal was to see to it that future contests would be conducted as "National Ski Tournaments." With this event came the founding of the National Ski Ass'n. The original association had 17 charter members, all from the Midwest.

The first world-wide ruling body for the sport of skiing, Federation Internationale de Ski (FIS), was formed in 1910. Through this group's direction, competition on an international scale in downhill, slalom, jumping and cross country became a reality.

Chamonix, France was selected to host the first Winter Olympic Games in 1924. The ski events, held under the guidance of the International Olympic Committee (IOC), have since become a regular part of the Winter Olympics.

During the 1920's skiers were

few in number but made up the deficit with sheer enthusiasm. There were between 3,500 and 4,000 skiers and about 75 ski clubs. All were concentrated mostly in the northern Midwest, upper New England and north sections of New York State and northern California.

The awarding of the 1932 Winter Olympic Games to Lake Placid, New York, set the stage for the first big-time showing of skiing in the United States. The Olympics exposed many, many people to ski exhibitions for the first time. As a result, the excitement and thrill caught their fancy and they returned home determined to try this unique and wonderful sport.

The growth of the association was steady going into 1932. There were clubs in just about every state that had skiing and during that year there were many interclub and regional championship tournaments, attracting no small interest locally.

In the mid-1930s skiing was gaining in both national and international popularity. One ski exhibition at Chicago's Soldier Field drew 57,000 people. The 1936 Games at Garmisch-Partenkirchen in the German Alps were attended by some 155,000 spectators.

Throughout these years the ski association supervised the expanding horde of skiers, influenced the creation of ski areas where none had ever been thought of, and began to develop top-rate ski teams for international competitions.

In 1950 the association name was changed to the United States Ski Ass'n to better identify the organization to international ski bodies. In a few short years the association has become a respected and listened-to member of the FIS and the U.S. Olympic Committee.

The USSA is composed of eight regional divisions. All are self-supporting and administer their own competitive programs. National headquarters for the association are in Denver.

USSA proudly works closely with the National Ski Patrol System, the Professional Ski Instructors of America, the National Ski Areas Ass'n, U. S. Ski Writers Ass'n, Ski Industries America,

the U.S. Forest Service and the National Parks Service.

Some time ago the objectives of the U.S. Ski Ass'n were put down. They are worth reviewing because they represent the goals each and every officer and director of the association works toward.

1. To create, develop, promote and maintain the sport of skiing in the United States and to encourage formation of local ski clubs and divisional associations of ski clubs in all parts of the nation.

2. To standardize rules governing ski competitions, races and other ski events.

3. To cooperate with affiliated divisional associations in arranging most effectively and economically for visits of skiers from the clubs of one division to tournaments of another division.

4. To establish and maintain uniform standards of amateurism among skiers and to preserve skiing on the plane of pure amateurism in conformity with the highest ideals of gentlemanly sport.

5. To create and maintain a board of arbitration to consider and decide disputes between divisional associations affiliated with the Association or other cases referred to it by divisional associations.

6. To establish and maintain cooperative relationships with other national and international skiing or other winter sports organizations; to promote international exchanges of skiers for the good of the sport in the United States; and to foster good-fellowship

among skiers in this and other countries.

The association involves itself in a myriad of tasks and efforts. Far West members of USSA, for example, have put countless hours into the current Mineral King ski area battle. Their voice, which represents the majority of the skiers, is being heard and will influence the outcome.

The association has the responsibility of raising funds that support and field our U.S. Ski Team. These funds not only come from large corporations and ski manufacturers, but also come from the association members. USSA also supports and maintains the National Ski Hall of Fame in Ishpeming, Michigan.

The USSA has an impressive storehouse of talent. This talent is used to teach young kids about racing. It's used to put together low cost accident and ski theft insurance policies for the members. And it's used to create better ski areas and safer skiing.

What does the future hold for the ski association? As the sport of skiing grows and expands, the role of the association becomes even more important and clear. As a true and interested representative of organized skiing, the association will not only continue to field the best ski teams it knows how, but will also concentrate its efforts toward ski legislation, increased membership, new benefits to members, and a total dedication to keep skiing the unique and personal sport that it is today.

One thing for sure. As long as you see someone taking time to address a ski club about a current problem, to coach young kids, to help raise funds, and to see to it that a top notch ski team proudly represents the U.S. on foreign snow, there will be a strong and significant USSA.

Reach the Top

Austria's triple Olympic gold medal winner
shows how to make parallel turns and wedeln — his way

by Toni Sailer

The parallel swing begins after the first quarter of the stem christie or the stem swing. At this point, you are able to initiate all your higher-speed turns with some sort of a stemming movement during the first quarter. If you now substitute something to make that stem disappear completely, you will be able to perform a full turn with your skis in the parallel position from beginning to end. Such a turn is called the *parallel christie*.

Start from the normal traverse position. As you approach the point at which you will start your turn, sink down sharply into your knees, momentarily setting your edges, advancing the downhill shoulder and planting the pole. Now, with a definite up-motion, take advantage of the brief period of unweighting to shift your weight to the outside ski. There is no stemming movement at this point in the parallel christie. Instead, the pronounced unweighting lightens the ski tails enough to permit you to flatten the edges, advance the inside ski, shift the weight and start the tails sliding outward for the characteristic heel-slipping action of all christies. As the heel slip starts, begin to apply the

PARALLEL CHRISTIE. The parallel christie starts from the parallel running position (1). With a down motion, the pole is planted and the skis are checked with a brief edge set (2). Come up on the pole and flatten the edges, forcing heels out to begin the christie movement (3). Weight is shifted to outside ski and, as heels slip, this brings you around in the new direction (4). As turn ends, drop down again and edge (5). The amount of edge set determines whether you stop or continue on in another traverse (6).

edges again. The turn finishes with a down motion as you approach the new traverse in the same manner you finished your stem christies and parallel swings.

It is important to develop your timing in parallel turns. Everything should occur in proper sequence as if the turn was one flowing movement. As you re-apply the weight in the middle of the turn, be sure your hips coordinate to swing the body around through the turn and to exert sufficient force to steer the ski tips into the arc of the turn. The inside shoulder and ski remain advanced from the time the weight shift is started. Again, you should practice parallel christies in both directions and then put them together into a series of linked turns, just as you did with the parallel swing. Work first at moving from one turn into a traverse and then the next turn. Then move from one turn directly into the next without the traverse, gradually making the turns shallower and closer to the fall line. Such a series of tight parallel turns is called *short-swinging*.

There are several good exercises that will help you to develop your parallel turns. Try traversing diagonally across the slope, periodically letting your heels slip downhill and setting your edges in a checking movement, then immediately unweighting and resuming the traverse. Another good exercise is to run a series of parallel swings or short swings close to the fall line on a rather gentle slope. On each turn, lift the tails of both skis off the snow and move them around, across the fall line, in a smooth motion harmonized with your hip movements. The tips, of course, remain on the snow. This *tip dance* variation is especially effective in deep snow and is very elegant. It will prepare you for the next and final maneuver—*wedeln*.

Wedeln (literally "wagging the tail") is the absolute, final product of skiing. There is no other maneuver left. It epitomizes all you have learned and permits you to ski anywhere in any conditions. It is best described

TIP DANCE. This wedeln exercise is made with skis together. Plant each pole successively, unweight sharply and lift tails off snow, swinging them to one side. Then repeat to other side.

WEDELN. The wedeln maneuver is a series of short, quick, rhythmical parallel swings in which the tails of the skis swing from one side of the fall line, across it, to the other. There is *no traverse between swings. As one swing ends, the next swing begins, as shown in the photos above. Pole action, weight shift, precision of edging and timing* *must be perfected before you ca[n] execute wedeln successfully. Bu[t] the reward is high—with wedel[n] you can ski terrain of practicall[y] any degree of difficulty.*

Short-swings are a series of high-speed parallel turns made close to fall line.

Each turn is a short swing. The skis move in a series of rounded arcs from one turn to next, snakelike.

I check to start a turn, come up into the turn, and immediately check to start the next.

I'm up again and coming around, then down into still another short-swing turn.
Note that there has been no traversing between my turns: this is the essence of short-swing.

Wedeln is a series of short, incomplete parallel turns performed in the fall line at fairly good speed.

The skis swing from one side of the line to the other. Each swing ends with a brief edge set.

Weight shift, pole plant and edge set, which starts next swing, occur almost simultaneously, in rhythm.

Upper body remains facing squarely downhill throughout the entire maneuver. It is the skis and the lower body, in wedeln, which swing back and forth across the fall line and bring you down the slope.

as an extremely short parallel swing with little shoulder work and plenty of hip motion. Your line of movement goes straight down the fall line. Your upper body faces straight down the hill while your hips and legs produce the turns. Unweighting, proper edge and pole movement, and precision timing are its essential ingredients. Practice it first on gentle slopes until your rhythm and timing are perfected.

Start in the fall line, skis together and pointed straight down the hill. Try never to leave the fall line throughout the series. As you begin each turn, use an up-motion to unweight your skis. Touch the inside pole lightly in the snow for an instant, being careful to keep your shoulders square across the fall line, facing down the slope, as your hips, legs and skis accomplish the turning. Actually, wedeln is not a "carved" turn. Instead, the tails of your skis brush from side to side across the snow surface to cause the change of direction. At the end of each swing, drop down briefly for a quick setting of the edges to arrest the swing and start the next movement to the opposite side. Your knees, of course, must always be together and flexing as you rise up and sink down in each turn. Most of the weight is on one ski or the other during wedeln, never completely on both skis together. A ⅔ : ⅓ ratio is about right.

In addition to being the most graceful and advanced skiing maneuver, wedeln has practical uses. As you have already seen, it is a most efficient means of skiing down or close to the fall line. Its brief edge set at the end of each swing provides a means of controlling speed—without changing direction. This makes it valuable for skiing down very steep or narrow trails or through moguls or interrupted terrain. It is also the easiest and safest way to negotiate deep, wet or soft snow.

When you have mastered wedeln, you will find it the most satisfying maneuver in your skiing repertoire. It means you have reached the top.

The Best Way to Flunk Out of Ski School is in Two Days

by Peter S. Prescott

Prologue: The rump end of March. Where snow no longer covers my lawn, I can see that snow mold has discolored my grass. This is what snow is: It covers something or it kills something. Today, however, there is a smell of warmth at the core of the wind, and reasonable men who have wintered on beaches at Acapulco and Grenada think of restringing their tennis rackets. Not I. In answer to my question, a ski salesman tells me I must indeed attach my foot to my ski boot before I attach my ski boot to my ski.

It is news to me. My assignment is to go to a fashionable ski camp that promises to teach me how to ski in five days. I imagine easy days of cautious movement across flat or gently rolling lawns of snow. I will anchor one ski firmly in the crust and, like a mountain climber, gracefully slide the other up to, and even beyond it. Next season, perhaps, I will climb on a chair lift and come sailing down a hill.

So, on a Sunday afternoon, I squeeze into my car my demonstration skis, my rented boots and poles, my baggy borrowed ski clothes, a flyweight typewriter and a bottle of unblended Scotch. I drive north, and reach the inn by dark. In my room, I notice a sign that says no lunch is served at the inn. To maintain a lifetime habit of eating at the middle of the day, I am actually going to have to go out to the mountain, which looms more ominous than ever, its sides shaved in streaks like an Iroquois Indian's skull.

The first day: Snow falls as I get up, and continues intermittently all day. Cheers, a reprieve. No sane man would ski as snow falls — but in fact we do. There are five girls and another man in my beginners' class. Heinie, our Austrian instructor, appears in a red jacket and bronze face. "You have your boots on wrong," he tells me, "but your skis on right. Ha! Dot is something." Ha, indeed: As it happens, I am the only one in my class who has never skied before. The other man has skied for years but wants to learn the new techniques. The girls are all married to expert skiers who swoop over the suicidal paths in the morning and then, after Rhine wine and fondue, coach their wives in the afternoon. We move off, shuffling toward our practice snow. I fall three times getting there, but the girls in my group ski politely around me.

The snow slams down. Our primary practice slope has a terrifying downward cant to it. My sunglasses, bought in Barbados, fog up as I push down from the slope, and that, of course, is why I wipe out so quickly. "Bend your knees!" Heinie shouts as I push off. Too late: I have fallen again, very fast and on my back, only my skis erect. The rest of my patrol skis gracefully down, slowly snowplowing to standing stops. "Don't try so hard," Heinie says to me.

Later, Heinie gives me a private lesson. "Don' worry about them," he says. "They have all been on skis before." The proper skiing position, it seems, is that of a woman in labor: knees and ankles bent as far as possible and spread out, pelvis thrust forward with the back straight, and arms limp. Pausing for breath, I watch a couple scramble for a seat on the lift and fall off in a tangle of skis. A baby too young to stand zips past me. "How *old* are you?" I ask him later. "I'se twee-an-a-half," he replies.

Notes written later the first

day: The fear of it: This is what the instructors refuse to acknowledge, but the older expert skiers do. It is terrifying simply to stand on a slope this first day, and look down, knowing you have to go, knowing you can't control your speed or direction of descent. "Confidence is all," an expert skier told me. "You go through periods when you lose it. Like me and ice." That day, he had hit ice, fell, and slid a hundred yards on his back. "The teachers," he said, "they never recognize how scared you are when you ski."

After one day, I am an expert at putting on and taking off my skis, but skiing itself seems to be controlled skidding, and my problem is I cannot skid slowly. I finish by practicing with a nice girl from my class. She does graceful turns as I work on the snowplow. "I don't know why I do this every year," she says. "I don't like skiing. I don't like cold. I come from Los Angeles." Her husband, however, spent the day flashing down the expert trails with the pros. "I don't know why you married me," she says to him over drinks. "I keep thinking you'll meet another girl on top of one of these mountains."

"Another girl!" her husband says, "I can't even afford you!"

The second day: The fog is so low I can't see the top of my car, but soon there is a massive assault from spring. The temperature rises, and everywhere there is running mud and slush, snow sliding from roofs, haze, and blankets of yellow Cézanne sun. Skiing today is a sweaty business, and yet I am not as sore as I would have thought. It may be true that booze in quantity pacifies the aching muscles.

Class begins with a girl telling me how, on the first day, she had gone up the lift and down the hill three times. I remember her from yesterday, sliding past me and wishing me good luck, with a clip, clip, and modest turn to the right as I lay cooling my elbows and hipbones in the snow. Heinie slushes up to announce that we will all follow him in neat curves downhill. Unfortunately, I have not learned *how* to make a turn; in fact, I have forgotten the snowplow I mastered yesterday and fall twice. Heinie politely pretends not to notice. Then he announces we will go up the lift, and describes the disasters awaiting those who get on or off the lift too casually. I wait and nod, and then resign. Heinie nearly sighs with relief. After a lesson and a quarter, I have become a ski-school dropout.

Heinie and I meet again at noon for another private lesson. To my horror, Heinie insists we go up the lift. "Look, Petah," he says as he drifts backward before me, "does my body move when I turn? I hold it still and lean this way . . . and . . . that way . . . and I turn. But you!" If words fail him, gestures do not; Heinie imitates me flailing around the turn. "You try too hard," Heinie says. "All the time you are thinking! Don't think! Relax. You should have two brandies before you ski!" I go down the hill, really quite fast, and it's fun. I don't fall, but I hear Heinie shouting behind me: "Turn, Petah! Turn!" Turn, hell. This is fun.

Last testament and final reflections of a retired skier: This is not a simple thing to do that only I cannot do; it is a damn difficult thing to do, and everyone around me can do it. What's more, my emotions are involved; I feel fear and rage, pain and frustration.

If I don't make *this* run properly, there is something wrong with me. "For heaven's sake," a girl in my class told me, "skiing isn't *everything*!" But it is! It is! My wife and kids are hundreds of miles away — to heck with them — I am flunking a test of manhood.

At lunchtime, I lie back on a terrace and let the sun sink into my skin. There, firmly anchored to cement, I watch the matchstick figures twisting down the courses. "Look at that," says the man on my right, pointing to two grinning instructors carrying an unconscious boy. "Think positive," he says, "you won't get good enough soon enough to be hurt that bad."

His wife guessed that I had borrowed my baggy ski pants, "but," she said, "stretch pants cost $60 or $70. I didn't think they were worth it. I mean, if you fell and broke a leg, the instructor had to cut them away, and there goes $70. But now instructors are trained to cut the slacks away only at the *seams*."

Sitting there, drowsy in the sun, I thought of my tourist round trip up the gondola to the top of the mountain where the world stretches out to where the haze begins and skiers pause, for a moment, just looking at the wonder of it all. There is a sign there that says I am in a national park and assume the risks of being there. Yes.

"Then off, off forth on swing," Gerard Manley Hopkins wrote, "as a skate's heel sweeps smooth on a bow-bend." I could see the skiers glide away, but then I remembered Heinie's last sight of me, as I pushed in a door that opened outward. And then I thought of Falstaff's words: "Can honor set to a leg? No. Or an arm? No." And I went home.

Prominent 1968 Olympic ski racers: Nancy Greene, Canada, Jean-Claude Killy, France, Bill Kidd, U.S.

Alpine Skiing

MEN

Downhill
1948—HENRI OREILLER, France
1952—ZENO COLO, Italy
1956—TONI SAILER, Austria
1960—JEAN VUARNET, France
1964—EGON ZIMMERMANN, Austria
1968—JEAN-CLAUDE KILLY, France

Slalom
1948—EDI REINALTER, Switzerland
1952—OTHMAR SCHNEIDER, Austria
1956—TONI SAILER, Austria
1960—ERNST HINTERSEER, Austria
1964—PEPI STIEGLER, Austria
1968—JEAN-CLAUDE KILLY, France

Giant Slalom
1948—HENRI OREILLER, France
    (Alpine Combined)
1952—STEIN ERIKSEN, Norway
1956—TONI SAILER, Austria
1960—ROGER STAUB, Switzerland
1964—FRANCOIS BONLIEU, France
1968—JEAN-CLAUDE KILLY, France

WOMEN

Downhill
1948—HEDI SCHLUNEGGER, Switzerland
1952—TRUDE JOCHUM-BEISER, Austria
1956—MADELEINE BERTHOD, Switzerland
1960—HEIDI BEIBL, Germany
1964—CHRISTL HAAS, Austria
1968—OLGA PALL, Austria

Slalom
1948—GRETCHEN FRASER, U.S.
1952—MRS. ANDREA MEADE LAWRENCE, U.S.
1956—RENNE COLLIARD, Switzerland
1960—ANNE HEGGTVEIT, Canada
1964—CHRISTINE GOITSCHEL, France
1968—MARIELLE GOITSCHEL, France

Giant Slalom
1948—TRUDE JOCHUM-BEISER, Austria
    (Alpine Combined)
1952—MRS. ANDREA MEADE LAWRENCE, U.S.
1956—OSSI REICHERT, Germany
1960—YVONNE RUEGG, Switzerland
1964—MARIELLE GOITSCHEL, France
1968—NANCY GREENE, Canada

Nordic Skiing

MEN

Cross-Country—18 Kilometers
1924—THORLEIF HAUG, Norway
1928—JOHAN GROTTUMSBRAATEN, Norway
1932—SVEN UTTERSTROM, Sweden
1936—ERIK-AUGUST LARSSON, Sweden
1948—MARTIN LUNDSTROEM, Sweden
1952—HALLGEIR BRENDEN, Norway

Cross-Country—15 Kilometers
1956—HALLGEIR BRENDEN, Norway
1960—HAAKON BRUSVEEN, Norway
1964—EERO MAENTYRANTA, Finland
1968—HARALD GROENNINGEN, Norway

Cross-Country—30 Kilometers
1956—VEIKKO HAKULINEN, Finland
1960—SIXTEN JERNBERG, Sweden
1964—EERO MAENTYRANTA, Finland
1968—FRANCO NONES, Italy

Cross-Country—50 Kilometers
1924—THORLEIF HAUG, Norway
1928—PER E. HEDLUND, Sweden
1932—VELI SAARINEN, Finland
1936—ELIS VIKLUND, Sweden
1948—NILS KARLSSON, Sweden
1952—VEIKKO HAKULINEN, Finland
1956—SIXTEN JERNBERG, Sweden
1960—KALEVI HAMALAINEN, Finland
1964—SIXTEN JERNBERG, Sweden
1968—OLE ELLEFSAETER, Norway

MEN

4-x-10 Relay Races
1936—Finland
1948—Sweden
1952—Finland
1956—USSR
1960—Finland
1964—Sweden
1968—Norway

MEN

Biathlon
1960—KLAS LESTANDER, Sweden
1964—VLADIMIR MELANIN, USSR
1968—MAGNAR SOLBERG, Norway

MEN

15-Kilometer Race—70-Meter Jump
1924—THORLEIF HAUG, Norway
1928—JOHAN GROTTUMSBRAATEN, Norway
1932—JOHAN GROTTUMSBRAATEN, Norway
1936—ODDBJORN HAGEN, Norway
1948—HEIKKI HASSU, Finland
1952—SIMON SLATTVIK, Norway
1956—SVERRE STENERSEN, Norway
1960—GEORG THOMA, Germany
1964—TORMOD KNUTSEN, Norway
1968—FRANZ KELLER, W. Germany

WOMEN

Cross-Country—5 Kilometers
1964—CLAUDIA BOYARSKIKH, USSR
1968—TOINI GUSTAFSSON, Sweden

Cross-Country—10 Kilometers
1952—L. WIDEMAN, Finland
1956—LYUBOV KOZYREVA, USSR
1960—MARYA GUSAKOVA, USSR
1964—CLAUDIA BOYARSKIKH, USSR
1968—TOINI GUSTAFSSON, Sweden

3-x-5 Relay Races
1956—Finland
1960—Sweden

Gold Medal Winners

1964—USSR
1968—Norway

MEN
Ski Jump
1924—JACOB T. THAMS, Norway
1928—ALFRED ANDERSEN, Norway
1932—BIRGER RUUD, Norway
1936—BIRGER RUUD, Norway
1948—PETTER HUGSTED, Norway
1952—ARNFINN BERGMANN, Norway
1956—ANTTI HYVARINEN, Finland
1960—HELMUT RECKNAGEL, Germany
Ski Jump—70 Meter
1964—VEIKKO KANKKONEN, Finland
1968—JIRI RASKA, Czechoslovakia
Ski Jump—90 Meter
1964—TORALF ENGAN, Norway
1968—ULAD BELOUSSOV, USSR

Figure Skating
MEN
1924—GILLIS GRAFSTROM, Sweden
1928—GILLIS GRAFSTROM, Sweden
1932—KARL SCHAEFER, Austria
1936—KARL SCHAEFER, Austria
1948—RICHARD BUTTON, United States
1952—RICHARD BUTTON, United States
1956—HAYES JENKINS, United States
1960—DAVID JENKINS, United States
1964—MANFRED SCHNELLDORFER,
      West Germany
1968—WOLFGANG SCHWARTZ, Austria

WOMEN
1924—MRS. OTTO VON SZABO-PLANK,
      Austria
1928—SONJA HENIE, Norway
1932—SONJA HENIE, Norway
1936—SONJA HENIE, Norway
1948—BARBARA ANN SCOTT, Canada
1952—JEANETTE ALTWEGG, Great Britain
1956—TENLEY ALBRIGHT, United States
1960—CAROL HEISS, United States
1964—SJOUKJE DIJKSTRA, The Netherlands
1968—PEGGY FLEMING, U.S.A.

PAIRS
1924—HELEN ENGLEMANN, A. BURGER,
      Austria
1928—ANDREE JOLY, PIERRE BRUNET,
      France
1932—ANDREE & PIERRE BRUNET, France
1936—MAXIE HERBER, ERNST BAIER,
      Germany
1948—MICHELINE LANNOY, PIERRE
      BAUGNIET, Belgium
1952—RIA & PAUL FALK, Germany
1956—ELISABETH SCHWARZ, KURT OPPELT,
      Austria
1960—BARBARA WAGNER, ROBERT PAUL,
      Canada

1964—LJUDMILLA BELOUSOVA, OLEG
      PROTOPOPOV, USSR
1968—BELOUSOVA/PROTOPOPOV, USSR

Speed Skating
MEN
500 Meters
1924—CHARLES JEWTRAW, U.S.
1928—CLAS THUNBERG, Finland
      BERNT EVENSEN, Norway (tie)
1932—JOHN A. SHEA, U.S.
1936—IVAR BALLANGRUD, Norway
1948—FINN HELGESEN, Norway
1952—KEN HENRY, U.S.
1956—EUGENY GRISHIN, USSR
1960—EUGENY GRISHIN, USSR
1964—TERRY McDERMOTT, U.S.
1968—ERHARD KELLER, W. Germany
1,500 Meters
1924—CLAS THUNBERG, Finland
1928—CLAS THUNBERG, Finland
1932—JOHN A. SHEA, U.S.
1936—CHARLES MATHIESEN, Norway
1948—SVERRE FARSTAD, Norway
1952—HJALMAR ANDERSEN, Norway
1956—EUGENY GRISHIN, USSR
      YURI MIKHAILOV, USSR (tie)
1960—EUGENY GRISHIN, USSR
      ROALD AAS, Norway (tie)
1964—ANTS ANTSON, USSR
1968—KEES VERKERR, Netherlands

MEN
5,000 Meters
1924—CLAS THUNBERG, Finland
1928—IVAR BALLANGRUD, Norway
1932—IRVING JAFFEE, U.S.
1936—IVAR BALLANGRUD, Norway
1948—REIDAR LIAKLEV, Norway
1952—HJALMAR ANDERSON, Norway
1956—BORIS SHILKOV, USSR
1960—VIKTOR KOSICHKIN, USSR
1964—KNUT JOHANESSEN, Norway
1968—FRED ANTON MAIER, Norway
10,000 Meters
1924—JULIEN SKUTNABB, Finland
1928—IRVING JAFFEE, U.S.
1932—IRVING JAFFEE, U.S.
1936—IVAR BALLANGRUD, Norway
1948—AKE SEYFFARTH, Sweden
1952—HJALMAR ANDERSEN, Norway
1956—SIGGE ERICSSON, Sweden
1960—KNUT JOHANESSEN, Norway
1964—JOHNNY NILSSON, Sweden
1968—JOHNNY HOEGLIN, Sweden

WOMEN
500 Meters
1960—HELGA HAASE, Germany
1964—LIDIYA SKOBLEKOVA, USSR
1968—LUDMILA TITOVA, USSR

1,000 Meters
1960—KLARA GUSEVA, USSR
1964—LIDIYA SKOBLEKOVA, USSR
1968—CAROLINA GEIJSSEN, Netherlands
1,500 Meters
1960—LIDIYA SKOBLEKOVA, USSR
1964—LIDIYA SKOBLEKOVA, USSR
1968—KAIJA MUSTONEN, Finland
3,000 Meters
1960—LIDIYA SKOBLEKOVA, USSR
1964—LIDIYA SKOBLEKOVA, USSR
1968—JOHANNA SCHUT, Netherlands

Bobsled
TWO-MAN
1932—United States
1936—United States
1948—Switzerland
1952—Germany
1956—Italy
1960—No competitions held
1964—Great Britain
1968—Italy

FOUR-MAN
1924—Switzerland
1928—United States (5 men)
1932—United States
1936—Switzerland
1948—United States
1952—Germany
1956—Switzerland
1960—No competitions held
1964—Canada
1968—Italy

Luge
ONE-SEATER RACE
MEN
1964—Thomas Koehler, East Germany
1968—Manfred Schmid, Austria
WOMEN
1964—Ortrun Enderlein, East Germany
1968—Erica Lechner, Italy
TWO-SEATER RACE
MEN
1964—Austria
1968—E. Germany

Ice Hockey
1924—Canada
1928—Canada
1932—Canada
1936—Great Britain
1948—Canada
1952—Canada
1956—USSR
1960—United States
1964—USSR
1968—USSR

WHAT THE SKI PATROL IS ALL ABOUT

"HELP WANTED — Man or woman over 18 for seasonal outside work. Must take 40 hours classroom training plus yearly 8-hour refresher for week-end work. Job training required at no pay. Must be in good physical condition, able to do heavy manual labor and be a capable skier. No company-paid fringe benefits or salary but workers receive a complimentary ski lift pass. Must work long hours during coldest months of year. Must buy their own uniforms and equipment and provide personal transportation. Remuneration includes respect, smiles and occasional thank-you letters. Interested parties should inquire at their local ski areas."

by Harry G. Pollard *National Director, National Ski Patrol System*

If the National Ski Patrol System (NSPS) ever had to advertise in the help-wanted section of the paper, their ad might read something like that. Luckily, for everyone who skis, there are many dedicated people who enjoy giving their time and talent. Last year, 20,000 ski patrolmen proudly wore the rust-colored parkas with the distinctive gold cross that identify them as members of NSPS.

These men come from all walks of life with one common bond. They enjoy skiing, they want to help their fellow man, and they are willing to work hard. About 90 per cent of them are volunteers who consider ski patrol work a stimulating avocation.

How do you become a member of this prestigious fraternity? There is a multitude of physical and mechanical requirements that a patrolman must meet. Foremost, a candidate must have a real desire to serve his fellow skier.

When C. Minot "Minnie" Dole, Roger Langley, Roland Palmedo and others organized the NSPS more than three decades ago, the rules were not only framed around skill and astuteness, but also attitude and desire. A patrolman's wish to be of service must go beyond even the splinting of a fracture or being front man on a toboggan.

Back in 1938 when it all started, there was only a handful of ski patrolmen. But then there were only a few alpine skiers, too. Ten years after the organization got its start, 3,700 patrolmen registered nationally. By 1965 there were 8,900 and the 1970 count of 20,000 marks an all-time high.

One patrolman put in words why he belongs to the NSPS:

"Unlike many service or community activities," the Midwesterner said, "patroling enables one to see immediate results; a look of thanks, a relief from pain, an expression of real appreciation. It is tangible."

Before a patrol candidate may proceed with any formal training and testing, he must first have both standard and advanced American Red Cross (ARC) first aid training. Armed with a current ARC card, he then contacts the NSPS leader at the ski area where he generally skis. He will then be assigned to a regular patrolman and begin the training sessions.

Each candidate is instructed in toboggan handling and other important rescue techniques. The training period which varies from area to area also is designed to prepare the individual for the actual test administered to all candidates before they can wear the rust parka. The test is national in scope in that certain minimum requirements and standards are established. It includes six phases covering basic proficiencies such as toboggan handling, on-the-hill first aid, general ski ability, packed snow skiing, unpacked snow skiing and endurance.

The tester, who is a ski patrolman himself and has gone through the same program, looks for strong and stable skiers rather than a candidate who skis as "beautifully" as a ski instructor. A patrolman must be strong to wield a 70- or 80-pound sled down a 45-degree slope or haul it across a long flat.

"Many skiers look at patroling as a glamorous pastime. But there's a lot of sweat, too," said one old-timer who has patroled several ski areas west of Denver for 15 years.

Once a candidate passes the test — and about 60 per cent

do — he will be "on trial" for a year with the local area patrol where members keep a close tab on attitude, ability and performance.

In the fall of each year, every patrolman must take an ARC eight-hour refresher course before he can be re-registered with the national NSPS office in Denver. Additionally, the patrolman must take an on-the-hill refresher at the area where he patrols.

Patrolmen at work are of little value to a ski area unless they are at the top of the hill or skiing the mountain looking for people in trouble. Consequently areas provide them with complimentary lift passes and the privilege of loading on the lifts as soon as they reach the bottom. In that way they are always in circulation and ready to go. Some ski areas provide discount prices on food and lodging for their patrolmen.

"But," said a five-year veteran, "it's a helluva tough day's work for a so-called free ticket and fringe benefits."

And there are those who do join the NSPS for the free lift ticket. But after the first year the "free-loader" usually has had enough and doesn't come back.

The most tangible benefit of belonging to the NSPS is the deep satisfaction of helping someone. The physical part of becoming a patrolman is not that difficult. It is the desire and attitude that make a National Ski Patrolman different.

So, whether the "Help Wanted" section of the newspaper will ever have to be used or not, a skier can be assured that the man in the rust parka and the blue first aid belt is on the slope to help him. He hopes you'll never need him, but if you do, you can count on him to do a good job.

ABOUT THE AUTHOR
Harry G. Pollard, Jr., 62, is the fifth national director in the 30-year history of the System. Other national directors include Charles Minot "Minnie" Dole of Greenwich, Conn.; Edward F. Taylor of Denver; William R. Judd of Lafayette, Ind., and Charles W. Schobinger of Denver.

Pollard served as Eastern divisional chairman from 1963 until his election as national director. He was appointed National Ski Patrolman #66 in February, 1939 and has been section chief and regional chairman in the System. During his time as division chairman, he visited more than 150 areas in his division which had 345 ski patrols and 6,000 ski patrolmen.

The question of money is paramount when the skier thinks of equipment. Good equipment costs money and bad equipment costs pleasure.

Possibly the simplest solution at first is to rent one's skis, poles, and boots at a rental shop near home or at the ski area. This is one way out for the new skier. He may decide against the sport after a try, in which case his investment is minimal. But there are pitfalls. The rental shop may be good or it may be bad. Many of them are bad.

The skier's best bet is to rent from a shop near home. This shop knows that the skier is a local person and consequently might serve his needs better than a shop at a ski area. (To be sure, there are plenty of good rental shops at ski areas.) The second advantage in renting from a store nearby is that the skier can go in during the week, get fitted, get the binding setting checked (most important!), and get financial dealings over with — all before he reaches the ski area. This saves him up to 25 per cent of his skiing time, for he is not going to be standing in line all weekend.

The critical feature of rental equipment is the release binding. Most rental places, unfortunately, use cheap release bindings, which is like buying cheap insurance: it doesn't protect you where you need it most.

Second, the rental boot, which is item number two in a skier's equipment priority list, is usually fairly soft and doesn't fit well. This isn't dangerous, merely uncomfortable.

One way out of the dilemma is to rent a pair of short skis, preferably the two-and-a-half-footer. The short skis don't really need a safety binding, and the stiffness and fit of the boot are not nearly so important on short skis. The skier is introduced to the sport without having to manipulate six- and seven-foot boards on his feet. (Note: the four-foot ski should have a release binding, although this is not critical, and the five-footer definitely should have release bindings.)

For about the same money as it might cost to rent a two-and-a-half-footer for a couple of weekends, the skier can buy a pair with simple bindings ($15 to $25). He doesn't need to rent poles at all, and so he saves there as well.

It must be noted in all fairness that there are not likely to be more than a small minority of skiers at any area wearing two-and-a-half-footers. If a skier is worried about appearances, it may be that he would rather struggle with the full-length ski — and he might learn faster just through sheer will-to-win. The middle way is to rent a pair of five-footers or buy a pair ($25 and up for wood, around $100 for metal).

Let us assume now that the skier has decided to go skiing at least ten weekends, over a period of two years, often enough to justify an investment in equipment. Figuring that minimum expense for a ski weekend will come to fifteen dollars a day, exclusive of equipment, and, given ten ski weekends, investment in

COMMON SENSE GUIDE TO BUYING EQUIPMENT

*What to look for in skis, boots, poles and bindings. Renting vs. Buying.
How to get the most security from your bindings. How to
dress. Mittens vs. Gloves. Glasses and Goggles. Undergarments, too.*

by Morten Lund

the sport will be $300 for those ten weekends. More likely it will be nearer $500. In light of these considerations, the expense of equipment assumes its proper proportion. It is almost like the old saying about a yacht: if you have to ask what the yacht costs, you can't afford it. If the skier has to worry excessively about investing in equipment, he might not be able to afford to ski regularly. (He can afford to sample it, via a weekend or two on rental equipment, however.)

BUYING BINDINGS The first item to consider is the least glamorous, the bindings. More than 85 per cent of the bindings today are release bindings. The reason is that a well-designed release binding will get the skier out of trouble almost 100 per cent of the time if they are set properly.

Trouble can come when the ski, for some reason, such as a fall, twists or bends the ankle. Even if the skier escapes with nothing more than a scare, the feeling that one's ankle has been twisted hard is a psychological detriment. With a release binding working properly, the binding will let go of the boot before the skier feels too much of a twist.

On a given day, two skiers out of a thousand will have some injury that requires medical attention. This figure could be cut in half, or better, if release bindings were all properly designed and maintained. Two out of a thousand is not a high figure, but over ten weekends it adds up to two per hundred, or 2 per cent of skiers skiing weekends. My motive in mentioning these figures is only to assure you that release bindings are necessary and that, of the people who get hurt, almost 100 per cent asked for it. Either they were skiing

out of control or they had bad release bindings, or, as is usually the case, both.

When you buy bindings, ignore all setups that don't have a release at both the toe and the heel. Both are needed. The heel release is usually designed to let go in a forward fall, and the toe in a sidewise fall, although with some bindings both releases are designed to let go in all kinds of falls.

The "unit" bindings, costing $25 and up, come with toe and heel together, as a unit. They usually require boot plates, or metal plates on the boot heel and toe. They should be shop-mounted, even if you are a good shop-man yourself.

Other kinds of bindings are sold as separate heel and toe releases.

On these, the new type of heel binding, which does away with the long spring cable that has been a standard feature of bindings for years, is preferable. The long cable has to be threaded through cable leads along the sides of the ski, and the cables sometimes stick in these leads and will not release.

The new heel releases are of two types: first, the "step-in" type, more expensive, and the "short-cable" type, which are less expensive.

Bindings ordinarily should be mounted by a ski shop, unless you know what you are doing. But the shop itself should have a good reputation with the binding-maker. There are shops that mount some bindings properly, others improperly. The safest way is to write to the binding manufacturer, once you have picked the binding, and ask them to recommend a shop in your area. It is worth a trip to get bindings mounted the way they should be. Otherwise you may be taking

a lot of the "release" potential out of the binding.

CHECKING YOUR BINDING There are a few very practical things you can check to make sure the binding behaves up to its potential.

(1) Make sure that the top of the toe piece doesn't "squeeze" the tip of the boot sole. Your boot should be held in the binding by the forward pressure exerted by the heel binding, not by excessive downward pressure at the toe piece. Too much downward pressure on the boot at the toe may cause a binding to stick. If the boot is being squeezed, you will find an adjustment — if the binding is of a reputable make — enabling you to raise the toe piece. The toe piece should "touch" the top of the boot toe but not squeeze it down.

(2) Once the boots are fitted to the binding in the shop, keep the left boot in the left binding and the right boot in the right binding. Don't switch skis from foot to foot unless you readjust the bindings. Boots might be slightly different in length. (Mark one ski in some way to distinguish it.)

(3) Make sure that, if you have your boot notched to fit the binding, that the notches are of equal depth. Unequal notch depths will cause the boot to release more easily in one direction than the other, and you can never get the binding at its best setting.

(4) Make sure that the boot is centered in the binding when you ski. If the boot is in off-center, it will release hard to one side.

(5) Don't let the nailheads or screwheads protrude from the ski or from the soles of the boots. They will block the release mechanism.

(6) If you are using a cable,

keep it at a low tension, so that it doesn't "mash" the boot against the toe piece in front. Too much pressure against the front toe piece will raise the release threshold of the binding. (With too little pressure, of course, the boot won't stay in.)

(7) If you have a long cable, the rear side hitches or leads should not be more than two-thirds of the way back along the boot. If they are farther back than that, they may "kink" the cable and foil release.

(8) Use a leather strap or thong to help support the boot and just to keep the ski from running off if it releases (this is a very good thing to have — you may lose the ski otherwise); attach it to the cable back of the rear side hitches, not in front, otherwise your may foul up the cable release.

(9) You can lubricate the working parts of your release bindings with graphite to make sure they don't stick.

(10) Check the settings of the release bindings frequently.

A little more detail on this last point: There is a way to check the toe release, roughly. That is to buckle a boot onto one ski and then try to push the empty boot out with the thumbs of both hands. This test should determine whether you have sufficient pressure to keep you in if you are an intermediate skier. If you are a hard skier and need more pressure to hold you in, you can set your toe piece.

There is a much more scientific way of doing this. Buy a $15 gadget called Release Check, made by a designer named Gordon Lipe. The gadget will give you a reading on your toe release that will be much more accurate and will check the release on both sides. Release Check will teach you a lot about

safety and safety bindings.

As for checking the heel release, the proper way is to put one ski on and then simply try to pull your heel up out of the release by main force, pulling forward. You should be able to pull your heel out without resorting to a forward lunge.

No release binding will safely cover all ranges of skill and weight with one setting. For instance, if you are an expert skier, you would probably want to tighten the toe and heel release more than indicated in the test above. You might want your toe binding set so that your thumbs can't cause the boot to swing it out. In that case, you will be eliminating some of the release potential at the low end of the scale. You could not get out of the binding in a "slow-twist" fall, in which the ski slowly twisted around while you fell. On the other hand, the ski would stay on if you wanted to make some twenty-foot jumps and come down hard. You have to make a choice.

I have dwelt on bindings at length, because of their importance and because badly designed bindings and badly set bindings hold skiing back. Not many beginners come back to the sport after an injury. Gordon Lipe has tested various brands of release bindings and has found that most best-selling brands are pretty good releases and that there are dozens of cheap off-brand release bindings that are no good at all.

BUYING BOOTS In terms of pure comfort, however, the boot is the prime factor in skiing. Also, it is the most important factor in edge control and in governing the direction of the ski. The skier's foot performs hundreds of little reflex actions every run to keep the ski running in the direction the skier wants to point

BUCKLE UP FOR GOOD SKIING

An improperly buckled ski boot will make it difficult for you to transmit "orders" to skis through your boots.

For maximum efficiency and comfort, follow these simple buckling-up steps: Before you leave the lodge, put your boot on from a standing position and flex your knee forward to drive your heel into the heel cup. With your knees still flexed, buckle the bottom two closures snugly. Straighten your knee now and fasten the third buckle — the one which crosses your instep. With this moderately tight, flex the knee again to finally seat your heel. Now straighten up and buckle the top one or two buckles comfortably. At this point the bottom two buckles may feel loose. If so, take them up a notch or two until they feel secure again.

It's perfectly all right to loosen buckle boots when taking short breaks or while riding the lifts, but it is advisable to loosen only the instep buckle and the uppermost one. If you open all of the buckles, it will be necessary to repeat the entire fastening process before you descend.

For lift-riding or short breaks, loosen the ankle and instep buckles of your boots. Undo more and you'll have to reseat your heel before skiing.

it. If this seems strange, take a pair of cheap rubber ski boots (such as are made in Japan and sell for about six dollars) and try them. You will find that the ski won't go where you point it. The reason is that the boot doesn't adequately transmit the reflex actions of the foot to the ski. On the other hand, the skier with the rubber boot can edge a ski fairly well.

The deductions from this experiment are that the most important function of the boot is steering, not edging, and that the boot should fit very closely over the whole lower foot, particularly at the ball. Thirdly, stiffness of the ankle of the boot, while helpful in edging, is not so important as the close fit at the low part of the foot where the "steering" is done.

Fit is important to comfort, too. If your boot hurts, you won't want to ski. Your feet are very delicately constructed, but they carry great pressures. Overload one area of the foot and the pain becomes excruciating. If bad fit ends in a blister or "bone bruise," your skiing is over for a while.

There is hardly a boot worth wearing that costs less than thirty dollars, and you probably ought to spend forty dollars at a minimum. The boots form the connection between the skis and the body and they should take most of the strain of the job off the feet. The boot has to be rugged, and rugged material is expensive. So is good workmanship.

Some boots lace and other boots buckle. Buckle boots are the modern alternative. They have the great advantage that you can buckle them down in cold weather and unbuckle them on the lift to let the blood circulate and warm the feet. This enables you to keep your boots good and tight in cold weather, which is hard to do with lace boots.

Also, the buckle boot can be tightened up in seconds when the boot warms and stretches from the heat of the foot, as happens with any leather. This means you don't have to take time out to relace. In an ordinary lace boot, relacing can take ten to fifteen minutes, several times a day.

On the other hand, the buckle boot costs more, and it has to be chosen very carefully. The buckle boot fits tight: a poorly fitting buckle boot will cause blisters and sore spots very easily. The advent of "poured" boots this season may well eliminate this problem by making it possible to custom-fit every skier with boots.

When buying boots, particularly buckle boots, take your time. Visit at least three stores and try on various brands. Each brand is made over a different last, and, where one boot may not be "right" for your foot, another may be. Some lasts have a high instep, others a low instep. The instep is particularly critical, because you want to be able to put pressure on the top of the instep, back of the ball of the foot to make sure that the boot is tight at that point; otherwise the "steering" is lost. But if you put pressure on top of the instep and the boot does not fit under the instep, you will have an uncomfortable boot.

The second critical point is at the heel. The boot should be tight enough so that the heel cannot readily be raised off the sole of the boot, even if someone holds the boot heel and you try to pull the heel of your foot upward. However, this is not quite so critical as the first point. If you have a boot that is very snug and tight over the top of the instep and around the ball of the foot, you can accept a little "give" at the heel.

If you have a typical "American foot," narrow-heeled and wide across the ball, or a long, narrow foot, you may be better off getting a made-to-order boot. But sending your boot measurements to a boot-maker (they are nearly all in Europe) is no guarantee of a fit. These made-to-orders frequently come back badly fitting. The only sure ways are either to have it done while you are in Europe so that the fit can be checked or to send a plaster cast of your feet. Any good orthopedic foot doctor and some orthopedic stores will make you a cast.

When you are trying on boots, wear one thin sock and one thick sock on each foot. This is the best combination for the slopes, and you should wear it when being fitted.

The skier must bend forward at the ankle when he skis, to down-unweight and to execute other moves. There is no sense, then, in getting a boot that is too high at the ankle. It will cut into the shin bone when the skier bends forward at the ankles. This is particularly true of stem skiers. Their ankles are bent forward a good deal of the time. In fact, most stem skiers are better off with the top buckle or the top lacings of most types of boot undone.

Unless you are a hard skier, do not buy a hard boot. Buy a medium-stiff boot. Only those skiers who ski a great deal of the time can afford the luxury of breaking in a very stiff boot. It takes time, and you have to do it gradually, shifting to older and more comfortable boots to give your feet a rest.

The skier who doesn't have time for this and who is stuck with a very stiff boot can soak his socks in water, put the boots on over the wet socks, and walk around until the socks are dry. This "shapes" the boot; the same thing takes place, but more slowly, when the boot is being broken in gradually. In effect, the skier has bought a too-stiff boot and has to take some of the life out of it to use it at all. It is better to get a not-so-stiff boot to begin with. As mentioned, however, the boot manufacturers are currently working to perfect several varieties of the "poured-to-fit" plastic boot. Though expensive, these boots will eventually solve many of the problems traditionally associated with ski boots.

BUYING SKIS There are really two main choices when it comes to skis. First, length: short or long? Second, material: wood, metal, or fiberglass?

We have debated the question of length sufficiently. The question of material is a matter of cost. A set of wood skis will perform fairly well, provided you are willing to pay something above $25 for them. But they have a tendency to warp over the summer, which means that your skiing will get lopsided: you turn more easily in one direction than in the other. And they lose their "life" or resilience very soon.

Metal skis, which begin somewhere around $100 (for the cheap ones), will not warp, won't wear out nearly so soon, and can be resurfaced, top and bottom, for less than it costs to buy new. Also, metal skis can be designed to turn more readily than the wood. Beginner's metal skis are designed just that way. Head and Hart are the two major American metal-ski manufacturers. Head is renowned for its great speed in repairing and replacing its skis if either is needed. Hart sells its skis somewhat less expensively. Each brand has its partisans.

Buying a metal ski from a foreign manufacturer involves the usual risk that the manufacturer won't back up the ski with service if the skier needs repair or replacement. Also, the resale price of the ski will depreciate much faster. There is a good used-ski market for Head and Hart skis here if you want to "trade up."

The more expensive domestic skis go to about $175-$200. The beginner's models, although they turn well and easily, do not track so well as the more expensive "expert" models. On the other hand, the expert models are harder to turn. You can't have it both ways. A beginning skier is much better off with the beginner's models.

The last material choice is among the fiberglass skis. These are made of everything from 100 per cent fiberglass to a 10 per cent fiberglass covering on wood skis. Good fiberglass skis are being made, and the best are very smooth-skiing products, easy over the bumps and steady in tracking.

Some of the expensive wood skis are still used for slalom racing by expert skiers, who like the "spring" of the wood ski. But the ski loses this spring, and its best skiing qualities with it, after a year or two of use.

BUYING POLES It may be comforting, after all this, to know that the best buy in ski equipment is the poles. Excellent aluminum poles can be had for $12 to $15. There are lovely light aluminum-alloy poles at $25 to $35, but it takes an expert skier to appreciate them.

The main question regarding poles is height. I favor a long pole for the recreational skier. Stand the pole on the floor. The handle should come up hard against the underside of the arm, next to the body, when the skier stands normally. The slalom racer may like a shorter pole for ma-

HOW TO KEEP A WELL-OILED CABLE BINDING

A forward release cable binding must be lubricated periodically at several key points. A silicon spray or grease, which will outlast ordinary household oil, is recommended and usually easier to apply.

First, lubricate the front throw where the cable is secured and adjusted. The pivot point on the throw as well as the adjusting threads on the cable harness should be treated.

Most toepieces have three critical points: the adjustment screw, the swivel unit which makes contact with the boot, and the base on which the top swivels during a release.

Heel release units should be lubricated at all points of movement.

If bindings have been exposed to road grit and grime or salt, a light oiling will flush impediments. It's especially important to tend to your maintenance rules and regulations when travel and exposure are factors.

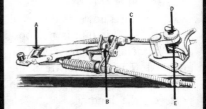

The important lubrication points on a conventional cable release binding are as follows: A, front throw pivot point; B, tension release adjusting screw; C, cable adjusting threads; D, toe-piece height adjuster and E, toe-piece swivel shaft.

HOW TO NOTCH BOOT TO BINDING

The toe pieces of many bindings require, or at least work more satisfactorily with, notching on the toes of the boots. The two small notches in the boot fit the two small "posts" on the binding *(drawing)* and basically serve two purposes:

1) prevent premature or unnecessary release of the binding by giving a secure fit, and

2) permit an identical positioning of the boot in the ski each time the skis are put on.

To properly notch boots, the skier should first mark the position of the notches by actually getting into the bindings with the boots on. The boots should be positioned exactly where you want them — unless you tend to be slightly "duck-footed" or "pigeon-toed," they should be centered exactly on the ski. Then mark the spot for the notches and file the notches into the boot with a file or grinding wheel.

If your boots are already notched, check to see that the "V" is nice and clean. If wear and tear has made the "V" ragged, the toe of the boot should be filed down smooth and renotched, or, if that is not possible, a metal toeplate should be attached. These plates are made with indentations that will fit the posts on the binding.

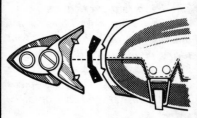

neuverability, but the recreational skier uses the pole for support while standing and while unweighting. If the pole is too short, he'll have to lean over too far to use it. The skier also uses the pole to push himself along the flat and to climb. Here again, length, up to a certain point, is good.

The other pole consideration is the hand strap. The strap should be adjustable—and broad enough so that it won't cut into the hand when the skier leans on it.

The proper position for the hand inside the strap is one in which the skier grasps both strap and pole and lets the strap take the strain, rather than holding the pole handle in a death grip. The skier should be able to use the pole with the fingers unclasped if he is utilizing the strap to take the strain in the proper manner.

WARMTH AND SKIING

The sport of skiing is built up partly of a series of interdependent judgments on equipment and clothes. If the skier starts out with good, functional clothes, the rest of the sport becomes easier. If the skier has warm underclothes, for instance, he won't have to wear markedly heavy sweaters and parkas. He will be freer to move. Also, if the underclothes keep the central part of the body warm, the hands will be warm and the skier will move the poles better. And he will have warmer feet, which means they'll be more sensitive to the proper edge needed for the skis.

The eastern skier particularly needs warm undergarments. Temperatures in the east can go below zero. If there is a wind, it is impossible to ski comfortably in below-zero weather without quilted underwear. This is rather

bulky, soft, pliable stuff, and it doesn't hinder the skier's movements. It is built along the same principles as the quilted parka. A full suit of this underwear costs about ten to twenty-five dollars and can save a weekend. Quilted underwear makes it possible to ride a chair-lift at 15 degrees below zero in a 25-mile-an-hour wind and still be comfortable.

The next-warmest kind is net underwear, and after that, double-ply long underwear. Both are useful in temperatures from zero to 25 above, but below zero, they are no substitute for the quilted. The ski instructor, who is at the area all week long, has time to become acclimated to the cold and probably does not need anything but net underwear. The recreational skier *does* need it, unless he sleeps outdoors on his porch all week to get acclimated.

STRETCH PANTS Stretch pants do make the wearer more attractive (in most cases), and because they are close to the skier's skin, they help him to get the feel of the correct positions more easily. Stretch pants run from $25 to $65. The most crucial point about stretch pants is whether the stirrup, which goes under the foot, is broad enough to hold the pants down without cutting the skier's instep. It should be at least two inches wide at the narrowest point and should be made of stretch material like the pants themselves.

The alternative to stretch pants is knickers. They are less expensive and more comfortable. If you are riding a long distance to the slope in ski clothes, they are *much* more comfortable. And they are as acceptable as stretch pants. Levis are acceptable, as well, particularly for those under 25. The levis are open at the bottom, however, and you should expect your socks to get wet if the temperature is above freezing.

With proper underwear, the skier needs only a parka and a sweater. If you have a mountain parka, which is quite bulky and filled with eider down, you won't need more than a medium-weight sweater. Mountain parkas have been coming on the market lately in response to a sensible demand for warmer clothes. Fashion people are so imbued with the idea of "the thin look" that there has been a minor revolt on the part of some skiers. The thin look is great when the sun's out and the temperature stands at twenty-five or so, but below that, it is forbiddingly cool to ski in a "thin look" outfit.

The mountain-type parka filled with eider down makes sense in another way. The parka is cut to allow plenty of movement, and the skier can wear a light sweater under it. This makes for ease of adjustment; if the parka gets too warm, it can be zipped down. On the other hand, if the skier is cold and has nothing to put on, he is in bad situation.

The cost of the mountain parka is somewhere around fifty dollars.

The standard padded, insulated, or quilted parka is about half as warm and costs around half as much. On cold days it has to be supplemented by a good thick ski sweater underneath. The thinner, more fashionable "thin-look" parka is also quilted or insulated, but it is not really warm enough, as I have said, for the run of eastern skiing, although it might fare better under the milder Western conditions or in Europe. The east, by and large, has the coldest recreational alpine conditions in the world.

All parkas ought to have a hood for riding the chair lift. No amount of warm clothing replaces the wind-breaking action of the hood on a parka.

Standard wear under the sweater is a turtleneck T-shirt, and standard headgear is a knitted hat or headband.

MITTENS AND GLOVES
The remaining item of importance is mittens or gloves.

Some wear mittens and some wear gloves. Gloves enable you to handle the poles better, and to work on the bindings without taking the gloves off. But to wear gloves below twenty above, you either have to be well acclimated or wear very warm clothing to keep the circulation going to the hands. The average skier should have a good pair of leather mitten covers and wool liners for the cold. It is no good to ski with cold hands. It distracts you from concentrating on skiing.

Of the leather mittens available, there are two types, insulated mittens and non-insulated mitten covers. The insulated make more sense. If you have adequately warm clothing, you can wear a well-insulated mitten without any liners or undermitten cover at temperatures below zero. The undermitten is made of knit wool. An undermitten plus the leather mitten cover makes the hand a bit cumbersome on the pole handle. It is also clumsy to take off and put on a mitten-cover-undermitten combination. But at zero and below, it is worth it.

There are lighter mitten covers for warm weather. For instance, there are mitten covers made of light poplin. But, even with an undermitten, these aren't much good under 20 degrees.

It is a good idea to have a pair of gloves around, even if you own mittens. When the temper-

KEEP YOUR EDGES SHARP

You'll be surprised how properly sharpened edges — really sharp — can make all the difference in the world in the way you perform on the slopes. This is especially true for skiers in New England and the Midwest where rocks, hardpack and ice round out the sharp edges needed to really turn well.

It's easy enough to keep edges sharp. At the start of each season, make it a practice to have the edges professionally sharpened at your ski shop. Then, for in-season maintenance, equip yourself with one of several models of portable edge-sharpeners available for about $5. Plan on sharpening the edges yourself (*drawing*) once every four times you ski.

Don't try to sharpen the edges with a common file as you won't be able to keep the file at an absolute right angle. Files especially designed for ski edges are not costly and they do the job well.

ature goes above freezing, most mittens get pretty warm. And rather than ski barehanded, it is advisable to have a pair of gloves on. If you fall, you won't skin your knuckle if you are wearing gloves — and some of the ice patches that lie on the slopes can give the knuckles quite a skinning.

GLASSES AND GOGGLES

Glasses and goggles are standard ski equipment for most skiers. The wind, flying flakes, too much sunlight, fog — all require some help for the eyes.

Goggles fog, even though they protect you from flying flakes better than glasses. Even the best goggles fog. (So do glasses, but they don't fog so easily.) There are a couple of good fog-preventive liquids on the market, and a lot of bad ones. Try to find one that works for you, whether you use glasses or goggles.

Except for extreme conditions, such as high (40 miles per hour) speed and high wind, high-quality dark sunglasses and yellow fog glasses are better than goggles. These "ordinary" glasses give you better peripheral vision, they fog less easily, and they are more easily wiped clean of fog or snow. Only racers really need goggles for windless days; in high wind, almost every skier needs them.

Dark glasses should be of high quality. Don't buy cheap sunglasses. Cheap plastic dark glasses don't screen out the ultraviolet, and you get headache and eyestrain. Buy a pair with "optical-grade" plastic lenses sold by opticians. These cost ten dollars or so, but they screen out the rays that should be screened out. Good-grade optical plastic lenses will not shatter, although they will scratch up easily. Better a few scratches than shattered glass near your eyes.

If you wear prescription glasses, you can have the prescription ground into an optical-grade plastic lens. Ordinary flat lenses are better than wrap-arounds, because the wrap-arounds distort peripheral vision and fog up more easily.

The best way to wear glasses is to secure them. Drill a very small hole through each earpiece, and then pass a fishline "leader" through both earpieces. Tie the leader so that you can barely squeeze the glasses over your head; then, even if you make a violent movement, the glasses will not wander very far out of place.

The worst snow condition, as far as vision is concerned, occurs when flakes of wet snow settle on the lenses. The best solution for this is to wear a "sun shield" over the regular glasses. The shield can be pushed up when too much snow gets on it, and you can then continue until the glasses underneath also become covered with snow. This combination gives you twice as long a run before you have to stop and wipe off the shield and glasses.

Yellow glasses are best for gray days and fog.

If you wear prescription glasses for distance vision, have the prescription made in optical grade plastic, plain glass, so that you can use them for dull-day skiing. They serve just as well on a dull day as yellow glasses.

Don't buy cheap sunglasses; don't ski with nonplastic prescription glasses (they will shatter); don't ski with glasses unless they are tied to a thread looped around your head (you'll lose them in a fall), and don't use goggles unless you ski so fast that you need them, because they are hard to wipe and because they cut down on your peripheral vision.

RESHAPE BOOTS TO FIT THE FOOT

Boots that basically fit well may still give skiers pain or discomfort at certain pressure points, due to the fact that no two feet are alike, to say nothing for being perfectly formed. Here are a few minor fitting problems that can be solved by having boots reshaped slightly at a good ski shop.

—tightness across the ball of the foot, causing pinching at the little toe or some pressure at the base of the big toe, or both.

—pressure of the stiff material under the lining of the boot against the bones on the inside of the foot.

—pressure of the cup-shaped rear portion of the boot against the ankle bone.

Good re-shaping equipment will change the contours in the boot's construction sufficiently to eliminate any of these pressure points. In effect, this process, coupled with a sound diagnosis of the fit problem, permits you to get a custom fit in a pair of boots mass-produced for Mr. Average.

Hopefully, the new form-fitting techniques will eliminate the aches and pains from wearing ski boots.

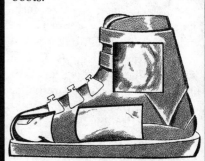

"Windows" on boot show where pressure points often develop.

When it comes to buying ski equipment, it pays to shop around—through the following pages of the *Buying Guide,* before you set foot in a ski shop. It's possible to lay out huge sums of money on equipment. Some prices have soared into the stratosphere, with skis—the most expensive item—going as high as $350, and with $200 a fairly common denomination. Good boots, bindings, and poles also carry high price tags.

But it's not really necessary to go for broke in buying ski equipment. One thing to avoid is over-buying. If you're a hotshot skier who heads for the top every weekend plus during a couple of weeks' vacation, then you would be wise to invest in the best engineered and manufactured equipment you can possibly afford—equipment made to give you the performance and long life that you demand.

But on the other hand, if you're a sort of permanent-intermediate who gets out on the slopes only a few times a year, it's foolish to buy equipment designed to do things you'd never ask of it.

From the *Buying Guide* you'll see how prices run for different types of equipment, and from the capsule descriptions of each item you'll get some idea of why one ski sells for $100 and another for twice that price. Bindings are the most technically complex of the ski equipment, and the most important. Skis are also masterpieces of engineering and craftsmanship, each model differing in some way from all others. Boots, too, have made giant technological steps forward.

Data in the *Buying Guide* were supplied by manufacturers and distributors. Prices are *suggested retail* only, and you may find variations when you go to buy.

We suggest that you read carefully through these pages and use the *Buying Guide* as just that—a guide, an additional help in finding your way through the complicated world of ski equipment. Then put your faith in a shop that carries a reputation you trust.

SKIER'S DIGEST OF NEW EQUIPMENT

A descriptive guide to the latest skis, boots, bindings and poles. Special section on ski touring gear.

SKIS
FIBERGLASS REINFORCED PLASTIC

ATTENHOFER

Fiberglass — multi-laminated fiberglass over wood core, sandwich construction; for expert skiers; also SL model...... **$180**
Glassflex—Fiberglass-metal over wood core sandwich construction
.... **$130**
Topglass—Fiberglass over wood core sandwich construction. **$100**
Glasstar—Fiberglass over synthetic core **$90**

AVANT

Glas Combi—Fiberglass ski with aluminum top protective edge, medium flex **$55**

Glas Master—Fiberglass with aluminum top protective edge, medium flex **$60**

BLIZZARD

Formal Total—Fiberglass with 2 vertical aluminum stabilizing bars for strength **$190**
Formal Racer—Giant slalom model is metal designed for great speed **$100**
Slalom model is fiberglass for quickness and lightness ... **$175**
Exclusiv—Core of prestressed and pressed fiberglass lamination and one-piece steel cracked edges
.... **$80-$120**
Formal Static—Fiberglass embedded in epoxy resin to make supporting upper and lower sheets **$150**
Super Epoxi—Fiberglass lamination sandwiched between rubber layers to dampen skiing chatter.
.... **$140**
Fascination—Upper and lower layer of metal and layer of fiberglass under top surface of metal, for beginner to intermediate ....
.... **$100**
Fiberglas Special—Core completely enclosed in fiberglass shell; quickest and most responsive in its class **$100**
Alu Glas—Inner core reinforced with epoxy fiberglass with upper layer of aluminum for strength .
.... **$90**

CONY

Glass All-Round—Fiberglass with aluminum top protective edge, medium flex **$60**
Glass Master—Similar to above, medium-firm flex **$90**
Glass Super Flex—Similar to above, cracked-edges **$145**
Olympic '72—Fiberglass and metal competition ski, medium firm flex, cracked edges ... **$175**

DARTMOUTH

Derby—Fiberglass top and bottom, multi-laminated core . **$40**
Royal—Fiberglass top and bottom, multi-laminated core . **$45**

Silverline—Epoxy fiberglass top and bottom sheet **$65**
Champion—Epoxy fiberglass top and bottom plates.... **$70 - $75**

DYNAMIC

Dynamic 70—Fiberglass torsion box construction, elastic aluminum sidewall; for competition or expert recreational use ... **$210**
VR-17—Glass-reinforced polyester torsion box over laminated wood core

Downhill	**$200**
SL & GS	**180**
Combi	**110**

ELAN

Competition fiberglass and aluminum over hardwood core . **$150**
Dynaglass—Fiberglass over lightweight, epoxy-bonded core. **$100**
Professional—Fiberglass top and bottom sheets over epoxy-bonded wood core **$50**
Impulse—Fiberglass laminate over hardwood core; competition ski **$175**
Snow Star—Fiberglass laminate over hardwood core; recreational ski **$160**

ERBACHER

Sonic V—Epoxy fiberglass layers over laminated wood core; a racing ski for experts

RS	**$225**
SL	**250**

Sonic II—Fiberglass and light metal alloy over laminated wood core; for advanced skiers and racers

A	**$235**
RS	**200**

Lancet—Fiberglass over laminated wood core; for experienced skiers

RS	**$175**
SL	**200**

Ultra S—Epoxy-fiberglass layers over laminated wood core; for expert skiers **$185**
Club RS—Plastic parts, and aluminum layers over laminated wood core; for expert skiers ....
.... **$150**

Delta RS—Plastic-metal compound in sandwich construction over wood core; for good recreational skiers **$135**
Epoxi 80—Epoxi fiberglass laminated over wood core; for beginners through advanced skiers
. . . . **$100**
Epoxi 50—Epoxy fiberglass laminated over wood core; for beginners **$70**

FISCHER

Imperator—Fiberglass and aluminum layers laminated over lightweight wood core **$250**
Fischer Superglass—Fiberglass layers over laminated wood core, aluminum edge protectors around top fiberglass layer **$180**
Fischer Glass GT—Two layers of fiberglass over laminated wood core **$145**
Fischer 707—Two layers of fiberglass over laminated wood core
. . . . **$120**
Silverglass—Sixteen bands of fiberglass run length of wood core, plastic top
      Senator **$95**
      Pioneer, for beginners
      to intermediate **$75**

FRITZMAIER

Giant Slalom—Fiberglass construction **$210**
Slalom—Fiberglass construction
. . . . **$210**

GERDAU

Fiberglass 990—Two layers of fiberglass epoxy and plastic bonded to laminated hardwood core with plastic spacer over bottom layer
. . . . **$110**
Fiberglass 440—Three layers of fiberglass epoxy and plastic bonded to laminated hardwood core **$80**

FRANKLIN

Hanover GL 11—Epoxy fiberglass construction **$45**

HART

Javelin XXL—Layers of glass and metal surround laminated wood core; for racers and aggressive parallel skiers **$210**
Javelin—Bonded layers of aluminum, steel, and fiberglass for experts and good intermediates . . .
. . . . **$185**
Cutlas—Bonded layers of glass and metal; for racers, advanced skiers, and better intermediates .
. . . . **$165**
Camaro—Layers of fiberglass and metal, featuring fairly soft tip and stiff tail, equally good on powder and ice; for intermediate skiers on up **$145**
Jubilee—Layers of fiberglass and metal; for competent novices to parallel skiers who ski only a few times a year **$130**
Spoiler—Layers of fiberglass and metal; for beginners, occasional or casual skiers **$115**

HEAD

Killy 800—Fiberglass and metal layers over laminated wood core; 3 models for Giant Slalom, Slalom, and Downhill; for adventure skier, intermediates and experts; 1 year guarantee **$200**
XR-1—Completely fiberglass ski processed in unique one-shot molding operation; prototype worn last year by some U.S. World Cup competitors; for racers; 1 year guarantee **$250**
HRP—Sheets of unidirectional fiberglass wrapped around a lightweight wood filler; for adventure skier intermediates, 1 year guarantee **$185**
660—Four thick sheets of fiberglass bonded to lightweight wood core; for adventure skier intermediates; 1 year guarantee **$175**
606—Three layers of fiberglass; wider and more flexible than the 660; for pleasure skier intermediates; 1 year guarantee . . **$165**

HOLZNER

Astral—Combi model, fiberglass-epoxy with wood core, plastic top sheet; 1 year guarantee **$80**
Solar—Fiberglass-epoxy with

Advanced Pointer

POLE LIKE THE PROS

The everyday uses of ski poles are well-known to most: climbing, walking, even leaning on. To many they are just one more thing to wave around on the way down the hill. But watch the racers or the pros sometime, those skiers to whom each unnecessary movement represents valuable time or speed lost, they wield their poles with all the precision and dexterity of a surgeon with a scalpel.

One of the most important uses for the pole is in the parallel turn which, after all, is really the basis of modern skiing. As the turn is begun, the pole is planted near the tip of the downhill ski at the same time that the knees are abruptly forced forward and into the hill. This causes the edges to "set" and the body to take on an angulated position such that it is arced toward the pole. Seemingly stopped for an instant, though actually with great forward momentum, the skier travels past the set pole. As he passes it, his body straightens and unweights from its "low" point at the time the pole was planted. The jolt of planting the pole and interrupting the rhythm is a great aid to unweighting. The shock has also stopped the downhill shoulder, thus helping the uphill side of the body to lead the turn.

To be able to flick your poles accurately and comfortably, they must be snug at the grip; a loose strap will not give positive control. They should be held from 12 to 15" away from the body with thumbs up, as in grasping a steering wheel. The hand must be positioned properly, lest a sudden jolt deflect the pole toward the skier's body dangerously.

wood core, cracked edges; 1 year guarantee **$105**

Sorcerer—Combi model, fiberglass-epoxy with wood core, plastic tip sheet; 1 year guarantee **$140**

Spectral—Fiberglass-epoxy with wood core; cracked edges; 1 year guarantee **$170**

Cheetah—Fiberglass-epoxy with wood core; cracked edges; a super ski; 1 year guarantee . **$196**

KASTLE

Grand Prix—8 layers of fiberglass and metal bonded over lightweight wood core; for intermediate or advanced skiers . **$200**

CPM-T1—Series for racers; 7 layers of fiberglass and metal bonded over lightweight wood core; Giant Slalom, Hard Slalom, and Soft Slalom models . . . . **$175-$180**

Special—7 layers fiberglass and metal over lightweight wood core; for instructor and ski patrolman **$165**

CPM-70—7 layers of fiberglass and metal over lightweight wood core; recreational skier from beginner through advanced . **$155**

CPM-50—Fiberglass and metal over heavier ashwood core for slightly heavier, less expensive recreational ski **$135**

LaFemme—Ultralight ski with softer flex, especially for women **$145**

Topglass—Fiberglass layers above and below laminated wood core **$95**

Rally 8—8 strips of fiberglass laminate above and 8 below wood core **$80**

Rally 4—4 strips of fiberglass laminate above and 4 below wood core **$65**

KNEISSL

White Star Super RS—Epoxy-reinforced fiberglass plates in sandwich construction; no wooden core; for the advanced, expert, racer; 2 year guarantee . . **$250**

White Star Racer—Epoxy-reinforced fiberglass plates in sandwich construction; for expert recreational skier **$215**

White Star —Epoxy-reinforced fiberglass plates in sandwich construction; for advanced intermediate to expert **$210**

Red Star—Epoxy-reinforced fiberglass plates in sandwich construction; for advanced intermediate through expert **$185**

Blue Star—Less demanding version of White Star, for skier from intermediate to advanced . . **$165**

Slalom Racer—Epoxy-reinforced fiberglass plates in sandwich construction **$135**

Magic 77—Epoxy-reinforced fiberglass plates in sandwich construction; for learning skiers **$115**

KRYSTAL

Glas Formula—3 layers of full-length glass fibers over laminated wood fiber core; cracked edges; 2 year guarantee; racing ski . **$160**

Slalom—2 layers of unidirectional fiberglass; cracked edges; 2 year guarantee **$115**

SL—2 layers fiberglass epoxy laminate hardwood core; cracked edges; 1 year guarantee . . **$110**

Giant Slalom—2 layers high-density fiberglass; 2 year guarantee **$100**

Kombi—Similar to Slalom and GS, but modified for all-around use; 2 layers fiberglass, 2 year guarantee **$80**

Solo—2 layers fiberglass epoxy over laminated hardwood core; 2 year guarantee **$65**

LAMBORGHINI

Fuego Ice—Fiberglass ski, cracked edge, competition model **$195**

Ambassador—Fiberglass ski, metal top edges **$120**

Diplomat—Fiberglass ski, one-piece edges **$100**

Aristocrat—Fiberglass ski, one-piece edges, recreational . . **$90**

MAXEL-BARRECRAFTERS

Aluminum-fiberglass lamination over polymer core; unconditionally guaranteed for 1 year.

Alpha—For advanced skiers, patrolmen, instructors, competitors **$185**

Gamma—For serious regular skiers **$170**

Delta Giant Slalom **$160**

Sigma Combi **$145**

MILLER

Custom Pro—Handmade, fiberglass-metal construction . . **$189**

Professional — Handmade fiberglass ski with bamboo core, top metal edge **$149**

DeLuxe—Fiberglass construction **$80**

NORTHLAND

Stein Eriksen

X-11—All-glass ski; fiberglass molded over a fiberglass-impregnated foam core into one integral unit for recreational skier . . **$170**

Pro/Glas—Laminated fir plywood sandwiched between layers of fiberglass and aluminum alloy, for expert and competitive skiers **$175**

L-21—Aluminum alloy layers laminated to fir plywood core, for intermediate to advanced recreational skiers **$150**

National—Plastic top over aluminum skins and core of fir plywood; for all skiers, all conditions **$115**

V-10—Similar to National, but lighter in weight **$90**

X-7—Fiberglass body molded around fiberglass-reinforced foam core; for beginners or occasional recreational skiers **$90**

Glass 300—Epoxy fiberglass and laminated plywood construction **$70**

GT 1000—Laminated fiberglass and wood bonded with epoxy; for beginners **$50**

OLIN

Mark I—Fiberglass laminated to

lightweight wood core; for wide range of recreational skiers **$155**

OSTRYKER

Elastique 90—Fiberglass over extended plastic core, cracked edges, 1 year guarantee . . . **$115**

#990—Lamination of fiberglass, epoxy, and aluminum; 1 year guarantee **$75**

#660—Fiberglass with metal over wood core; 1 year guarantee **$50**

Zenith #550—Epoxy fiberglass laminate **$35**

PERSENICO

Cappa del Mondo—Four layers of fiberglass-epoxy on bottom, two layers on top of laminated ash-wood core; competition ski (1 year warranty) **$130**

Glass 400—Fiberglass on top and bottom over laminated ash-wood core; 1 year warranty **$75**

Glass 300—Laminated ash-wood core reinforced with fiberglass; 1 year warranty **$60**

Epoxy-Metal 600—One layer fiberglass on top, one on bottom of laminated ash-wood core; 1 year warranty **$95**

ROSSIGNOL

GTA—Fiberglass and metal with a hollow core structure **$240**

Strato 102—Stratified glass-epoxy over wood core; competitive ski **$170**

Strato AR—Same basic construction as Strato 102; for the expert skier **$165**

Stratix 112—Same basic construction as Strato, for intermediate and advanced skier . . **$140**

Stratoflex—Same basic construction as Strato at moderate price **$120**

Concorde—Same basic construction; for beginners and advanced occasional skiers **$95**

St. Anton—Fiberglass-reinforced plastic import **$43**

SOHLER

Black and White—Eight layers

of fiberglass-epoxy, cracked edges **$195**

Blue Bird—Plastic and metal compound, racing ski **$160**

Spyder—Metal and Fiberglass combination **$140**

Red and White—Five layers of fiberglass-epoxy, cracked edges **$145**

MK 700—Three layers of epoxy-fiberglass in economy model **$100**

MK 800—High glass content, with rubber dampeners for added control **$115**

MK 900—Epoxy-fiberglass, for up to the most advanced skier **$130**

MK 1000—Epoxy-fiberglass, with cracked edges **$175**

SPALDING

Sideral—Multi-layers of epoxy-fiberglass over wood core; for racers; 2 year guarantee . . **$200**

GS-Glass—Epoxy-fiberglass layers over wood core; for expert skiers; 2 year guarantee . . **$150**

SL-Glass—Epoxy-fiberglass layers over wood core; like GS, but designed for fast turns; 2 year guarantee **$150**

GM Compound—Combination of metal and glass reinforcement over wood core; for beginners and intermediates **$115**

ALU Compound—Metal and plastic layers over wood core; for novice skiers **$110**

GR-Glass—Epoxy-fiberglass layers over wood core; for beginners; 2 year guarantee **$85**

SPALDING/DYNASTAR

S430—Fiberglass and epoxy resin layers, wood core surrounded by fiberglass and polyester resin; top racing ski **$180**

S230—Wood core surrounded by fiberglass and polyester resin; for expert skiers, but easier to handle than S430 . . . . **$150**

GTS—Fiberglass and epoxy resin layers over wood core; recreational ski for intermediates **$125**

TIPS DOWN FOR TRACKING

Watch any good skier as he returns to the ground after being air-borne. If he's skiing properly and with the maximum control, the tips of his skis will be the last thing to leave the ground and the first to return. Or watch an instructor jump a mogul. As he leaves the ground he goes into a "tuck," the degree depending on the size of the mogul, his speed and snow conditions. At the high point of the jump, his tails will be between his waist and shoulders with tips lower.

The reason is simple. As in every turn, it is the tips which "carve" the path for the body and rest of the skis. By landing first they assure a more stable course just as a plane touches its nose wheel first.

Landing tails first will always have a tendency to drag your weight back on your skis. This is bad enough in any maneuver, but becomes almost suicidal when you're out of control.

In slower maneuvers, such as the hop garland, don't take your tips off the snow at all. Leave them there while pressing forward with your knees. You'll find you've executed a more precise stable turn and that you are always in a position to take any "corrective measures" necessary.

THE QUICK CLOSE

Parallel skiing is nothing more than learning to ski on one ski at a time. Since the downhill ski is dominant, the uphill ski goes along for the ride, bearing only enough weight to keep it operational and to help maintain balance. It, therefore, "lays in" next to the downhill ski.

By employing the quick close technique to the stem turn, you can learn the sensations of parallel skiing faster. In short, the less time you spend stemming, the more time you will be skiing parallel. Pick a slight bump and stem on your approach to it. At the very top of it, shift weight to the stemmed ski and immediately "close." That is, place your unweighted ski beside your downhill ski. If you find that you are in a forward side slip, great! That's what you seek. Hold the slide and keep enough forward pressure on so that the tips of your skis will be leading the turn. As your skis cross the fall line, increase angulation and traverse.

This simple exercise can bring your form into sharp focus because it doesn't excuse any shortcomings in the basics. More important, you will know it too.

If this is too tough for you at the start, begin more gradually by quick closing from a straight snowplow. Begin by weighting the downhill ski as you would for a snowplow turn. While still straight in the fall line, close the skis as suggested. Don't leap into the air when you close. Straighten up and then return to a flexed knees position. Keep after it using the poles for balance when needed.

TITAN

T 3—Fiberglass competition ski; SL and GS **$135**
Carousel—Lightweight fiberglass ski; for all levels of ability . **$95**
LaFemme—Lightweight, soft, flexible fiberglass ski for women
. . . . **$85**

VOIT

Spectra CT 6—Fiberglass filament wound over urethane center; for recreational skier **$150**
Spectra CT7—For more advanced recreational skier **$165**

VOLKL

Explosion—Torsion box construction with wrapped fiber glass and polyurethane foam core, cracked edges; outstanding visual pattern **$350**
Zebra—Torsion box construction with wrapped fiberglass, polyurethane and ashwood core, cracked edges; all-around ski
. . . . **$230**
Perfection—Torsion box construction with wrapped fiberglass, laminated. wood core, cracked edges, for all types of skiers **$150**
Perfection L—Torsion box construction with wrapped fiberglass, lightweight wood core; very light ski for good skiers **$148**
Sapporo—Torsion box construction with wrapped fiberglass, lightweight wood core; light, easy-turning slalom ski **$130**
Explosion—All-plastic; fiberglass wrapped around fiberglass channel embedded in polyurethane; distinctive explosion design
Epoxi 2000—Epoxy-aluminum-fiberglass lamination over ashwood core; low-priced for beginners on up

YAMAHA

Paramount—Fiberglass-epoxy laminate over wood core construction; for racers **$169**
Hi-Flex—Fiberglass-epoxy laminate over wood core construction; for intermediates **$139**

All-Around III—Fiberglass-epoxy laminate over wood core construction; for general skiers
. . . . **$99**
All-Around II—Construction similar to III, for serious beginners **$84**
All-Around I—Fiberglass-epoxy is principal material **$69**

ZENITH

#880—Two layers of metal with 3 layers of fiberglass over a plywood core; 1 year guarantee . **$70**

METAL

ATTENHOFER

Superjet—Racing ski with 3 metal layers (limited supply) . **$160**
Jet 55—Metal sandwich construction for giant slalom, fast skiers, racers **$125**
Jet 33—Metal sandwich construction for hard-packed and soft snow **$120**
Jet 22—Metal sandwich construction for beginners and intermediates **$110**
Jet 11—Metal sandwich construction, easy-going ski . . **$90**

AVANT

ALU Combi—Metal combination ski, medium flex, one-piece hidden edge **$90**
ALU All-Round—Metal ski with clear aluminum top, medium flex, one-piece hidden edge **$80**

BARRECRAFTERS

The Pleasure Ski—Aluminum with wood core, guaranteed for 1 year **$110**

BLIZZARD

Fan 2000—Lightweight metal ski for beginners and intermediates who like feel of metal ski . **$70**

CONY

Metal Combi—Metal ski, plastic top, medium flex **$80**
Standard—Similar to above . **$90**
GS—Metal ski, medium-firm flex,

cracked edges **$125**
Deep Powder—Metal ski, soft flex **$110**

ELAN

Silver Star—Aluminum sandwich construction; for recreational skier **$100**
Super GSL—Aluminum sandwich construction over hardwood core **$140**

FISCHER

Imperator—Aluminum and fiberglass bonded to lightweight wood core **$250**
President—Aluminum bonded to lightweight wood core
RSL—Giant slalom racer **$215**
Combi—recreational model **$205**
Alu-Steel—Aluminum bonded to lightweight wood core
RSL—Giant slalom racer .. **$150**
Combi—recreational **$150**
Alu-Standard—Aluminum bonded to wood core, for recreational skier **$125**
VP—Aluminum bonded to wood core, for recreational skier **$120**

GERDAU

Metal 770—Aluminum alloy top and bottom sheets bonded to laminated hardwood core **$140**
Metal 550—Same as 770 but lighter and more maneuverable; full year breakage guarantee **$125**

HEAD

240 STD—Aluminum over laminated wood core, plastic topped; the standard for beginners; 2 year guarantee **$110**
320 Yankee—Aluminum over wood core; designed to help stem skier to make transition to parallel; 2 year guarantee **$145**
360—Aluminum over wood core; for pleasure skier, beginners and intermediates; 2 year guarantee **$155**
720—Metal construction; won Silver Medal at Grenoble Olympics; for intermediates and experts **$170**

KASTLE

Perradur—Aluminum laminate over wood core, for skier of every degree of ability **$130**

KRYSTAL

Siren—2 layers of aluminum alloy bonded to laminated hardwood core, Swiss-made; 1 year guarantee **$88**
Metlski—2 aluminum laminations bonded to laminated hardwood core, Swiss-made; 1 year guarantee **$88**
ALU-X4—Aluminum sheets over laminated hardwood core; plastic top, 1 year guarantee **$85**

LAMBORGHINI

LTD—Metal with segmented edges **$140**
Maxima II—Metal with polished metal top edges **$130**
Ultima II—Metal, with recreational flex **$120**
Futura—Metal, with recreational flex **$110**

OSTRYKER

Metal #1000—Laminated aluminum and epoxy with hardwood core; for good skiers, 1 year guarantee **$95**

P + M

Silver 1000 GS—Aluminum sheet on top and bottom of ashwood core; competition ski; 1 year warranty **$115**
Silver 1000—Combination model, construction same as Silver 1000 GS, 1 year warranty **$115**
Triplo Metal 500 — Reinforced aluminum strips over laminated ashwood core; 1 year warranty. **$90**

ROSSIGNOL

Allais Major—Metal sandwich over wood core; racing ski **$145**
Allais GP—Metal sandwich over wood core; recreational ski **$100**

SPALDING

TF-Aluminum — Aluminum top and bottom sheets over laminated wood core; all-around recreation-

TRAINING TIPS FOR TRAVERSING

The living room carpet may not be your idea of the toughest skiing conditions imaginable, but it can serve as a secluded sanctuary to practice the traverse without the obvious hardship of real snow or a hair-raising mountain.

Actually it doesn't even have to be a secluded carpet, for on many occasions a ski buff, chockfull of the merriment of a festive occasion, or just the meeting of a fellow skier, has sprung up and landed in the ideal "parallel" traverse position. Of course this one act identifies him immediately as a skier. In fact, one of great devotion, skill and accomplishment. To those who did not recognize this display, well, they don't matter anyway.

But practicing the traverse in privacy can well prepare you for the correct position on the hill. At the same time it will condition the muscles used in traversing.

Begin as if you were on the slope wearing skis. If it is convenient, put your ski boots on. Although this is not vital, it does familiarize you with pressures caused by your feet against the boots. And it helps to toughen your feet to the boots themselves.

When you have assumed the position, flex the knees and ankles, angle the upper body more over the downhill ski.

After you have repeated this three or four times advance the other foot and get into the opposite traversing position. Repeat several times to each side. Do this often enough and it will eventually become thoroughly familiar.

al ski **$125**

SPALDING/DYNASTAR

MV2 Equipe—Aluminum casing around wood core; for experts **$180**

MV2 Rubis—Similar to Equipe model, for slalom **$150**

MV2 Argent—Aluminum casing around wood core, for intermediates **$125**

TOMIC

Ultra-Lite—Metal ski for recreational or competition use... **$85**

TREVISO

Parallel—Metal ski **$96**

WOOD

A & T

Blitz — Laminated hardwood, plastic finish **$22**
Skikee—"Shortee" miniaturized ski 3', 4', 5' .... **$20** 6' ... **$27**
Aspen—Laminated hardwood, sheet plastic top **$25**
Innsbruck—Austrian import, sheet plastic top **$30**

DARTMOUTH

Schuss Super — multi-laminated wood with plastic top **$26**
Trailmaster — Multi-laminated wood with plastic top **$30**
Grand Prix — Multi-laminated wood with plastic top **$40**
MK-500 — Multi-laminated ashwood with plastic sheet top. **$32**
Triumph—Multi-laminated ashwood with plastic sheet top. **$32**

FISCHER

Quick Super—Plastic-topped, 22 laminations **$45**
Red Master—Plastic-topped 22 piece laminated hickory core, for novices to intermediates **$35**

GERDAU

Jaguar — 31 laminations, alumi-

num top edges **$52**
Apollo — 5 laminations, plastic top edges **$45**
Polaris—25 laminations, plastic top edges **$40**
Torino GT—25 laminations, plastic top edges **$40**
Grand Prix—25 laminations; one year warrantee **$35**

HOLZNER

Futura—Multi-laminated first-quality ash, 1 year guarantee .... **$29.50 - $39.50**
Adventurer — Multi-laminated first-quality ash, 1 year guarantee .... **$35.00 - $45.00**
Lancer — Multi-laminated first-quality ash, 1 year guarantee .... **$35.50 - $39.00**
Challenger—Multi-laminated first-quality ash, fiberglass reinforced bottom, 1 year guarantee .... **$50.00 - $57.50**

KASTLE

Sprint — Plastic top over wood, for recreational skiers ... **$42.50**

KRYSTAL

Grand Prix—28 piece laminated, plastic top, 1 year guarantee **$35**
Europa — 17 piece laminated, plastic top; German-made, 1 year guarantee **$35**
880 LTD—20 piece laminated **$25.50**

NORTHLAND

Cobra—Hickory and ash laminated construction, plastic top **$42.50**
Skilark—Laminated wood core, plastic top sheet......... **$35**
Supreme—Laminated wood core, plastic top sheet **$29**

TREVISO

Innsbruck—25 hickory and ash laminations **$30**
Aspen—25 hickory and ash laminations **$32**
Mark IX—Plastic top over 25 hickory and ash laminations **$35**

BOOTS

A & T

Injecta-Foam—Liquid plastic injected into a double lining within a plastic outer boot shell; plastic changes to polyurethane foam in under 10 minutes, molding itself to the exact configuration of wearer's foot within the boot; 5 buckle shell **$135**

BATEMAN

Ski — 5 buckle, plastic uppers, men's and women's **$40**

ACHILLES

300 — 5 buckle plastic boot, men's **$25**
200—4 buckle plastic boot; women's **$20**

CABER

Delta 100—Injection molded shell, hand-lasted inner boot, 5 buckles, suede heel lining **$115**
Supreme—Plastic outer, foam inner lining, 5 buckles; for intermediate skier **$45**
Milan—Plastic laminated, 5 buckles **$39.95**

DARTMOUTH

"Wetlook" Sapphire — Polyurethane "flatmold" upper, shearling lined; women's **$70**
Pro Fibermold—Five-ply plastic upper, felt lined; men's..... **$67**
"Wetlook" Pro — Polyurethane "flatmold" upper, felt-lined; racing class; men's **$72**
Brown Fibermold Standard — Plastic upper, five buckles, lined and padded; men's and women's **$45**
Deluxe Fibermold — Five-ply plastic upper, five buckles, glove-lined, men's and women's .. **$55**
Sapphire Fibermold—Plastic upper, shearling-lined; women's **$62**

DOLOMITE

372—Plastic boot, 5 buckle, leather lined; women's **$45**
111—Plastic boot, 5 buckle, shearling lined; women's . **$55**
'36—Similar to above **$65**
99—Pre-molded plastic, 5 buckle. women's **$75**
510—5 buckle, grained plastic, men's **$40**
3121—Similar to above ... **$50**
505—5 buckle, pre-molded plastic; men's **$60**
567—5 buckle, molded hinge and cuff; men's **$70**
560—6 buckle, high-shaft, molded hinge; men's **$80**
808—5 buckle, pre-molded, high shaft; men's **$90**
GJSS—6 buckle, extra high shaft; men's **$135**

GARMISCH

W80 — Polyurethane leather bonded uppers, 5 swivel buckles, shearling lining **$83**
W75—Same as above, leather lining **$80**
W65—Plastic bonded leather, 5 spring-loaded buckles **$63**
W50—Plastic uppers, 5 spring-loaded buckles **$48**

GERDAU

DeLuxe—Molded rubber with 5 buckles **$25**

HEAD

Special—Polyurethane-fiberglass laminate, single-boot construction, 5 buckles; medium-stiff, moderate forward lean for average skier **$100**
Superior — Polyurethane-fiberglass laminate, double-boot construction, 5 buckles; for advanced, more aggressive skiers **$115**
Challenger—Polyurethane-fiberglass laminate, double-boot construction, 6 buckles, exaggerated forward lean for advanced skiers and racers **$130**

HENKE

Competition Plastic—Plastic construction, leather lining, 5 buckles; for expert skiers and racers; men's **$140**
Imperial — Plastic construction; for all skiers; men's and women's **$80**
Comfort — Plastic construction, shearling and leather lining; men's and women's **$70**
Rocket — Plastic construction, leather lining; men's and women's **$60**
Holiday—Plastic construction, leather lining, men's and women's **$50**
Toronado—Plastic construction, leather lining, top quality; men's and women's **$115**
Parallel — Plastic construction, leather lining, rugged; men's **$110**
Fashion—Plastic construction, beaver lamb lining, 7 color combinations; ladies **$85**

HOCHLAND

9410—Injection-molded plastic shell with 5 buckles, inner boot, and leather lining; men's . **$105**
9420—Similar to above; men's **$115**
9320—Plastic construction, single boot, 5 buckles; men's and women's **$49.95**
9330—Similar to above **$60**
9340—Similar to above, full beaverlamb lining **$75**
9350—Similar to 9330 . **$82.50**
9370—Similar to above, beaverlamb lining **$87.50**
9380—Plastic construction, single boot, 5 buckles, full beaverlamb lining; women's . **$87.50**
9390—Plastic construction, single boot, 5 buckles; women's **$105**
9400—Plastic construction, single boot, 5 buckles; women's **$115**

HUBER

Kreuzeck—Plastic uppers, spring buckles; men's and women's **$40**

SKI WITH THE MOGULS

For some, skiing moguls is a luxury, for others a necessity, but whichever situation you're confronted with, it's a good idea to know how to ski them properly and let them "work for you." Unfortunately, many skiers still glide up to the top and slide down the backside as they were taught 'way back when that was the way to make parallel turns. This roller-coaster ride may be diverting, but it can't compare with running the gullies between the moguls and turning on the uphill sides of each.

It's easy if you start your first turn over the top of a mogul and then let your tips wend their way through them. Set your edges against the uphill side. As you continue forward, your skis will probably have changed direction and you'll be on the bottom side. As you approach the inevitable next one, repeat the edge set.

This maneuver is especially helpful as mogul tops are good chances to pick up nicks and gouges in your ski bottom.

Moguls are fine places to practice two-pole turns. As you begin to set your edges, place both poles equally at the tips of your skis. Your shoulders should remain forward while your lower body rotates. As your set takes hold, throw yourself forward through the poles. Exert the forward pressure on the tips of your skis, allowing them to "steer" you around.

As you get the rhythm down, increase your lower body rotation. The edge set will have to increase proportionately. This maneuver also limbers up the lower body.

Kreuzeck Deluxe—Same as above, fur lining; women's **$45**
Lady Plastica—Similar to above, fur lining; women's **$55**
SKS-70—Similar to above; men's **$49.50**
Buckle Lady Streif—Similar to above, lambswool lining; women's **$65**
Buckle Master Streif—Similar to above; men's **$59.50**

HUMANIC

Coverite 707—Double layer of plastic with coating, fiberglass reinforced, five buckles, leather lining; competition boot; men's **$125**
Coverite 606—Double layer of plastic with coating, fiberglass-reinforced, leather lining; five buckles; for expert recreational skiers; men's **$100**
Coverite 505—Similar as above, for beginners to advanced intermediates; men's and women's **$80**
Coverite 404—Multi-layered synthetic construction, 5 aluminum buckles; loden or lambskin lining; men's and women's ... **$65**
Coverite 303—Similar to above; for beginners and intermediates; men's and women's **$55**

KASTINGER

Futura—Polyurethane injection-molded, leather lined, 5 buckles **$100**
Mark VII—Plastic uppers, 5 spring-loaded buckles **$70**
Mark VI—Polychrome upper, 5 spring-loaded buckles, lambswool lined; women's **$60**
Mark V (Star)—Similar to above, without wool lining; men's **$60**
Mark IV (Slalom)—Polychrome upper, 5 spring-loaded buckles; men's and women's **$50**
Mark III—Polyplast plastic upper, 5 buckles; men's and women's **$42.50**

PETER KENNEDY

PK Foam-N-Fit — Lightweight, all-plastic, 5 buckle boot shell, filled with liquid polyurethane foam; foot in rubber sock is inserted into boot, and foam forms around foot; men's and women's

Black **$135**
Color **$140**

KOFLACH

Expo Competition—Fully plastic molded shell, inner leather boot, loden lining, 6 buckles; for pros, experts, racers; men's **$130**
Expo Master—Plastic outer shell, leather inner boot; 5 buckles; men's and women's **$115**
Silver Star—Plastic laminate construction with leather lining; 5 buckles; men's and women's **$80**
Jet Star—Flat molded plastic shell with loden lining; men's **$75**
Five Star—Plasti-coat material, leather lining; men's and women's **$70**
Red Star—Flat molded plastic shell; loden lining for men **$65**
Fur lining for women **$70**
Swing Star—Plastic-coat material, lined in lamb's wool; for intermediate to advanced; women's **$62.50**
White Star — Plasti-coat material, 5 buckles, men's and women's **$55**
Artic — Plasti-coat material, 5 buckles; women's **$55**

LANGE

Lange-Foam Standard—Shell of flexible epoxy; liner holds foot in alignment while boot is being fitted and foamed with high-density, closed-material; also available with Lange-flo liner **$120**
Lange-Foam Pro—Similar to above **$145**
Lange-Foam Competition—Similar to above **$175**
Competite—Women's boot with cutaway arch, pronounced heel, 4 wide buckles; shell of flexible epoxy with "Lange-flo" inner liner that conforms to individual foot **$135**

MILLER

Custom Pro—Plastic, 5 buckles, 14-degree forward cant, for advanced skier ..... **$ 99.50**
Sizes 14 and 15 .... **114.45**
Venus Competition—Molded plastic, 5 buckles for advanced skier **$69.50**
Sizes 14 and 15 .... **79.90**
Olympic Model—Plasticized uppers, 5 buckles, for recreation skier **$49.50**
Sizes 14 and 15 ..... **56.90**

MONTEVERDE

5902 — Laminated plastic, 5 spring-loaded buckles, leather lined; men's **$90**
5918 — Laminated plastic, 5 buckles; women's **$64**
5920—Laminated plastic, 5 telescopic buckles, leather-lined; men's and women's **$64**
5910—Laminated plastic, 5 adjustable buckles, leather-lined; men's and women's **$52**
5973 — Leather, 5 adjustable buckles, suede lining; men's and women's **$37**
5975—Leather, 5 telescopic buckles, leather lining, men's and women's **$44**

NORDICA

Astral Super—Injection molded outer shell, 5 wide buckles, adjustable back hinge, leather lined **$115**
Astral Pro—Similar to Astral Super, without back hinge **$100**
Astral S—Similar to Astral Pro with standard buckles **$88**
Astral Ladies—Similar to Astral S, with lamb's fur lining **$90**
Velox—Plastic laminated outer, reverse leather lining **$58**
Comet—Plastic laminated outer, 5 adjustable buckles **$50**
Sestriece—Plastic laminated outer, 5 buckles **$42**

NORTHLAND

Supreme—Plastic construction, leather lining, 5 buckles . . . **$50**
Prima—Plastic construction, 5 buckles for beginner or intermediate **$40**

P & M

758—Chrome-tanned leather, 5 buckle, orthopedic insole; men's and women's **$32.50**
   with shearling lining . . **37.50**
768—Plastic-laminated leather, injection-molded construction, 5 buckles; men's and women's
. . . . **$37.50**
826—Similar to above; men's and women's **$45**
830—Similar to above; men's and women's **$52.50**
831—Similar to above, shearling lining; men's and women's . . **$54**
840—Similar to above; men's **$62.50**
845—Similar to above; men's and women's **$63.50**
850—Similar to above; men's
. . . . **$65**

RAICHLE

Fiber Jet Comp—Center-opening fiberglass, 4 closures, leather inner boot, for competition skiers; men's and women's . **$140**
Fiber Jet II Standard—Center-opening fiberglass, for advanced recreational skiers; men's and women's **$110**
Formula I—Textured micro-cellular rubber with leather collar; for competition skiers; men's and women's **$90**
Le Mans—Plastic over leather; for serious recreational skiers; men's and women's **$80**
Rally—Plastic over leather; for experienced weekend skiers; men's and women's **$70**
Vogue—Metallic-toned plastic over leather; shearling-lined; women's **$65**
Monte Carlo—Plastic-laminated leather; for recreational skiers; men's and women's **$60**

Cresta—Plasticized leather, for beginners; men's and women's
. . . . **$50**

RIEKER

Doleboot—Rigid outer shell of magnesium; inner boot injected with urethane elastomer; 3 buckles, adjustable hinge for forward lean **$165**
Unifit—Rigid outer shell; inner boot injected with urethane elastomer **$135**
Orbis G2—Plastic shell, 3 buckles, adjustable hinge for forward lean; men's **$150**
Orbis G1 Jet—Plastic shell, 5 buckles, leather lined inner boot; men's **$115**
Orbis G1 Fur—Plastic shell, 5 buckles, lambskin lined; men's and women's **$100**
Orbis G1 Thermo—Plastic shell, 5 buckles, thermo-felt lining; men's and women's **$95**
Orbis G1 Standard—Plastic shell, 5 buckles, leather lined inner boot; men's and women's . . **$90**
J 800—Plastic-covered leather, 5 buckles, leather lined; men's to size 14 . . . . **$80**
J 700—Similar to above, with lambswool lining; women's **$70**
J 600—Synthetic bonded to nylon, leather lined, 5 buckles; men's and women's to size 14
. . . . **$60**
J 500—Chrome-tanned leather, plastic reinforced, 5 buckles; men's to size 14 and women's
. . . . **$50**
J 50B—Plastic and leather laminate, 5 buckles, fur lined, men's to size 14 and women's . . . **$45**

ROSEMOUNT

Classic—Fiberglass shell, side entry, inner strap for fit, leather lining, Corfam cover; men's **$150**
Fastback—Similar construction, with variable forward-lean adjustment up to 25 degrees **$170**
Lady Rosemount—Fiberglass shell, Corfam cover, side entry,

leather lining, variety of colors; women's **$155**
ST-100 — Fiberglass shell, 2 buckle top entry, inner boot, leather lining **$110**

ST. MORITZ

Silver Medal—5 buckles, swivel loops; men's and women's .. **$55**
Gold Medal—5 swivel buckles, constant-pressure spring loops; men's and women's **$60**
Grenoble — Thermo-plastic; 5 swivel buckle loops; men's and women's **$40**

SAN MARCO

Val Gardena — Molded plastic boot with plastic inner boot, suede lining, men's and women's **$89.95**
Gemini—Molded plastic boot with plastic inner boot, suede lining; 2 buckle construction; men's **$125**
Cristallo—Medium-stiffness plastic, suede lined; men's .. **$69.95**
Davos—Plastic uppers, leather lining, for intermediate skier; men's **$49.95**
Mariella—Plastic coated leather, shearling lined; women's **$59.95**

Contessa—Leather, shearling lined, medium-stiffness; women's **$59.95**

TECNICA

Galaxy—Plastic-laminated leather, 5 buckles, suede lining .. **$90**
Meteor—Plastic-laminated, 5 buckles, suede and shearling lining **$80**
Komet — Fiberglass-reinforced plastic, leather lining, 5 buckles **$70**
Dama—Plastic-laminated leather, full shearling lining, 5 buckles; women's **$60**
Gardena—Plastic, heavy-duty, 5 buckles **$50**
Sapporo—Plastic shell, suede lining, 5 buckles **$60**

TRAPPEUR

Pro—Polyurethane shell bonded to leather, 5 buckles, shearling lined in front; men's **$120**
Femina — Plastic laminated to leather, 5 buckles, full lambswool lining; women's **$85**
Slalom—Polyurethane shell lined with leather, shearling in front, 5 buckles; for intermediate and advanced skier; men's **$90**
SM—Polyurethane shell, shearling lined, 5 buckles; men's and women's **$70**
Quick V—Plastic shell lined with wool and leather, 5 buckles; for novice and intermediate; men's and women's **$50**
Slalom Shell—Rigid plastic shell with extra reinforcement for custom foam fit; 5 buckles.... **$85**

TREVISO

969—Top-grain leather, 5 buckles **$37**
1069 — Top-grain leather, 5 buckles, injection molded soles **$45**
2070—Injection-molded plastic, leather lined, 5 buckles **$52**
3070—Laminated plastic and rubber, 5 buckles **$64**

TYROL

T-Boot—Rigid plastic outer shell, leather lining, front opening with metal contact plates, two ratchet type closures in front, one in back for forward lean **$160**
Banff — Plastic-leather lamination, 4 buckles, leather lining; heavier construction for "working" skier **$95**
Royal Plastique — All-plastic, 4 buckles **$85**
Royal Competition—All-plastic, 4 buckles **$95**
Canadian — Plastic-leather lamination, 5 spring loaded buckles, leather lining **$75**
Quebec—Plastic-leather lamination, 5 spring loaded buckles, shearling lining **$65**
Mt. Tremblant — Plastic-leather lamination, 5 spring loaded buckles, fleece lining **$55**

Plastique — Plastic-leather lamination, 5 spring loaded buckles, fleece lining **$45**

VOLKL

Ulrich—Plastic uppers, fur lining, 5 interchangeable buckles; men's and women's **$45**
Lech—Plastic uppers, 5 interchangeable buckles; men's and women's **$62.50**
Lady Bavaria—Plastic uppers, 5 spring buckles; lambswool lining; women's **$69.50**
Lady Bavaria Comfort—Same as above, with flexible heel; women's **$75**
Innsbruck—Racing model, plastic uppers, felt or leather lining, 5 interchangeable buckles; men's and women's **$75**
P - U Plus—Plastic uppers, combination felt or leather lining, 5 interchangeable buckles, racing design. **$85**

ZERMATT

Plastica—5 buckles **$69.95**
Plastica—6 buckles **$79.95**
660—6 spring buckles .. **$69.95**
665—5 spring buckles **$55**
465—5 buckles, Velcro corset, crossed buckle straps..... **$50**
555—5 buckles, crossed buckle straps **$47.50**
540—5 buckles **$45**
510—5 buckles **$37.50**

BINDINGS

ATTENHOFER

Starflex Combi—Flexible safety toe piece, step-in heel binding **$45**
Cobraflex Combi — Swivel toe piece, step-in heel binding **$31**

CUBCO

Standard—Step-in type; toe releases in any direction or upwards; heel releases in forward fall **$22**

COBER

Tigre—Step-in heel unit. run-away strap **$25**
Cougar—Step-in heel unit **$15.95**
Sferico—Spherical toe piece **$18**
Super Blitz—Toe piece . . **$14.95**
Sicur Blitz—Toe piece . . . **$9.95**

DOVRE

"40" Concorde — Self-centering step-in model with visual release adjustment **$29.95**
"40"—Step-in model with visual release adjustment **$29.95**
30—Step-in model, length and heel height adjustment . **$19.95**
"K"—Step-in model, lateral re-lease **$19.95**
30 R—Rugged, step-in model **$15.90**

ECKEL

Royal—Automatic release step-in binding, many angles of re-lease **$55**

ESS

ESS-3—Step-in heel release with shock-absorber, all-angle release **$30**
Twist—Toe-piece with visible tension adjustment **$9**
Trimatic—Step-in heel, simple adjustment **$20**
U-2—Step-in heel, visible ten-sion adjustment **$22.50**

GERDAU

SH40—Step-in heel unit; full forward fall release; visual ad-justment **$16.50**
S301—Step-in toe unit; double-action release; toe resets auto-matically to prevent premature releases **$5.50**
1000 Dynamica — Step-in heel unit; full forward fall release **$18.50**
Toe unit; double-action **$10.50**

GERTSCH

6D Elite—Toe unit, heel plate, and release plate **$50**
4D—Similar to above **$35**

GEZE

Top Master — Self-seating cup-type toe holder, shock absorp-tion system **$17.50**
Step Master—Step-in heel, visual tension setting device **$35**

HOPE

Salvaguard — Step-in heel, ad-justable **$15**
Salvaguard III—Step-in heel, ad-justable **$13**
Salvax—Toe piece **$7**
Unimax—Toe piece **$6**

KHAZZAM

Mark II Autoway—With self-centering toe piece....... **$25**

KRYSTAL

XK Kombo — Step-in binding; heel unit has tension indicator, coin-adjustable release toe **$19.50**

LOOK

Grand Prix—Step-in heel release with forward fall release and 360 degree swivel **$31**
Nevada II—Elastic toe release, self-centering, forward release **$15**
Look 55—Toe release, self-cen-tering, visible adjustment . **$12**
Flash II—Step-in heel release, elastic system **$21**

MARKER

Simplex DL—Toe binding, dial settings from beginners to ex-perts **$16.95**
Elastomat—Step-in heel binding, with lateral fall protection, for ruggedest skiing **$49.95**
Rotamat FD—Releasable turn-table **$37.95**
Rotamat—Similar to above **$27.95**
Telmat—Step-in binding, adjus-ments require no tools . . . **$21.95**
Junior System—Jr. toe binding and Jr. Rotamat heel for young-sters **$34.90**

MILLCO

SL-4—Toe piece self-centering, requires no boot notching; ten-sion controlled by piston spring

Advanced Pointer

ON HANDLING BOILER PLATE

Western skiers may not en-counter this vexing condition too often, but it is very much a part of eastern skiing. The proper name is "frozen granular" but "boilerplate" is more accurate.

Many skiers, faced with such circumstances, retire to a warm fire and a hot toddy. But learning to handle yourself on ice will in-crease your proficiency and fun.

It is vitally important that you maintain a fairly erect stance, well forward and in a position to push your skis into the surface. Never get too far "hung out" over your skis; always be ready to compensate for a sudden patch of ice. You must be ready to react immediately to a sudden change in conditions.

Weight must be kept almost exaggeratedly far forward as the skier who sits on his tails will quickly find himself out of con-trol. What's really needed is "turning power" from the legs and feet.

If you uncork a turn and noth-ing happens, don't panic and, above all, don't split back into the snowplow position. Simply in-crease your lateral ankle bend and drive your edges into the ice.

The first requirement for skiing boilerplate, however, is a pair of skis with mighty sharp edges.

With sharp edges, confidence and guts, ice skiing can be fun. Many think the "eastern hard pack" is more challenging than the kind of powder skiers enjoy in the west where all you have to do to turn is change your mind.

. . . . **$24.95**
Heel piece, step-in style with built-in shock compensating device **$29.95**
Ski Free—Toe piece with micromatic adjustment **$7.50**
Step-in heel piece adjusts with single screw **$12.50**

MILLER

M1-A—Fully automatic step-in binding **$24.50**
M2-A—Automatic step-in; racing toe front affords heavier toe release **$24.50**
Ambassador—Release from every possible angle of stress; $500 guarantee against leg fracture **$39.50**
Competition—Full Miller binding **$39.50**

NORTHLAND

Endus Step-In—Forward release heel, impact-absorbing toe . **$45**
Deluxe Ski Free/Free Thro — Cable binding, forward release heel, lateral release toe . . **$12.50**
Deluxe Ski Free/Heel Free — Step-in binding, multi-angle forward and lateral release **$20**
Northland—Step-in binding, multi-angle release **$18**

P & M

Z-69 Front Step—Step-in binding with five different release angles; visual tension settings **$47.50**

ROSEMOUNT

SE 1—Toe binding, designed for non-leather boots, with special toe clip, anti-shock design **$22.50**
SE 2—Heel unit, step in type, controlled upward release **$27.50**
Synergistic System—Toe and heel units described above, plus LO-TORK anti-friction device **$52.50**

SALOMON

S-505 Heel—Dial adjustment for tension, 2 independent spring systems **$30**
S-505 Toe—Calibrated release

setting, self-centering cup . . **$20**
S-404 Heel
    Toe
        for beginners and intermediates **$27.95**

THUNDER

Super—Complete step-in binding **$20**
Standard — Complete step-in binding **$16.50**

TREVISO

K-7—Toe piece, adjustable **$5**
88—Toe piece, concealed screw adjustment **$3.50**
SH—Step-in heel **$6**
1000—Automatic step-in heel **$13.50**

TYROLIA

2000—Shock-proof release toe, spring powered release, microadjustment **$14.95**
3000—Heel with horizontal, vertical and lateral elasticity **$34.95**
500—Toe with parallel elasticity system **$12.50**
Rocket 100—Shock proof release toe **$9.95**
Skimeister 752—Self-centering **$6.95**
Clix 90—Heel with adjustable tension setting **$22.50**
Clix 55—Heel with vertical and horizontal elasticity **$14.95**

POLES

A & T

707—Aluminum alloy pole, adjustable leather grip **$20**
747—Aluminum alloy pole, contour rubber grip, rubber ring **$25**

ALLSOP

Olympic-Red—Aluminum alloy pole, plastic grip, plastic basket, nylon strap **$30.00**
Olympic-Blue—Same as above with plastic strap **$25.00**

ATTENHOFER

Arosa—Aluminum, bi-conical shaft, plastic grip, plastic basket **$11.95**
Davos—Light metal bi-conical shaft, plastic grip. plastic basket **$15.95**
St. Moritz—Aluminum, bi-conical shaft, middle part square, rubber grip, plastic basket **$22.50**
Elite 1—Cylindrical steel shaft, plastic grip, rubber basket **$8.95**
Elite 2—Similar to above . . **$9.95**

BARRECRAFTERS

AP-5—Aluminum pole, leather grip, plastic basket—for beginners **$4.50**
AP-30 — Aluminum pole, soft vinyl racing grip, aluminum and rubber ring **$7**
AP-33—Polished aluminum, vinyl racing grip, rubber and aluminum ring **$12**
SP-50—Steel coated with nylon shaft, vinyl grip, aluminum and rubber ring **$12**
SP-70—Steel shaft, "quick flick" grip, rubber and plastic ring **$19**
AP-71—Aluminum pole, "quick flick" grip **$19**
Swing-Lite—Strong, light shaft, integrally molded ring, "quick flick" grip **$26**

BLIZZARD

Gold Crown—Aluminum shaft, contour rubber grip, aluminum and rubber basket **$24.95**
Tru Balance—Steel shaft, contour rubber grip, aluminum and rubber basket **$19.95**
Monarch—Steel shaft, contour rubber grip, aluminum and rubber basket **$14.95**

COBER
(baskets separate)

Airone—Light alloy, chrome finish shaft **$10.95**
Porthas—Aluminum alloy, black finish shaft **$8.95**
Aramis — Aluminum alloy, chrome finish shaft **$6.95**

Gemini—Aluminum alloy, red and black shaft **$15.95**
Gardena—Aluminum alloy, square shaft **$19.95**
Sapporo—Aluminum alloy, hexagonal shaft **$25**

ECKEL

7075—Metal alloy shaft, sword grip, 5 spoke plastic basket **$34.50**
Steel Deluxe—Steel shaft ½ gold plated, multigrip, 5 spoke basket **$39.50**
Duraflex Super — Lightweight shaft, sword grip, 5 spoke basket **$27**
Fantasia — Lightweight colored metal, colored multigrip, geometric design **$19.50**
Steel Deluxe — Chrome polish steel shaft, multigrip **$16.50**
Steel—Steel shaft, color plastic coating, plastic grip **$15**

FTC

Jamboree—Chrome-plated steel shaft, vinyl grip, rubber/metal basket **$8**
Avant — Aluminum shaft, vinyl grip, rubber/metal basket .. **$10**
Locus Great—Aluminum shaft, vinyl grip, rubber/metal basket **$12**

GERDAU

BK-52—Dual taper aluminum alloy shaft, contour rubber grip, rubber and aluminum basket **$16.50**
801 J—Steel shaft, rubber grip, rubber and aluminum basket **$11**
701 J—Similar to above .. **$8.50**
401 — Aluminum shaft, plastic grip, aluminum basket **$9**
201—Similar to above .. **$7.60**

GIPRON

Parabolic/70 .... **$18**

KERMA

Equipe—Metal alloy shaft, molded finger grips, plastic baskets, 5 prong tip **$30**
   With conventional tip.... **$25**

Slalom—Similar to above, maneuver shaft **$19.95**

KRYSTAL

Strato Pro — Aluminum shaft, contour grip **$15**
Varsity—Aluminum shaft, dual tapered **$10**
Red Hot—Aluminum shaft, thermo grip **$8**
Duralite—Aluminum shaft, thermo grip **$7**
Special—Aluminum shaft, thermo grip **$5.50**

MILLCO

Red Baron—Aluminum alloy shaft, vinyl contour grip . **$25**
Grand Prix—Aluminum alloy shaft, vinyl contour grip **$19.95**
Titan — Aluminum alloy shaft, vinyl contour grip **$13.95**
Nike—Plated steel shaft, vinyl contour grip **$10.95**
Galaxy—Aluminum alloy shaft, vinyl contour grip **$9.95**

MILLER

Deluxe — Lightweight, molded grip **$6.95**

NORTHLAND

Alolite—Aluminum shaft, custom left and right grip, aluminum/rubber basket **$18**
Rocket—Similar to above .. **$15**
Regal—Steel shaft, custom left and right grip, aluminum/rubber basket **$13**
Peerless—Aluminum shaft, molded grip, aluminum/rubber basket **$9**
Special—Similar to above **$6.50**

PRISMATIC

Blue—Hexagonal aluminum shaft; racing finger or standard contour grip; aluminum and rubber hexagonal basket ... **$24.50**
Gold—Hexagonal aluminum shaft; plastic contour grip; aluminum and rubber hexagonal basket **$18.50**

ROSSKOPF

Dual taper aluminum shaft, contour grip **$9.95**

SIDESLIPPING

Every ski patrolman knows the value of sideslipping, especially when bringing a toboggan down a steep slope.

Without a toboggan you can practice sideslipping that will pay off many times. Pick a slope with a decent pitch. If it happens to be icy, so much the better. Assume the traverse position and unweight to release your edges. Your descent should be straight. Now reset your edges and release them in a regular pattern. You should be literally walking down the slope with your skis together.

When you have the "action" down the way you want it, try a forward traverse. Release your edges as before as you run across the hill. Now set and release them to create a "fishtailing" pattern in the snow. (The skis fishtail, not you.) Add pole-planting on your next run by stabbing your downhill pole into the snow at or near the tip of your downhill ski. At the opposite end of the slope let your sideslip drift a little longer and then set your edges and at the time of your pole plant: unweight, thrust your heels across the fall line and — you know the rest.

SANDVIK

Tourist—Steel shaft contour grip, plastic basket **$9.50**
Sport—Steel shaft, finger grip, rubber basket **$12.50**
Elite — Chrome-plated steel shaft, finger grip, rubber basket **$15.50**

SCOTT

Olympia — Strong aluminum shaft, finger grip **$35**
Competition Superlight — Extra light aluminum shaft, finger grip, 4 prong ice point **$35**
Deluxe Steel—Lightweight steel, gold-plated top half, finger grip **$27**
Deluxe Aluminum — Aluminum shaft, finger grip **$27**
Model A—Aluminum shaft, contour grip **$25**
Standard Aluminum—Aluminum alloy shaft, finger grip . . . **$19.95**
Standard Steel—Lightweight steel shaft, finger grip **$19.95**
Basic Aluminum—Aluminum alloy shaft, contour grip **$14.95**
Basic Steel—Chrome over nickel plating, steel shaft, contour grip **$14.95**

TELEPOLE

Adjustable-length aluminum shaft, contour grip, metal/rubber basket **$13.95**

TOMIC

Dual Delux — Aluminum shaft, dual taper, finger grip, aluminum/rubber basket **$25**
Dual Standard—Similar to above, but not heat-treated **$18**
T-2 — Aluminum shaft, single taper, finger grip, alminum/rubber basket **$16**
T-3—Similar to above **$14**
T-5—Similar to above **$10**
Super Steel—Steel shaft, lightweight racing ring **$10**

ZENITH

#308 — Hexagonal steel shaft, contour molded finger grip, steel/rubber basket **$10**
#305—Chrome-plated steel shaft, molded rubber grip, aluminum/rubber basket **$8**
#304—Enamellized steel shaft, molded rubber grip, aluminum/rubber basket **$5**

CROSS COUNTRY, TOURING EQUIPMENT SKIS

ATTENHOFER

Lightweight wood skis with scaled base for easy climbing and gliding **$58.00**

BONNA

Similar to Trysil-Knut; hickory bottom, lignostone edges for light touring **$40.00**

BONNA

Snow Star—plastic top and bottom **$15.00**

HARTOLAN

Touring model, laminated birch **$30.50**
X-C model, same construction . . . . **$22.50-$29.50**

JAAKARHU

Plastic impregnated bottom, for light touring **$30.00**

LATU-KARHU

Birch bottom, hickory edges **$27.50**

LUMI-KARHU

Birch bottom, hardwood edges **$25.00**

REX

Similar to above **$25.00**

SILVA

40 Touring—laminated birch . . . . **$15-$21**
43 Touring—Birch with beech top, hickory edges . . **$27-$29.50**
75 Touring—Very strong hickory and birch, lignostone edges . . . . **$42-$47.50**
44 Mountain Touring—Laminated birch, beech top, steel edges . . . . **$38-$42**
42 Touring—Laminated birch, lignostone edges . . **$35-$37.50**

SPORT HOUSE

#120—Laminated birch, hickory edges **$26.00**
#150—Laminated birch with adjustable cable binding . . **$26.25**
Asnes—Hickory sole, lignostone edges **$37.00**
Sandstrom—Mountain ski, steel edges, wood base **$41.00**

TITAN

Super Racer—Epoxy laminates reinforced with thin steel wires, birch running surface **$27.50**
Combi Wood **$23.50**
Combi Fiberglass—Fiberglass laminates encase lightweight wood core **$50.00**

TRYSIL-KNUT

Hickory bottom, lignostone edges for light touring **$40.00**

TRYSIL-KNUT

All hickory bottom **$30.00**

BOOTS

ALPHA

For toe or heel **$30.00**

HENKE

Lightweight waterproof boot, also can be used for hiking **$28.95**

KARHU-KILPA

For toe bindings only **$22.50**

KARHU-LAPPI

For toe or heel bindings . . **$32.50**

KARHU-LATU

For toe or heel **$27.50**

KARHU-RETKI

For toe or heel bindings . . **$26.00**

KIKUT

For toe and heel bindings . **$32.50**

MONTEVERDE

Cross-country, leather upper and sole **$23.00**
Touring boot, leather upper, rubber sole **$24.50**

SILVA

Ski Jogger—Lightweight leather, composition sole **$30.00**
6241—Women's lined boot **$36.00**

SPORT HOUSE

Europa—Leather lined, medium weight **$26.90**
Marco—Rugged, for racing or touring **$27.90**
Turino—Lightweight, for light touring **$21.00**

VEPO

96—Lightweight leather boots (racing) **$30.50**
W188—Touring boots .... **$28.50-$29.50**

BINDINGS

ATTENHOFER

Light touring **$6.95**

EDSBYN-KABY

Adjustable toe plates, heel protector **$7.50**

GRESSHOPPA

Heel binding **$8.00**

KANDAHAR LOYPE

Heel binding **$8.00**

KANDAHAR LOYPE LETT

Heel binding **$10.00**

KILPA KARHU

Toe binding **$6.00**

KYMPPI

Y-shaped adjustable binding **$5.75**

MM KARHU

Toe binding **$6.00**

ROTTEFELLA FENIX

Toe binding **$6.00**

ROTTEFELLA SNABB

Toe binding **$6.00**

SEKUR

Touring bindings, cable with adjustable front throw release ....
.... **$9.00**

SILVA

Ski Jogger—Lightweight, adjustable toe piece and cable . **$8.95**

SPORT HOUSE

Touring Binding—Fully adjustable cable; adapts many outdoor boots for touring **$7.95**
Clamp Binding—"Rat trap" style leaves heel completely free . **$5.00**

VILLOM

Toe binding **$6.50**

POLES

ATTENHOFER

Bamboo pole **$6.95**

HARTOLAN

Bamboo pole, bent spike tip ....
.... **$7.90**

KARHU 1206

Leather handle, plastic ring ....
.... **$6.50**

KARHU 1216

Same as above, with broadened handle and layer basket ... **$7.00**

NORGE-SKI

According to length . **$5.50-$8.00**

SCOTT

Aluminum shaft, cork grip ....
.... **$25.00**

SILVA

Ski Jogger—Tonkin cane shaft, molded grip, plastic and leather basket **$6.00**

SANDVIK

Tourist—chrome-plated steel shaft, plastic grip **$9.50**

SPORT HOUSE

#302—Tonkin cane shaft, cork handle **$6.55**
#310—Bamboo cane shaft, plastic cover **$4.60**
Olympic—Fiberglass reinforced, cork handle, plastic basket ....
.... **$19.00**

Advanced Pointer

WARM-UP FOR WEDELN

Most athletes take time to warm up before starting out in any activity. Skiers should, too. Here is an exercise tieing in with snowplow turns that even the most advanced skier can profit from. It's not just to limber up those stiff muscles, but is a quick way to improve timing.

Starting in the straight snowplow, begin two or three snowplow turns in the fall line. As you gradually build up speed, employ more angulation of the upper body and more edging of the downhill ski. Let your skis come closer together as you pick up still more speed.

Plant your pole before each turn which, by now, should have developed into a stem christie, with enough side-slip between turns to keep you in the fall line. If your rhythm and form are correct at this point, you can let your skis come parallel and, by proper unweighting between turns, your wedeln should be in full bloom.

Be sure to pick a smooth and fairly open slope. If you find yourself "stepping out of a turn," stop right there and start over again. The completed run requires about 50 yards and can be confined to a 10-foot width. Repeat this sequence two or three times.

COME TOUR WITH ME

What a weekend of ski touring is like, and why

No one has been counting ski-tourers lately, but it looks like there are a whole lot more of them around than when Rudolph Mattesich first started promoting the sport, a recreational version of cross country, via his Ski Touring Council in 1962. Its current popularity, Mattesich believes, is the result of the new American thirst for physical fitness, on one hand, and the increasing cost and crowdedness of downhill skiing, on the other. And he points to convincing evidence that the sport really has caught on: Sales of touring equipment have jumped dramatically. Many ski areas now make room for tourers (Snowmass-at-Aspen offers trips daily, and Lake Placid recently opened 20 miles of touring trails).

The U.S. Ski Ass'n has launched a nationwide program of touring trips and workshops. The Boy Scouts of America recently added the activity to its winter camping program. And the operators of youth hostels and national parks are showing interest in tieing into the sport. Pictured here are scenes from a ski touring weekend sponsored by the Dartmouth, N. H., Outing Club. Photos were taken by Peter Arnold.

FRIDAY Ski touring itself is not nearly as structured as a ski touring *workshop* which educates newcomers about the sport, and helps veterans brush up on their techniques. About 200, many having traveled fair distances, showed up for this one and, after signing in and sitting through a lecture on touring basics, got down to the nitty-gritty — preparing their skis for the next day. In some cases this involved minor repairs like relocating the bear-trap bindings, in others, giving the ski bottoms their annual pine-tarring, with the help of a blowtorch.

SATURDAY A.M. Up bright and early to put running wax on the skis, maybe give them another lick with the blowtorch, and then go over to the local golf course and practice the quickly-mastered ski touring stride. There you also find out, by judging whether your skis slide too quickly or too slowly, if you've used the right wax on your bottoms. Maybe you should not have followed that chap's advice ("Oh, that's no good, put on a little more red Klister"). Ski tourers, like downhillers, can have grave discussions about what wax is best for conditions, and some even bring along thermometers to stick in the snow.

SATURDAY P.M. After lunch, the skiers break up into small groups, each led by one or two experienced guides, and go off on an extensive tour of the golf course, crossing fairways like crazy. Beginners fall once in a while because they are unused to the narrowness of the skis, or because a ski catches a root or something under the snow, but injuries practically never result. Touring speeds are slow, and when one does fall, the foot in its loose heel binding moves with the fall, avoiding strain. That night, a wild square dance, for tourers only.

SUNDAY By now everyone knows all there is to know about the sport, except the many wild and beautiful woodland places it can take you. Major tours are organized for the three-mile hike to the Fred Harris Cabin at the base of Moose Mountain, where a box lunch awaits, and back again. The woods are dense with birches and underbrush but the trails are well-maintained and a low-hanging branch is your major inconvenience. In defense of their sport, tourers always speak first of the satisfaction in being off in a quiet place remote from the world of men and affairs. If you are lucky, you will see rabbits, a few birds, and you may even spot where a bear has sharpened his claws on the side of a tree. It makes the day.

by **Karin Everson**

SKI TOURING IS A GROWING WINTER WORLD

How and why more and more Americans are strapping on those funny-looking, economical, easy-to-handle, mind-expanding cross country skis

Anyone can ski X-C. Cross-country skiing is new to America. But in Norway whole families, ages two to 92, spend days ski-touring through the forests and across mountains. Canadian Finns put their children on skis almost as soon as the children can walk. Five-year-olds race over a mile track for ribbons and cups.

With thin, light skis, ski touring (alias cross-country, ski jogging, and Nordic skiing) is more like jogging through the woods than crashing down an icy slope or plowing across a powdery hill.

Simple, inexpensive equipment makes ski touring available to anyone. Unlike downhill ski

equipment, only the toe of the light (one pound) X-C boot attaches to the ski (one and a half pounds). It is a soft-soled, flexible boot, comfortable for walking. The ski is about six feet long, and two to three inches wide. The binding is a simple clamp on the sole of the boot-toe, or a spring circling the heel. Poles help guide and propel the skier.

A family can be permanently equipped for ski touring for less money than one person would pay for a ski weekend in Aspen. Complete X-C equipment for one person costs less than $50. Children's equipment is even less — about $12 for skis and bindings.

Adult-size skis with bindings cost between $15 and $30. Boots are about $25, though a non-professional skier can do very well wearing galoshes or rubber boots. Downhill and X-C poles are interchangeable. Army surplus stores sell old touring equipment for even less.

X-C is a do-it-as-you-like-it sport. A tee shirt, sweater and light windbreaker with ski pants, or jeans with long johns are sufficient in the coldest weather. Dad's baggy old sweater is as fashionable as the latest slick plastic . . . perhaps even more so, because X-C is one of the least pretentious sports ever discovered.

The Washington's Birthday X-C jog in Marlboro, Vt., draws more entrants every year, many of them simple winter souls (as opposed to hardy competitive sorts) with a yen for the whiteness, silence and exhilaration of their sport.

Gaudy splendor has no part in X-C. Individual, aesthetic strength and an appreciation of natural beauty come to be central.

But X-C skiing is hard sport to find. There are no pamphlets describing the location of X-C haunts. It is a sport learned through experience not lessons.

Snow is the only prerequisite for exhilarating X-C skiing. A

What is the age range for cross country skiing? Ask Canada's Herman Smith Johannsen, aged 93, or Norway's Mette Seyersted, aged 2, here shown touring at Sun Valley.

backyard or a creekbed make excellent X-C ski territory. Skiing on a level or uphill is as natural as skiing down. Carving around a swing set, clothes pole, and across a small garden, the skier darts lightly forward. He steps alternately from one foot to the other, poling with each step. Repeated circling of the yard packs a solid two-groove track. The yard might be at home, around a dorm, or in a small park adjacent to a business area.

In a residential area, a ski loop could be set two or three blocks long through neighboring backyards. For the beginning skier it means no broken bones or twisted ankles. For the experienced skier it is a chance to ski when no one else can. For the dedicated jogger it is the perfect winter equivalent of a running workout.

Colleges and high schools are beginning to encourage trackmen to participate in X-C activities. This lengthens the training season, as well as providing an opportunity for distinction in two sports. And the fun is contagious. Professors in a small northern Michigan college ski cross-country to classes.

But X-C skiing need not be limited to backyards and spare moments. The banker who takes several loops before breakfast, and the student who slips into skis between classes have only begun.

A tour through a park or across fields is a mind-expanding experience: spending hours skiing alone on self-made paths, seeing a forest as no one has ever seen it, being a living, breathing part of the forest. One slips lightly along over drifts and across streams where a snowmobile would flounder.

In the almost unnoticeably light, flexible skis, one moves many times faster and easier than a man walking or in snow shoes. Nothing slows him but his own inclination to stop and listen to the silence of the trees.

Taking friends on an all day ski tour is as simple as a trip to a city park. And the more people involved, the easier it is to break a trail.

Several colleges around the country coach X-C skiers: in Colorado, Vermont, Macalaster in Minneapolis. High school students in Cloquet, Minn., have a well coached junior team. These teams travel hundreds of miles to race against individuals and other teams from all over the country.

The fastest way to find another X-C enthusiast is to contact regional offices of the U.S. Ski Ass'n (USSA) which increasingly is taking an interest in this phase of the sport.

Races are often held near popular downhill ski areas. X-C equipment is usually available in downhill shops. A few dealers still ask "X-C? What's that?" and try to sell downhill equipment instead. But with increasing demand, ski shops are stocking more X-C equipment. They are learning quickly that the spirit of the sport is new and refreshingly different from that of any other sport known today.

For a time yet the X-C skier will be an uncommon, unconventional occurrence on the American ski scene. But the weekend is fast approaching when the backyards and forests will be crisscrossed with as many ski trails as there are people on the slopes today.

ABOUT THE AUTHOR

The author, 23-year-old Karin Everson, was a member of the class of 1970 graduates at Mackinac College, Mich. She began skiing four years ago as part of the college's winter physical education program. She started racing cross-country in 1967. In 1968 she trained with the American women's Olympic cross-country ski team and in 1969 won the Central X-C Skiing Championship, Women's Division.

by Louise A. Colby

I'D WALK A MILE FOR A . . .

What it's really like to partake of
one of the most talked-about (if least frequented) adventures in skiing
—the trip to Tuckerman Ravine

It's a phenomenal creation of nature, a paradise for the die-hard skier, where the skiing season opens in April and extends through Memorial Day. It has a base of ±40 feet of snow, no ski lifts, and betweeen runs you can bask in the sun clad in your bathing suit. It's Tuckerman Ravine.

Located in northern New Hampshire at Pinkham Notch, Tuckerman is a huge snow bowl reached by hiking three miles up the state's highest mountain, 6,-288-foot Mt. Washington, and it offers challenging runs rated from expert to super-expert. The Headwall in the Bowl is .1 - .2 miles in length with a maximum pitch of 55°, the little Headwall has a run of 75 yards, 35° maximum pitch. Only a super-expert would attempt to ski over the Lip of the Bowl into the Headwall.

Skiing usually ends Memorial Day weekend, but there have been years, 1969 for instance, when skiing was extended into July due to continuous storms depositing additional feet of snow into the Bowl. Volunteer patrols advise you by megaphone if you're in an unsafe area. Skiing is permitted until 4 p.m.

You start by parking your car at the Appalachian Mountain Club base lodge. Accommodations are available at the AMC lodge or you can "rough it" by gathering your pack-frame, air mattress, sleeping bag, skis, boots, poles and suntan lotion, and hiking up the trail from the lodge. Suntan lotion is a necessity because of the rays from the sun and the reflections from the snow. Be sure to apply lotion to *all* exposed areas of your body. Take along your camera to capture extraordinary shots. It's advisable to wear hiking boots that have a thick sole and are at least ankle high. If you tie your skis onto your pack-frame, try on your pack at the base to make sure they're tied high enough so that the ends of your skis won't be digging at the back of your calves, but not so high that they clip

branches overhanging the trail. Either way you will be off balanced. Be sure your sleeping bag is rolled tightly and securely tied onto your frame. Use your poles as walking aids. The total preparation takes at least a half hour. When you're ready to start hiking, take a deep breath, don't rush and after 2½ to 3 hours you will reach the area (2.4 miles up) where sleeping accommodations are available at a small charge. There are several open-front shelters which in all can house 100 people. Facilities also include a shack available for gas cooking, tent sites, toilets, and a hut nicknamed "Howard Johnson's" where various snacks and

ski items may be purchased.

One April night my husband and I arrived at the base of the trail to Tuckerman. I had taken this route once before and I assured my husband we'd have no trouble finding sleeping space in the shelters. We prepared our gear in the parking lot aided by our headlights. It was a night of the total eclipse of the moon. It was very dark and very chilly. We started hiking at 9:30 p.m., each carrying a 50-pound pack, each guiding ourselves by flashlight.

If you were to climb the trail just for the day without much gear, you most likely would not have too difficult a time, but when you're weighed down, it be-

Hippies, oldsters, straight college kids, married folk and any other type you can imagine, gather every Spring to share in the warm and windy outdoor world of Tuckerman, one of the few places left in the ski world where a lift ticket means nothing.

comes a tedious process.

Just past the start of the trail, a sign is posted warning hikers not to attempt this climb unless they're in top physical condition.

We heard the roar of waterfalls and around the first bend, we arrived at the Crystal Cascade, which we would only be able to appreciate in daylight. Around the next bend the upgrade began. Breathing deeply with every couple of steps helped us from running short of breath. We forged on until we came to the first bridge about an hour later. Rather than remove our packs, we sat on the wooden rail of the bridge by first bending forward and aiming the ends of our skis over the water

and then sitting down, reminding each other not to lean backwards.

One-third of the journey was over. Another bridge was ahead followed by a few mild upgrades and we would be there . . . but it was still a long way off. We hadn't passed any hikers yet and this was an encouraging sign that there would be spaces available in the shelters to choose from before the weekend crowd arrived early the next morning. In the climb from the first to the second bridge, we had difficulty with slipping in the granular snow.

The last lap of the hike was very slow. We were getting progressively tired and it was approaching midnight. Finally we

turned the last bend and pushed onward until shortly after midnight we reached the clearing where the majestic snow-covered walls were in view. Our hike was over for the night.

But I had made a miscalculation. We checked out the various shelters and discovered the weekend crowd was *already* there. The college students were on vacation; it was a "No Vacancy" situation. Other weary hikers were scavenging the area. Two were sacked out beneath a picnic table surrounded by their gear in an attempt to shield themselves from the wind. We caught sight of the First Aid hut and decided to sleep inside of it, but found a patrol toboggan in storage. With *one* air mattress and two sleeping bags, we bundled up *under* the First Aid hut with a few sharp rocks to keep us company. The temperature went below freezing and the wind blew in gusts through my lightweight sleeping bag. People who don't think an air mattress is a necessity, should try sleeping outside on the ground below freezing temperatures at an elevation of over 3,800 feet without one. Those people back in the lodge didn't know what they're missing.

The next morning we arose to the sound of rifles shooting down the excess ice in the Headwall area to prevent hazardous slides.

After breakfast of fried eggs and ham, we donned our ski boots, gathered our skis, poles, camera and winebag and hiked the remaining half mile to the Headwall Floor. Once you're on the Floor of the Wall, it's a short climb to the Lunch Rocks where you can leave your belongings. We sat on the Rocks for an hour before we had built up enough courage to take our first run. We took our first steps up the Wall, stepping in the already frozen formed steps. We kept looking back, and after a few dozen steps, we decided we were high enough—for it was getting steep. Putting your skis on before you're ready to take your run isn't a good idea. It can cause slipping, falling, or having second thoughts of whether you'll ski down after all or walk back down and join the audience.

Our skis were adjusted, but before descending, I got the camera out from my kidney bag around my waist and took a picture of the Headwall area.

Our first run was a cautious one as we tried our best to keep in good form. After a run, which takes but a few minutes, you're hiking up the Wall again. We took a rest period of a half hour

before we made a couple more runs. There were hundreds of skiers there that weekend, and it was such a thrill watching the more expert skiers that we advanced to the Lunch Rocks and spent the rest of the afternoon sun-bathing and cheering the crowd on.

Occasionally onlookers will yell out in unison warnings such as "ICE," when it falls loose from the cliffs, or "LOOSE SKI," as a runaway zooms down the wall.

Memorial Day weekend brings out the exhibitionists, both the truly expert skiers who display their talents and the pretend-experts who display their foolishness. For example, on one such weekend we saw two men slide down the Wall in slickers, some came down on one ski, bikini-clad girls got whistles and applause for a run well done, and one daredevil accomplished a complete somersault in the middle of his run. But there was also the man who skied down the Wall not paying heed to the crossed sticks indicating a hole, and fell in head first. His skis, clipped crosswise on the surface, prevented him from completely disappearing. A pretend-expert who checked out the Lip area to connect to the Headwall ignored the patrol's warning relayed by megaphone. Onlookers, with hearts beating double-time, saw him fall over the Lip, over the rocks, and down to the Floor. The crowd and patrol rushed to him, but the skier got on his feet, brushed off the excess snow and walked away for another run with just a few scratches on his face. Fortunately nothing so exciting happened on that warm April day.

Towards late afternoon we descended back to the First Aid hut to gather our gear and look for more comfortable sleeping quarters. We found them to the rear of the Forest Ranger cottage below

the Lower Snowfield, next to a stream with a pile of hay available for our sleeping bags.

After a hearty meal of steaks, fried onions and peppers, we settled down in the dusk to enjoy the sounds of singing voices and guitars and the glow of campfires scattered throughout the area as we reminisced about the events and triumphs of the day.

It was considerably warmer than the previous night, warm enough to sleep in the open air very comfortably.

Sunday was another beautiful day, part of which we spent exploring the surroundings. Parallel to the connector trail between the Headwall and shelters is a trail more snow covered than the first. You have to be extremely careful not to side-step onto what seems to be hard packed snow. At this time of the year, melting is rapidly occurring below the surface and you might step on a soft spot and find your leg completely buried.

My husband and I were sun-bathing on the large boulders off the main connector when he heard running water. He put an empty water jug in his pocket and went to find the stream. He headed for the slope to the rear and descended below the rocks, stepping carefully, but suddenly he sank feet first to his waist. Only grabbing bushes growing near-by kept him from disappearing. I tried to banish all thoughts of what might have been the result had he not caught the bushes.

Our weekend was now more than complete. We gathered our goods, weighing considerably less.

The hike down was no trouble at all. It was daylight and we captured a few scenes with our camera. At the end of the trail we felt as if we had just left a different world. We had golden tans, and pictures to remind us of the enchantment of Tuckerman Ravine.

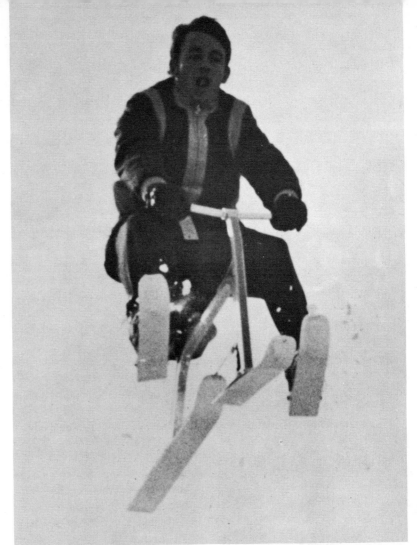

LET'S CALL IT A SKIBILL SKIBEN SKIBOB

The bikes-on-skis known as skibobs appear to have become permanent fixtures on the American snowscape, chiefly because they're fun

At a scattering of ski areas in recent winters, people saw skiers sitting down, not on the tails of their skis, but on skibobs. For many, the first glimpse of a skibobber was a surprise, a source of amusement and, finally, an invitation to try the winter world's newest sport themselves.

The same thing undoubtedly will happen again this season, only on a larger scale. Some areas will be offering skibobs for rent for the first time, and others will have at least a couple of the bicycle-like skiing machines around as an "experiment." Finally, a new organization—the American Skibob Assn. (ASBA) —will busy itself promoting the sport nationally.

Skibobbing's growing popular-

ity stems partly from the ease with which it can be mastered. The skibob itself is a metal or wooden frame with a seat and handlebars, mounted on two short skis front and rear. You wear even shorter skis on your feet in operating the contraption. Technique consists only of keeping your knees near the skibob, elbows near the body and foot skis parallel to the skibob skis. You steer with the handlebars; you slow down by pressing the heels of your foot skis into the snow. With a half hour's practice, anyone at any age can learn to skibob well enough to descend an intermediate trail as quickly and smoothly as an intermediate skier.

Actually, the first skibob was

invented by an American before the turn of the century, but it was not until Englebert Brenter perfected a model in Austria in 1947 that the sport took hold anywhere. Since then, skibobbing has grown by leaps and bounds in Europe, where an international skibob race circuit draws much spectator interest and press publicity.

The bulk of the estimated 300,000 European skibobbers, however, are the people who take it up for fun, not for glory, and a similar development may occur in this country. While skibob races have been held here, most of the sport's new adherents are recreational types.

Some ski areas look askance at skibobbing, perhaps in part because of the proletarian quality of a sport that can be learned in minutes, and mainly because of the tremendous maneuverability of the bike-on-skis. The turns a skier makes are predictable because he visibly prepares for every turn. Skibobbers, however, can turn in any direction almost

instantly. As a result, there is little danger that a skibobber will run into a skier. Conversely, however, because of the unpredictable path of the skibobber, it is more likely that he might be run into by a skier.

Some of the more ingenious participants in the new sport have built their own skibobs from old bicycle frames, but the homemade rigs don't compare with the European imports, primarily those from Austria which are the products of many years' experience. Presently, these imports cost from $50 for a junior model up to $200 for a top-flight adult model.

Skiers, as a group, think skibobbing is too easy to be fun. But those who try it have a ridiculous grin on their faces by the time they reach the bottom of the trail.

Views on this page are of skibobbing for pleasure—down a dramatic ridge in Europe, and on a chair in U.S. Opposite, competitive skibobbing, including a ragged turn by Jean-Claude Killy.

Andy Williams pushed off and started down an intermediate run at California's Mammoth Mountain. Eyes glued on the trail, he tried to remember all he had learned in ski school that morning. Without warning, a female skier zoomed into his path and came to an abrupt halt. Andy, normally more relaxed than a sleeping infant, lost his cool. He took a swan dive and half disappeared into the packed powder. As he checked to see if he was in one piece, the perpetrator of his spill herringboned over.

"I thought she was going to offer some words of comfort and apologize," Andy recalls. "Instead she gurgled, 'I finally caught you — now you've *got* to give me your autograph.'"

Unnerved, the golden-throated tenor hit a few off-key notes as he sang the blues at this autograph hound.

Such occurrences are becoming more and more common because scores of movie, TV, recording, and nightclub personalities have become addicted to skiing.

Gamboling in the Utah powder last season were Jane Powell, the Monkees, James Arness, Donald O'Connor, Natalie Wood, Adam West and Robert Redford. Taking the plunge at Aspen were Barbara McNair, Gregory Peck, Lucille Ball, Dan Dailey, Lee Marvin, James MacArthur, Eddie Albert, Herb Alpert, Elvis Presley, Katharine Ross, Mamie Van Doren, and John Wayne.

Schussing at Sun Valley were Jim Garner, Janet Leigh, Art Linkletter, Henry Mancini, Kim Novak, Jimmy Stewart, Robert Wagner, and Raquel Welch.

Heavenly Valley was the ethereal scene for Cliff Robertson, Debbie Reynolds, Ed Ames, Buddy Hackett, and Robert Goulet while bombing the Squaw Valley slopes were former ski instructor

SKIING AMONG THE STARS

Not all film folks spend their leisure time lolling around a swimming pool. More and more are discovering the delights of the snow-covered mountain and the "wide-open, clean feeling" of skiing

by Walt Roessing

Noel Harrison and Paul Newman.

Some of these beautiful people, and many more, also cavorted at such popular pads as Sugarbush, Vail, Banff, and in Europe.

Why has the Hollywood Set adopted skiing as its newest ritual?

Glenn Ford says, "Skiing is exciting, challenging, and it gets the adrenalin going." William Shatner, who spent three years in outer space on TV's "Star Trek," emphasizes, "It gives me the same thrill as flying, racing across the California desert on my motorcycle, or scuba diving." Art Linkletter tells his surfing friends, "It's like riding a 9,000 foot wave." Andy Williams says, "I like the wide-open, clean feeling, which gets me away from the rigors of TV, the concert trail, and recording sessions." Many, like "The FBI's" Efrem Zimbalist, Jr., enjoy the sport for its "sheer escapism from the real and often bitter world of the over-populated, polluted cities."

Box office giant Steve McQueen was 1970's most distinguished inductee into the skiing ranks.

Dorice Taylor, Sun Valley's proficient publicist, told me, "Steve McQueen was phenomenal as a beginner. He left the beginners' slopes in three days and was skiing fearlessly on Baldy. Since this was something of a record, a photographer was sent to get a picture. Steve refused. With his natural ability as an athlete at stake, he wasn't going to have his technique recorded until it was perfect. He told our photographer, 'You let me take a picture of you riding a motorcycle first.' The idea came across clearly and he wasn't bothered again."

Frequently victims of a bad press for their tantrums on the hyperactive Hollywood scene, personalities always seem at their best behavior in the serene surroundings of the mountain playgrounds.

A high-flying slats artist, who soared off a mogul and crash landed, forgot his pain riding down the Heavenly Valley tram to the first aid room thanks to the comical seven-minute monologue performed by Debbie Reynolds. The mischievous actress also kept the employees in hysterics by answering the manager's phone and identifying herself as the new secretary—Debbie Reynolds.

While trying to catch up in technique with his family at the same Lake Tahoe resort, Buddy Hackett gave Yiddish lessons to his Austrian instructor.

Producer Ray Stark of "Funny Girl" fame has supported Sun Valley's junior racing program for the last two years. He made the films "Funny Girl" and "In His Majesty's Secret Service" available for fund raising showing in the Opera House.

"The star of a TV series must devote himself to perfect health," professes Zimbalist. "A serious injury could cost a studio millions. For this reason, I don't ski with great abandon."

Songstress Kay Starr had to give up the sport after suffering a spiral fracture of her right leg, Eddie Albert incurred a broken shoulder, and Natalie Wood cracked one of her curvaceous ankles.

However, you might say that the limbs of all male skiers are

At top: TV's Cartwrights in an early version of the snowmobile. Middle row: James Garner, Efrem Zimbalist, Jr., of FBI fame, and lovely Kim Novak. Bottom row: Andy Williams and wife, and John Wayne, riding a new hoss.

in danger when beauties like Natalie, Barbara McNair, Kim Novak, Raquel Welch, Claudine Longet, Katharine Ross, Mamie Van Doren, and Janet Leigh slither onto the slopes. Control skiing would seem impossible, under the circumstances.

Dick Barrymore has seen the most spectacular sights in Skidom as a globe-girdling cinematographer-producer. But he loses his cool when he talks about the contours of Jill St. John. "She is unbelievable in ski clothes," he growls. "And she can ski, too."

However, the zenith of fashion is reportedly Janet Leigh.

A fashion writer hurried to her electric typewriter after first seeing Janet skiing in a completely black outfit — black fur parka, black pants, black hood — and then in the evening noticing her at a cocktail party in a mind-boggling gold mini-skirt. She wrote, "Colors are out, black is definitely the thing, and for evening wear, mini-skirts have taken over from apres-ski pants." The next day the fashion writer was thrown an unexpected curve when Janet appeared as colorful as a canary in a bright yellow outfit — and that night wore apres-ski slacks with a brocaded top.

Maybe the most envied woman in or out of a ski suit last season was French actress Danielle Gaubert. The Gallic beauty is an accomplished skier, to be sure. But her traveling companion and ski instructor at Squaw Valley was an up-and-coming personality named Jean-Claude Killy.

More stars: top row: Janet Leigh and Adam (Batman) West; middle row: David McCallum and Paul Newman; bottom row: Art Linkletter in pre-race prayer, and Buddy Hackett.

IT'S A BIRD ...IT'S A PLANE ...IT'S A ...SKI JUMPER?

*Whatever the viewpoint—
on the ground or in the air—
jumping is one of the
big thrillers in ski competition*

by Frank Elkins

...SKI JUMPER

Notwithstanding the phenomenal development of downhill and slalom running, ski jumping continues unchallenged as the most spectacular and dangerous of winter sports.

Ski jumping calls for more nerve than any sport we can think of, flying, polo, bob-sledding and motor-car racing not excepted. It is a lone wolf game. The jumper climbs to the roof of the world and catapults himself down a precipitous runway into an aching, dazzling void of sun-reflected whiteness. He must choke down an overpowering sense of isolation as he toes the mark at the top of the speedy inrun. Even veteran flyers don't care to hang around the starting line too long, peering into the abyss below. It gives them the fidgets.

There are two important phases to a typical ski jump hill. The first half of the downrun (chute) is called the inrun. This may be either a natural slope or an artificial slide buttressed by steel or wooden trestles. It usually measures 300 feet in length, depending upon the length and profile of the hill, and cants downward at a pitch calculated to give a fly the vertigo.

Upon this declivity, the ski jumper whips up momentum for the actual take-off, the platform leading into space.

At the lower extremity of the starting hill is a snowcovered platform, either raised on stilts or built up about ten feet or more above the ground. It may also be a natural "take-off" as the platform is called.

The platform is the jumping-off place, the stage from which the skier must hurtle into nothingness. At that moment, in his express-train descent, he hasn't time to do much worrying. He couldn't stop if he wanted to. For him, it is the edge of the world, and beyond lies an expanse of emptiness comparable, at least in the jumper's imagination, to the Grand Canyon.

Below and beyond the take-off lies the second phase of the hill, which slants down at a dizzy grade of 35 degrees or more to a level terrain some three or four hundred feet ahead.

The ski rider soars along a breathtaking parabola, high above the steep slope of the landing hill as distinct from the starting hill, which gave him impetus. By the aid of the approach and a powerful self-actuated lift, the jumper glides into space entirely free and unhindered. The air buzzes as in a storm while all the lower run is scanned for a satisfactory landing space on the transition.

He covers about 800 feet, depending upon the hill's profile, to the spot where the jumper finally comes to an end with a stylish "Telemark" or "Christiania" turn. The thrilling journey involved a vertical drop of about 400 feet.

The jumper's skis actually cleave empty space for about three to five seconds, though to the onlookers below he seems to have suspended in mid-air during that many minutes. The illusion of an interminable flight heightens suspense as breaths are sucked in and fingernails dig into palms.

It is not only the spectator who is thrilled with a graceful jump on skis. The fact is the skier himself is vastly more thrilled. It is an experience electrifying to every nerve. True, the sensation lasts but a few seconds, but it feels like an eternity. Even so, after the surest and steadiest landing, disappointment mingles with joy: Oh, that it might have lasted, yet a little longer!

Preceding page shows John Balfanz, America's strongest ski jumper, now retired, in action. Opposite top left, is a view, from the top, of Lake Placid's Intervales Hill, long a training ground for U.S. jumpers. Below, Bjoern Wirkola of Norway prepares to unleash another record-setting leap. Wirkola, perhaps the world's greatest jumper, is also shown at top right, above photo of fellow countryman, rival, Lars Grini.

TIPS FROM GREAT INSTRUCTORS

If you've ever had the feeling you could learn to ski better *faster* if there weren't quite so many students in your class or—ultimate luxury—if you had an instructor all to yourself, then consider this: *10* of the country's top ski instructors, directors of the 10 most prestigious ski schools, each with a special suggestion to help you improve your technique.

Need to improve your co-ordination? Paul Valar describes some helpful exercises to do before you reach the slopes. Swiss champion Roger Staub points out the importance of the hips in skiing. Wondering how to handle powder? Alf Engen tells you. Bob Gratton explains ways to treat moguls as a bonus instead of a bugaboo. Olympic champion Penny Pitou and husband Egon Zimmermann offer special advice for women who need to put more aggression in their skiing for better control. Suggestions for over-40 beginners who lack confidence come from Taos Valley's Ernie Blake.

Sometimes the advice is philosophical, as when Neil Robinson adds an off-the-cuff reminder, "You can't ski all day and drink all night and expect to do either well." Sometimes it's mechanical, like Luggi Foeger's admonition to "Keep your fanny forward." Sometimes it may sound funny, like madcap mentor Fred Iselin's advice to leap like a ballet dancer, and Jack Nagel's talk-to-yourself technique. But all of it is practical, designed to get you down the hill faster, safer, and more gracefully than you've ever done it before.

Some of the ski school directors featured in this section are, clockwise from the top: Bob Gratton, Roger Staub, Fred Iselin, Neil Robinson, Ernie Blake, Luggi Foeger and Egon and Penny Pitou Zimmermann.

SHAPE UP
WITH SHORTSWING JUMP

Paul Valar, CANNON MOUNTAIN, NEW HAMPSHIRE: *"Most adults today come to an instructor to learn co-ordination, which they could learn faster, better, and cheaper with the right exercises on the living room floor."*

The Shortswing Jump is an excellent pre-season conditioner which simulates the body's movements during a parallel turn. To do it, stand erect with feet together and knees bent, arms slightly out to the sides and upper body slightly forward. Swivel on your toes quickly from side to side, moving your feet as a single unit and covering about six inches with each jump. As you jump to the left, land so that your heels are slightly farther away from center than your toes. The upper body remains almost stationary, though the shoulders swing around, counter to the knees, to create the distinct comma position. Arms move from side to side, opposite the knees, as in an exaggerated traverse. When this becomes easy, try lifting your inside foot from the floor at each jump.

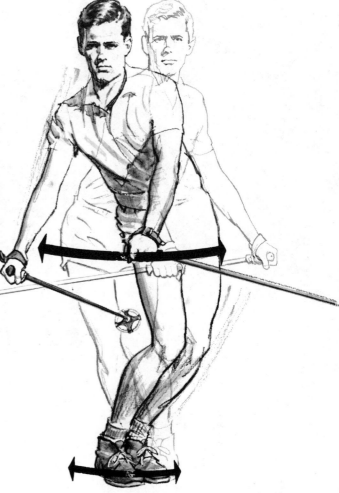

...AND THE HEEL-AND-TOE WALK

For strong supple legs, practice this one: Stand erect with feet together. Take a step forward, placing your weight on your left heel. Follow with a step landing on your right heel. Now a step landing on the ball of your left foot, then your right, then back to your left heel, and so on. This exercise is particularly good for women as it stretches the Achilles tendon which is often contracted from walking in high-heeled shoes.

Five minutes a day or two or three 15-minute sessions a week is enough for these exercises.

USE
YOUR HIPS FOR CONTROL

Roger Staub, VAIL, COLORADO: *"Your hips are perhaps the greatest source of power in turning, traversing, and straight running. But your hips must be positioned properly for them to do any good."*

If you ski with knees and ankles properly flexed but with your upper body bent forward and your hips out behind, you are giving up much potential turning power. The proper way to make a turn and to hold a good traverse is to use your hips as the central power source. If you're trying to hold a clean traverse, you must have your downhill ski clearly weighted. If your hips are forward with their weight concentrated over your boots, you'll feel the pressure along the outside calf of your downhill ski. Ride farther back, though, and the pressure disappears and the next thing you know you've got your weight on the uphill ski. The forward position does not reduce the need for the "reverse," with the hips facing down the hill.

Correct hip placement is important from the standpoint of positive skiing and comfort. The illustrated figure is shown in the desirable position for straight-running. For a traverse, the hips would remain substantially the same, but the knees would press into the hill to achieve angulation. The outlined figure depicts what many consider an acceptable stance, but his exaggerated forward lean radically reduces the turning power of his hips.

Rotary action with the hips is most important, but since it doesn't come naturally it must be learned. You can be physically fit and still not have supple hips. Side-to-side stretching exercises can help remedy the situation.

MAKE THE HOP TO SKIDDED TURNS

Neil Robinson, GLEN ELLEN, VERMONT:
"Suppleness and speed make all the difference between 'steered turns' and 'skidded turns'."

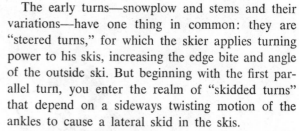

The early turns—snowplow and stems and their variations—have one thing in common: they are "steered turns," for which the skier applies turning power to his skis, increasing the edge bite and angle of the outside ski. But beginning with the first parallel turn, you enter the realm of "skidded turns" that depend on a sideways twisting motion of the ankles to cause a lateral skid in the skis.

The illustrated figure has just come down in his turn and his skis will just now begin to skid. The ragged marks to the left of the figure depict the path made by a steered turn. The ski tracks are heavier than those left by the parallel skier and are more exhausting.

In order to achieve sufficient unweighting for the skidded turn you must carry some speed. At higher speeds your skis seem to leave the ground almost by themselves and skid effortlessly to the new direction. But when you're going slow you have to really pick them up to unweight them and yank them around to make them skid.

A good exercise to practice is the "hop," the actual physical lifting of the tails of the skis off the snow. The knees are vital to all skiing and especially to unweighting. The down-up motion involves the knees to great measure. You must have the suppleness and fluidity to sink for the unweighting and then spring up and forward on the actual unweighting.

WATCH SHOULDER POSITION IN A TURN

Alf Engen, ALTA, UTAH: *"Whether it's powder or hardpack, you ski them basically the same—the difference is in degree. In either situation, if you drop one shoulder, your weight is badly distributed."*

Proper shoulder position in a turn is with the downhill shoulder slightly back and with both shoulders parallel to the surface of the slope, as in the illustrated figure. In the outlined figure, the skier has dropped his inside shoulder and has held them "square" over his skis, which makes proper weight distribution impossible.

...AND WATCH YOUR WEIGHT IN DEEP POWDER

Weight placement is different when you ski powder. Concentrating your weight on your ski tips as you do in hardpack would cause them to dive too deep in powder. So you make your ski-snow contact through the balls of your feet. This doesn't mean you sit back on your heels. Keep a good knee and ankle bend and a straight back, but ride somewhat farther back on your feet until you plane through the powder at the proper depth.

Unweighting is different, too. In powder it's as if you have a surface all around your skis, not just beneath them. So instead of the violent unweighting and edge-setting used on hardpack, change your course gently. Do this in the beginning with a small unweighting movement accompanied by a rolling of the knees in the direction you wish to turn. This results in establishing a new surface on which to slide. The upward curve of your ski tips guides the skis in a new direction.

SKI MOGULS TO IMPROVE TECHNIQUE

Bob Gratton, MT. SNOW, VERMONT: *"Skiing* over *moguls is a good way to learn to start your turns, but skiing* around *them is a great way to improve balance."*

Contour skiing means skiing with the hill and making your turns flow in a logical rhythm. It is achieved by skiing the "valleys"—picking turns to cut against the sides of moguls so that the moguls form a platform of resistance. In that way, you can ski faster and at the same time under better control than if you skied the moguls with a straight up and down body position, as in the outlined figure. The key to contour skiing is positive edge control; you must keep your skis tracking cleanly at all times as you round the mogul. The knees press forward during the turn and the hip stays out over the edges to compensate for centrifugal force.

Skiing *over* the moguls is a very good way to learn to start your turns, a phase of parallel skiing of great importance. As you ski across the top of a mogul, there comes a time when only the portion of the ski beneath your boot is touching the snow; the tip and tail are not in positive contact with the snow. At that instant the resistance to changing direction is much less than normal; you can pivot or turn your skis easily.

Of course, in practice you combine both kinds of contour skiing in a single run.

AIM FOR
GOOD FORWARD BALANCE

Luggi Foeger, SKI INCLINE, NEVADA: *"It is almost impossible to ski well, especially in parallel turns, with your weight on your heels. Keep your fanny forward!"*

A good natural position on skis is one which closely resembles a relaxed position when standing on the ground. When you stand, you don't stick your rear end out, and your weight is evenly distributed with the majority of it on the forward part of your feet.

If you are sitting back on your skis, which means with knees bent and fanny sticking out behind you, your weight—or power—cannot act on the tips of your skis. This also means that your weight is being supported by your muscles, rather than your bones, which is very tiring. But this doesn't mean you should stand up like a stick and just lean forward. It is important that your knees be bent, but not so much that they force your fanny out behind you.

A proper downhill stance finds the skier with knees and ankles flexed to act as shock absorbers, upper body comfortably erect and hips forward. In this position the skier's weight is concentrated on the balls of his feet to afford precise tracking, clean turns, and increased stability. The outlined figure represents the common—though incorrect—body position found in many learning skiers. Though knees and ankles are flexed, the upper body is exaggeratedly forward and hips are back. Weight is concentrated on heels which results in poor turns, wavy tracking, and increased likelihood of backward falls.

FALL LINE

CHECK INSIDE POSITION OF SKI

Ernie Blake, TAOS SKI VALLEY, NEW MEXICO: *"Adults who are learning to ski often have trouble with the unweighting necessary for parallel turns. There is a way to overcome this."*

Adults, because of a certain amount of stiffness and some understandable apprehension, often learn to ski more slowly than children. They progress all right to the point of parallel turns, but then many confront a specific problem: unweighting their skis so they can get into the air and make their turns through the fall line. An exercise for overcoming this, of value to any beginning parallel skier, whether you're 15 or 55, is the position check.

Unweight your skis and start the turn. Then, as you're arcing around, lift the tail of your inside ski four to six inches off the snow. If you're in the proper position, with weight concentrated on the outside or downhill ski and hip and shoulders correctly placed, you can do it without losing balance—as in the illustrated figure. But if, as in the outlined figure, you're splitting your weight between the two skis, you'll feel insecure and start to fall. A good comma position, knees and hips into the hill, shoulders facing downhill, will make it possible to do this exercise without losing your balance.

PRACTICE
THE CHECK HOP GARLAND FOR
EDGE CONTROL

Egon and Penny Pitou Zimmermann,
GUNSTOCK, NEW HAMPSHIRE: *"To ski precisely, use your edges to begin and end each turn sharply. Women skiers, particularly, need to learn to use their edges."*

Women are neither as strong nor as aggressive on skis, and it's hard for them to ski well under adverse conditions, like ice. Women also have a tendency to sit back on their skis. They must learn to use their edges.

The check hop garland is one of the best exercises available for improving edge control—for men as well as women skiers. Move across the slope in a shallow traverse (heavy dotted line) with your body in the normal edging position of the figure in the sketch. At the start you are moving forward only; there's no sideslipping action at all. After a few feet, release your edges so that the tails of your skis slide below the line of your traverse (heavy arrow). Then, planting your downhill pole, raise yourself up —unweight—and "hop" the tails of your skis back to or slightly above your original traverse line (dotted arrow). Do the exercises in series, and you will obtain an excellent feeling for edge control.

Edges are like brakes; if they're not strong, or you don't trust their ability to stop you, you'll sit back on your skis because you won't dare lean out over them. When you feel you can rely on your edges, you'll acquire a greater degree of control in your skiing, and more confidence.

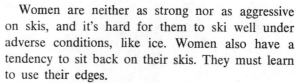

FALL LINE

"FLOAT" THROUGH YOUR TURNS

Fred Iselin, ASPEN HIGHLANDS, COLORADO: *"Get light on your skis, like a ballet dancer. That's the only way you can get* lift *at the beginning of your turns."*

FALL LINE

Floating through a turn means unweighting your skis after the check phase to the point where all but the tips leave the snow. Once airborne, it is a simple matter to deflect the now weightless skis with hip and heel thrust. Intermediate skiers will want to practice this maneuver against a mogul. As you approach the bump, set your edges on the near side as you sink to coil your body. Then, instead of simply coming up enough to unweight your skis, actually leap up and *forward* (arrow), twisting your skis as you rise.

When you go up and forward you float, and that is the way to ski!

"TALK" YOURSELF TO PARALLEL

FALL LINE

DOWN . . .

UP . . .

AROUND . . .

Jack Nagel, CRYSTAL MOUNTAIN, WASH-INGTON: *"We explain skiing maneuvers in catchy phrases the student can remember. I call it the Cadence Method."*

The Cadence Method has been developed to answer one of the biggest questions most students have: "How do I turn?" It is an aid to the mind more than the body, since it represents a different "approach" to turning rather than a different "technique." The Cadence Method explains ski maneuvers in terms of catchy little sing-song phrases that are easy to remember as you "talk" yourself through a maneuver.

The parallel turn, for example, is broken down into four operational phases: edge set, unweighting, shift through the turn, and the final edge set which ends one turn and begins the next. This is translated into "Down-Up-Around-and-Down" in a syncopated meter timed to the turn itself. Here's how to do it:

While you are skiing, you count off in a syncopated beat DOWN (to set the edges, bend the knees, and plant the pole); UP (to extend the legs, unweight the skis and remove the pole); AROUND (to deflect the skis from their course and begin them skidding through the fall line); and finally, DOWN (to reset the edges and return to a new traverse). The final DOWN, which has been omitted from the illustration, is the same as the first one and starts the next turn.

WHAT AM I AND MY WATER BOTTLE DOING TONIGHT?

by Lora Heller

So this is the year you've decided to start skiing. Be forewarned that most of skiing is absolutely detestable. The single, really beautiful thing about skiing is actually *skiing,* coming down the mountain. And that is so beautiful, such a thrilling use of flesh and bone, that in order to do it some 10 or so times in a given day, most skiers will put up with all the wretched rest of it — the getting up at a foul hour in the morning, the getting dressed in clothes that threaten to make you anoxic (short on oxygen). the loading up of gear, and the driving over icy mountain passes in total whiteouts. Lugging your skis, poles, and boots from the parking lot to the base lodge will generally be enough to make you feel you've already over-exercised and hyper-ventilated for the day.

And it's only 9:30!

Waiting in lift lines will give you agoraphobia, the lunchroom will give you claustrophobia, and riding the chairlift will give you vertigo.

If, after taking all this into account, you are still determined to start to ski this year, permit me to offer a few words of advice not generally found in ski magazines or on the back of your lift ticket.

EQUIPMENT No matter what conservative, practical types tell you, you should immediately sink as much money as you possibly can into your equipment. Never mind the quality, just make sure it costs an awful lot. Do this *before* your first lesson. The first lesson is an absolute horror, but if you've got $120 invested in your boots alone, you won't *dare* quit.

The second lesson is worse — you will be required to ride the lift. If you've got $180 sunk in your skis alone, you won't dare *not* ride it.

CLOTHING The skier's most important article of clothing is the zipper. With a good zipper you can get at your money, cigarettes, comb, and tissue. Without money, cigarettes, comb, and tissues, it won't matter much what you're wearing.

With a good zipper you can use the bathroom. If you can't use the bathroom, it won't matter much what you're wearing.

Novice skiers, especially women, would do well to avoid wearing ski pants in colors like shocking pink. The snowplow does not bring out the best in you. As a matter of fact, next to childbirth, it is about the most graceless position life will probably ever demand of you.

Except for minor variations on the theme, everyone on the slopes looks basically like everyone else. It's one of the pleasant things about skiing — this democratization of dress — for those who can afford it.

CONDITIONING Do at least half of the following exercises daily for 10 months before the season opens:

1. Oil your zipper.

2. Holding your poles in your inside hand, look over your outside shoulder while someone slams a heavy iron chair into the backs of your knees.

3. Put on your ski boots and side-step down the bowling alley.

4. Smear your nose with zinc oxide ointment and sling a wineskin jauntily over your see-through cocktail dress.

5. Put on your thermal underwear and herringbone up the tennis court.

6. Practice doing kick turns in a hotel elevator.

7. Paste a fresh "Think Snow" sticker on your bumper.

8. Eat skimpy, dried out, lukewarm hamburgers for lunch.

9. Put your skis on and swim two lengths of the pool.

THE KIDS Since you're a novice, everyone on the slopes will ski better than you. It doesn't hurt so much to admit to yourself that your instructor's form is, perhaps, a bit more graceful than yours; what does hurt are those six year old kids! There are two factors that enable little kids to ski straight down the fall line of any slope in a racing crouch. The first is that the anatomy of a six-year-old skier is 90 per cent ankles. They're *made* of ankles (the other 10 per cent is puppy dogs' tails). The second factor is that six-year-old kids are stupid. Not fearless — don't look at it that way — they're just plain stupid. For instance they haven't any idea at all of how many bones in an adult's body can break, twist, splinter, crunch, fracture, grind, crush, pop, or split — or of the myriad variations and combinations thereof. Ask any little kid — he thinks a bone is something you pull apart to make a wish on.

Obviously no kid should be allowed on the ski slopes until he has sympathy for and veneration of his elders.

MAIDEN VOYAGE There's no trick to it at all — if you can somehow get the operator to stop the chair as you get on and again as you get off. However, since non-novice skiers don't like to have the lift constantly stopping, there has to be a good cause for the operator to do it. He will stop the lift for you if —

1. One leg is in a cast.

2. You are carrying a bottle of imported French rosé. (I haven't any idea why the lift was stopped for me that day — unless it was out of respect for the wine.)

If nothing else seems to work, you might consider threatening the area management with a ski-in, for which you organize a group of skiers who noisily gather around the ski school bell, present their demands, chant, "No siree! We won't ski!" and defiantly burn their lift tickets. Lots of luck.

LESSONS Ski lessons are absolutely essential. For one thing, by providing useful work, they keep ski instructors, those handsome devils, off the streets.

For another, as everyone knows, there's a right way and several wrong ways to do everything. Ski lessons will show you the *right* way to break your leg.

Choose your lesson group carefully. Nothing is so detrimental to a novice skier's self-confidence as being hopelessly outclassed by his cohorts. Choose a group in which there are no six-year-old kids made of steel ankles, no athletic young men in far better physical condition than you, and no women at all more attractive than you. If you can manage to get in with the Dade County Golden Age Ski Club, you've got it made.

Choose your instructor equally carefully. You'll have to live with him for a whole hour, but it will seem closer to 10 years.

In the student-instructor relationship, it is essential for the survival of whatever is left of your ego that you immediately assume control. If you don't, the instructor will take you up to the top of something and — unbelievable as it sounds—*make you ski down!* Instructors not only do that but apparently even take some perverse pleasure in doing it. To avoid it, there are a number of remarks you can make, all guaranteed at the least to throw him off stride and, if you're lucky, to break his spirit completely.

1. On meeting him, look him slowly up and down, smile gently, and tell him you happen to *like* older men with a bit of a paunch. Really you do.

2. On the lift, with the mountain a-dazzle below you, ask him what is a nice guy like him doing in a dump like this.

3. Ask him to show you how to do the Telemark.

4. Tell him that skiing Suicide Schuss is against your religion; you happen to be an Orthodox Chicken.

5. Pinch your nostrils together yell "Death before dishonor!" and leap off the chairlift.

The last may seem a bit overdramatic, but it seems a lot less so when you remember the alternative — that if you let him get you to the top of something, he'll *make you ski down!*

If you take these ski tips to heart, you will be sitting on top of the world — with no way of getting down! But it's amazing how many people have learned to ski under just these circumstances.

HIGHLY SPIRITED SKIS

They may not show as much form as your better recreational long-ski type, but wine-barr

A graceless, thoroughly idiotic, and sometimes mildly painful off-shoot of ski racing is appearing on western slopes from California to Colorado. Called barrel-stave racing, it is mushrooming in popularity because it provides a laugh a second for spectators and participants, features bizarre costumes in team encounters, and gives rank beginners as much chance to win as an expert skier.

There are two particularly wacky aspects to this so-called sport.

First, instead of using skis, you race on two rounded staves from barrels. In many western areas, the staves come from 50-gallon wine barrels belonging to Paul Masson Vineyards, which sponsors a racing program. Killington Ski Area in Vermont, creator of the sport in the east, uses solid oak slats originally designed for making whisky barrels. In any case, the 30-inch-long staves offer virtually no support.

"Ridiculous things happen to the best skiers when they first try to ski on staves," reports Jim Friedman of Paul Masson. "As there are no edges, and since the ski base is curved like a rocking chair, the normal forward lean of a skier promptly rolls him head first into a snowbank. If he sits back, he gets the same reaction, only he falls on his caboose. It gets hilarious."

However, some advanced technology has been adopted. Until

recently, you merely prayed that your feet would stay on the staves as your tootsies were held perilously in place by loose-fitting toe straps and shoestring-thin thongs. Many staves now feature steel edges, cable bindings, and plastic bottoms.

The second wacky element surfaces during the team encounters. When two competing racers attempt to simultaneously swing through a common gate from opposite sides, it's havoc.

Some barrel-stavers actually reach the finish line in a normal, upright position. But most either crawl across the finish on all fours, ski across on one stave, or do a little of both with one or two broken staves lashed to their ankles. Often, when team races are exceptionally close, spectators will leap onto the course and tackle a member of the opposition.

Obviously these are spirited encounters. In fact, it might be worth staging a meet between East, strapped into whisky barrel staves, and West, with its wine barrel staves. May the highest spirit win.

A typical barrel-stave race at Bear Valley, Calif., featured the usual display of fallen bodies and dubious slalom styles. Since most of the participants crossed the finish line on their hands and knees, there frequently were grave discussions with race officials about the rules.

stave racers, like blondes, sometimes have more fun **by Walt Roessing**

STATUS REPORT ON

SNOWMOBILES by Seth King

Twilight shadows were darkening around the Chanticleer Inn, Eagle River, Wis., and the clean, feathery north woods snow thickened the heavy silence.

Suddenly the quiet exploded. Volleys of noise shook the snow-plastered spruce and birch trees, and three snowmobiles, belching gasoline fumes and trailing sleds filled with shouting children, churned off toward the inn's network of snowmobile trails.

A year or two ago the likelihood of seeing five adults and nine children charging through the 20-degree evening air just for the fun of it would have been rare.

But today this group of enthusiasts from nearby Eagle River was only one of many among the 60,000 Wisconsin residents who now own snowmobiles. The adjoining state of Minnesota has just issued its 108,000th snowmobile permit, and by the end of 1969, in the "snow belt" states from Washington to Maine, 225,000 had been sold, eight times as many as had been sold five years ago.

The multiplication of the sleek little vehicles has meant a new and exuberant form of recreation for thousands in areas where the snow piles up from late November till early April and below-zero temperatures help form the life style.

"What else would we be able to do around here except sit in front of the television and snarl

Pleasure snowmobilers almost always travel in groups, as at left.

at the children?" asked Jack Armstrong, an Eagle River radio broadcaster who heads the local snowmobile club. "We wouldn't want to miss such a nice evening when we have machines like this in our front yard."

The enthusiasm of Armstrong has been echoed across the northern United States by newly mobile ranchers, repairmen, housewives and policemen. It has also spurred a new multimillion-dollar industry and has evoked nightmares for skiers, conservationists, municipal officials and property owners along some snowmobile routes.

Ten deaths in snowmobile accidents were reported in Minnesota last winter. One of these occurred when the snowmobile broke through some thin ice and the rider drowned. Another rider was struck by a Great Northern Railway train on a right-of-way, and elsewhere a 12-year-old girl piloting a snowmobile got her scarf caught in the treads and was strangled. In Michigan, 11 snowmobile deaths and 550 injuries were reported during a recent winter.

With concern growing about the vehicles' safety as well as their noise, the snowmobile industry has become increasingly worried over demands for more stringent regulations.

Through the relatively simple combination of a light, two-cylinder engine, a fiberglass body, skis and a tank-like driving tread, the manufacturers have produced a conveyance that can spin over all but the deepest and softest snow at more than 50 miles an hour.

To drive a snowmobile one needs only to squeeze the throttle lever on one handlebar and hang on. The vehicle can climb formidable slopes, and an experienced rider can keep it upright on a rolling, pitching surface.

While a snowmobiler's thirst for exposure may be hard for some to understand, it has been clearly demonstrated all over the nation by family picnics in the deep woods, moonlight jaunts across the meadows, and enormous gatherings for races.

Last season members of a Denver snowmobile club made a 70-mile trip over Cottonwood Pass in a blizzard.

In one of the newest diversions in the Far West, the Ellensburg, Wash., snowmobile club has been ferrying mountain climbers up to the 6,000-foot level of 12,300-foot Mount Adams. From there the climbers put on snowshoes for a weekend of winter mountaineering, made possible by the snowmobiles, which in a few hours eliminated an approach march that would take a day or two on foot.

In Eagle River the town's adult snowmobilers frequently gather on the outskirts just before the cocktail hour and roar off to the White Stag, 10 miles across the fields, or to another of the area's many taverns and restaurants, some of which were once open only in the summers but now remain open all winter.

In Acadia National Park at Bar Harbor, Me., the old car-

riage roads built in the 1920's by John D. Rockefeller Jr. are now open to snowmobiling families who have new access to some of Maine's most spectacular winter scenery.

Before the snowmobile, the immense acreage of Yellowstone Park was locked in snow in winter, with only one road across the northeast corner open to automobiles. This winter the park rangers expect more than 7,000 people to ride snowmobiles deep into the park to the spectacular winter setting of the geyser basins and through the thousands of deer, elk, and buffalo that retreat to the valleys from the high mountains for the deep winter.

The swift expansion of snowmobiling across the northern United States is in the same pattern as the growth of the automobile — from skepticism, through promotional racing, to sport and recreation and, finally, utility.

"Back in 1960, people around Rhinelander called it Fred's Folly when I borrowed $2,500 to buy a few of the very first ones," said Fred Gates, one of the first snowmobile dealers.

"Well, last year my gross went over $500,000," he went on. "Hell, I'll sell 600 new Ski-Doos this year. And on top of that we

Far left, a pair comes in after a long day cruising the forest. Above at left, a typical scene in the Middle West, where sociable snowmobilers make tracks from inn to inn. Left, men mark spot where scientists reached North Pole on snowmobiles after 44-day trek over the frozen Arctic Ocean.

sell these new thermal-lined snowmobile suits, in Ski-Doo's yellow colors, and boots, helmets, visors, attaching sleds and trailers to haul them. I even sell knitted sweaters and tight pants, in Ski-Doo yellow, of course."

A testimonial of the influence of snowmobilers, the average family machine of 200 to 300 pounds sells for about $1,000. An attaching sled, cushioned, costs about $130 and a small flat-bed trailer can be bought for about $200.

Back in 1964, Gates, with John Alward of the Chanticleer Inn, organized the first snowmobile "marathon," 22 miles cross-country from Rhinelander to Eagle River, both of which now call themselves the snowmobile capital of the world.

"We figured this was the best way to publicize these things," Gates explained. "Well, that was an amateur affair and the first prize was a fifth of brandy. Today the drivers are all professionals from the manufacturers. Last year our snowmobile derby drew thousands from all over the area, and the prize money went over $40,000."

Like Gates, other dealers across the country (there are now more than 50 manufacturers of snowmobiles) still advertise the vehicles primarily for recreation. But snowmobile owners are finding other uses.

The Nassau County (N.Y.) police this year acquired eight of them for emergency and rescue work. The Erie County (Buffalo) sheriff, Michael A. Amico, has deputized 31 snowmobilers to form a special emergency unit.

From the Upper Michigan town of Cheboygan the rural mail is being delivered by snowmobile to homeowners along unplowed back roads. Housewives in such areas often find the family snowmobile the easiest means of getting their children to the school bus stops on the main highways.

National forest rangers in many parts of the country cruise timber areas by snowmobile. Ranchers in Wyoming and Montana use them to check fences and sometimes to herd cattle to safer pastures.

The snowmobile is neither quiet nor odorless. Nor are all snowmobilers gentle or discreet. With the steadily mounting numbers, there have been a growing number of complaints.

"When you get a pack of those things roaring through your village at 1 o'clock in the morning, it makes you mad," a resident of a Minneapolis suburb complained recently.

In New Hampshire some snowmobile clubs have been handing property owners red cloth signs with the picture of a snowmobile and the word "no" on them.

"They hoped maybe the traffic and noise would be cut down some this way," Mike Cady, a state police dispatcher in Concord, said. "But, even so, four or five of 'em get together and bust down a fence or rip down a road. Some nights we get eight or 10 calls complaining about them."

With snow-covered railroad rights-of-way offering enticing thoroughfares for snowmobilers, railway officials in the upper Middle West have complained of highway crossing switches being cut and of snowmobiles being hit by trains. The Soo Line has reported two snowmobiles demolished by fast freights.

Game wardens have already had to increase patrols, on snowmobiles, to prevent chasing of big game by snowmobilers.

In the wilderness areas of the national parks and forests, where all motors are barred, the potential for poaching and intruding has been enough to send the rangers out on more frequent patrols—by snowmobile.

Many owners of summer cottages in this area once closed them for the winter, secure in the knowledge that hardly anybody could get through the snow to them. Last winter an increasing number of cases of vandalism were reported and, in the Eagle River area, some cottage owners hired watchmen (owners of snowmobiles) to make twice-weekly checks for break-ins or weather damage.

A number of states have regulations for registering, operating and equipping snowmobiles, and others are debating the matter.

"But so far, we've had a generally happy experience with our snowmobiling families, who are finding a new way to see the forests in winter," Gary Keppen, district ranger of the Nicolet National Forest in Wisconsin, said.

"Anyway," he added, "around here the best trails are between the taverns."

NEW WINTER BREED:

THE SNOWMOBILE RACER

Attracted by the thrill of moving and the sound of a rapping engine, snowmobile racers, you get the feeling, are the old motorcycle packers grown up

by John Sherman

NEW WINTER BREED

Snowmobiles, with faces like giant sea bass, pushed and shoved along the invisibile starting line between two old automobile tires, waiting for the red flag to swing down on the second running of what was called the New England Championship Snowmobile Rally.

The national anthem, bruited from a blue sound truck, had just marked the opening of the rally. For the rest of the afternoon it would content spectators and stimulate racers with a fare of Sousa marches and Hank Williams ballads.

The brightly-garbed riders wound their engines to a screaming pitch. Stinking racing oil smoke poured from exhaust pipes and fizzled white in the cold air. Spectators pressed against the snow fence.

When it seemed the racers could be held no longer, the starter dropped the flag, setting 17 power sleds bolting down the first icy yards of the two-mile course, set among the snowcovered fairways of a golf course in Plainville, Conn. A red-faced man with a new clipboard, from the sponsoring Plainville Jaycees, estimated that 125 riders from four states had registered for the rally, and 3,000 persons had paid admission. It seemed more like 1,236, but 3,000 is a rounder figure.

Six hours later, mechanic Joe Wilkerson, splendid in his black racing suit, stepped forward in the evening darkness to receive what amounted to the best-in-show trophy, for accumulating the most points in the three main events of the day; slalom, sprint and cross country (a "Powder Puff" race was also held for seven lady snowmobilers who showed up). Wilkerson, a member of the six-man Tri-State Racing Team from Lee, Mass., had brought his yellow Ski Doo, with a modified 70-horsepower engine, to speeds up to 85 miles an hour on the long, powdery straightaway in the last cross country heat. Wilkerson and teammates were experienced riders who knew how to shift weight and approach turns at just the right tilt. As a result, the Tri-State Racing Team copped all the important awards of the day.

Snowmobile racing, first popular in Canada and the Midwest, carries none of the pomp of other sports like horse racing or sports car racing. There are no Astors or Vanderbilts, no popular heroes, like Arcaro or Andretti, in it. But the sport is rapidly growing, and it has a large field of ordinary snowmobilers to draw upon for support. According to the snowmobile industry, there are more than 300,-000 machines (from more than 60 different manufacturers) in use today, something like a tenfold increase over the past four years, and there may be twice that number around by next winter.

The day's riders at the Plainville rally were a mixed lot attracted, they said, by the "thrill of moving," the sound of a rapping engine, and the rushing wind of competition. Talk to them long enough and you get the feeling they are the old motorcycle packers grown up.

Gone are the swastikas and the skulls, the studded jackets and leather boots. In their place are less ominous images carefully painted on the snoots of the machines—a pink roadrunner bird on one, "BOBBY AND MARY JONES & CHILDREN" on another. Many riders running the three or four most popular makes wore the slick racing suit and colors of the manufacturer, with matching double-layered boots.

For some, like Pete Lucas, the day of racing provided a first taste of the sport. A bulldozer mechanic by trade, Lucas is a weekend stock car racer in season. He bought a snowmobile a year ago "to make the winter go by faster." He said racing spirit doesn't change with the weather: "It's still a man and his machine running against another man and his machine." Lucas took home no trophies that day, but he had already registered for a second race a week later.

Another novice, driven to sport by the winter doldrums, described

Scenes on opposite page are from various races, including the major Eagle River snowmobile derby held annually in Wisconsin. The snow-covered flatlands of the Middle West have been ideal sites for numerous cross country snowmobile competitions which have attracted enthusiasts from throughout the country.

his attraction to the snowmobile: "Once you get on, you can't get off." A New Hampshire rider swore it was the "only" winter sport.

For some riders, one snowmobile in the garage was just not enough. One competitor who drove down from New Hampshire that morning said he had four machines, "a couple for racing and a couple for fun."

"They never trade one in on a new model," said Fred LaGrant, snowmobile distributor and the major underwriter of the Tri-State Racing Team. "They keep it for their kids and get the new one anyway. Some of them sell their second cars so they can buy a *third* snowmobile."

A great, bearded driver in a red sweatshirt bulled into a turn out on the course, briefly hung halfway off his seat, but regained balance in time to avert a spill. LaGrant frowned. "Anyone who's got a machine thinks he's a driver, but they just don't know what they're doing."

Snowmobile racing, LaGrant explained, is moving to the oval county fair tracks which can more safely bear the 100-mile-an-hour speeds recorded by some of the modified machines.

LaGrant was interrupted by one of his racers, who complained that one of the machines needed an adjustment. He hurried to the pit and buried his hands in the engine in an effort to get it running before the slalom began. He did, and the rider roared to the line.

HOW TO BE AN EXPERT AT 13

*Join the
Buddy Werner League*

A nine-year-old boy named Chris stared intently from the starting gate. He studied the combination of red, blue and yellow flags that were fluttering quietly on the race course. He shuffled his feet slowly and adjusted his goggles which were a little big because they belonged to his older sister. The starter began his slow and methodical count. "Two, one, go!" He pushed hard on his poles. As he started down the course shouts of encouragement came from his teammates and coach. Chris might have been thinking about the words of Buddy Werner: "There are only two places in a race and I only want one of them."

One of America's greatest skiers, Wallace "Buddy" Werner, voiced this thought shortly before his untimely death in 1964. Because of it, however, his excitement and competitive drive is continued in a learn-to-race program called the Buddy Werner League. The program was organized in 1967 and is now na-

tionwide in scope.

The Buddy Werner League is organized and administered by the United States Ski Ass'n. Direction comes from the USSA board of directors and a national committee made up of three members from the Alpine coaching staff, the eight USSA divisional chairmen and the junior racing chairman. USSA junior program officials stress, "The league is designed to fit into existing programs, not to replace them or to compete with them. Our at-tempt, when the USSA formed the league, was to promote racing and provide good coaching to the kids, before they pick up bad habits."

The key to the Buddy Werner League program is that it operates only at the local level. Basically it is a learn-to-race program that coordinates nicely with other existing divisional programs. Since the competition is held at nearby ski areas, Chris's parents don't have to worry about the high cost of travel with their

Photos show the Werner League program in action at Round Top Mountain in Plymouth Union, Vt., an area that decided to sponsor the League simply because of the high enthusiasm for ski racing already present among the youngsters patronizing the area.

young and aggressive racer. Nearly all competition is among the teams that are formed under a local league at the area.

Shortly after Chris started skiing, he began to watch and imitate older boys who held slalom

practice at the ski area. The winter he turned eight, he and some friends signed up for the local Buddy Werner League and were soon drafted by one of the coaches for a new team that was forming at their area.

The boys reported to fall training and their new coach began teaching them what ski racing was all about. They practiced, running on foot, through a dry-land slalom course and learned the difference between an open gate and a hair-pin. The boys played soccer, jumped hurdles and did other muscle-building exercises. By the time the first snow fell they were in good physical condition and had a pretty good idea what ski racing was all about.

Being an expert at eight years old can be dangerous, as Chris soon found out! His first race against another team was disaster. He fell three times on the first run and was finally disqualified for missing a gate. That kind of thing could be pretty hard to take for a young lad just getting started. Luckily, his friends didn't do much better and the coach was very understanding. Teams race against teams, and although individual performance is important, the overall team standing is the only thing tallied.

New leagues are springing up all around the country and part of the reason is the low cost of joining. Very little travel is involved, uniforms are at a minimum and the youngsters are not encouraged to buy the most expensive equipment available. The local leagues are sanctioned by USSA and pay only $20 to $35 to their divisions. Team members join for individual costs of less than $2! Each team finds its own sponsor among local businesses and, by keeping costs down, many more youngsters are

becoming avid skiers.

How much do the kids learn about ski racing? They learn a lot and they learn it fast. Teams are small — no more than 15 members. Each team has its own coach and they do a lot of racing. Since they don't need to travel to compete, some teams can race as much as twice a day.

The coaches work hard, too. They consult with one another in the league and rely on information and techniques developed by the Buddy Werner Ski League Coaching Center, established at Johnson State College in Johnson, Vt. At the center, three control groups are available at all times for the testing and evaluation by comparison of generally accepted teaching and coaching methods. The result is a carefully controlled national effort to develop high quality ski racers.

Now that Chris is nine, he is already a seasoned veteran of many races. His plans? His short range goals are to win as many races as possible for his team and to get some goggles that fit! His long-range plans are for a berth on the U.S. Olympic Team in 1984 when he'll be 22. If he learns to like girls, he says he may get married, "or something like that."

What is the Buddy Werner League all about? Perhaps the reason for it was best summed up by former U.S. Alpine team coach, Bob Beattle. "That the program was named after the late Buddy Werner is natural," he said. "Buddy received his start in a similar program in Steamboat Springs, Colorado. He was always the idol of youngsters and went out of his way to help them. He'd be pleased with this program since he always felt skiing should be exciting, competitive and fun. Buddy Werner League skiing is all three."

ANYBODY FOR SNOWSHOEING?

A neglected winter sport that can be fun for the skiing family

by Nelson Bryant

Snowshoeing is a sorely neglected sport. People who brave summer's heat, black flies, deer flies, gnats and mosquitoes to hike woodland trails find an entirely different atmosphere when they are deep in snow.

Yet the use of the snowshoes, an invention of the American Indian, is limited mostly to bobcat hunters, trappers, timber cruisers and other men whose occupations call them into the woods in winter.

Family snowshoeing parties are a delightful way to spend a winter's day. A campfire, for warmth or cooking, can be built with no danger to the woods. Small children can be towed behind on a toboggan, and there is no better time to introduce them to the pleasures of deciphering animal signs left on the snow.

Basic snowshoe styles are trail, bear paw and pickerel. The trail shoe is very long and narrow with an upswept toe and designed for use on deep snow in open country. The bear paw is nearly round and flat intended for traveling in dense woods. The pickerel is a shorter version of the trail shoe.

One of the best for general use is a modified trail shoe sold by L.L. Bean of Freeport, Me. Regular Alaskan trail shoes aren't really needed by the casual user, and the bear paw can drive a neophyte to distraction if the snow is fluffy and deep.

It only takes a few minutes to learn how to use snowshoes, although one shouldn't, unless he's an athlete, try for more than two miles the first time out.

The snowshoer's gait is shambling, but it doesn't have to be spraddle-legged. As you walk, the top of one snowshoe actually rides a few inches above the other and clears it when the stride ends.

Ski poles are helpful when climbing with snowshoes. Without them, it is necessary to crab up steep inclines.

When possible, keep your snowshoes outside or in a cold place if you are planning to use them the next day. If they are warm when you start, snow will stick to them, making each step an ordeal.

Bindings are a matter of individual preference, but all good bindings hold the toe of your foot firmly on the snowshoes and allow the heel to ride up and down. Any good outdoor boot can be worn with snowshoes, and many people get by with ordinary overshoes over street shoes.

The cost is not great: You should be able to buy a good pair of snowshoes with bindings for about $30.

ABOUT THE AUTHOR

Nelson Bryant writes "Wood, Field and Stream" for The New York Times.

Mittersill (Franconia, N.H.) ski instructor Ira Litke vaults up and over a snow roller during obstacle race on snowshoes, an untypical but enjoyable application of this winter footwear.

by Michael Strauss

THE MAN-MADE BEASTS THAT BEAUTIFY THE HILLS

Snowmaking technology continues to come up with bigger and better ways to lengthen the season and soften your sitzmarks

Once upon a time, ski area operators, having cleared the stumps and rocks from their slopes and oiled up their rope tow machinery, used to sit and wait for winter to come. They hoped it would arrive with swirling white flakes which would continue to swirl until the arrival of spring.

All too often, however, their vigil proved long and frustrating. Mother Nature frequently refused to cooperate. There would be skimpy snow-producing winters in which the only machinery in constant operation at ski centers were those producing red ink. In a number of cases, the lack of snow proved a short cut to bankruptcy.

Then, about two decades ago, the story goes, someone forgot to turn off the sprinkler spouting water on a day in which the

Brodie Mountain (above) in the Berkshires of Massachusetts is one of many Eastern ski areas that rely on snowmakers. At right, compressors at Snow Bowl, N. J.

thermometer was hovering around the freezing point The weather turned even colder, the spray from the sprinkler began producing white flakes and before long there lay a mantle of snow on ground which had been bare only a few hours earlier.

This episode, as it developed, was to provide another installment in skiing's remarkable success story. An installation at the Concord Hotel in New York's southern Catskills in 1951 confirmed that highly pressurized water ejected from thin nozzles on sub-freezing days could produce snow as surely as the summer sun produces sunburn. The "Banana Belt" was in the ski

business to stay.

"Banana Belt"? For almost 20 years, this had been the scornful expression applied by many of the sport's cognoscenti to those regions located south of such presumably Arctic reaches as Maine, New Hampshire and Vermont. In the west, any sections harboring ski centers in the foothills of the Rockies or the Sierras often were placed in the same uncomplimentary category. The "Banana Belt" was identified among the in-set with its lack of sufficient, durable cover.

But with the advent of the snowmaking machines, Ski Country, U.S.A., like little Topsy, began to grow and grow. Soon centers, fortified by equipment that could produce blizzards at the turn of a switch — when the weather was cold enough — began appearing all over the landscape.

Small resort complexes only 40 miles from New York, 15 miles from Boston and 30 miles from Hartford, Conn., began operating on a daily basis. Later came artificial snow developments near New Haven, Philadelphia and even Baltimore. But what made even the non-skier sit up and take notice was the appearance of ski areas in Tennessee, North Carolina, Southern New Mexico and even a short distance from Los Angeles.

Today, snow-running resorts, scores of them, are thriving in such states as Pennsylvania, Ohio, Michigan, Wisconsin, Minnesota and North Dakota among others. And while many of the areas in these precincts have small hills, they have base lodges that would do justice to the Alps. Adding stature to the entire snowmaking situation is the fact that some Canadian developments and such important New England resorts

as Mount Snow, Stratton Mountain, Killington and Sugarbush are finding the machine indispensable.

One of the most crushing rejections of nature took place a few years ago when Sepp Ruschp, the astute Austrian entrepreneur from the high Alpine country and the major domo of the pioneer Stowe (Vt.) center, decided to install a snow making system. The step was particularly noteworthy because for years this popular Vermont retreat had thrived on the slogan of "When you think of snow, think of Stowe." Bear in mind what was meant was "natural" snow.

"But we had to make an adjustment," Ruschp told me a few years ago shortly after Stowe had adjusted its snow sights. "We took the step to insure skiing during the early season. Ski business has become so big that it seems foolhardy to take a chance of missing the lucrative Christmas trade just because nature fails to produce."

Jack Riley, the present American sales representative for an Italian lift company, but then the manager of Sugarbush, was heard howling shortly after nozzles began spewing snow at his Vermont resort.

"It's so expensive," he lamented. "When you get finished figuring the cost of compressors, the miles of pipe, the temperamental nozzles and the overtime pay for night-time crews, it runs into big money."

"We agree," was the laconic answer by a spokesman of the Larchmont Engineering Company of Concord, Mass., which at that time enjoyed a snowmaking machine production monopoly. "But think of the big money it costs you on those days when you have no snow and can't sell lift tickets."

Actually, there are two sides to the story. What about those winters in which nature doesn't need a nudge from science? It's a question frequently raised by potential purchasers of the machines.

There was the winter of 1968-69, for example, when it began snowing in mid-November and snowed regularly right into mid-March. Ecstatic about nature's bountiful helpings of the white gold was none other than colorful Hans Thorner, the creator of Magic Mountain in Vermont's high country.

The Swiss-born Thorner, who had come to the United States back in the depression years as a skimeister, had been successful in making Magic a lucrative resort — without the help of snow machines. Through the years he had been one of leading lights in pooh-poohing suggestions that Vermont's mountains might need "mechanized weather."

"Not here," he often told me. "This is the Green Mountains. The state's statistics prove that snow is never a stranger to Vermont. Except for exceptional years, nature always has been our most reliable snow machine. And nature doesn't charge a cent."

But came the Christmas season of 1967 and some winter resorts at many upper New England ski centers came within a few snowballs of being considered distress areas. There were some exceptions — those fortified with the "expensive" snowmaking systems.

For Thorner, this revolting development was doubly difficult to take. Two of Magic's neighbors, Stratton and Big Bromley, were doing turn-away business while poor old Magic lay almost bare and deserted by its usual patrons, The reason? Both Stratton

Jay Peak, Vt., (top) and Hidden Valley, Ont., boast high fake-snow capability.

and Bromley had installed snowmaking machines.

Then and there Thorner took the pledge. He promised himself that by the following winter he would have similar equipment on his slopes.

"It isn't so hard for me to take it when my mountain doesn't have snow," he explained. "But

when my two neighbors have it and I don't, that's almost demoralizing."

So Thorner installed a $250,000 snowmaking plant that fall in anticipation of a busy winter in which he would have added insurance — the machines. What happened? He didn't need them. It snowed so much that season that Thorner used his new equipment only five times.

"Honestly," he told me while seated in his office just before that spring's skiing season was approaching. "Most of the few times we used the equipment we did so only to make sure it was working."

At Cannon Mountain, a ski resort owned and operated by the state of New Hampshire, a total of $500,000 was dumped into snowmaking that same winter. And, as at Magic, Bill Norton, the manager of Cannon, had little opportunity to use it because of the abundance of natural snow that year.

Last winter, however, the weather in New Hampshire was so unreliable that deep freezes were followed by mild thaws. Several times Norton saw his expensive man-made snow float back to the lake at the base of the mountain from whence it originally had been pumped to make the snow.

"It was like watching a horse, leading in the stretch by a wide margin, drop dead a few yards from the finish," reminisced Norton with a grimace. "Just when we would think we had the elements licked with a deep cover of carefully nurtured snow, along would come one of those thaws to pour us right out of business."

Through the years, fickle weather causing man-made snow to melt back into water, has been only one of the problems plaguing snow area tycoons. Among other shortcomings have been the inclination of pipes to freeze and the difficulty in obtaining labor for shifts in the wee early morning hours when snowmaking conditions are at their best.

Nevertheless, it is acknowledged that snowmaking at many ski areas, particularly in the lowland country, is the item that keeps cash registers at lift ticket windows ringing regularly. Expensive? There's no doubt about it. Necessary? In many cases it's like what oxygen is to lungs.

Besides, help in coping with costs may be coming soon. Goesta Wollin, a Swedish-born inventor, who is associated with the Lamont-Doherty Geological Observatory of Columbia University as an oceanographer, has conceived a machine which he maintains will do away with the need of expensive compressors. He insists that his machine will reduce the cost of snowmaking by 75 per cent.

Wollins's contraption, which will cost only $1,500 a unit — at least until big-scale production makes them less expensive — is driven by a five-horsepower motor that weighs only 100 pounds. The new snowmaker, in experiments last winter, converted as much as 20 gallons of water a minute into snow.

What will happen if Wollin's wonder proves successful? It probably will etch a whole new image on the ski recreational picture. Since the machines should cost only about $1,000 when made in quantity, a brand new market will open that will cater to skiers who have anything resembling a slope in their backyards.

Sure it won't be like skiing in the high Sierras or the awesome Alps. But for a slide down a hill from your own back door — there will be nothing like it.

FAKE SNOW, PART II

Meanwhile, back at the mad inventor's lodge, a completely different approach was devised for providing skiability when the weather failed to cooperate. This approach required facing snowless conditions head-on, and produced such ingenious devices as the TurfSki (above), a carefully engineered land ski which can be used on any grassy slope. It works less well in actual snow, of course.

Also devised has been a variety of artificial slopes, perhaps best typified by Sno-Mat, a plastic European import here negotiated by former U.S. Ski Team racer Rip McManus, on a preseason slalom course set up at Great Gorge, N. J.

ENGLISH ACCENT IN THE ALPS

*The author, a founding father of modern
Alpine skiing, tells of the challenge in getting recognition for a sport
once considered proper diversion only for women*

by Sir Arnold Lunn

The first country to organize a national championship to be decided on a downhill ski race was Great Britain, in January, 1921. Until then all national championships were awarded, as in Norway, on the combined result of a langlauf, (cross country meet) and a ski jumping competition. In 1920 my proposal that the British championship should be awarded on the combined result of a downhill ski race and a style competition was accepted and I was entrusted with the organization of this event.

On January 6, 1921, fifteen competitors started together from the summit of the Lauberhorn in Switzerland, and raced down to a point below the Scheidegg. Leonard Dobbs won both the downhill ski race and the combined championship, and Miss Olga Major, who was fifth in the open championship, won the ladies' championship with ease.

This was in 1921. It was not until 1929, eight years later, that another Alpine country, Austria, followed our example. The first Arlberg-Kandahar race had already been held in St. Anton, but the Austrians in authority were not as far-seeing as Hannes Schneider, and apparently still regarded a downhill ski race as an inferior form of competition, only suitable for ladies. No downhill ski championship for men was organized at this meeting. The ladies' downhill ski racing championship was won by Inge Lantschner.

Leonard Dobbs, who won the first historic British championship, was one of the best British racers in the twenties. When the British ski championship was held at Adelboden in 1924, an Adelboden photographer who was also a very good skier, remarked to Captain H. Marriott that he intended to photograph the start and then ski down to the finish and watch the British competitors arriving. After the race he told Captain Marriott that he doubted whether Leonard Dobbs' time, eight and a half minutes for the 4,000 foot descent, would be improved.

TOWARDS SLALOM The style competition in the first British ski championship meeting of 1921 was a failure, but I did not abandon my attempt to invent a ski competition which would test those skiing qualities inadequately tested in a downhill race.

In January 1920 I had already organized a ski competition in which competitors were taken on a tour, and the cup was awarded to the best Alpine runner among the competitors, hence the name of the cup, Alpine Ski Challenge Cup. Marks were given for speed, steadiness and control. E. C. Pery, later the Earl of Limerick, was the winner. J. A. Joannides, who was second, described a slalom in which he had taken part at Klosters, and which had hardly anything in common with the modern slalom which was first held at Murren.

In the Klosters slalom marks were given for style, and competitors were required to do a particular turn round a particular flag. The modern slalom is a race in which nothing but time counts. In the old slalom the competitors had to turn round single flags instead of through gates consisting of a pair of poles.

Again, the modern slalom has virtually nothing but the name in common with the old Norwegian one, a competition which died a natural death. The word 'slalom' was used in Norway for a steep run which necessitated turning. Fitz Huitfeld in *Kria,* his famous book on skiing published in 1908, describes a Norwegian slalom. 'For such a track,' he wrote, 'no kinds of preparation were made. Everything remains as in nature.'

The great Austrian pioneer, Mathias Zdarsky, was the first to produce an intelligible analysis of a stemming turn, and the first to start a school to teach the art of skiing on steep Alpine ground. He might justly be called the father of Alpine skiing. On March 19, 1905, Zdarsky organized a competition consisting of a descent of some 750 meters on a heavily controlled course. It was a test of mountain skiing. Everybody who covered the course within a fixed time received a prize. Competitors carried rucksacks, and there was no restriction on stick-riding.

In 1922 the Alpine Ski Challenge Cup was transformed into a slalom race: I set the first modern slalom on the practice slopes at Murren on January 21, 1922. The Alpine Ski Challenge Cup, which is now the world's senior challenge cup for slalom racing, was won by J. A. Joannides.

The first rules for slalom racing were published in the *Public Schools Alpine Sports Club Year Book,* in 1922. The slalom became an integral part of the British ski championship in the championship meeting which opened in Gstaad on January 2, 1926.

LADIES FIRST

H. B. Luttman-Johnson once remarked to me that in his opinion the greatest contribution of the British to competitive skiing was not the invention of the modern slalom and the promotion of downhill racing but putting lady skiers on the map.

In 1923 I suggested to my wife and her friends that it was about time somebody founded a ladies' ski club. In January 1923, the Ladies' Ski Club, which is today the world's senior club for lady ski-runners, was founded at Murren by Lady Mabel Lunn, Doreen Elliott and Mrs. Duncan Harvey. I am not a member of the Ladies' Ski Club, but I have been presented with a club badge to symbolize my illegitimate association with this distinguished club. My official title is "Sinister Father of the Ladies' Ski Club."

Six years later, in 1929, Elsa Roth founded a club for the Swiss ladies, the Schweizerische Damen Ski Club (S.D.S.). She was present at one of the very best parties in my life, my 80th birthday party organized in Murren by my friend Godi Michel. In her speech she paid a notable tribute to the British ladies. In Switzerland at that time lady skiers had no real status: it was the precedent set by our British ladies which determined the Swiss to follow their example. In the early days of downhill racing our girls were in a class by themselves. The Ladies' Ski Club under the captaincy of Greta, Lady Reaburn, won three friendly matches against the Swiss Ladies' Ski Club.

THE KANDAHAR

The Kandahar Ski Club, the mother club of Alpine racing, was founded at Murren on January 30, 1924, to raise the standard of downhill and slalom racing, and to secure international recognition for these events.

At the foundation meeting my suggestion to call the club after the oldest of downhill races, the Roberts of Kandahar, was adopted with enthusiasm. Various suggestions for a badge were put forward. Somebody thought that a bit of a mountain would be rather nice as a background. "No," said A. H. d'Egville, usually known as 'Deggers', "nothing of the kind. Just a simple 'K'."

'But your badge,' somebody protested, 'has nothing to suggest skiing. Nobody will know what the "K" stands for.'

'Well, if they ask you,' replied Deggers, 'you just say, "If you want to know what 'K' stands for, you can bloody well find out for yourself." And they bloody well will find out for themselves.'

Among the original members of the Kandahar was Andrew Irvine, who disappeared on Everest later in the year. He rowed for Oxford in 1922 and in 1923, and spent the winter of 1923-1924 at Murren, in the course of which he won the Strang Watkins Challenge Cup for slalom racing. No man enjoyed skiing more. 'When I am an old man,' he wrote, 'I will look back on Christmas 1923 as the day when to all intents and purposes I was born. I don't think anyone has *lived* until they have been on skis.'

Irvine was chosen by Mallory as his companion for an attempt on Everest. Somewhere below the summit their bodies lie—thousands of feet above the loftiest of all the unnumbered graves of unnumbered generations.

A GREAT YEAR

1924 made a greater contribution to skiing history than the centuries in which men have skied before 1924 and the decades in which they have skied since 1924. The Kandahar Ski Club was founded at Murren on January 30, and in the same month the Federation Internationale de Ski, usually referred to as the F.I.S., was founded at Oslo, and the First Winter Olympic Games were held at Chamonix in which the only skiing events were langlauf and ski jumping. None of the organizers of the Olympic ski events could have foreseen the day when the chief interest in the Olympic Winter ski events would be ski competition originally sponsored by an Englishman of whom they had never heard, and developed at a Swiss ski center which few of them had ever visited.

In the same month, January 1924, the founder of the Kandahar organized the first international event to be decided on the Alpine combination, downhill and slalom.

Nobody was more interested in the British developments of competition skiing than two young Swiss, the brothers Max and Walter Amstutz, whose family at that time ran a hotel in Murren. Walter Amstutz who, as a boy, had skied with interned British officers at Murren, is one of those people who can see a coming thing before it actually hits him, with the result that he was to be our first continental ally in the campaign for the recognition of the Alpine races.

Walter Amstutz is not only a first class skier but is still a first class mountaineer. At the age of 65 he carried through some important climbs in the Andes.

1924 was a memorable year in my life not only because it was in 1924 that I founded the Kandahar Ski Club but also because in June of that same memorable year Walter Amstutz, his friend W. Richardet who was later killed in the mountains, and my friend Fritz Amacher of Grindelwald, made the first ski ascent of the Eiger, an expedition which had its link with the development of Alpine racing. That great mountaineer, Frank Smyth, who later climbed the Eiger by this route, described it as 'extremely dangerous', but conceded that our expedition 'from the purely sporting point of view was one of the most skillful ski-aided expeditions ever carried out'.

It was while resting on the Eigerjoch that Walter confided to me that he proposed to found in the autumn a Swiss University Ski Club to cooperate with the British in the campaign for the recognition of Alpine racing, and also to select a team to race against the British. Thus it was in November 1924 that Walter Amstutz founded at Bern, a club, *begotten* at Murren, the Swiss University Ski Club, which was to have a decisive influence on the ultimate recognition by the F.I.S of the Alpine races . . .

NEW FORMS To the young racers of today the description in the *British Ski Year Book* of some of the races in the 1920s would certainly seem faintly bizarre. The most important races of the twenties

were the British ski championship which has been, and the first Arlberg-Kandahar which will be, described:

The Oxford and Cambridge I was given the job of organizing the first Oxford and Cambridge ski race which took place on January 2, 1922 at Wengen. The Oxford team included two Norwegians, Tor Klaveness and C. Stang. The Norwegians demanded and obtained from the judges a good measure of level and uphill racing in the course. Klaveness completed the course in 30 minutes, a clear three minutes ahead of Stang who was second. Leonard Dobbs, the Cambridge Captain, was third, and the result was an easy victory for Oxford.

In January, 1925 Oxford won what was perhaps the most decisive victory in any skiing team race. The last Oxford man finished a minute and a half ahead of the first Cambridge man. Christopher Mackintosh was the individual winner.

I had hoped that the modern slalom would prove to be a school for and a test of mountain skiing. In the early days of slalom racing at Murren, the first part was held on hard snow and the second part on powder snow, the order of starting in the second part being determined by the order in which competitors finished in the first part on hard snow. Moreover, in those days the racers had to use their judgment where to put in an extra turn in what were known as Alpine figures. In the modern slalom the racer's line is virtually dictated by the slalom setter, for he has only to turn *through* the slalom gates instead of occasionally putting in an extra turn on the open slopes between the gates.

The Scaramanga Roped Race In 1925, J. C. Scaramanga, an original member of the Kandahar, and a member of the Alpine Club, offered a cup for roped racing in order to encourage ski runners to master the technique of roped running, and thus to increase their safety in glacier running. I won the first Scaramanga Roped Race, held at Murren, with Adrian Allison as my partner, and the third Scaramanga Roped Race with Christopher Mackintosh. Our time from the Maulerhubel to Test Finish was two minutes and 45 seconds. As the result of practicing for these races, I was not only far steadier but far faster when skiing roped on the glaciers.

No-Fall Races The No-Fall race was invented by Vivian Caulfeild, a leading member of the Downhill Only Club. It would hardly be an over-statement to describe Caulfeild as the father of modern skiing,

Opposite page, Walter Amstutz executes a flawless jump turn off of a cornice in Murren.

for he was one of the first vigorously to condemn stick-riding, certainly the first to produce a brilliant analysis of the different skiing turns in his book *How to Ski.*

On January 7, 1927 the first No-Fall race was held for *The Sunday Times* Cup, from the top of the Bumps to Inner Wengen, and was won, appropriately enough, by Berry Caulfeild, Vivian's son.

The Bracken No-Fall race is still popular at Murren.

The Inferno Race The Inferno Race from the summit of the Schilthorn (9,754 ft.) to Lauterbrunnen station (2,615 ft.) is now organized by the Murren Ski Club, but the race, which was first held on January 29, 1928, originated with Harold Mitchell, Antony Knebworth, Pelham Maitland, Patsy Richardson and Bunny Ford, all members of the Kandahar Ski Club. Forty years later my dear friend Mimi von Allmen of the Eiger Hotel, Murren, remarked to me, 'I suppose you got the Murren Ski Club to organize the race.'

'The organization,' I replied, 'consisted of one man, Patsy Richardson, who had sprained his ankle, and was therefore unable to compete. He was at the finish. All competitors were, of course, to start together. The actual starter, A. L., who was also competing, synchronized his watch with Richardson's before the race, and on arriving sixth out of the eighteen competitors at the finish, informed Richardson when the race had started. The donors had stipulated that the race should start from the Col just below the actual Spitz, but I persuaded them to allow the race to start from the actual summit. It was arranged that those who did not want to race from the summit should join in as the competitors who started from the top swept past. So much for the "organization".'

The snow was, of course, untracked, and the course included a short climb and a langlauf section along the railway. Harold Mitchell won in one hour and 12 minutes.

The Inferno remains today the only important Alpine race which is a real test of Alpine skiing, for though there is usually a *piste* down to Murren, the rest of the race to Lauterbrunnen is almost always run on natural snow.

RECOGNITION When the Kandahar was founded, competitive skiing was still dominated by Norway and Sweden. The langlauf race developed naturally out of Scandinavian terrain. Though Norway has some fine skiing mountains, the greater part of the country is typical langlauf country. Prior to

the Kandahar revolution, skiing (apart from ski jumping in which alone the aesthetic criterion was admitted in the awarding of style marks) was regarded as a means of getting about the country. *How you got from point to point did not matter.* There was no prejudice against stick-riding in difficult country. Victory in a langlauf race depended primarily on speed along the level and uphill. In an official booklet issued to Norwegian race officials and competitors, the following advice to competitors is included: *'When going downhill one should regain breath and rest as much as possible.'*

I attended the F.I.S Congress in February, 1928 in St. Moritz formally to propose that downhill and slalom races should be internationally recognized, and that for these races the British Rules, which had been worked out by the Kandahar at Murren, and approved by the Ski Club of Great Britain should be adopted.

The prospects were not encouraging. A famous English skier told me that it would be time enough to demand recognition for our British rules for Alpine racing when the British had entered some skiers in international competitions, which were then restricted to langlauf and ski jumping.

I could not even count on the whole-hearted support of the Alpine countries though they had most to gain from the international recognition of the Alpine races. Toni Hiebeler, who interviewed me on my 80th birthday for that famous Munich paper *Alpinismus*, recalled the fact that Carl Luther, whom he describes as 'the German Ski Pope', was at that time my bitter opponent.

Major N. R. Oestgaard, the Norwegian vice president, asked me what I would think if Norwegians tried to alter the rules of cricket, but was apparently disarmed by my reply, which he quoted with amusement to a Norwegian friend of mine, 'I wish to heaven you would. We might have fewer draws.'

The F.I.S. appointed a special committee to con-consider our proposals, a committee which was presided over by a Swiss, Dr. Danegger. An article in *Sport* of Zurich had proved decisive in influencing Swiss opinion. *Sport* at that time was edited by Colonel Fritz Erb who had entered for a slalom at Murren and had been converted to its value.

The Czech on this F.I.S committee said that the racing program was already so overcrowded that

Top photo was taken at the Roberts of Kandahar race in 1927 and reveals at a glance the various straight racing styles practiced at the time. Below is a 1940 view of the author, Sir Arnold.

no new races could possibly be added. The Finns said that Finland was flat, and so the Finns were not interested in downhill racing. The Norwegian said that he thought the British restriction on stick-riding very artificial: 'The object of a race should be to determine which man gets to the finishing post in the shortest time. It is absurd to try to prevent stick-riding.' Dr. Karl Roesen of Garmisch, Germany, fortunately gave us his unqualified support. Roesen had attended the first university international meeting at St. Moritz, and had been impressed. He was a man of great character, for he resisted all efforts to entice him into the Nazi Party: at the end of the Second World War he was largely instrumental in preventing a Bavarian village from being bombed, for he managed to cross the lines and get in touch with the American commander of the artillery. He introduced himself by producing a letter which I had written to him before the war (to an address in Davos) congratulating him on his anti-Nazi stand. The American officer was a skier, and the introduction worked.

The Polish Ski Ass'n adopted the F.I.S suggestion that the national associations should experiment with the British rules for the Alpine races, and decided to include a downhill race in the program for the World Championship meeting at Zakopane which they were organizing on behalf of the F.I.S.

I wrote and asked if the downhill race was open to all comers, and on receiving an affirmative reply, promptly entered our two best Kandahar ladies, Doreen Elliott and Audrey Salt-Barker, now Countess of Selkirk. The Poles objected that there was no precedent for entering ladies in an open race. I might have replied, as I did on a similar occasion, that there were two kinds of people, those who followed precedents and those who created them, but I contented myself with pointing out that there were many precedents for ladies competing in open British events, and that as we were the popularizers of downhill racing, it was our precedents which mattered. There were 60 competitors, Czech of Poland won, and Bracken, the British captain was second. Guy Nixon was sixth, W. J. Riddel eighth, F. P. Maitland tenth, and E. W. A. Richardson twelfth.

The sensation of the meeting was the performance of the two girls, Doreen Elliott who finished 13th and Audrey Sale-Barker who finished 14th, beating 45 men. The Poles were thrilled by the courage which they showed in taking a particularly villanous icy glade dead straight, strewed as it was with tree stumps. Their fame spread throughout Poland, and when they entered a restaurant in Warsaw all those present stood up and cheered.

I was confident that downhill ski racing would be officially recognized by the F.I.S Congress which was to meet at Oslo at the end of February, 1930, but I knew that the opposition to the recognition of the slalom would be formidable. In the January before the Congress, my first Norwegian ally, Captain, now Colonel, Christian Drefting, a former winner of the Norwegian Military Ski Championship, visited Murren. On leaving Murren he wrote an article for *Aftenposton,* Oslo, which had a considerable influence in securing the acceptance of the British proposals by the Congress which met a few weeks later. He wrote: 'It was an alluring thought to come to Switzerland as a Norwegian and show these newcomers to our sport what skiing really was . . . We laugh at English skiing and say that the English only take trains uphill and come down the nursery slopes behind the hotels and practice a lot of pecular twists and turns, and we think they understand nothing of what skiing really is. This was how I looked at things when I arrived in blissful ignorance.'

He then continued, 'The name downhill racing gives an average Norwegian a very faulty conception of what happens. This is natural as we conceive of hills as hills and not as practically vertical drops. I stood at the different points where the races started and felt quite giddy looking down. *To get down in the usual Norwegian way was quite out of the question*—that would be tempting Providence too much . . . The Roberts of Kandahar race was an imposing sight—to watch these plucky young Englishmen coming down these steep hills with an incredible speed . . . it kindled in me an ambition to be able to master those hills as well as these men did. I had long ago given up the idea of being able to impress by my Norwegian knowledge of skiing.' (Italics mine.) A generous tribute by a great Norwegian.

In the *British Ski Year Book* I created a storm in Norway by stating that 'the average standard of downhill skiing among visitors to Norwegian centres was deplorably low'. I also gave offense by remarking that the steepest parts of a Norwegian langlauf course were gentle by Alpine Standards. On my arrival in Norway I learned that Eric Horn had been assigned the task of looking after me. I did not know that he had been instructed to push me down the steepest parts of the traditional Holmenkollen langlauf course in the hope that a few falls would inspire me with more respect for Norwegian terrain. There was nothing on the course comparable with the stunt straight runs at Murren which I had often held without falling. Eric in despair deviated from the course and led me to the top of a steepish slope covered with trees and bushes. Horn took it straight and would have held it had he not tripped in a bush at the end. I put in four cautious S-turns, and whereas I was impressed by Horn's courage, he was impressed by my S-turning, for the art of continuous S-turning was at that time little known in Norway because unnecessary in normal Norwegian terrain.

In 1946 when Eric met my son Peter he recalled the incident. 'Your father,' he said, 'did some slalom turns which were more economical'—that is, economical of falls. This demonstration of 'economy' and some copies of the *Year Book* which I sent him, transformed Eric Horn into an ardent pioneer of Alpine racing. A few years later he won the classic Galdhopiggen race, the Roberts of Kandahar of Norway. Eric Horn, Einar Bergsland and Jacob Rytter-Kielland are the creators of the modern school of Norwegian skiing. Their only problem was to convince the Norwegians that they had something to learn.

'When we told them,' said Kielland to me in 1946, 'as you did in 1930, that the average standard of skiing at places like Finse and Fefor was very bad, we were regarded as skiing Quislings.'

Fortunately for our British proposals both Colonel, later General, Ivor Holmquist, the Swedish president, and Major, later Colonel, N. R. Oestgaard, the vice president of the F.I.S, were men who attached far more importance to the unity of the F.I.S and to the good of the sport than to their personal doubts about the slalom. Oestgaard's position was particularly difficult because he was persistently attacked by Norwegian skiing die-hards who controlled most of the important papers. He was well aware that the vote he intended to give in favour of recognizing the Alpine races would be interpreted as a further surrender to Central Europe.

Dr. Danegger, an ex-president of the Swiss Ski Ass'n, proposed the recognition of our rules in an effective speech. A delegate rose and began to criticize the rules in some detail. I dreaded a long discussion, the effect of which might have been to postpone ratification of our rules until the next Congress.

The flags of the different nations had been placed in front of the delegates. The Norwegians were familiar with the red ensign which they saw flying on the merchant ships entering their harbours, and it was a red ensign which was placed in front of me. I fiddled nervously with it while the delegate was speaking. Suddenly the flag tumbled down. *Absit*

omen, I murmured. The delegate prosed on. The president glanced in my direction, but I was determined not to speak unless it was essential. The president, as I hoped, suggested to the delegate that he should put his views before the special downhill slalom committe for which I had asked.

'Does anybody else wish to speak?'

Nobody stirred. Up went the chairman's hammer, and still he hesitated.

'*Angenommen* (agreed),' said the President. Down went his hammer and up went the red ensign, a ritualistic gesture and my only contribution to a debate which was the culminating point of a ten years' campaign.

WORLD CHAMPIONSHIP The British were entrusted with the organization of the first world championship in downhill and slalom racing which opened at Murren on February 19, 1931. At the time this event was called the F.I.S. championship, and was officially changed to world championship in 1936. The names of previous winners of what was always in effect the world championship are described in records as world champions. This was, if I remember right, the result of a resolution which I proposed to the F.I.S downhill/slalom committee of which I was for some time the chairman.

The British teams were admirably coached at Murren by Colonel de Lande Long. Doreen Elliott, the captain, was prevented from racing by a strained ankle. The championship unfortunately coincided with snowfalls unprecedented in Swiss experience.

The world championship opened with the ladies' slalom in which the British won five out of the first six places. In the downhill race next day the British ladies took four out of the first five places. Miss Esmé Mackinnon won the first world championship for ladies in downhill racing, and also an unofficial race from Murren to Lauterbrunnen, the full Inferno course being too dangerous because of heavy snowfalls. Miss Mackinnon had thus brought off the hat trick by winning all three races at this meeting.

The men's downhill race resulted in an overwhelming victory for the Swiss who took the first four places. In langlauf races no competitor who has not reached the age of 18 is allowed to compete, and the inclusion in the British team of a boy of 16, Peter Lunn, provoked mild protests from the Scandinavians. Peter Lunn, as it happened, was the second best British racer in the downhill (13th) and

Gina Hathorn, who placed fourth in slalom at Grenoble, is a contemporary British force in ski racing.

in the slalom (7th).

The slalom, which had to be postponed because of the bad weather, was held after some of the competitors had left, and was regarded as unofficial.

The little Inferno from Murren to Lauterbrunnen was won by G. Lantschner of Austria, Christopher Mackintosh of Great Britain being second, and Paumgarten of Austria being third. The race was held before any of the competitors had left Murren, and was a far more exacting test of downhill racing than the official downhill race for the world championship.

It was inevitable that the first reactions of the Scandinavians to the British proposals for the recognition of the Alpine races should have been critical, and it is greatly to their credit that they were so ready to revise their views. On his return from the first world championship at Murren, Major Oestgaard wrote a series of articles for *Aftenposten* of Oslo which were greatly favorable.

I also received a very charming letter from Colonel Holmquist in which he explained how much he had been impressed by the *Abfahrt Kanonen,* and added, 'We Scandinavians are very grateful to you for the unprecedented development of downhill skiing technique for which we have to thank you.'

One of the greatest compliments ever paid to the Kandahar Ski Club was the acceptance by the Norwegians of a cup to be called the Norwegian-Kandahar Challenge Cup. Certainly one of my happiest recollections is of presenting the cup to the first winner, Stein Eriksen, in an Oslo restaurant.

In 1936, Winter Olympic Games were held in Garmisch-Partenkirchen and for the first time in the history of the games a downhill slalom combined event was held. Birger Rund of Norway, who had been living in Germany for two winters, won the downhill race, and the ladies' downhill resulted in a surprise victory for Froken Laila Schou-Nilsen, also of Norway, a girl of 16. The combined results of downhill and slalom resulted in a triumph for Germany, Franz Pfnur and Christel Cranz, both Germans, being the individual winners of the slalom and of the combined. Peter Lunn, 12th in the combined, and Jeannette Kessler, eighth, were the best for Great Britain.

I was asked to broadcast my impressions of the slalom, which I had refereed. The games had been exploited as propaganda for Nazism, and my mind travelled nostalgically back to Murren, the cradle of care-free skiing, and all I could bring myself to say was, '*Germans, may I tell you a little secret. There are still some people who ski for fun.'*

*Nastar is the new and highly
successful program for the recreational skier
who has a little bit of the racer in him*

Skiing
Against Par

by Gloria C. Chadwick

NASTAR NATIONAL COORDINATOR

This season an estimated 50,-000 skiers at as many as 75 ski areas throughout the country will take part in something called Nastar. What is it, and why has it grown so rapidly since its inception in 1969?

Nastar means National Standard Race and it refers to a competitive racing program that was conceived by Ski Magazine especially for the recreational skier. The competition takes place on an easy-to-ski giant slalom course at any of the sponsoring areas. The course is designed to test the ability of beginners and, at the same time, to permit experts to use technical skills to get down the hill faster. Basically, it is a run that is fun for skiers of every ability. The courses are between 25-30 gates and are designed to be run in 30-50 seconds.

By paying a $2 entry fee and running the course against an electric timer, a skier establishes a racing handicap — similar to the handicap in golf — and obtains a measurement of his racing skill that can be compared with skiers who entered Nastar programs elsewhere in the country.

Anyone, regardless of age or ability, is eligible to enter Nastar. Last season the youngest to complete a Nastar course was four years old, and the oldest 78. Nearly 30,000 recreational skiers participated in Nastar at 39 ski areas last year. A pilot program in 1969 involved 3,000 skiers at eight areas. Bob Beattie, former U.S. Olympic ski coach, is commissioner of the Nastar program.

How does Nastar test ability? Each ski area selects a top pro to be a pacesetter. He races against pacesetters from all the other Nastar race centers to establish his handicap. A zero handicap would mean he is the fastest pacesetter, his time becomes the national standard against which you and all other skiers can compare yourselves.

The pacesetter's time is translated into a national standard by having a special pacesetters' race early in December. Each pacesetter runs 15 trial heats. The 10 best runs are averaged and compared to one another to determine percentage ratios. From these the pacesetter receives his season's handicap. During the course of the season the pacesetter's handicap will be checked to be sure he is still consistent with the national standard.

For his area's Nastar races the pacesetter will take two runs, and his best time, which is corrected by his earned handicap will be "Par," the goal for that day's race. Example: a pacesetter with a national three handicap running the course in a 30.10 will have a "par" time of 29.20. It is the "par" time that all participants' handicaps are based on. The handicap compensates for differences in terrain, snow condition, even the pacesetter's mood.

Nastar is not a "who won" type of race. In Nastar you race against "par" just as in golf. The Nastar handicap is the percentage points by which your time run is slower than the national standard. A 21 handicap means you are 21 percentage points slower than the national standard. Everyone entering a Nastar race has the opportunity to qualify for the attractive Nastar gold, silver and bronze award pins. These pins are awarded by coming within a certain percentage of "Par."

Gold: men 20 per cent of par; women 25 per cent

Silver: men 35 per cent of par; women 40 per cent

Bronze: men 55 per cent of par; women 65 per cent

For the first time this coming season special consideration will be given juniors and veterans in order that they will be able to qualify for junior Nastar and veteran Nastar pins.

Plans for the 1970/71 season include holding regional as well as final competitions. Other special Nastar competitions will be held for deaf and amputee skiers. Team competitions between ski areas, clubs, ski shops will be encouraged. Nordic Nastar will be tried as a pilot program. Nastar participants will automatically be enrolled in the Nastar Club and receive the Nastar newsletter to make their Nastar participation more meaningful and a continuing one.

For additional information and a complete list of 1970/71 ski areas and their schedules write: Nastar Program, Gloria C. Chadwick, National Coordinator, 126 Cresta Road, Colorado Springs, Colorado 80906.

ABOUT THE AUTHOR

Gloria Chadwick has long been active in organizational skiing. Prior to taking her present position as national coordinator for Nastar, she served for eight years as executive secretary of the U.S. Ski Ass'n. Prior to that she worked for the Eastern Amateur Ski Ass'n for seven years. In her spare time, she enjoys working in the USSA ladies' cross country program, and painting.

by **Eileen Holm Matthew**

HOW TO ENTERTAIN OTHER SKIERS

Give them nectar, ambrosia and gemütlichkeit, *prepared exactly as follows*

Drinks never taste as good as they do after a thirst-building day on the ski slopes. There's something about coming inside to warm surroundings, propping up your feet, and bending your elbow with other skiers that makes "happy hour" the best time of the day.

Although there is nothing wrong with having a drink at the lodge bar or at some other après ski establishment, it's often more fun to come equipped with a small private stock. Such foresight can be a necessity when skiing in dry states such as Utah.

Inviting friends for cocktails in your cabin or room before dinner or during the evening is cozy and friendly. Having your own "mini-bar" can save you the bother of running out to the lounge, or the time wasted in waiting for room service. Buy ice if you can; if not, a wastebasket full of snow will do just as well. And it's the best way I know of to chill champagne. Drinks taste better in glasses than in paper cups, so don't be shy about asking everyone to bring one from his room if

necessary. Foam cups are fine for hot drinks.

In order to serve your guests in great style, you'll need certain items of equipment: an electric blendor, a small coffee pot to warm hot drinks, and the basic jigger, spoon, and opener. I have seen a molded luggage-style travel bar that comes complete with a small electric coffee pot. Of course, many lodge and motel rooms are furnished with water heating appliances these days. If you don't have a travel bar, tall airline bags are inexpensive and just the right size for toting bottles, blendor, and whatever. We often simplify things by preparing favorite formulas at home, and bringing them pre-mixed in bottles.

Punch is undoubtedly the easiest refreshment to serve to a large gathering. A plastic wastebasket or bucket makes a great punch bowl for after-ski parties. Without that luxury, you might use the bathroom washbasin *after* checking to be sure the drain stopper is a tight one. One spring vacation at Sun Valley, I saw served punch that had been made in a bathtub.

Here, then, are some suggestions for making potions to melt the ice:

HOT DRINKS

GLUH WEIN
1 cup dry red wine (Burgundy, claret, Chianti, etc.)
2 teaspoons sugar
1 strip orange peel
1 strip lemon peel
1 cinnamon stick
Heat all ingredients, do not boil. Strain into heated mug. (An easy way to heat a mug is by soaking it in hot water.) Add cinnamon stick, float lemon slice on top.

SCHUSSBOOMER'S GLOGG
2 ounces dry red wine
2 ounces sherry
1 ounce brandy
1 tablespoon sugar
3 dashes Angostura bitters
Heat all ingredients, do not boil. Pour mixture into heated mug. Garnish with two or three raisins and an unsalted almond.

HOT BUTTERED RUM
1 ounce light rum
1 ounce dark rum
2 cloves
Pinch each of ground cinnamon and nutmeg
½ teaspoon brown sugar
3 ounces heated apple cider
Small pat of butter

Place first five ingredients in a heated mug or pewter tankard. Add heated cider, float butter on top, and stir well.

WARMING HUT
1½ ounces light rum
1½ ounces dark rum
3 ounces dry red wine
2 teaspoons sugar
Twist of lemon peel, or a slice of lemon
Place ingredients in a heated mug, add boiling water, stir well.

LANGLAUFFER'S LEMONADE
1½ ounces rum
Juice of ½ lemon
1 teaspoon sugar
Place rum, lemon juice, and sugar in a heated cup or mug. Fill with hot water, float a lemon slice on top. A can of frozen lemonade reconstituted and heated may be substitute for the lemon juice, sugar, and hot water.

GIN GARLAND
3 ounces gin
2 teaspoons sugar
Juice of ½ lemon
Place ingredients in a heated cup or mug. Add boiling water as desired.

HOT SAKE
1 bottle sake (Japanese rice wine)
Pour sake into a heatproof container such as a baby's bottle or the server from a sake set. Heat container in a pan of hot water until the sake is quite warm. Serve a small amount at a time in sake cups or demitasse coffee cups, leaving the rest in the container to stay warm. Allow about six ounces per person. In a pinch, the top of a double boiler (preferably glass) may be used to warm the sake.

LONGTHONG
1½ ounces light rum
1½ ounces dark rum
   (or 3 ounces brandy, gin, or whisky)
1 teaspoon curaçao
Juice of ½ lemon

2 teaspoons sugar
1 tablespoon water
Dissolve sugar in water in a saucepan. Add rum, curaçao, and lemon juice. Heat, but do not boil. Serve in warm wine glass.

COFFEE DRINKS

SKI SLOPE
½ ounce vodka
1 teaspoon instant coffee
5 ounces prepared hot chocolate
Place vodka and instant coffee in a heated mug, add prepared hot chocolate. Shake powdered cinnamon on top.

IRISH COFFEE
1½ ounces Irish whisky
2 teaspoons sugar
1 cup strong, hot coffee
Whipping cream
Place whisky and sugar in a warm mug, or stemmed goblet. Fill to within one inch of the edge with hot coffee. Float very slightly whipped cream on top.

RUM NEW ENGLAND
1½ ounces dark rum
1 teaspoon sugar
1 teaspoon lemon juice
Hot tea
Place rum, sugar, and lemon juice in a heated cup. Add hot tea. (O.K., so it's not a coffee drink!) Float a lemon slice on top.

CAFE ROYALE
Brandy
1 lump of sugar
1 cup strong, hot coffee
Balance a silver spoon over a demitasse cup full of strong, hot coffee. Drop a sugar lump into the spoon, and fill the spoon with brandy. Allow the brandy and sugar to warm; then ignite. As the flame dies, stir the brandy and sugar into the coffee.

HOT PUNCHES

ANGEL FIRE PUNCH
   (8 Servings)
2 cups dry red wine (Burgundy, claret, Chianti)
2 cups tawny port

1 cup brandy
Orange peel
10 cloves
4 cinnamon sticks, broken up

Remove the skin from a large orange in one long curl; stud the curl with cloves. Place all ingredients in a chafing dish pan, and heat almost to a boil on the kitchen stove. When the punch is hot, carry the pan to the serving table and set aside. Light the alcohol or Sterno flame for the chafing dish. Dip a metal ladle full of punch, and hold it over the flame until it is very hot. Ignite the punch. (The secret of flaming is to get the punch very hot and keep it hot). Quickly put the pan over the flame, and pour the flaming liquid from the ladle into the pan. The fire will spread over the surface of the punch. Now put on a show for your guests by dipping a flaming ladle full of punch, and pouring a line of fire back into the pan from a foot or so in the air. Serve punch in cups before the flame goes out.

APPLEJACK FLAMER
(10 Servings)
1 quart applejack
½ ounce Angostura bitters
1 cup sugar
Lemon peel
1 quart boiling water

Place applejack, bitters, sugar, and lemon peel in a chafing dish pan. Heat almost to a boil on the kitchen stove, stirring until sugar is dissolved. When mixture is hot, carry pan to serving table and place over chafing dish flame. Ignite, then pour boiling water over mixture while it is flaming. Ladle into heated mugs.

COLD DRINKS

SLALOM SLING
2 ounces gin
1 ounce cherry brandy
1 dash Benedictine
1 dash Angostura bitters
1 teaspoon sugar
Juice of ½ lemon

Pour all ingredients into blendor with a little cracked ice. Turn on blendor briefly to mix and chill drink. Serve with straws in a tall glass. Add club soda to taste, if desired.

SITZMARK
1 ounce dark rum
1 ounce light rum
1 ounce orange curaçao
½ ounce Orgeat syrup
Dash of Angostura bitters

Mix ingredients in blendor with a small amount of cracked ice. Serve in a large, chilled Old Fashioned glass.

SNOW MAN
2 ounces light rum
2 ounces lemon juice
1 teaspoon simple syrup
3 pineapple chunks

Combine ingredients in blendor. Add a small amount of cracked ice and blend until drink is mixed and chilled. Serve in a chilled cocktail glass.

BETWEEN THE SHEETS
1 ounce brandy
1 ounce Cointreau
1 ounce light rum
(Juice of ½ lemon, if desired)

Mix ingredients in blendor with a small amount of cracked ice. Serve in chilled cocktail glass.

SKIER'S MIST
1½ ounces Scotch

Fill an Old Fashioned glass with snow. Pour in whisky. Garnish with a twist of lemon peel.

DAMN THE WEATHER
2 ounces gin
1 ounce sweet vermouth
1 ounce orange juice
Dash of Curacao

Mix ingredients in a blendor with a small amount of cracked ice. Serve in a chilled cocktail glass.

DOWNHILL SPECIAL
1½ ounces rye
1 teaspoon simple syrup
Dash Angostura bitters

Pour into chilled Old Fashioned glass. Add ice cubes and a twist of orange peel.

MOGUL CHASER
1½ ounces Southern Comfort

Fill an Old Fashioned glass with snow. Pour in Southern Comfort. Add a twist of orange peel.

AFTER DINNER DRINKS

SNOWBUNNY'S DOWNFALL
3 ounces brandy
¾ ounce Curaçao
Dash of Angostura bitters

Pour into a chilled Old Fashioned glass. Add ice cubes and a twist of lemon peel.

STINGER
½ ounce crème de menthe
1 ounce brandy

Mix in blendor with a small amount of cracked ice. Serve in chilled cocktail glass.

GUN BARREL
1½ ounces brandy
½ ounce sweet vermouth
Dash of Angostura bitters

Mix in blendor with a small amount of cracked ice. Serve in chilled cocktail glass.

THE WAY TO A SKIER'S HEART

Dining out at a ski resort can be a memorable part of après ski activity. There is usually a choice of atmospheric dining spots which feature a wide variety of culinary masterpieces. The only problem to the repeat skier without stretch dollars is that the meals are usually as expensive as they are delicious.

Skiers who take to the slopes regularly often find accommodations with cooking facilities. Self-prepared meals can be both easy and elegant.

Some of these dishes may be fixed ahead of time, and warmed

up when needed. Others may be quickly prepared after a day on the ski slopes. Some recipes are money-savers, others are elegant splurges. All of them are winners. Here are a few of my favorites:

CHEESE FONDUE

Swiss cheese fondue is easily the most sought-after recipe in the skiing world. It is sometimes called the "national dish" of Switzerland. Fondue is good either for dinner, or as a late evening snack. This authentic recipe was brought to me by a friend who spent a season in the Swiss Alps.

Fondue is most easily cooked and served with the aid of a fondue set consisting of a cooking pot over a burner, and a set of long, wooden-handled forks. A casserole or a pan heated over a hot plate or on the stove will do quite well if you lack the more elegant equipment.

The best fondue is made from a mixture of about one-half Gruyère and one-half Emmenthaler cheese. You can get by with the common American type "Swiss" cheese if you combine it with at least one-third Gruyère cheese to retain the proper consistency.

Shred 6 ounces of cheese per person, and place it in a cooking utensil which has been well rubbed with a clove of garlic. Add a "nut" of butter (exact amount not important) and pour in about ½ cup of dry white wine for each pound of cheese used.

Heat the fondue mixture, stirring constatly. Fondue must be stirred continuously from the instant it begins cooking, until it vanishes into the last hungry mouth. It should be served at the exact moment it is ready, and should be stirred by the eaters with their forks while it is being eaten.

As soon as the fondue begins to cook, stir in a liqueur glass of good kirsch (or cherry

brandy) in which you have dissolved two teaspoons of corn starch (for a four-person batch) and a little grated nutmeg. Add salt and pepper to taste. A dash of bicarbonate of soda at the last moment will make the fondue lighter.

When the cheese and wine have melted smoothly together, the fondue is ready to serve. Place the utensil over low heat on the table so that the fondue will continue cooking during the meal.

Each hungry skier should be equipped with a long-handled fork, a plate, and a pile of bite-sized chunks of good sourdough French bread. (Be careful not to cut the bread into too tiny pieces. Leave some crust on each one.)

A piece of bread is speared with the fork, stirred around in the fondue, and eaten. Some people like to drop it on the plate first, for a cooling-off period. But if the bread falls off the fork in the fondue pot, watch out! The penalty is a kiss.

BEEF FONDUE

Beef fondue has long been the rage at ski resorts on the Continent. Give it a try and you'll see why.

Beef fondue requires the same props you use with the cheese version — long-handled forks and a fondue cooking set. I think an electric saucepan is even better than a conventional fondue cooker because it keeps the oil at the ideal temperature, which happens to be 375° F. Most people like to have two forks — one for cooking (which gets hot), and one for eating (which stays cool).

You'll need about a half pound of beef per person, a pint of salad oil for cooking, and a tempting assortment of condiments and sauces. Cut the beef into one inch cubes. Pat them dry with paper towels. Heat the oil to 375° F. (check it

with a fat thermometer) and place the cooking utensil over a low heat in the center of the table. Group the condiments around the fondue pot so that every guest can reach them.

Each person cooks his own fondue by spearing the meat with a fork and dipping it into the hot oil until it is done enough to suit him. Then it is dipped into a sauce and eaten. I like to give each person a huge paper or cloth bib to protect clothing from possible oil spatters.

For sauces and condiments, you can serve anything that suits your taste. Various types of mustard, catsup, chile sauce, garlic butter, pickles and pickle

relishes, olives, mayonnaise mixed with horse-radish, sour cream and chives, onion slices, chutney, and potato chips or corn chips are all delicious.

Complete the meal with a good red wine, a crisp salad, a rich dessert, and coffee. It will be an evening to remember.

SKIER'S BEEF

Here is a man's recipe for a gourmet après-ski dish that is both delicious and simple to prepare. Serve it with rice pilaf (the instant variety will speed things along), red wine, green salad, hot biscuits (from a tube or a dry mix) and coffee. The amounts given here will serve six people.

3 or 4 pounds lean beef, cut in 1 inch cubes and marinated in

red wine
2 packages dried onion soup mix
1 or 2 cups of whole fresh
mushrooms
¼ pound of butter, melted

Place a layer of beef cubes in a casserole. Cover it with one package of dried onion soup mix. Add a layer of uncooked fresh mushrooms, either whole or sliced. Spoon over half the melted butter. Repeat layers of beef cubes, mushrooms, and butter. Cover the casserole with foil or with a tight lid, and bake at 350 degrees for two hours or so, depending upon the cut of beef selected.

This dish can be cooked ahead of time, and reheated after skiing.

SCHUSS KEBAB

If you're lucky enough to be staying in a ski cabin or a room with a fireplace, it's great fun to cook dinner over the fire while prospective diners gather around and watch. You will need a long-handled double grill which holds the food inside, so that you can turn the whole thing over to cook both sides of the meat. An asbestos barbecue mitt and a basting brush are handy, also.

Schuss Kebab can be made at home on disposable bamboo skewers, and packed along, soaking in a tasty marinade. When no kitchen facilities are available for making salad and pilaf, you can complete the meal with your favorite canned foods heated in their containers right next to some of the hot coals in the fireplace. Be sure to remove the can lids, however, to let the steam escape. During a trip to Canada I learned this the hard way by having a can of beans explode like a bomb. I half expected to be arrested by the Mounted Police, but fortunately none were within earshot at the time.

A bottle of dry white wine, chilled in a snowbank, is really a necessity with Schuss Kebab.

SCHUSS KEBAB
5 or 6 chunks of lean lamb per person
3 whole mushrooms per person
½ onion cut into 3 wedges per person, or 3 small whole onions
Plenty of small cherry tomatoes
MARINADE (Increase amount as needed.)
⅓ cup sherry
2 tablespoons salad oil
1 teaspoon oregano (crushed a little in the palm of your hand)
½ teaspoon freshly ground pepper
1 teaspoon salt

Thread meat, onion, and mushrooms on skewers. Marinate overnight. Cook slowly over hot coals, turning frequently and basting with marinade. Thread the tomatoes on separate skewers and cook over coals for a lesser period of time.

BEEF BROCHETTE

Beef Brochette is similar to Schuss Kebab, except that beef is substituted for lamb on the skewers. You may wish to add bacon and green pepper to the skewer line-up of meat, onions, and mushrooms. Rice, a crisp salad, and Rosé wine packed in snow are excellent with Beef Brochette. Or you may warm canned foods in the fireplace when there are no other cooking facilities.

Daring cooks may wish to try roasting ears of corn or potatoes on the coals. You can prepare these at home by brushing them with melted butter, and wrapping them in double thicknesses of heavy duty aluminum foil. The idea is to knock the gray ash off the coals, and lay the potatoes or corn right on top. Potatoes take about an hour to roast, while corn is usually done in ten minutes. I must admit I have had varying degrees of success with roasting corn and potatoes, and I heartily recommend that you try it at home first.

BEEF BROCHETTE
MARINADE (Increase amount as needed.)
½ cup salad oil
¼ cup soy sauce
4 teaspoons Worcestershire sauce
½ teaspoon salt
1 teaspoon dry mustard
1 teaspoon freshly ground pepper
3 tablespoons wine vinegar
1 crushed garlic clove
4 teaspoons fresh lemon juice

Combine ingredients in marinade. Mix well, add beef chunks, and refrigerate until needed. Prepare Beef Brochette in the some manner as Schuss Kebab.

SKIER'S SKEWERS

One of the easiest skewer loads to prepare is Skier's Skewers, which simply alternates cubes of boneless canned ham with canned pineapple chunks. Follow the cooking directions for Schuss Kebab, using this marinade-basting sauce.
MARINADE
½ cup honey
¾ cup lemon juice
½ teaspoon ground cloves
3 teaspoons soy sauce
½ teaspoon M.S.G.

Combine ingredients in a screw-top jar. Shake to mix well and pour over ham cubes.

ABOUT THE AUTHOR

Eileen Holm Matthew learned to ski in California's Sierra Nevada mountain range while she was earning her A.B. and M.A. degrees from Stanford University. She has taught physical education in California and in Pennsylvania, and she has traveled widely in most of the 50 states, as well as numerous foreign countries. Her work as a free-lance writer and photographer has appeared in many popular magazines. She presently lives in Grants Pass, Oregon, and skis regularly at nearby Mt. Ashland with her husband and small son.

HOW TO ENTERTAIN YOURSELF

GO How much après-ski, can an après-skier après-ski if a skier isn't all fagged out by skiing before après-skiing? This is the true account of mid-Manhattanite Kitty Lutz, a story teller for the New York City Public Library, who came to visit Stowe, and close friend Ted Ross. Ted introduced Kitty to only a few of the 27 Stowe establishments that own liquor licenses, the largest collection of après-ski spots in one ski village in the East. Here is the blow-by-blow account of their evening. It was exhausting and a lot of fun and it delayed their early morning skiing by just a few hours.

4:15 Skiing is finished at Spruce, where Kitty took lessons. Ted picked her up for a quick trip to *The Den,* attached to The Lodge at Smuggler's Notch. Here is where the ski instructors and skiers stop for a warm drink before heading down the mountain. Clientele, outside of the ski school, is usually middle-aged marrieds and hot buttered rums move quickly, although ski instructors like their beer. Kitty's comment: "The drink is real smooth." Ted's comment: "If we sit with the ski instructors, we get our drinks at half price." Hot buttered rums are $1.00 but seeing Ted was in on the half price (he is an occasional ski instructor at Stowe), he bought a round: 6 Schlitz at .30 each, 2 HBR's at .50 each for total of $2.80. Add .12 for tax and .50 for tip, and he and Kitty walked out for $3.42, after bidding goodbye to Phinias, a ski instructor who likes to argue for the Austrian technique.

When home remedies fail, when you're not group-bound, and above all when you have $43.47 in your pocket, just swing, as did this young couple in Stowe, Vt., one merry winter night

Text and Photos by Peter Miller

5:00 Just a mile down the road is the *Matterhorn* which at one point in its history sold more beer than any other pub in Vermont. It still is famous for draft beer and attracts the younger set for a few pops and a pick-up. On weekends the place is jammed from 4:30 on. Ski bums congregate, during the week, and behind the bar is Roger, who claims to be part Indian and who has the reputation of being an able trout fisherman. The Matterhorn, besides being famous for wild evenings, is also well known for its large roast beef and tuna sandwiches. Draft is .50. Ted had his usual, Canadian Club on the Rocks, Kitty had a draft, and the two ski bums in the picture sneaked two drafts out of Ted. Drafts at $1.50, one CC at $1.00, .50 tip for Roger—total of $3.00.

5:45 Favorite spot for a longer drink after skiing is *The Shed.* Proprietor Ken Strong serves fondue made with cheese and white wine as a free tidbit from 4:00 to 6:00. He is also famous for his Shedburgers, hamburgers soaked in beer and grilled. In be-

tween bites of fondue and chat with Ken ("skiing was pretty good today, sort of granular but nice and slick"), Ted and Kitty had a drink, then bought four drafts for acquaintances met on the slopes: two men from Detroit who just met two gals from Boston who were just planning their evening ("We understand all the action's at the Black Gull later on? See you there?"). Kitty, on her first watering stop, found that the sliding door to the john area was mystifying; she tried to pull it open. Ted gallantly showed her that it would facilitate matters to slide it open. Kitty liked the Shed. "It's real comfy but there's no fireplace." Ross paid up ($4.10—.85 for the CC, $2.00 for four drafts, .75 for Scotch and Water, .50 for tip, and nothing for a mouthful of fondue) and led her out.

7:00 The downstairs lounge of the Green Mountain Inn, located within Stowe Village, is called *The Whip.* It is decorated with horse whips and carriage lamps, and did have Kitty's current desire: a large fireplace burning brightly. Local businessmen who consider themselves important to the economy of Stowe stop here for an after-work snort and gossip with their cronies. Skiers usually fill the bar. Jimmy, the red-coated bartender, coaxed Ted and Kitty into the $1.50 specialty of the house, a Whip—extra large quantities of bourbon and a few other mixtures, including oranges marinated in liqueur. Kitty's comment, after a cuddle and a snort by the fire, was "Wow!" Ted paid ($3.10 includ-

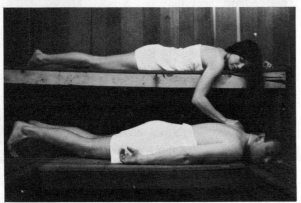

ing tax and .30 tip) and said he was getting a little drunk.

7:40 For a sobering and warming experience, Ted decided on a sauna at *The Centre,* now also known as Jack Straw's Inn. Cost is $2.00 per person and with a little inhibition Kitty and Ted slapsticked a few faces on the door of the sauna before the 180° heat warmly sobered their giggles. Kitty: "This is soooo nice! I could stay here all night." Ted: "Rub my back, Kitty. Thank you." Kitty: "I think I'll go to sleep." Ted: "You better take a cold shower."

They did. She said "Eeek!", and, dressed again, they hopped upstairs for a quick drink before heading home for a quick change before dinner. Cost—CC on Rocks-$1.00, Scotch and Water, $1.00, tip .40, total cost with sauna, $6.40.

8:30 It was time to eat, so Ted took Kitty to *La Bicoque,* a French restaurant that specializes in Provence cooking with the theory that garlic is refreshing. M. and Mme. Jaubert, both of

them enthusiastic skiers, do their own cooking and serving with the help of a daughter and a nubile friend. On the wall are Mme. Jaubert's paintings, impressionistic with the bright colors of her southern France home. La Bicoque is one of the few restaurants in town that keeps its kitchen open until 11:00. The service is slow, the cocktails heavy, and the atmosphere relaxed, friendly, and even a bit romantic. Specialties are Broiled Shrimp served with a garlic and mustard sauce, Seafood Bisque, Quiche Lorraine and, for dessert, small cakes or Peche Melba served with a rum sauce. A spartan meal of broiled shrimp and Mateus came to $12.50 with tax, and Ted left a $1.75 tip.

10:40 The meal was spartan because Ted and Kitty were late for a rendezvous with friends at *Stowe Stables* for a mile-and-a-half sleigh ride. Duane Cobb is the driver, and for $15.00 he will drive one of his buckboard sleighs (filled with bales of hay), around the mowings behind his stable, a trip that takes from an hour to an hour and a half, depending upon how Mr. Cobb feels. The sleigh takes up to 12 people and heavy clothes, comforters, and warm potables are recommended. Included in this trip was a jug of hard cider that Ted Ross had made (take 10 gallons of apple cider in a keg, sweeten with 10 pounds of sugar, let it sit three months, add potato peels to clear it, tap and drink).

Mr. Cobb said it was the finest he had tasted in a long while, and he looped his horses around again. Under a moonlit sky, Mr. Cobb's sleigh ride is straight out of *Dr. Zhivago*. At $2.50 per couple, the price was cheap.

12:15 Ted and Kitty's next stop was *Sister Kate's* where a Princeton graduate-proprietor, Rock King, sings, plays the piano, and tells the funniest off-color jokes ever heard in Vermont. It's good to be a little loaded for his show. The show room is a large, sit-down affair, but the upstairs is smaller, designed for coffee, Sunday brunch, after-hours (2:00 a.m.) buffets, or just a good belt. Edwardian Red, Tiffany Lamps and Victorian head shots of long-gone Vermonters provide the motif. Cost—$2.30 for his CC, her Scotch and Water.

12:50 Then they walked to *The Black Gull,* Stowe's leading night spot where Gene Cipriano's trio keeps a fast hot beat and the dancing is correspondingly furious. It is the favorite pick-up place. There is a long bar, and upstairs and downstairs lounges. The atmosphere is partly Yankee as the building itself is a converted barn. Here is where one lone male tried to pick up Kitty before Ted moved her to safer grounds on the dance floor. For two drinks each, their last stop cost Ted $4.60.

STOP After some conversation on the front stoop, Ted and Kitty ended their après-ski jaunt, and this account, with a kiss.

Fifty Recommended Mountains in North America

Call them the "tops:" fifty of the world's finest ski mountains, all located in the United States and Canada. Each has something very special to offer the skier.

Maybe it's the terrain, with an assortment of dazzling runs and wide-open slopes. Some are meccas for superskiers, hotshots who demand spine-tingling trails. Others are great "teaching mountains," the place to go if you want to learn how under the best conditions, with the best instruction. Some are swathed in the most delicious powder snow under the sun. Some boast the longest season. Some are a mere ski-jump from a metropolitan area, and others are away-from-it-all worlds unto themselves.

Après ski is considered as important as uphill facilities, and the life styles are as distinctive as the mountains themselves. Some are for families who want good meals, bright fires, and quiet companionship before turning in early. Others swing all night. Some areas offer a little bit—or a lot—of everything.

Among these fifty there's a mountain to suit your skiing ability, your life style, and your budget. But one note of caution: Generally speaking, the data are as up-to-date as we could make them at press time. But prices do have a way of changing, usually upward, and new trails are constantly being built and lifts added or improved. If you're considering spending more than a weekend at any of these mountains, it's always wise to write ahead for the latest information.

Sugarloaf
MAINE

Boasting one of the longest seasons in the country and some rather magnificent snow-fields, Sugarloaf attracts a serious crowd that is willing to sacrifice frills for fine skiing.

THE MOUNTAIN: Altitude - 4300'; Vertical drop - 2600'; Exposure - N./N.W.; Annual snowfall - 13'; Longest trail - 3¼ mi.; Slopes and trails - 8 exp., 10 int., 6 nov.; 30 mi. x-c; Total acreage - 2000.

LIFTS: 1 gondola, 1 double chair, 5 T-bars; Fees - $6.50 weekdays, $8 weekends.

SKI SCHOOL: Harry Baxter, director; 12 instructors, American tech.; Cost of lessons - 2-hr. group, $5; 1-hr. private, $8.

FACILITIES AND SERVICES: Ski shop, rentals, cafeteria, restaurant, bar, entertainment, children's nursery (min. age, 2).

ADDITIONAL SPORTS AT AREA: Ice skating, ski-bobbing, snowmobiling.

ACCOMMODATIONS: 100 beds at area, 800 in vicinity; Contact for information - Sugarloaf Area Association, Kingfield, Maine 04947.

LOCATION: Nearest town - Kingfield; Nearest major city - Waterville or Bangor; Nearest airport - Carrabasset-Sugarloaf.

ATMOSPHERE: There are 1200 chalets, all privately owned and all season ticket-holders, who establish this as a family place, but not to the exclusion of a "progressive element." Apres-ski includes all kinds of music and some unusual theatrical entertainment.

Cannon Mountain
NEW HAMPSHIRE

A pioneer Eastern ski center since 1930, state-owned Cannon Mountain was the site of the nation's first racing trail, the first organized ski school, and the first aerial tramway on the continent. Present history includes snow-making equipment to take advantage of the varied terrain.

THE MOUNTAIN: Altitude - 4200′; Vertical drop - 2130′; Exposure - N.E.; Annual snowfall - 14′; Longest trail - 2 mi.; Total acreage - 164; Slopes and trails - 9 exp. (4 mi.), 18 int. (18 mi.), 11 nov. (5 mi.), 3 x-c (4 mi.); Snow-making machinery.

LIFTS: 2 double chairlifts, 1 tramway, 4 T-bars; Fees - $9 weekends, $7 weekdays.

SKI SCHOOL: Paul Valar, director; 15 instructors, American tech.; Cost of lessons - 2-hr. group, $5; 1-hr. private, $12.

FACILITIES AND SERVICES: Ski shop, rentals, 2 cafeterias, restaurant; children's nursery nearby (min. age, 1 yr.).

ACCOMMODATIONS: 1500 in vicinity; Write for information - Ski 93, Lincoln, N. H. 03251.

ATMOSPHERE: Some, with New England bluntness, claim its après-ski life is "lousy." Others say it's what you make of it, and what appeals to you. Whatever it is, it's not at the mountain but in near-by hostelries, of which there is no shortage.

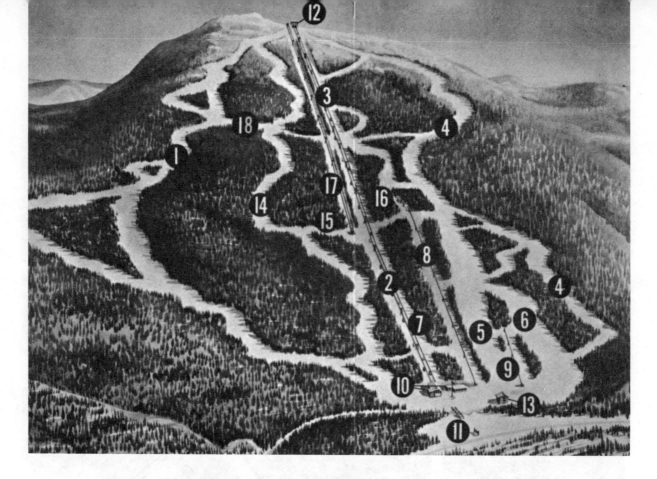

Wildcat Mountain
NEW HAMPSHIRE

Wildcat is in the midst of a huge expansion program designed to take greater advantage of its natural endowments: its location in the heart of the White Mountain National Forest with a spectacular view of Mt. Washington, one of the greatest annual snowfalls in the east, and a long, long season.

THE MOUNTAIN: Altitude - 4100'; Vertical drop - 2100'; Exposure - North; Annual snowfall - 14'; Longest trail - nearly 3 mi.; Slopes and trails - 8 exp., 7 int., 7 nov.

LIFTS: 2 double chairs, 1 gondola, 2 T-bars; Fees - $9 weekends, $8 weekdays.

SKI SCHOOL: John R. Winn, director; 13—24 instructors, American tech.; Cost of lessons - 2-hr. group, $5; 1-hr. private, $10.

FACILITIES AND SERVICES: Ski shop, rentals, cafeteria; restaurant and bar planned; children's nursery (min. age, 2 yrs.).

ACCOMMODATIONS: 5000 in vicinity; Contact for information - Mt. Washington Valley Assoc., North Conway, N. H. 03860.

LOCATION: Nearest town - Jackson; Nearest major city - Portland, Me.; Nearest airports - Portland; Berlin, N. H. and Fryeburg, Me.

ATMOSPHERE: People who ski almost every free day they can—from the first snowflake to the first dandelion—are the kind of folks who like Wildcat. Apres-ski life is plentiful and varied with a wide choice in atmosphere, sound, menu, and cost.

Mt. Sunapee
NEW HAMPSHIRE

Like Cannon, Mt. Sunapee is state-owned, and New Hampshire takes good care of its skiers. It's also the southernmost of the major ski areas, making it a "commuter's mountain."

THE MOUNTAIN: Altitude - 2743′; Vertical drop - 1450′; Exposure - N.W.; Longest trail - 2½ mi.; Slopes and trails - 1 exp., 14 int., 5 nov.; Total acreage - 190; Snow-making machinery.

LIFTS: 5 double chairlifts, 2 T-bars, 1 rope; Fees - $9 weekends, $7 weekdays.

SKI SCHOOL: Walter Graf, director; 20 instructors, American tech.; Cost of lessons - 2-hr. group, $4.50; 1-hr. private, $12.

FACILITIES AND SERVICES: Ski shop, rentals, cafeteria; children's nursery, Wednesday through Sunday.

ADDITIONAL SPORTS AT AREA: Ice skating, ski-bobbing.

ACCOMMODATIONS: None at area, 1000 in vicinity; Contact for information - Lake Sunapee Board of Trade, Mt. Sunapee, N. H. 03772.

LOCATION: Nearest town: Newbury; Nearest major city - Concord; Nearest airport - Lebanon.

ATMOSPHERE: Leans to the do-it-yourself kind of fun, with inns and lodges providing most of the impetus.

Loon Mountain
NEW HAMPSHIRE

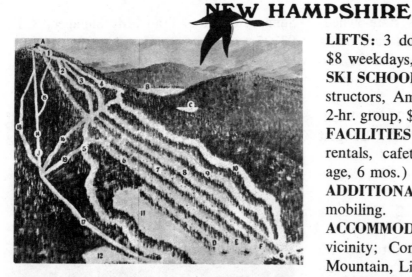

One of the most imaginative ski areas in the country, Loon brings in all types of skiers, but it's the families who love it most.

THE MOUNTAIN: Altitude - 3000'; Vertical drop - 1700'; Exposure - North; Annual snowfall - 4'—8'; Longest trail - 2 mi.; Slopes and trails - 4 exp., 7 int., 7 nov.; 5 mi. x-c; Total acreage, 120.

LIFTS: 3 double chairs, 1 gondola; Fees - $8 weekdays, $9 weekends.

SKI SCHOOL: John Wilson, director; 10 instructors, American tech.; Cost of lessons - 2-hr. group, $5; 1-hr. private, $12.

FACILITIES AND SERVICES: Ski shop, rentals, cafeteria, children's nursery (min. age, 6 mos.)

ADDITIONAL SPORTS: Ice skating, snowmobiling.

ACCOMMODATIONS: 110 at area, 1000 in vicinity; Contact for information - Loon Mountain, Lincoln, N. H. 03251.

ATMOSPHERE: The homesite area (you can ski down to the lifts) is being rapidly occupied by families building nice homes with a good sense of community. Lift ticket sales and season passes are limited. Good food, dancing, and quiet atmosphere are there, but swingers usually end up somewhere else.

Mount Cranmore
NEW HAMPSHIRE

Brainchild of the late Hannes Schneider, Mt. Cranmore is a sort of New England tradition, and the excellent ski school carries on in Schneider's manner.

THE MOUNTAIN: Altitude - 2000'; Vertical drop - 1500'; Exposure W./S./E.; Annual snowfall - 5'—10'; Longest trail - 2 mi. Slopes and trails - 6 exp., 8 int., 2 nov., 1 x-c.

LIFTS: 3 double chairs, 1 poma, 2 trestle-track tramways; Fees - $7 weekdays, $8 weekends.

SKI SCHOOL: Eduard Mall, director; American tech.; 20—45 instructors; Cost of lessons - 2-hr. group, $5; 1-hr. private, $10.

FACILITIES AND SERVICES: Ski shop, rentals, cafeteria, bar, restaurant.

ACCOMMODATIONS: None in area, 3500 within 10-mi. radius; Contact for information - Mt. Washington Valley Office, North Conway, N. H. 03860.

LOCATION: Nearest town - North Conway; Nearest major city - Portland, Me.; Nearest airport - Portland, Me.

ATMOSPHERE: Middle income skiing families and vacationing students with all levels of skiing ability find a niche in these marvelously varied slopes. Dancing, movies, live entertainment, and a lighted night skating rink give after-ski life the same variety.

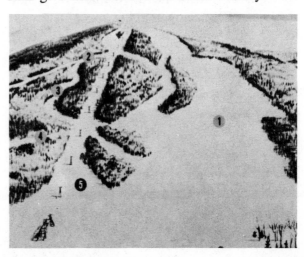

Waterville Valley
NEW HAMPSHIRE

Take your choice at Waterville Valley: Mt. Tecumseh, with runs for intermediate and expert skiers, or Snow's Mountain, an older and smaller ski area open weekends and holidays only, for the less proficient skier who also likes the intimacy of a small area.

THE MOUNTAIN: MT. TECUMSEH—Altitude - 3850'; Vertical drop - 2020'; Exposure - E./N.E.; Annual snowfall - 15'; Longest trail - 2½ mi.; Slopes and trails - 10 exp., 12 int., 4 nov., 10 mi. x-c; Total acreage - 175; Snow-making machinery.

LIFTS: 5 double chairs, 1 T-bar, 1 J-bar; Fees - $9 weekends, $6 weekdays.

SNOW'S MOUNTAIN—Altitude - 2170'; Vertical drop - 650'; Exposure - S.W.; An-

nual snowfall - 12'; Slopes and trails - 2 int., 2 nov., 10 mi. x-c; Total acreage - 18; Night skiing.

LIFTS: 2 T-bars, 1 pony-lift; Fees - $5 weekends.

SKI SCHOOL: Paul Pfosi, director; 25 instructors, GLM and American Tech.; Cost - 2-hr. group, $4; 1-hr. private, $10.

FACILITIES AND SERVICES: Ski shop, rentals, cafeteria, restaurant; children's nursery (out of diapers).

ADDITIONAL SPORTS: Ice skating.

ACCOMMODATIONS: 550 in area, 800 in vicinity; Contact for information - Waterville Valley Associates, Waterville Valley, N. H. 03223.

LOCATION: Nearest town - Campton; Nearest major city - Plymouth; Nearest airport - Laconia.

ATMOSPHERE: Still in the building stages, a complete pedestrian village with the ski lift rising out of the village center is the goal—the kind of place that will attract a steady crowd returning to its condominiums.

Mount Snow
VERMONT

Name it, and you can find it here: outdoor swimming pools, indoor skating rink, an "air car" from lodge to lifts, Japanese hot and cold baths—plus "four worlds of skiing," including a man-made glacier for superb spring skiing.

THE MOUNTAIN: Altitude - 3600'; Vertical drop - 1900'; Exposures - S., E., N.E., N.; Annual snowfall - 18—20'; Longest trail - 3½ mi.; Slopes and trails - 7 exp., 24 int., 10 nov., 1 x-c; Total acreage - 5000; Snow-making machinery.

LIFTS: 10 double chairs, 2 gondolas, 1 T-bar, 2 ropes; Fees - $9 weekends, $7 weekdays.

SKI SCHOOL: Robert Gratton, director; 80 instructors, Modified American tech.; Cost of lessons - 2-hr. group, $5; 1-hr. private, $12.

FACILITIES AND SERVICES: Ski shop, rentals, 5 cafeterias, 2 restaurants, 2 bars; children's nursery (min. age, 2).

ADDITIONAL SPORTS AT AREA: Swimming, ice skating; snowmobiling nearby.

ACCOMMODATIONS: 1000 at area, 1200 in vicinity; Contact for information - Valley of the Inns, Wilmington, Vt. 05363.

LOCATION: Nearest town - Wilmington; Nearest major city - Brattleboro, Vt.; Nearest airport - Albany, N. Y.; Mt. Snow (private).

ATMOSPHERE: This all-around-the-year all-around area attracts a number of non-skiers as well as skiers with its something-for-everybody philosophy. Apres-ski life runs the gamut from folk to rock.

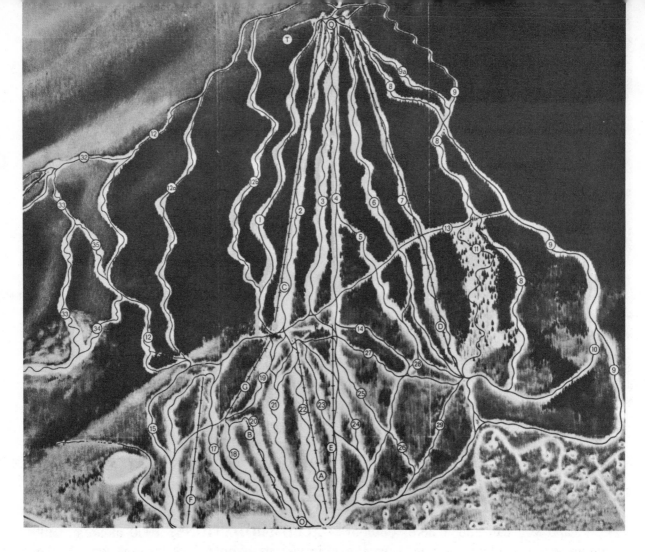

Stratton
VERMONT

It's a nice place to ski, even if you don't own a chalet here—as do a good many Fairfield County, Connecticut, executives and their families who continue to flock to one of the biggest "in" places in Southern Vermont.

THE MOUNTAIN: Altitude - 2000'—4000'; Vertical drop - 2000'; Exposure - N.E.; Longest trail - 1400'; Slopes and trails - 11 exp., 14 int., 16 nov., 2 x-c; Total acreage - 400—500; Snow-making machinery.

LIFTS: 6 double chairs, 2 T-bars, 1 pony-lift; Fees - $10 weekends, $9 weekdays.

SKI SCHOOL: Emo Henrich, director; 45—95 instructors, American Tech.; Cost of lessons - 2-hr. group, $3.75—$5.50; 1-hr. private, $12.

FACILITIES AND SERVICES: Ski shop, rentals, cafeteria, restaurant, bar, nightclub, entertainment; children's nursery (min. age 1—3); children's ski schools (age 3—5, and 6—11).

ADDITIONAL SPORTS: Snowmobiling a few miles away.

ACCOMMODATIONS: 350 rooms at base, 100 inns in vicinity; Contact for information - Green Mountain Resort Association, Londonderry, Vt. 05148.

LOCATION: Nearest town - Bondville; Nearest major city - Bennington, Brattleboro; Nearest airport - Rutland; Albany, N. Y.

ATMOSPHERE: Apres-ski life runs the gamut from Tyrolean music each evening in the base lodge to at-home entertainment in the private chalets and apartments to all-out nightclub swinging . . . and every shade and flavor in between.

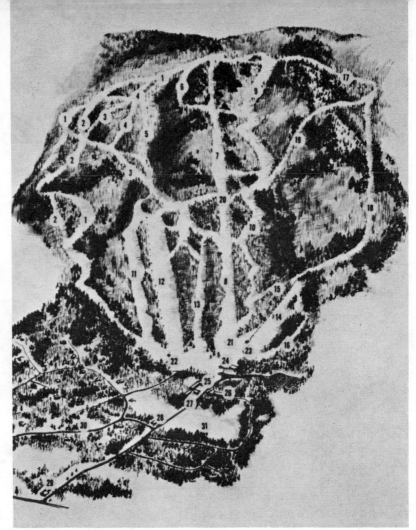

Magic Mountain
VERMONT

This is the place for swingers, who really dig that Abracadabra Room, and also maybe the really fine skiing, and some of the shortest lift lines in Southern Vermont.

THE MOUNTAIN: Altitude - 3000'; Vertical drop - 1550'; Exposure N./N.W.; Longest trail - 2½ mi.; Slopes and trails - 6 exp., 9 int., 5 nov.; Total acreage - 200; Snowmaking machinery.

LIFTS: 2 double chairs, 1 T-bar; Fees - $10 weekends, $8 weekdays.

SKI SCHOOL: Hans Thorner, director; 20 instructors, FUN Tech.; Cost of lessons - 2-hr. group, $5; 1-hr. private, $12.

FACILITIES AND SERVICES: Ski shop, rentals, cafeteria, restaurant, bar, nightclub, entertainment; children's nursery (min. age, 3 yrs.).

ADDITIONAL SPORTS: Ice skating, swimming; ski-bobbing in mid-week.

ACCOMMODATIONS: 500 at base, 5000 in vicinity; Contact for information - Magic Mountain Corporation, Londonderry, Vt. 05148.

LOCATION: Nearest town - Londonderry; Nearest major city - Rutland; Nearest airport - Rutland.

ATMOSPHERE: VERY lively, what with all the "imaginative" people the area seeks to attract. A limit of 1500 skiers keeps things in line and keeps the place intimate and friendly as well as swinging.

Big Bromley
VERMONT

With snow-making machinery supplying what Old Man Winter forgets on 80 per cent of the mountain, Big Bromley remains one of the great Green Mountains of Southern Vermont, easily holding its own fine reputation among the young whippersnappers that have sprung up all around.

THE MOUNTAIN: Altitude - 3284'; Vertical drop - 1334'; Exposure - South; Annual snowfall - 4'; Longest trail - 2 mi.; Slopes and trails - 6 exp., 9 int., 8 nov.; Total acreage - 1000; Snow-making machinery.

LIFTS: 3 double chairs, 5 T-bars, 1 poma; Fees - $9 weekends, $8 weekdays.

SKI SCHOOL: Hermann Gollner, director; 60 instructors, American and GLM tech; Cost of lessons - 2-hr. group, $5.50; 1-hr. private, $12.

FACILITIES AND SERVICES: Ski shop, rentals, 2 cafeterias, restaurant, 3 bars, nightclub, entertainment; children's nursery (min. age 3, on weekends; infants taken during week).

ADDITIONAL SPORTS: Ice skating and snowmobiling nearby.

ACCOMMODATIONS: 4000 in vicinity; Contact for information - Chamber of Commerce Booking Service, Manchester Center, Vt. 05255; and Green Mountain Resort Association, Londonderry, Vt. 05148.

LOCATION: Nearest town - Manchester Center; Nearest major city - Rutland, Bennington; Nearest airport - Rutland, Bennington, Albany.

ATMOSPHERE: Good restaurants and good night life abound in the neighborhood for the family that likes to live a little after the lifts close down. And it's very much a family place, with an excellent beginner program and a fine prep school for the juniors, and special events and races for all abilities.

Jay Peak
VERMONT

The Alpine Aerial Tramway lifts 60 skiers at a time to the peak in six minutes flat, treating them to fabulous views of Vermont, New York, Maine and Canada. Once at the top, skiers find trails scaled from easy to expert—there's even a trail for beginners all the way down from the top.

THE MOUNTAIN: Altitude - 3900'; Vertical drop - 2050'; Exposure - North; Annual snowfall - 10'; Longest trail - 3½ mi.; Slopes and trails - 6 exp., 8 int., 10 nov., 1 x-c.; Total acreage - 2000; Snow-making machinery.

LIFTS: 3 double chairs, 3 T-bars, aerial tramway; Fees - $8 weekends, $6.50 weekdays.

SKI SCHOOL: George Stepanek, director; 50 instructors, "Jay Way" International Tech.; Cost of lessons - 2-hr. group, $4.50; 1-hr. single, $10.

FACILITIES AND SERVICES: Ski shop, rentals, cafeterias, restaurant, 3 bars, nightclub, entertainment; nursery school (min. age, 2).

ADDITIONAL SPORTS AT AREA: Swimming.

ACCOMMODATIONS: 100 beds at area; 1200 in vicinity; Contact for information - Jay Peak Accommodations, Jay, Vermont 05859.

LOCATION: Nearest town - Newport; Nearest major city - Burlington; Nearest airport - Newport.

ATMOSPHERE: The ski school is a big thing here; Jay's diagnostic clinic is open to any skier whether he attends classes or not. Make an appointment for a video tape session. Instant replay lets you study your mistakes, and Director Stepanak will study it with you and give you pointers on your technique. Extra-curricular activities for snow scholars can best be described as "lively."

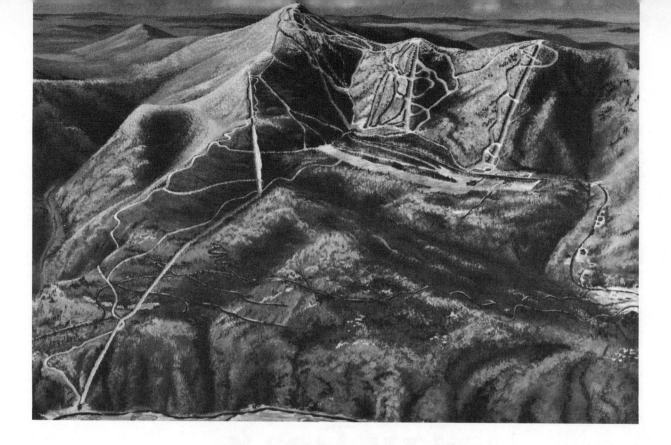

Killington
VERMONT

Actually six mountains instead of one. Day and night, Killington is expanding like mad. Item: New gondola is said to be the world's longest (3½ mile) ski lift. Item: Five new nightclubs opened in the neighborhood last year.

THE MOUNTAIN: Altitude - 4241'; Vertical drop - 3000'; Exposure - N.E.; Longest trail - 5 mi.; Annual snowfall - 17—23'; Slopes and trails - 14 exp., 11 int., 20 nov., 3 x-c; Snow-making machinery.

LIFTS: 1 gondola, 6 double chairs, 4 pomas; Fees - $9 weekends, $8 weekdays.

SKI SCHOOL: Leo Dennis, director; 42 instructors, American and GLM Tech.; Cost of lessons - 2-hr. group, $6; 1-hr. private, $12.

FACILITIES AND SERVICES: Ski shops, rentals, 4 cafeterias, 1 restaurant, 3 bars, dozens of nightclubs nearby; children's nursery (ages 3—8).

ADDITIONAL SPORTS: Snowmobiling at night; ice skating and swimming at some area lodges.

ACCOMMODATIONS: 4251 in vicinity;

Contact for information - Killington Lodging Bureau, Killington, Vt.

LOCATION: Nearest town - Sherburne; Nearest major city - Rutland; Nearest airport - Rutland.

ATMOSPHERE: Everyone is excited about the Graduated Length Method for producing proficient skiers in the shortest possible time. Extra-curricular activities are plentiful indeed.

Glen Ellen
VERMONT

Lifts were invented to get skiers uphill faster so more time could be spent coming down. That's what it's all about at Glen Ellen—and some of that coming-down part is among the most hair-raising in the East. Plenty of other, less demanding runs, too.

THE MOUNTAIN: Altitude - 4135′; Vertical drop - 2645′; Exposure - N.E.; Annual snowfall - 17′; Longest trail - 2½ mi.; Slopes and trails - 6 exp., 19 int., 14 nov.; Snowmaking machinery.

LIFTS: 3 double chairs, 1 poma; Fees - $9 weekends and weekdays.

SKI SCHOOL: Pierre Stamos, director; 25 instructors, French Tech.; Cost of lessons - 2-hr. group, $5; 1-hr. private, $12.

FACILITIES AND SERVICES: Ski shop, rentals, cafeteria, bar; children's nursery.

ADDITIONAL SPORTS: Ice skating, snowmobiling; swimming nearby.

ACCOMMODATIONS: 2500 in vicinity; Contact for information - Glen Ellen Corp., Box 111, Waitsfield, Vt. 05660.

LOCATION: Nearest town - Waitsfield; Nearest major city - Montpelier; Nearest airport - Montpelier.

ATMOSPHERE: Families with all kinds of skiing members are attracted by the separate areas for each level of ability, convenient yet apart. Nightlife abounds within a 5-mile radius.

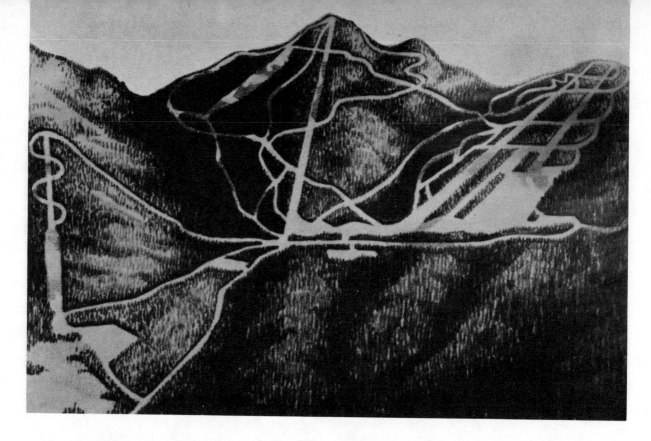

Madonna Mountain
VERMONT

On the *other* side of the mountain from Stowe, Madonna is like a kid sister growing up to be the beauty of the family, attracting more and more attention with her natural attributes — in this case, not one but three mountains, each for a different class of skier.

THE MOUNTAIN: Altitude - 3610'; Vertical drop - 2400'; Exposure - N.W.; Annual snowfall - 10'; Longest trail - 3 mi.; Slopes and trails - 7 exp., 9 int., 9 nov.; Total acreage - 152; Snow-making machinery.

LIFTS: 3 double chairs, 1 rope; Fees - $8.50 weekdays and weekends.

SKI SCHOOL: Dixi Nohl, director; 40 instructors, Austrian "Open Stance" tech., free video tape TV; Cost of lessons - 2-hr. group, $5; 1-hr. private, $10.

FACILITIES AND SERVICES: Ski shops, rentals, 2 cafeterias, 2 restaurants, 3 bars, 2 nightclubs; children's nursery; grocery store.

ADDITIONAL SPORTS AT AREA: Ice skating, ski-bobbing, swimming, tennis.

ACCOMMODATIONS: 550 at base, 450 in vicinity; Contact for information - Madonna Area Assoc., Jeffersonville, Vt. 05464; or Madonna Village, Madonna, Vt. 05464.

LOCATION: Nearest town - Jeffersonville; Nearest major city - Burlington; Nearest airport - Burlington.

ATMOSPHERE: Families enjoy the quiet after-ski hours, which often means just sitting around a cozy fire, although there is a nice kind of action in still-growing Madonna Village. And if it all gets just too quiet for your blood, there's always that *other* side.

Stowe
VERMONT

Since the first hardy few began climbing Mt. Mansfield in the Thirties for one or two glorious runs a day, through Sepp Ruschp's arrival from Austria and the installation in 1940 of the first chair lift in the East, Stowe has maintained its reputation as THE place to ski in New England with some of the toughest runs anywhere.

THE MOUNTAIN: Altitude - 4393'; Vertical drop - 2150'; Exposure - N.E./S.E.; Annual snowfall - 10'; Longest trail 4½ mi. novice; Slopes and trails - 6 exp., 25 int., 5 nov.; Total acreage - 800; Snow-making machinery.

LIFTS: 1 single chair, 3 double chairs, 1 gondola, 3 T-bars; Fees - $10 weekdays and weekends; coupon books, single rides also available.

SKI SCHOOL: Kerr Sparks, director; 60 instructors, Modified American tech.; Cost of lessons - 2-hr. group, $6; 1-hr. private, $15.

FACILITIES AND SERVICES: Ski shop, rentals, 5 cafeterias, 3 restaurants, 2 bars, nightclubs, entertainment; children's nursery in Stowe.

ADDITIONAL SPORTS AT AREA: Swimming, snowmobiling.

ACCOMMODATIONS: 200 at base, 3500 in vicinity; Contact for information - Stowe Area Association, Stowe, Vt. 05672.

LOCATION: Nearest town - Stowe; Nearest major city - Burlington; Nearest airport - Burlington.

ATMOSPHERE: Fun off the slopes ranges from the sheer elegance of the Lodge at Smuggler's Notch, to rock sound for younger skiers, and plenty of quietly atmospheric places for people who prefer that style.

Mad River Glen
VERMONT

Some call it "lovable." Even if that's not an adjective you'd pick for a ski area, Mad River Glen was the site of the National Giant Slalom Championships last spring, so it obviously has a lot that serious skiers find to love.

THE MOUNTAIN: Altitude - 3585'; Vertical drop - 1985'; Exposure - N.E.; Annual snowfall - 10'; Longest trail - 3½ mi.; Slopes and trails - 9 exp., 13 int., 7 nov.; x-c; Total acreage - 78.

LIFTS: 1 single chair, 2 double, 1 T-bar; Fees - $8.50 weekends, $7.50 weekdays.

SKI SCHOOL: Rudi Mair, director; 10 instructors, Austrian-American Tech.; Cost of lessons - 2-hr. group, $5; 1-hr. private, $12.

FACILITIES AND SERVICES: Ski shop, rentals, cafeteria, bar; children's nursery (min. age, 4 mo.).

ACCOMMODATIONS: 24 at base, 1500 in vicinity; Contact for information - Mad River Housing Office, Waitsfield, Vt. 05673.

LOCATION: Nearest town - Waitsfield; Nearest major city - Burlington; Nearest airport - Burlington.

ATMOSPHERE: Most of the entertainment at this strictly-for-skiers area is the "at-home" variety, and the style of life and leisure is strictly your own.

Sugarbush
VERMONT

A four-mountain massif at the summit of the Green Mountain National Forest — laced with challenging runs and loaded with glamour — that's Sugarbush.

THE MOUNTAIN: Altitude - 4013'; Vertical drop - 2400'; Exposure - N.E.; Longest trail - 3 mi.; Annual snowfall - 12'; Slopes and trails - 12 exp., 8 int., 8 nov.; 40 mi. x-c; Snow-making machinery on 46 acres.

LIFTS: 1 gondola, 4 double chairs, 1 T-bar; Fees - $9.50 weekdays and weekends.

SKI SCHOOL: Sigi Grottendorfer, director; Modified Austrian tech.; 25 instructors; Cost of lessons - 2-hr. group, $5; 1-hr. single, $12.

FACILITIES AND SERVICES: Ski shop, rentals, 3 cafeterias, restaurant, bar; children's nursery (min. age, 6 weeks).

ADDITIONAL SPORTS AT AREA: Ice skating, snowmobiling, swimming.

ACCOMMODATIONS: 80 beds at area, 2200 beds in vicinity; Contact for information - Sugarbush Valley Lodging Bureau, Warren, Vt. 05674.

LOCATION: Nearest town - Warren; Nearest major city - Burlington, Vt.; Nearest airport - Burlington.

ATMOSPHERE: Many of the people who come here to ski have stayed around long enough to build vacation homes, where a good part of the after-ski life is centered, but there is also a broad spectrum of away-from-home entertainment running from beer bars to dinner dancing. Many of the lodges conjure up special activities for the children, too.

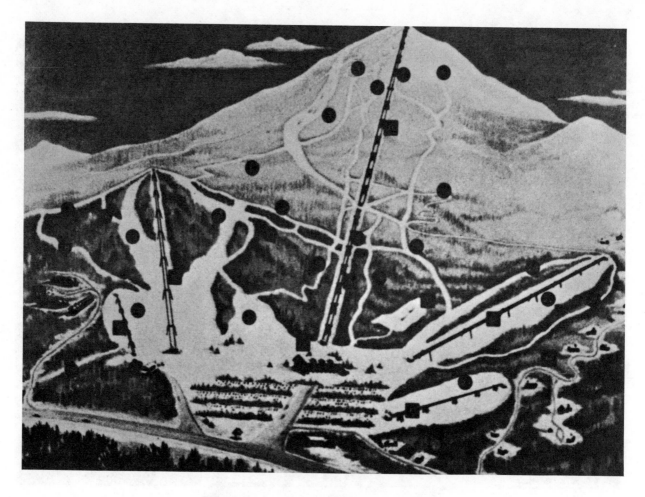

Pico Peak
VERMONT

"The Friendly Mountain" now goes all the way to the top with some breathtaking runs to challenge the experts as well as some trails to make novices feel at home on every part of the mountain.

THE MOUNTAIN: Altitude - 3967'; Vertical drop - 2000'; Exposure - North; Annual snowfall - 16—18'; Longest trail - 2½ mi.; Slopes and trails - 4 exp., 14 int., 7 nov.; Total acreage - 2200.

LIFTS: 3 double chairs, 3 T-bars; 1 new double chair to open; Fees - $8.50 weekends, $7.50 weekdays.

SKI SCHOOL: Alois Mayer, director; 12 instructors, Modified Austrian Tech.; Cost of lessons - 2-hr. group, $5; 1-hr. single, $12.

FACILITIES AND SERVICES: Ski shop, rentals, cafeteria, restaurant, bar, nightclub; children's nursery (min. age, 2 yrs.).

ACCOMMODATIONS: 300 at base, 4000 in vicinity; Contact for information - Rutland Regional C. of C., Merchants Row, Rutland, Vt. 05701.

LOCATION: Nearest town - Sherburne; Nearest major city - Rutland; Nearest airport - Rutland.

ATMOSPHERE: A strong group of loyal followers, including the Pico Ski Club, and an active racing program keep satisfied skiers coming back for more. There's enough variety in the after-ski life to satisfy most people, from a spot for "under 21s" to sophisticated supper clubs and night spots.

Brodie Mountain
MASSACHUSETTS

The atmosphere is from Erin, the ski season is the longest in the area, and over seven miles of trails, slopes, and glades make Brodie the largest night skiing area in the world.

THE MOUNTAIN: 2700'; Vertical drop - 1300'; Exposure - S.E.; Annual snowfall - 5'—7'; Longest trail - 2½ mi.; Slopes and trails - 15 mi., 6 exp., 4 int., 2 nov.; Total acreage - 2000; Snow-making machinery; Night skiing.

LIFTS: 2 double chairs, 2 T-bars, 2 ropes; Fees - $8.50 weekends, $7 weekdays.

SKI SCHOOL: Bill O'Connell, director; 40 instructors, American tech.; Cost of lessons - 2-hr. group, $4.50; 1-hr. private, $12.

FACILITIES AND SERVICES: Ski shop, rentals, canteen, cafeteria, restaurant, bar, nightclub, entertainment; children's nursery (min. age, 2 yrs.).

ACCOMMODATIONS: 47 at base, 2000 in vicinity; Contact for information - Berkshire Hills Conference, 48 Eagle Street, P. O. Box 1170, Pittsfield, Mass. 01201.

LOCATION: Nearest town - New Ashford; Nearest major cities - Pittsfield; Albany, N.Y.; Nearest airport - Pittsfield; Albany.

ATMOSPHERE: Long hours (Brodie is open for night skiing until 11 p.m.) attract all kinds of skiers from the nearby metropolitan areas who want a full day (and night) on the slopes. But there's also big entertainment for those who prefer to call it a day when the sun goes down and spend the evening where it's warm.

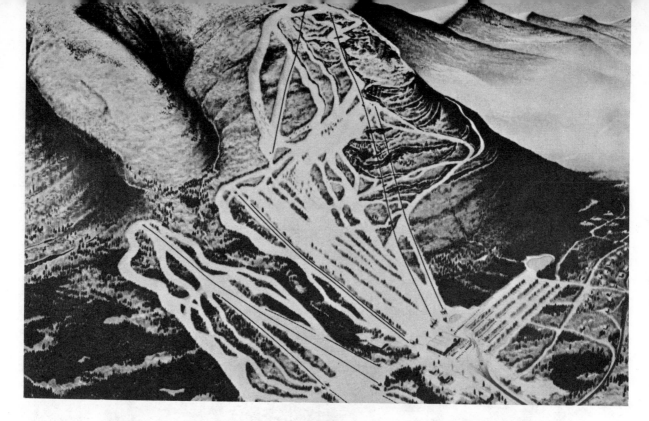

Hunter Mountain

NEW YORK

Everybody from New York City, and that includes Mayor John Lindsay and his ilk, skis at Hunter, which on weekends makes for busy, busy slopes. But the uphill facilities can cope and the snow-makers puff out nicely skiable stuff to make a much longer season than you might expect.

THE MOUNTAIN: Altitude - 1600'; Vertical drop - 1600'; Exposure - N./NE.; Annual snowfall - 7'—8'; Longest trail - 2 mi.; Slopes and trails - 5 exp., 14 int., 8 nov., 2 x-c; Total acreage - 140; Snow-making machinery; Night skiing.

LIFTS: 5 double chairs, 1 triple, 2 pomas, 1 T-bar, 3 ropes. Fees - $8 weekends, $6 weekdays.

SKI SCHOOL: Karl Plattner, director; 65 instructors, International tech.; Cost of lessons - 2-hr. group, $5; 1-hr. private, $12.

FACILITIES AND SERVICES: Ski shop, rentals, cafeteria, restaurant, bar, entertainment; children's nursery (min. age, 6 mo.); ski school nursery.

ADDITIONAL SPORTS: Ski-bobbing, swimming; ice skating and snowmobiling nearby.

ACCOMMODATIONS: 2000 in vicinity; Contact for information - Mountain Top C. of C., Tannersville, N. Y.

LOCATION: Nearest town - Hunter; Nearest major city - Kingston; Nearest airport - Hudson.

ATMOSPHERE: The Slutzky brothers have made Hunter all that it is (and it is plenty); they'd like everyone to know that apres-ski life is "the greatest." Just in case someone finds something to complain about, they've instituted a "courtesy patrol" who lend an ear and they try to do something about it.

Whiteface Mountain
NEW YORK

Whiteface is something of a sleeper—one of those wonderful places cherished mainly by skiing families and overlooked mostly by those whose sporting doesn't really begin until day's end.

THE MOUNTAIN: Altitude - 4870'; Vertical drop - 3216'; Exposure - East; Annual snowfall - 8—10'; Longest trail - 2+ mi. Slopes and trails - 12 exp., 4 int., 10 nov.; Snow-making machinery.

LIFTS: 4 double chairs, 1 T-bar, 1 J-bar; Fees - $7 weekends, $5 weekdays.

SKI SCHOOL: Karl Fahrner, director; 15 instructors, American tech.; Cost of lessons - 2-hr. group, $4; 1-hr. private, $10.

FACILITIES AND SERVICES: Ski shop, rentals, cafeteria.

ACCOMMODATIONS: 125 hotels and motels in vicinity; Contact for information - Wilmington C. of C., Wilmington, N. Y. 12997; Lake Placid C. of C., Lake Placid, N. Y. 12946.

LOCATION: Nearest town, Wilmington; Nearest major city - Plattsburgh; Nearest airports - Saranac Lake, Plattsburgh.

ATMOSPHERE: Although Whiteface is quiet, there is plenty of winter sports activity in near-by Lake Placid (bobsledding, figure skating, ski jumping, hockey, etc.) as well as apres-ski life.

Gore Mountain
NEW YORK

Boasting the only gondola in the state, Gore's four quite separate-but-integrated areas for skiing help keep lift lines relatively short, and the crowd remains "Ski-first, play-later."

THE MOUNTAIN: Altitude - 3600'; Vertical drop - 2100'; Exposure - N./NE.; Annual snowfall - 8'—10'; Longest trail - 2½ mi.; Slopes and trails - 8 exp., 5 int., 10 nov.; 2 x-c.

LIFTS: 5 double chairs, 1 T-bar, 1 J-bar, 1 gondola. Fees - $7 weekends, $5 weekdays.

SKI SCHOOL: Ray Allard, director; 40 instructors, American tech.; Cost of lessons - 2-hr. group, $4; 1-hr. private, $10.

FACILITIES AND SERVICES: Ski shop, rentals, cafeteria, restaurant, bar; children's nursery.

ADDITIONAL SPORTS: Ice skating, sled and toboggan slope.

ACCOMMODATIONS: 75 motels and hotels in area; Contact for information - Warren Co. Publicity, Lake George, N. Y. 12845.

LOCATION: Nearest town - North Creek; Nearest major city - Glens Falls; Nearest airport - Glens Falls (Warren Co.)

ATMOSPHERE: A quiet place, but apres-ski life is available to those who want it.

Great Gorge
NEW JERSEY

Only 52 miles from Manhattan, Great Gorge is the five-year-old Mecca for city skiers who can start the day at 8:30 a.m. and keep going right up to the 10:45 p.m. shut-down. The largest snow-making plant in the world compensates for its south-of-the-snowbelt location.

THE MOUNTAIN: Altitude - 1400'; Vertical drop - 1033'; Exposure - N./NE.; Annual snowfall - 4'; Longest trail - almost 2 mi.; Slopes and trails - 1 exp., 4 int., 4 nov., x-c.; Total acreage - 80.

LIFTS: 5 double chairs, 1 T-bar, 1 poma, 1 rope; Fees - $8 weekends, $6 weekdays.

SKI SCHOOL: Luis Schlafflinger, director; 30 instructors, Modified American tech.; Cost of lessons - 2-hr. group, $5; 1-hr. private, $10.

FACILITIES AND SERVICES: Ski shop, rentals, cafeteria, 2 restaurants, 2 bars, entertainment on weekends, summit lodge with cafeteria; children's nursery (ages 2—6).

ACCOMMODATIONS: 250 in vicinity; Contact for information - Great Gorge, Box 848, McAfee, N. J. 07428.

LOCATION: Nearest town - Hamburg; Nearest major city - New York; Nearest airport - Sussex.

ATMOSPHERE: A mixed bag, befitting its proximity to New York from whence pour families on weekends, housewives during the week, and students in the evening. After-ski life tends to be subdued rather than noisy: a quiet drink in the lounge or dinner overlooking the slopes. A Playboy Club-Hotel a-building in the area may change that. Great Gorge North is under development, too, adding to the scope of the existing area.

Camelback
PENNSYLVANIA

Philadelphians and New Yorkers have made this Pocono Mountain area THE place to learn to ski, but there's enough non-beginner terrain to satisfy all but the Really Big Mountain Boys.

THE MOUNTAIN: Altitude - 2200'; Vertical drop - 750'; Exposure - N.W.; Annual snowfall - 4'; Longest trail - 1¼ mi.; Slopes and trails - 4 exp., 3 int., 6 nov., 2 beginners; Snow-making machinery; Night skiing.

LIFTS: 1 double chairlift, 2 T-bars, 1 J-bar, 1 triple chairlift; Fees - $7 weekends, $6 weekdays.

SKI SCHOOL: Joe Amato, director; Multi-method tech.; 60 instructors; Cost of lessons - 2-hr. group, $4; 1-hr. private, $10.

FACILITIES AND SERVICES: Ski shop, rentals, cafeterias, restaurant, bar, nightclub, entertainment; children's nursery.

ACCOMMODATIONS: 10,000 in vicinity; Write for information - Camelback Reservation Service, Box 168, Tannersville, Pa.

LOCATION: Nearest town - Tannersville; Nearest major city - Stroudsburg; Nearest airport - Mt. Pocono.

ATMOSPHERE: All those city folks keep apres-ski life on the light and lively side at Camelback.

Big Powderhorn
MICHIGAN

Big Powderhorn, in the high country of Michigan's Upper Peninsula, combines Swiss-style architecture, Midwestern-style hospitality, and the greatest skiable vertical drop in the Midwest.

THE MOUNTAIN: Exposure - North; Annual snowfall - 17'; Longest trail - 1 mi.; Slopes and trails - 2 exp., 6 int., 4 nov. Total acreage - 135.

LIFTS: 3 double chairs, 1 T-bar, 2 ropes; Fees - $6 weekends, $5 weekdays.

SKI SCHOOL: Nick Terstenvak, director; 5—12 instructors, American tech.; Cost of lessons - 2-hr. group, $4; 1-hr. private, $10.

FACILITIES AND SERVICES: Ski shop, rentals, cafeteria, restaurant, bar, nightclub, entertainment; children's nursery.

ADDITIONAL SPORTS: Swimming.

ACCOMMODATIONS: 22 at base, 250 within ½-mi. of ski area; Contact for information - Big Powderhorn Mountain, Box 136, Bessemer, Mich. 49911.

LOCATION: Nearest town - Bessemer; Nearest major cities - Ironwood—Duluth, Minn.; Nearest airport - Bessemer.

ATMOSPHERE: A family ski-area where altitude and vertical drop are secondary to good snow and congeniality.

Boyne Highlands
MICHIGAN

The Highlands are part of Boyne Country that includes three other areas: Boyne Mountain, Thunder Mountain, and Walloon Hills, all friendly neighbors. Mid-Westerners flock here in droves, but the area is designed to handle all phases of the influx.

THE MOUNTAIN: Altitude - 1600'; Vertical drop - 625'; Exposure - N.E.; Annual snowfall - 10'; Longest trail - 1.8 mi.; Slopes and trails - 4 exp., 3 int., 5 nov.; Snow-making machinery.

LIFTS: 4 triple chairlifts, 1 T-bar, 1 poma-lift, 1 rope; Fees - $8 weekdays and weekends, interchangeable with all other areas in Boyne Country.

SKI SCHOOL: Othmar Schneider, director; 64 instructors (all areas).

FACILITIES AND SERVICES: Ski shop, rentals, cafeteria, restaurant, bar, nightclub, entertainment; baby sitters available.

ADDITIONAL SPORTS AT AREA: Ice skating, snowmobiling, swimming.

ACCOMMODATIONS: 250 at base lodge; others in neighboring areas and nearby towns; Contact for information - Boyne Highlands, Harbor Springs, Mich. 49713.

LOCATION: Nearest town - Harbor Springs; Nearest major city - Petoskey; Nearest airport - Pellston.

ATMOSPHERE: Michiganites make the most of what they have, and mid-westerners love it. Given the diversity of areas and facilities concentrated here, there's one word for apres-ski life: "Total."

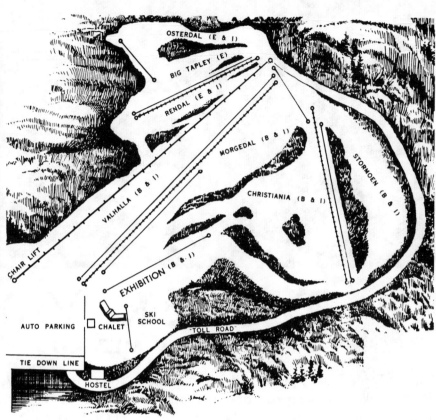

Mount Telemark
WISCONSIN

Which will it be, ski life or night life? Mount Telemark offers a lot of both. Wisconsinites aren't discouraged by unimpressive altitude and vertical drop figures, and many are settling down in one of the new Telemark Villages.

THE MOUNTAIN: Altitude - 1750'; Vertical drop - 370'; Exposure - N.E.; Annual snowfall, 7½'; Longest trail - ½ mi.; Slopes and trails - 3 exp., 4 int., 3 nov.; Total acreage - 100; Snow-making machinery; Night skiing.

LIFTS: 1 double chairlift, 3 T-bars, 8 ropes; Fees - $6 weekdays and weekends.

SKI SCHOOL: James Bauer, director; 12 instructors, American tech.; Cost of lessons - Group, $4; private, $10.

FACILITIES AND SERVICES: Ski shop, rentals, 2 cafeterias, 2 restaurants, 2 bars, nightclub, entertainment; children's nursery (min. age, 4 mo.).

ADDITIONAL SPORTS AT AREA: Ski-bobbing; snowmobiling, swimming nearby.

ACCOMMODATIONS: 50 at base, 1500 in vicinity; Contact for information - Telemark Company, Hayward, Wis. 54843.

LOCATION: Nearest town - Cable; Nearest major city - Duluth, Minn.; Nearest airport - at area.

ATMOSPHERE: A family kind of place with lively entertainment whether you're over or under 21.

Taos Ski Valley
NEW MEXICO

Taos is Ernie Blake's place, make no mistake. He has taken the steepest slopes in America (and among the highest), infused it with a liberal portion of Alpine charm, and limited the accommodations so that only 520 skiers at a time can enjoy the total absence of lift lines.

THE MOUNTAIN: Altitude - 9200′ to 11,800′; Vertical drop - 2600′; Exposure, N./N.E./E.; Annual snowfall - 7′—13′; Longest trail - 7 mi.; Slopes and trails - 9 exp., 7 int., 4 nov.! Total acreage - 5090.

LIFTS: 2 double chairs, 4 pomas; Fees - $7 weekends and weekdays.

SKI SCHOOL: Ernie Blake, director; 39 instructors; French + GLM = Ernie's Own Tech.; Cost of lessons - 2-hr. group, $4; 1-hr. private, $10.

FACILITIES AND SERVICES: Ski shops, rentals, cafeteria, restaurants, bars, nightclubs, nightly entertainment, saunas; children's nursery (min. age, 18 mo.).

ADDITIONAL SPORTS: Ski-bobbing, swimming (heated pool).

ACCOMMODATIONS: 600 at base, 650 within 21 mi. radius; Contact for information - Baron H. V. von Kretschmer, Box 266, Taos, N. M. 87571.

LOCATION: Nearest town - Taos; Nearest major city - Albuquerque; Nearest airports - Taos, Albuquerque.

ATMOSPHERE: Remote location eliminates transient crowds, and those who come are serious skiers who lap up the non-commercial attitude. Everyone is there for a "Learn to ski BETTER" week or more, and so everyone is automatically in the ski school. The food, served up by European chefs, is frankly fabulous, and apres-skiing is informal.

Mount Werner
COLORADO

Since the days of barrel-stave skis and "bear-trap" bindings, Steamboat Springs has been famous for its champagne-light powder. Its next-door neighbor, Mt. Werner, deep in Routt National Forest, is the kind of environment that's produced more international ski champions than any place in America.

THE MOUNTAIN: Altitude - 7000' to 10,650'; Vertical drop - 2850'; Exposure - N.W.; Annual snowfall - 15 feet at base; Longest trail - 3½ mi.; Slopes and trails - 13 exp., 20 int., 6 nov., x-c. Night skiing in Steamboat Springs.

LIFTS: 5 double chairs, 1 poma; Fees - $6 weekdays and weekends.

SKI SCHOOL: Skeeter Werner Walker, director; 35 instructors, American tech.; Cost of lessons - 2-hr. group, $4; 1-hr. private, $10.

FACILITIES AND SERVICES: Ski shop, rentals, cafeteria, restaurant, bar, nightclub, entertainment; children's nursery (min. age, 6 mos.).

ADDITIONAL SPORTS: Snowmobiling, swimming in Steamboat Springs.

ACCOMMODATIONS: 800 at base, 2500 in vicinity; Contact for information - Steamboat Springs Resort Service, Steamboat Springs, Colo. 80477.

LOCATION: Nearest major city - Denver; Nearest airport - Yampa Valley (daily flights from Denver and Salt Lake City).

ATMOSPHERE: Families and students make up the biggest part of the crowd because of special lift ticket rates. After-ski life is on the upswing, especially weekends.

ASPEN HIGHLANDS
Elev. 11,665

ASPEN MOUNTAIN
Elev. 11,212

CITY OF ASPEN
Elev. 7,980

Aspen
COLORADO

"Aspenglow" is the word for the pleasure of skiing three great neighboring mountains— Aspen (shown in general view), Buttermilk, and Snowmass—with a combined total of more than 200 miles of runs, trails, and deep, deep powder bowl.

THE MOUNTAINS: ASPEN—Altitude - 7930' to 11,212'; Vertical drop - 3300'; Annual snowfall - 25'; Slopes and trails - 50 mi., some over 2 mi.

LIFTS: 6 double chairs, 1 single chair.

BUTTERMILK — Altitude - 7868' to 9840'; Vertical drop - 2000'; Annual snowfall - 16'; Slopes and trails - 35 mi. of runs up to 2 mi.

LIFTS: 1 T-bar, 4 double chairs.

SNOWMASS — Altitude - 8230' to 11,700'; Vertical drop - 3500'; Annual snowfall - 25'; Slopes - 60 mi. of runs up to 3 mi.

LIFTS: 7 double chairs, 1 T-bar; Night skiing on Fanny Hill.

LIFT FEES: $8 weekdays and weekends, interchangeable among the 3 mountains.

SKI SCHOOL: Curt Chase, director; 200 instructors, American tech.; Cost of lessons: ½-day group, $6; 1-hr. private, $15.

FACILITIES AND SERVICES: Ski shops, rentals, restaurants, bars; children's nursery (min. age, 3).

ADDITIONAL SPORTS: Dog-sledding, ice skating, skimobiling, snow-shoeing, swimming.

ACCOMMODATIONS: 11,500 in Aspen area; 3500 in lodges and condominiums at Snowmass; Contact for information - Aspen Chamber and Visitors Bureau, Box 739, Aspen, Colo. 81611.

LOCATION: Nearest major cities - Denver, Salt Lake City; Nearest airports - Aspen, Denver.

ATMOSPHERE: Victorian Aspen has a rich mining-town heritage as well as more than a dozen night spots. At Snowmass the self-contained village is built right on the slopes.

Mt. BALDY
Elev. 13,162

SNOWMASS·AT·ASPEN

SAM'S KNOB
Elev. 10,645

ERMILK
Elev. 10,003

ASPEN AIRPORT Elev. 7,780

Aspen Highlands
COLORADO

Part of the big Aspen group, Aspen Highlands likes to be called the "Balanced Mountain" with a great variety of terrain for all types of skiers. The Maroon Bowl offers the greatest powder skiing in Colorado.

THE MOUNTAIN: Altitude - 11,800'; Vertical drop - 3800'; Exposure - N.W.; Annual snowfall - 15'; Longest trail - 3½ mi.; Slopes and trails - 17 exp., 21 int., 20 nov.; 58 trails covering 55 mi.; x-c.

LIFTS: 5 double chairs, 5 pomas. Fees - $8 weekdays and weekends.

SKI SCHOOL: Fred Iselin, director; 50—100 instructors, International tech.

FACILITIES AND SERVICES: Ski shop, rentals, 2 cafeterias, 2 nightclubs with entertainment; standard races; wine and cheese picnics.

ADDITIONAL SPORTS: Ice skating, snowmobiling, swimming.

ACCOMMODATIONS: 400 at area, 12,000 in vicinity; Contact for information - Aspen Chamber and Visitors Bureau, Aspen, Colo. 81611.

LOCATION: Nearest major city - Denver; Nearest airport - Aspen.

ATMOSPHERE: Clubs and groups find the atmosphere here friendly and congenial what with the wine and cheese picnics and beer parties arranged especially for them.

Purgatory
COLORADO

One area that makes no attempt to live up to its misnomer, Purgatory is a quiet family-style resort with relaxed skiing and even more relaxed apres-skiing. Management characterizes night-life as "poor" and is obviously proud of it.

THE MOUNTAIN: Altitude - 10,600'; Vertical drop - 1600'; Exposure - N.E.; Annual snowfall - 5'; Longest trail - 2½ mi.; Slopes and trails - 3 exp., 10 int., 4 nov., 1 x-c; Total acreage - 100 with trails.

LIFTS: 2 double chairs, 1 poma, 1 rope; Fees - $6 weekends and weekdays.

SKI SCHOOL: Fritz Tatzer, director; 20 instructors, American tech.; Cost of lessons - 2-hr. group, $4.50; 1-hr. private, $10.

FACILITIES AND SERVICES: Ski shop, rentals, cafeteria, restaurant, bar, entertainment; children's nursery on weekdays in Durango (min. age, 2 yrs.).

ADDITIONAL SPORTS: Ski-bobbing, swimming.

ACCOMMODATIONS: 115 at base, 1100 in vicinity; Contact for information - Durango Ski Corporation, P. O. Box 666, Durango, Colorado 81301.

LOCATION: Nearest town - Durango, Colo. Nearest major city - Albuquerque, N. M.; Nearest airport - La Plata Field.

ATMOSPHERE: Friendly personnel, windless days, and warm sun welcome skiing families who are content to turn in rather than turn on when dinner's over.

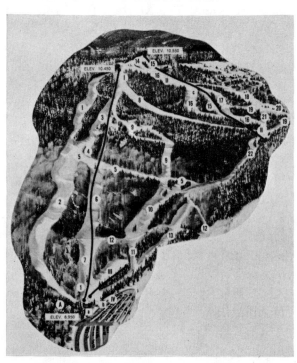

Vail
COLORADO

A little bit of Europe with a lot of skiing: Vail is Tyrolean all the way, beautifully planned and executed, in addition to superb skiing and uphill facilities that include two high-flying gondolas.

THE MOUNTAIN: Altitude - 11,250′; Vertical drop - 3050′; Exposure - N./S.; Annual snowfall - over 12′ base; Longest trail - 6 mi.; Slopes and trails - 37 mi. of cut trail on north side, open skiing; 19 exp., 19 int., 11 nov.; 17 x-c (121 mi.); Total area - 10 sq. mi.; Snow-making machinery.

LIFTS: 2 gondolas, 7 double chairs, 4 pomas; Fees - $8 weekdays and weekends.

SKI SCHOOL: Jerry Muth, director; 70—120 instructors, American tech; Cost of lessons - 2-hr. group, $6; 1-hr. private, $12.

FACILITIES AND SERVICES: Ski shops, rentals, cafeterias, restaurants, bars, nightclubs, entertainment; children's nurseries (minimum age, 6 months).

ADDITIONAL SPORTS: Ice skating, swimming.

ACCOMMODATIONS: 4500 beds at base, 6000 in vicinity; Contact for information - Vail Resort Association, Vail, Colo. 81657.

LOCATION: Nearest major city, Denver; Nearest airports - Eagle, Denver.

ATMOSPHERE: The young singles and young and middle-aged couples who come here can ski down into their lodges in the village at the base of the mountain. Night life is varied, from Austrian country music to hard rock to W.C. Fields and ski flicks to folk singers and a quiet cup of coffee.

Arapahoe Basin
COLORADO

For skiers who never know when to stop, Arapahoe boasts a fantastically long season (quittin' time last season was June 7). It's also the highest major area in the country.

THE MOUNTAIN: Altitude - 10,800'; Vertical drop - 3200'; Exposure - North; Annual snowfall - 28'; Slopes and trails - 7 exp., 7 int., 10 nov., 3 x-c.

LIFTS: 3 double chairs, 5 pomas; Fees - $6 weekdays and weekends.

SKI SCHOOL: (As of press time replacement for Willy Schaeffler, now U.S. Ski Coach, had not been named); 30 instructors, American tech.; Cost of lessons - 2-hr. group, $4; 1-hr. private, $12.

FACILITIES AND SERVICES: Ski shop, rentals, cafeteria, restaurant, bar, children's nursery.

ADDITIONAL SPORTS: Ski-bobbing.

ACCOMMODATIONS: 70 beds in area, 200+ in vicinity; Contact for information - Arapahoe Basin Lodge, Box 187, Dillon, Colorado 80415.

LOCATION: Nearest town - Dillon; Nearest major city - Denver; Nearest airport - Denver.

ATMOSPHERE: Families and young adults, mostly the better skiers, are attracted by the powder, the long season, and the low rates. And there's plenty going on in the area and nearby in the way of after-ski.

Jackson Hole
WYOMING

Jackson Holers think of this towering peak of the Teton Range as the Gentle Giant, but the gentleness of this behemoth of mountains depends largely on skiing ability. Rendezvous Peak is the really *big* challenge, and those who aren't quite ready for that will find things gentler on Après-Vous Peak.

THE MOUNTAIN: Altitude - 6000' to 10,450'; Vertical drop - 4138'; Exposure - East; Annual snowfall - 14'; Longest trail - 7 mi.; Slopes and trails - 18 mi. exp., 21 mi. int.; 4 mi. nov., National Biathlon x-c course.

LIFTS: 1 tram, 3 double chairs, 2 pomas; Fees - $7.50 weekends and weekdays.

SKI SCHOOL: Pepi Stiegler, director; 15 instructors, American Tech; Cost of lessons - 2-hr. group, $5; 1-hr. private, $12.

FACILITIES AND SERVICES: Ski shop, rentals, cafeteria, 7 restaurants, 4 bars, 4 nightclubs, entertainment; nursery.

ADDITIONAL SPORTS: Ski bobbing, snowmobiling, swimming, snow planes into Yellowstone, fishing excursions, sleigh rides.

ACCOMMODATIONS: 800 at base, 3000 in vicinity; Contact for information: Jackson Hole Resort Association, Teton Village, Wyo. 83025.

LOCATION: Nearest town - Jackson; Nearest major city - Salt Lake City, Utah; Nearest airport - Jackson.

ATMOSPHERE: This is the place for people for whom The Mountain is the thing—but not everything. Night life is perhaps not the most swinging, but what's lacking in Teton Village is made up for in Jackson.

Big Mountain
MONTANA

Powder snow at low elevation makes great skiing without waiting to get acclimated to the altitude. Skiing temperatures average a comfortable 22 degrees.

THE MOUNTAIN: Altitude - 7000'; Vertical drop - 2000'; Exposure - South; Annual snowfall, 15'; Longest trail 2¾ mi.; Slopes and trails - 7 mi. exp., 15 mi. int.; 3 mi. nov., unlimited x-c; Total acreage - 1500; Night skiing.

LIFTS: 2 double chairs, 1 T-bar, 1 poma, 2 ropes; Fees - $5.50 weekdays and weekends.

SKI SCHOOL: Karl Hinderman, director; 21 instructors, American tech.; Cost of lessons - 2-hr. group, $5; 1-hr. private, $10.

FACILITIES AND SERVICES: Ski shop, rentals, cafeteria, restaurant, bar, nightclub, entertainment.

ADDITIONAL SPORTS AT AREA: Snowmobiling.

ACCOMMODATIONS: 354 at base; 600 in vicinity; Contact for information - The Big Mountain, Reservations, Box 1215, Whitefish, Montana 59937.

LOCATION: Nearest town - Whitefish; Nearest major city - Spokane, Wash.; Nearest airport - Glacier Park International.

ATMOSPHERE: One of those friendly places where employees really seem to care. It's a place for young people, singles and couples, as well as serious skiers. After-ski hoopla is the relaxed, folksy kind, with employee-guest parties and professional entertainment.

Sun Valley
IDAHO

Sun Valley, virtually synonymous with skiing, has a 33-year-old tradition, a self-contained ski village, and a top-notch ski school where *everyone* comes to brush up his technique on what has been called "the most perfect teaching mountain in the world."

THE MOUNTAIN: Altitude - 9200'; Vertical drop - 3200'; Exposure - N./S./E./W.; Annual snowfall - 12'; Longest trail - 25,000'; Slopes - 1100 acres exp., 2100 acres int., 50 acres nov., 1 x-c course; Total acreage- 3150.

LIFTS: 6 single chairs, 5 double chairs, 1 T-bar; Fees - $8 weekends, $7.50 weekdays.

SKI SCHOOL: Sigi Engl, director; 145 instructors; tech. tailored to individual; Cost of lessons - 1-hr. private, $14; All-day group, $9.

FACILITIES AND SERVICES: Ski shop, rentals, cafeteria, restaurant, bar, nightclub, entertainment; children's nursery.

ADDITIONAL SPORTS: Ice skating, swimming, helicopters for rental into back country for skiing.

ACCOMMODATIONS: 1500 at base, 2600 in vicinity (Ketchum); Contact for information - Sun Valley, Idaho 83353.

LOCATION: Nearest major cities - Boise, Twin Falls; Nearest airport - Hailey/Sun Valley, 12 mi.

ATMOSPHERE: The one common denominator among Sun Valley skiers is: they really dig skiing, so there are serious skiers of all ages and income brackets. When the skis are put away for the day, there's still something for everybody: young and old swingers and the tea-and-goodies set all find their slots.

Park City
UTAH

An old mining town in Utah's rugged Rocky Mountains is the setting for this young and flourishing resort, which features in addition to light, dry powder, a 2½-mile gondola tramway, a "Skier's Subway" that takes you three miles inside the mountain (then up an elevator to the surface), and all the flavor of the Old West.

THE MOUNTAIN: Altitude - 7000' to 9400'; Vertical drop - 2400'; Exposure - North; Annual snowfall - 6'; Longest trail - 3½ mi.; Slopes and trails - 5 exp., 7 int., 6 nov.; Total area - 30 sq. mi.

LIFTS: 1 gondola, 2 double chairs, 1 T-bar, 1 rope; Fees - $6 weekdays and weekends.

SKI SCHOOL: Woody Anderson, director; 55 instructors, American tech.; Cost of lessons - 2-hr. group, $4; 1-hr. private, $12.

FACILITIES AND SERVICES: Ski shop, rentals, cafeteria, restaurant, bar, nightclub; children's nursery.

ADDITIONAL SPORTS AT AREA: Ski-bobbing, snowmobiling.

ACCOMMODATIONS: Over 1300 in vicinity; Contact for information - Reservation Center, Box 32 A.M.F., Salt Lake City, Utah 84101.

LOCATION: Nearest town - Heber; Nearest major city - Salt Lake City; Nearest airport - Salt Lake City.

ATMOSPHERE: Here you'll find the excitement and charm of an old silver mining town, the main drag lined with original restaurants, saloons, and fascinating shops, along with many new lodges and entertainment centers. The flavor is authentic and amusing.

Alta
UTAH

Nestled in the tops of Utah's Wasatch National Forest, Alta enjoys consistently ideal snow conditions with runs for every class of skier, from miles and miles of carefully manicured, machine-packed runs to high open slopes covered with the famous Alta powder.

THE MOUNTAIN: Altitude - 8550' to 10,550'; Vertical drop - 2000'; Exposure - North; Annual snowfall - 39'; Longest trail - 3 mi.; Slopes and trails - 25 mi. exp., 20 mi. int.; 5 mi. nov.; unlimited x-c.

LIFTS: 1 single chair, 4 double chairs; Fees - $5.50, weekdays and weekends.

SKI SCHOOL: Alf Engen, director; 108 instructors, American tech.; Cost of lessons - 2-hr. group, $4; 1-hr. private, $12.

FACILITIES AND SERVICES: Ski shops, rentals, 4 cafeterias, 4 restaurants, 6 bars, 1 nightclub; children's nursery at nearby lodge.

ADDITIONAL SPORTS AT AREA: Swimming.

ACCOMMODATIONS: 400 at area, 7000 beds within 30 miles; Contact for information - Alta, Utah 84070.

LOCATION: Nearest town - Sandy; Nearest major city - Salt Lake City; Nearest airport - Salt Lake City.

ATMOSPHERE: If the apres-ski life is quiet the skiing is wide awake. Skiers come from all over the country to feast their eyes on the high-up scenery and to revel in deep, silky powder snow so light you hardly know it's there.

Alpine Meadows
CALIFORNIA

Known as the family ski resort of the High Sierras, Alpine Meadows has secured for itself some of the most beautiful ski country in the world, and attracts those who enjoy a relaxed atmosphere.

THE MOUNTAIN: Altitude - 8637'; Vertical drop - 1600'; Exposure - N./N.E.; Annual snowfall - 30'; Longest trail - 8000'; Slopes and trails - 12 exp., 14 int., 5 nov., 1 x-c; Total acreage - 1400.

LIFTS: 5 double chairs, 2 T-bars; 5 pomas; Fees - $7 weekdays, $7.50 weekends.

SKI SCHOOL: Werner F. Schuster, director; 42 instructors, American-International tech.; Cost of lessons - 2-hr. group, $4.50; 1-hr. private, $10.

FACILITIES AND SERVICES: Ski shop, rentals, cafeteria, bar, children's day school (min. age, 2).

ACCOMMODATIONS: 40 beds at area, 6000 in vicinity; Contact for information - Alpine Meadows of Tahoe, Inc., Box 865, Tahoe City, California 95730.

LOCATION: Nearest town - Tahoe City; Nearest major city - Reno, Nevada; Nearest airport - Reno.

ATMOSPHERE: After dark after-ski life moves elsewhere in the greater North Lake Tahoe area for western hospitality with European influence. And then, of course, Reno is just an hour away.

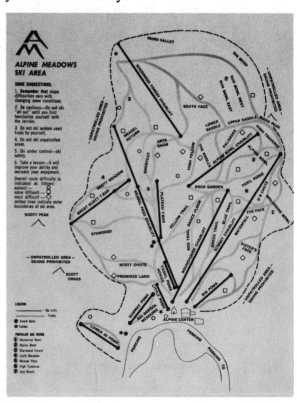

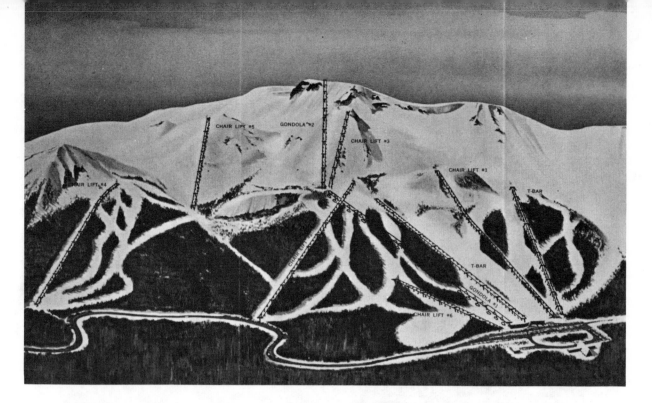

Mammoth Mountain
CALIFORNIA

Normally from November to June Mammoth slopes are covered with deep snows ranging from light, dry snow to packed powder in the open bowls and the untracked terrain above the timberline for more adventurous expert skiers. Temperatures are definitely in the comfort range.

THE MOUNTAIN: Altitude - 8400′ to 11,053′; Vertical drop - 2700′; Exposure: North; Annual snowfall - 10′ on ground; Longest trail - 2 mi.; Slopes and trails - 12 exp., dozens of int., 12 nov.

LIFTS: 9 double chairs, 1 poma, 2 gondolas, 2 T-bars; Fees - $8, weekdays and weekends.

SKI SCHOOL: Gus Weber, director; 30 instructors, Modified French tech.; Cost of lessons - 2-hr. group, $5; 1-hr. private, $12.

FACILITIES AND SERVICES: Ski shop, rentals, cafeteria, restaurant; bar, nightclub, and entertainment close by.

ADDITIONAL SPORTS: Snowmobiling.

ACCOMMODATIONS: 300 at area, 3000 in vicinity; Contact for information - Mammoth Chamber of Commerce, Mammoth Lakes, Calif. 93546.

LOCATION: Nearest major city - Reno;

Nearest airports - Reno; Mammoth Lakes Air Strip.

ATMOSPHERE: Skiers from all over the country are attracted to Mammoth for the great spring skiing. Bars with live entertainment, movies, and Forest Service programs twice weekly set the tone for the evenings.

Bear Valley
CALIFORNIA

The mountain playground of San Franciscans features the charm and sophistication of that city, done up with superb snow. Cars are taboo—allowed only to the fringe of the area, after which it's the Bear Train, — a policy in keeping with the "attuned to nature" philosophy of the mountain.

THE MOUNTAIN: Altitude - 6400' to 8500'; Vertical drop - 2100'; Exposure - N.E.; Annual snowfall - 45'; Longest trail - 3½ mi.; Slopes and trails - 14 exp., 3 int., 4 nov.

LIFTS: 4 double chairs, 1 rope; Fees - $7 weekdays and weekends.

SKI SCHOOL: Rick Carney, director; 35 instructors, French tech; instant replay TV; Cost of lessons - 2-hr. group, $5; 1-hr. private, $12.

FACILITIES AND SERVICES: Ski shop, rentals, cafeteria, restaurant, bar; children's nursery (min. age 3); bus service, sleighs.

ADDITIONAL SPORTS AT AREA: Ski-bobbing; snowmobiling nearby.

ACCOMMODATIONS: 500 at base, 2000

in vicinity; Contact for information - Central Reservations, P.O. Box 68, Bear Valley, Calif. 95223.

LOCATION: Nearest town - Arnold; Nearest major city - Stockton; Nearest airport - San Andreas.

ATMOSPHERE: After-ski life is diversified to suit the two main groups who come here (swinging singles, families) with a decidedly French flavor blended with San Franciscan cosmopolitan.

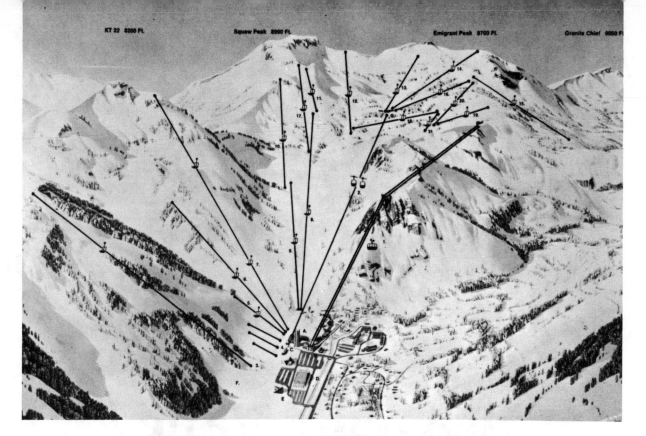

Squaw Valley
CALIFORNIA

One of the few places in the United States where European-style alpine skiing really exists, Squaw Valley was the site of the Winter Olympics in 1960 and is now the site of some pretty fantastic uphill facilities that spirit more than 22,000 skiers an hour to the top.

THE MOUNTAIN: Altitude - 6200′ to 9000′; Vertical drop - 2800′; Exposure - N./N.E.; Annual snowfall - 36′; Slopes - 30 square mi., all open slopes.

LIFTS: 18 double chairs, 6 pomas, 1 gondola, 1 tramway; Fees - $8.50 weekends, $8 weekdays.

SKI SCHOOL: Stan Tomlinson and Dec Daly, directors; 50 instructors, French and GLM techs. Cost of lessons - 2-hr. group, $8; 1-hr. private, $12.

FACILITIES AND SERVICES: 4 ski shops, 2 rental shops; numerous cafeterias, restaurants, bars, 4 nightclubs; Children's nursery (ages 3—8).

ADDITIONAL SPORTS: Ice skating in Olympic arena, snowmobiling, swimming.

ACCOMMODATIONS: 2—3,000 at area, 10,000 in vicinity; Contact for information- Chamber of Commerce, Tahoe City, Calif.

LOCATION: Nearest major city - Reno; Nearest airport - Reno.

ATMOSPHERE: Expert skiers head for the Olympic runs while vacationers from all over enjoy the California sunshine, the superb snow, and the swinging apres-ski life.

Heavenly Valley
CALIFORNIA

This unique two-state complex, one of the country's biggest ski areas, covers over 20 square miles of varying terrain, sits astride the towering Sierras with runs that plunge to the shores of Lake Tahoe on one side and sweep down into Nevada on the other.

THE MOUNTAIN: Altitude - 6600' to 10,040'; Vertical drop - California side, 3430'; Nevada side, 3700'; Exposure - California, N.W.; Nevada, N.; Annual snowfall - 15'; Longest trail - 7 mi. Slopes and trails - (6 exp. (7 mi.), 19 int. (30 mi.), 5 nov. (5 mi.), lots of x-c.

LIFTS: 11 double chairs, 2 pomas, 1 T-bar, 1 tramway; Fees - $8, weekdays and weekends.

SKI SCHOOL: Pepi Greimeister, director; 40 instructors, American tech.; Cost of lessons - 2-hr. group, $4; 1-hr. private, $10.

FACILITIES AND SERVICES: Ski shop, rentals, 2 cafeterias, 2 restaurants, 5 on-the-mountain snack facilities; touring by appointment; tram sightseeing rides; children's nursery nearby.

ADDITIONAL SPORTS: Swimming; ice skating and snowmobiling nearby

ACCOMMODATIONS: None at area, 6000 rooms in vicinity; Contact for information - Heavenly Reservations, P. O. Box 822, South Lake Tahoe, Calif. 95705.

LOCATION: Nearest major city - Reno and San Francisco; Nearest airports - South Lake Tahoe and Reno.

ATMOSPHERE: A general cross-section of the skiing public spreads out across this huge area, and apres-skiers go gaming in the casinos and enjoy big-name entertainment from sundown right around the clock.

Timberline Lodge
OREGON

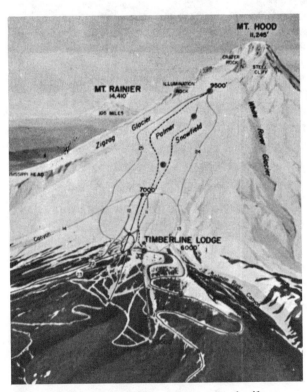

This massive wooden structure, built as a WPA project in the Thirties and remarkable for its tremendous beam timbers and half-ton door, is the focal point of Mt. Hood skiing. Snow-Cats take experts Waaay up for fantastic runs; racing schools operate here in the summer.

THE MOUNTAIN: Altitude - 11,246'; Vertical drop - 6000'; Exposure - South; Annual snowfall - 18'; Longest trail - 7 mi.; Slopes and trails - 5 exp., 12 int., 4 nov.

LIFTS: 3 double chairs, 2 pomas, 3 ropes; Fees - $6.50 weekends and weekdays.

SKI SCHOOL: Bud Nash, director; 75 instructors, American and French techs.; Cost of lessons - 2-hr. group, $4; 1-hr. private, $10.

FACILITIES AND SERVICES: Ski shop, rentals, cafeteria, restaurant, 2 bars, entertainment weekends and holidays; children's nursery (min. age, 2 yrs.).

ADDITIONAL SPORTS AT AREA: Ski-bobbing, swimming, whirly-birds.

ACCOMMODATIONS: 250 at area; Write for information - Timberline Lodge, Government Camp, Oregon 97028.

LOCATION: Nearest town - Government Camp; Nearest major city - Portland; Nearest airport - Portland.

ATMOSPHERE: The skiing is great, but the lodge is The Greatest. The atmosphere is simply *being* there. Nightlife is (on occasion) swinging.

Crystal Mountain
WASHINGTON

Washington State's Cascade Mountain Range is the setting for one of the Northwest's finest snow mountains, next door to Mount Rainier. The long season, stretching into May, gives Crystal some of the nation's finest spring skiing, providing the chance for advanced skiers to get out into the accessible high untracked valleys.

THE MOUNTAIN: Altitude - 4400' to 6872'; Vertical drop - 2472'; Exposure - North; Annual snowfall - 12'; Longest trail - 2½ mi.; Slopes and trails - 7 exp., 8 int., 6 nov., 2 x-c; Total acreage - 4500; Snow-making machinery; Night skiing.

LIFTS: 4 double chairs, 1 T-bar, 9 ropes; Fees - $6.50 weekends, $5 weekdays.

SKI SCHOOL: Jack Nagel, director; 200 instructors, "Nagel" technique; Cost of lessons - 2-hr. group, $5; 1-hr. private, $10.

FACILITIES AND SERVICES: Ski shop, rentals, cafeteria, restaurant, bar, nightclub, entertainment; children's nursery (min. age, 6 mos.).

ADDITIONAL SPORTS AT AREA: Swimming, ski-bobbing, snowmobiling.

ACCOMMODATIONS: 1060 beds at base, others in vicinity; Contact for information - Crystal Mountain Reservations, Crystal Mountain, Wash. 98022.

LOCATION: Nearest town - Enumclaw, Wash.; Nearest major city - Seattle; Nearest airport - Seattle-Tacoma.

ATMOSPHERE: Crystal boasts some of the best terrain in the Northwest and the most extensive area accommodations anywhere, attracting a cross-section of the skiing public.

Mt. Alyeska
ALASKA

Skiing on top of the world, at Alyeska (pronounced "Aley-eska"), is a bit different from anywhere in the "lower 49." A glacier above the chairlift preserves the slopes for year-round, MILD-WEATHER, low-altitude skiing.

THE MOUNTAIN: Altitude - 341' to 2400'; Vertical drop - 2200'; Exposure - North and South; Annual snowfall - 30'; Longest trail - 2 mi.; Slopes and trails - 5 exp. (6 mi.), 4 int. (6 mi.), 4 nov. (4 mi.), 2 x-c; Total acreage - 850; Night skiing.

LIFTS: 1 double chairlift, 1 poma, 3 ropes, 1 cable; Fees - $7 weekends, $5 weekdays.

SKI SCHOOL: Sepp Weber, director; 15 instructors, Austrian, French, and American techs.; Cost of lessons - 2-hr. group, $6.50; 1-hr. private, $10.

FACILITIES AND SERVICES: Ski shop, rentals, cafeteria, restaurant, 3 bars, entertainment on weekends; children's nursery (Wed., Sat. and Sun.; min. age, 6 mo.).

ADDITIONAL SPORTS AT AREA: Ice skating, ski-bobbing, snowmobiling, swimming.

ACCOMMODATIONS: 100 at area; Write for information - Mt. Alyeska Ski Resort, Girdwood, Alaska 99587.

LOCATION: Nearest town - Girdwood; Nearest major city - Anchorage; Nearest airport - Anchorage.

ATMOSPHERE: Not as rugged as you might think, Alyeska attracts an international set with the added inducement of fly-ins to the high glacier fields, dog-sled expeditions, and other adventures to write home about.

Mont Tremblant
CANADA

"Trembling Mountain" is *the* ski mountain of Eastern Canada's Laurentians, and it is the star around which the lesser satellites of the area revolve. It is the backyard "hill" of Mont Tremblant Lodge, a grandfather among "total ski resorts," and what a hill! There is, literally, something for every kind of skier and apres-skier.

THE MOUNTAIN: Altitude - 3001'; Vertical drop - 2200'; Exposure - S.W. and N.E.; Longest trail - 4 mi.; Slopes and trails - 5 exp., 14 int., 3 nov., 20 mi. x-c; Snowmaking machinery on 300 acres.

LIFTS: 2 single chairs, 3 double chairs, 5 T-bars; Fees - $5.50 weekdays, $6 weekends.

SKI SCHOOL: Georges Vigeant, director; 35 instructors, Canadian tech.; Cost of lessons - 2-hr. group, $4; 1-hr. single, $10.

FACILITIES AND SERVICES: Ski shop, rentals, 2 cafeterias, 2 restaurants, 3 bars, coffee shop.

ADDITIONAL SPORTS AT AREA: Ice skating, snowmobiling.

ACCOMMODATIONS: 400 at lodge, 1200 in vicinity; Contact for information - Mont Tremblant Lodge, Mont Tremblant, Que., Canada.

LOCATION: Nearest town - St. Jovite; Nearest major city - Montreal; Nearest airport - Montreal.

ATMOSPHERE: This old-fashioned French-Canadian village is wide-awake at night, with drinking, music, and dancing ranging from quiet through merry to frenzied.

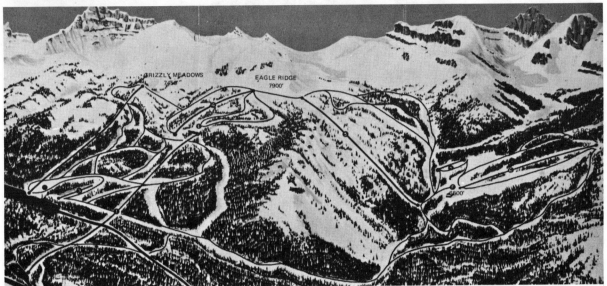

Lake Louise
CANADA

Excitement in the Lake Louise area of Banff National Park starts right on the Trans Canada Highway, 36 miles west of the town of Banff, with the lower terminal just off the traffic lanes and soaring high above beautiful Lake Louise.

THE MOUNTAIN: Altitude - 5000′ to 10,000′; Vertical drop - 5000′; Annual snowfall - 11′; Longest trail - 2 mi.; Slopes and trails - 2 nov., a number of int. and exp.; lots of ski mountaineering above lifts.

LIFTS: 1 gondola, 2 double chairs, 1 T-bar, 2 pomas, 1 pony lift; Fees - $6 daily.

SKI SCHOOL: Mike Wegler, director; 30 instructors, Canadian Ski Alliance tech.; Cost of lessons - 2-hr. group, $4; 1-hr. private, $8-$10.

FACILITIES AND SERVICES: Ski shop, rentals, cafeteria.

ADDITIONAL SPORTS: Ice skating, snowmobiling, swimming nearby.

ACCOMMODATIONS: 2000 beds in 35-mi. radius; Contact for information - Banff-Lake Louise Chamber of Commerce, P. O. Box 1298, Banff, Alberta, Can.

LOCATION: Nearest town - Banff; Nearest major city and airport - Calgary.

ATMOSPHERE: First and foremost there are the beautiful Canadian Rockies, lying under deep powder. After-ski life centers around the Banff Springs Hotel that caters to the skier and brings in top-notch entertainment. Otherwise, it's a 35-mile trek into Banff, a town with lots of enthusiasm.

by **Marilyn Levin**
and **Jess Maxwell**

RAISE HIGH THE WINTER-HOME ROOFBEAMS, CARPENTER

Pros and cons of owning a second home

Every weekend before you go skiing, do you spend an hour and a half packing the car?

When you take a winter vacation, does it cost you an arm and a leg for accommodations?

Do you have a family that likes to divide its time between skiing, snowmobiling, and sleeping?

Is your business getting big enough so you don't have to be there every waking minute?

Does your mother-in-law refuse to keep the kids while you and the wife sneak away to Tahoe for the weekend?

Does your wife refuse to keep the kids while you sneak away to Tahoe for the weekend?

An affirmative nod to any of the aforementioned means you should read what follows with some degree of attention. Not that what follows will act as a Dr. Clagworth's Cure-All, but it may help make your decision on

a second home a little easier.

Second homes are rapidly becoming a way of life with an ever increasing number of Americans and Canadians. In fact, there are now some 1,700,000 two-home families in just the U.S., and industry estimates say that in about 10 years there'll be over 4,500,-000 such families. And they're not necessarily the ones who have all the money. That's due in large part to the availability of pre-built homes. Homes that you buy in a store one day, and if you're lucky, have assembled on your lot before too many other days pass.

These homes come in all sizes and shapes, and range in price from $3,500 for a contemporary "A" frame, all the way to $44,-000 for a contemporary mini-mansion.

But, in either case, you can expect a home that isn't going to creak and bend with every wind that comes along. You can also expect a home as versatile and well equipped as the one you use most of the time. That is, if you're willing to pay for the work savers.

Things like washing machines, dryers, dishwashers, refrigerators, carpeting and TV sets just aren't included in the purchase price. But if there's a touch of horse trader in you, you might be able to get away with a real Finnish stove for your sauna.

These homes are available in most cities, and can be constructed on most sites with a minimum of time and trouble on your part. They eliminate architects, blue prints, and price haggling with plumbers, masons and carpenter.

One thing you might remember though, before you rush out and have one of these beauties sent to your lot in Northern British Columbia, is that the fab-

Building on or near ski slopes is usually an expensive proposition, but the convenience and the improvement in your life-style may be worth it.

ricating company usually charges you by the mile when calculating shipping costs.

It also behooves you to be a little talented with a hammer and saw. That is, if you're interested in taking advantage of one of the better reasons to buy a pre-built. That reason is called a "shell home."

Of course, there's always the possibility you'd rather leave the pre-builts to someone else and do all the building yourself.

If that's your bag, you're immediately faced with three major tasks. First, you have to find a site, or a lot. Second, you have to have plans drawn to fit. And third, you have to find a builder to put it together.

But, if the custom second home is the route you decide to follow

anyway, there are a few guidelines you can consider that could save some headaches.

First ask yourself, "how much can I afford?" Most property—with or without a structure on it — can be mortgaged. Land itself can be bought under a land contract, due and payable within two to seven years.

Fine. Then, you say, once you own the property, you'll build. This is the route many people choose to go. But don't forget, you'll be paying a lot of interest for those seven years. Example: Let's say you've selected a lot that costs $3,800. If you can pay cash, you'll probably get a discount and save maybe 10 per cent plus interest charges. But if you can only put $500 down on the lot, you'll have a balance of $3,300. That'll set you back about $50 a month with a seven-year land contract. Maybe the interest will be computed at seven

per cent annually. Over those seven years, you'll be paying $884.04 in interest, so actually the lot will be costing you $4,684.04. And don't forget the yearly taxes, assessments and fees you'll have to pay. But all that is not as bad as it sounds.

If your lot is in a good area, it'll probably appreciate quite a bit in those seven years.

Next question is, "where do I want to buy?" Maybe you've got a good idea already. But do you want to be within a few hours via freeway? Or within a few hours by jet?

OK, you say, I've decided on the general area. Now how do I actually find this place in the sun? Start writing some letters. To the local chamber of commerce in the general area you are interested. To ski area operators. To forestry or park officials. To real estate brokers. Subscribe to local newspapers. Buy outdoor

publications, if your state has them. Then, once an area begins to sound promising, plan a trip to it. Take along the wife and kids, as they'll play a big part in your decision. Plan to stay a few days. Roam around. Talk to people. Get a feel of the place.

And to help your decision along, there are certain people you can write to:

Real estate brokers. Much of the property in the vicinity of developed ski areas is privately owned. And much of it is listed by local realtors.

Developers. Development corporations may be found active near ski areas in almost every state. Normally, they purchase a large tract of land, install utilities and roads, plus maybe a swimming pool and clubhouse, then offer subdivided building sites. If you're looking for a recreation-oriented community, with a high probable resale or investment

value, this might be for you. But make sure the developer preserves the natural beauty of the area and does what he promises. Check out his references with banks, the local chamber of commerce, the Better Business Bureau, and with local citizens who've been around the area for awhile.

Lumbering companies. If you look carefuly, you might be able to locate a cabin site on lands owned by a lumber company. Each firm has its own policy about selling or leasing logged-over land, but it's worth checking out. Your state government can probably provide names and addresses to contact in your area of interest.

Tax lands. Try the county assessor at the county seat for lists of tax delinquent lands. Such property is usually sold by auction several times yearly.

Here are a few things you

Popular condominium life as led (from left) at Taos, N.M., Mittersill, N.H. and Winter Park, Colo.

should consider:

Accessibility. Is the property on year-round roads? That's a must for skiers. Is the road well-maintained? Does it slope? Sloping roads make it hard to get in and out in spring, fall and winter. Who maintains the road? You?

Location. Do you have a view of your favorite ski run? Or of a lake or stream? Remember, you'll be spending a lot of hours in your cabin. You won't care to look at the city dump or at a collection spot for well-used cars. Is the lot well situated to take advantage of the sun? Is it private? Protected from wind?

Utilities. Will you have to drill a well? Is city water available? If you'll need a well, make sure the water is tested for purity. Is sewerage service available or will you require a septic tank? Have

a perk test made on your soil before purchase. Is electricity available? Natural gas? All this may sound like too much detail, but thoroughness now could save you hundreds of dollars later.

Costs of building. Naturally, if you pick some remote spot near, say, Vail Pass in Colorado, it's going to cost you more to build than the suburbs of Denver. So check to determine where you can get building materials and the cost of transportation to your site. And don't forget labor. It's expensive anywhere, but out in the woods or mountains, well — it ain't cheap.

So friends, now that you've seen what can be involved in this second home thing, why not go back and re-read our questions at the beginning of the article. If you can still wholeheartedly answer "yes" to them, you and another home might really deserve each other.

"Gelandesprung" means "terrain jump" in German and excitement for skiers who like the feeling of being airborne. With ordinary alpine skis and poles, jumpers use the natural bumps for the lift-off and soar as far as 200 feet or more before they're down to earth again. The National Gelande competition held every spring in Alta, Utah, brings out entrants in professional and amateur categories divided into several age groups. There are 11-year-olds and younger who can match the pros with flights of 180 feet.

LOOK AT THEM LEAP

If downhill racing is the ultimate happening with gravity, then powder skiing is the ultimate aesthetic-sensual involvement with the primal elements of the sport, natural snow and an unprepared mountain.

Practice slopes and commercial ski trails are stepping stones into the mountains. Race courses are demonstration and performance arenas; playgrounds and gladiatorial fields. The idea is to learn to ski well enough to venture into the mountains and ski in snow.

You face that long, long steep slope all covered with deep, deep light snow, and the sun has just broken through to make it all sparkle, and there it all is, all smooth and deep with not a mark in it and you don't know if it will slide or not but you don't think so, so you go anyway and it doesn't, and it's so deep and light it comes up your chest and rolls over your shoulders and in your face and you don't see anything but snow but keep on skiing anyway even after it's over your head because even if it is a slide there's not much you can do about it now so might as well keep on skiing until something happens. And then you make it through into the sun again and it's not a slide, but because you get to laughing, laughing so hard at the feel of the snow and the sound and the rhythm and the synchronization of it all, you blow it three turns from the bottom and let yourself fall into it without even trying to recover.

But commercials for deep powder are like trying to advertise the most beautiful woman you know; she certainly doesn't need it, and you're not at all sure you want everybody to know, anyway.

Because the resistance to motion offered by anything over about 10 inches of new snow is such that most commercial ski slopes are rendered quite useless, the search for deep powder skiing inevitably leads one onto the steepest slopes that will hold snow; the narrowest chutes and the tightest lines through the trees. And because of this necessity to ski the steepest and sometimes narrowest and most challenging terrain, it is absolutely essential to develop a technique that results in the maximum control, stability and precision.

Just as there are many marginal varieties of natural snow other than perfectly crystalline dry powder, so there are many ways of skiing the powder, all of them more or less adequate to one or another set of conditions, until the maximum values of slope and snow depth are encountered. It is here that inability to control speed without expending large amounts of useless energy and consequent brutalization of the elements has led to the development of the so-called Black Orpheus Mellow Yellow Submarine Technique.

The essential principle of this technique is to let the resistance of the snow against the shovels of the skis cause them to flex of their own accord without the necessity of unweighting. This allows the skis to remain down in the snow at all times, and prevents the awkward porpoising action and abrupt acceleration-deceleration, "toe-stubbing," rhythm of

Skiing the Deep and Steep

An introduction to some of the risky, but rewarding,
problems of handling untracked powder, and how to overcome them with the
Black Orpheus Mellow Yellow Submarine Technique—no kidding

by Bob Chamberlain

more conventional techniques.

As to equipment, it is essential to use a ski having a very soft tip in order that the snow will be able to do the work of flexing the ski by itself. A short ski, 205 or less, with a broad, flexible shovel will stay down under the snow at all times, yet be capable of stability at moderate speeds. A short slalom ski with the softest possible tips, or an extremely soft downhill ski are other reasonable possibilities. When the snow is deep enough to become bottomless, the skis are free to dive deep or plane upward, seeking their own level in a truly three-dimensional medium, according to the speed of travel desired. You will find that the stiffer the ski, and/or the "stiffer" the snow, the more you must exert some positive muscular effort to cause the tips to flex properly. But in ideal conditions of light, dry powder, 10 inches or more in depth, the pressure of the snow alone should be sufficient in itself to cause the ski tips to flex, and, with the addition of lateral knee action to direct them, to turn, virtually without effort.

Thus the skier, descending a slope in deep powder, appears from below to be perfectly still, with only ski tips and knees oscillating in slow motion, punctuated by the leisurely planting of alternate poles.

DEEP POWDER TECHNIQUE Technically speaking, skiing in powder is simpler and easier than skiing on the piste. Learning to ski in the powder is in some measure un-learning certain reflexes built up through drill team maneuvers on practice slope gymnasium freeways.

If you are fortunate enough to learn to ski in an area that cannot afford mechanical packing equipment, or has the rare insight to use it judiciously on bad days, there is yet a possibility that you may learn to ski in snow from the very beginning.

Find, if you can, a gentle slope of uncut fresh snow, small and forgotten as it may be, and ride your skis straight downhill through the uncut snow—simply let yourself take a straight schuss down the fall line without doing anything. Let your skis take you on a trip. Give your attention to the feel of the snow resisting your skis and how they can only accelerate to a certain terminal speed regardless of the length of the slope. The depth of the snow and its resistance thus becomes your first source of control. Do not "sit back," regardless of how many times you have heard the old adage. Sitting back merely causes the tips to rise to the surface and scissor outward. Simply ride the skis through the snow evenly weighted dead center and parallel. Let

the snow grab at the tips if it wants to—push back against the resistance with your poles and blast on through.

Simply searching for beautiful patches of snow to let your skis trip through can involve you in the essence of powder skiing from the very first day. Running from a packed slope into a patch of powder and out again is an excellent way to make the transition to powder skiing, and it is here that most skiers have their downfall, begin to curse the beautiful elements, berate themselves unnecessarily, and call for the packing crew to be brought in. The key to this situation is that the skis must enter the snow exactly parallel in order to absorb the shock of deceleration dead center and head on with the flexible tips and shovels of the skis. The same principle applies to transitions, deep drifts, hidden moguls, buried logs, and any other irregular obstacles that may be encountered. As long as they are met perfectly straight on with skis parallel, the shock will be absorbed under the shovels and tips of the skis, and the worst that can obtain is coming to an abrupt and sudden stop, but still perfectly balanced on both skis.

Perhaps the strongest technical difference between packed and powder skiing, and the one most troublesome to advanced intermediate skiers, is that no edging is used in powder. Rather, the skis are skied flat as nearly as possible all the time. The instinct of edge-set built up in packed skiing must be replaced by that of flattening the ski to allow it freedom of lateral movement while buried in the snow, and applying tip pressure to fix the ski against the resistance of the snow. Thus control of the ski is shifted from edge-setting to "tip-flexing."

Another major change that occurs in powder skiing is one of timing. Due to the resistance of the snow and because every effort is made to keep the skis under the surface, they do not accelerate rapidly as one approaches the fall-line out of a traverse position. When the skis have entered the fall line one must wait quietly for them to pick up sufficient momentum with which to work the flexibility of the ski against the resistance of the snow. In so doing one may travel a considerable distance in the fall-line without anything happening. Time seems to slow down, turning and pole planting take on the tempo of an ultra-slow motion movie. Herein lies one of the hidden joys of deep powder skiing—the experience of time distortion or time suspension through motion—a relativity effect, the fourth dimension sensuously experienced.

Thus any given slope is effectively flattened out by a fall of deep snow, to the extent that above 10 or 12 inches even a formidable ski area can be reduced to novice and cross-country terrain. It is for this reason that the search for true deep powder skiing leads one inevitably onto the steepest slopes available, terrain that requires the utmost in control to be skied at all, and it is the achievement of this degree of control that elevated the submarine technique above all others.

The submarine body position can be described as keeping your back straight, chin tucked into chest, sitting in a chair that isn't there, toes curled up towards shins, and heels kept tucked back underneath the chair. Of these, the most important, strangely enough, is keeping the chin tucked into the chest. For keeping the chin tucked in automatically insures that the back is kept straight, but also gives one the all-important proper visual orientation directly down the fall-line of a very steep slope.

Starting at the top of a very steep slope in deep

"You get to laughing so hard at the feel of the snow and the sound and the synchronization of it all, you blow it three turns from the bottom . . . "

snow, the first operation is that of getting into the fall-line as directly as possible. If the snow is deep enough this means sticking the tails of the skis into the slope with tips projecting outward over the slope. Push off, assume the proper body position, concentrating visually directly down the fall line, and allow the skis to sink deeply into the snow. As they do, and the tips and shovels begin to flex upward from the resistance to the snow, begin to roll the knees to one side. This transforms the flex of the ski into an arc to one side, and the skis will turn in that direction. A split second before the extreme point of the arc is reached, the knees should begin rolling the opposite direction. This releases the ski from its arc and allows it to slowly return to the fall-line. As the fall line is reached the knees roll in the opposite direction, the skis are flexed into a new arc, and a "turn" in the opposite direction is described. More properly, there are not a series of turns at all, but rather one long serpentine track of continuous motion from top to bottom. It is essential that the rolling action of the knees remains continuous and uninterrupted, so that the skis continue to arc from side to side while the direction of motion remains directly down the fall-line, as fixed by visual concentration on the movie one is making through one's own eyes. As the snow begins to surge higher and higher, it is important to remember to breathe through one's nose, so as to keep from choking on inhaled snow or irritating one's dental work, both factors which may severely inhibit one's undersnow time. During the time one is completely submarining, there is little sense of time or motion, and it is important to remember to retain the proper body position and continue the serpentine motions uninterrupted. When lack of oxygen begins to be a problem, by all means surface for a look around.

Finally, when returning to the bottom of the mountain, do not expect your friends to give much credence to your tales.

BE CAREFUL Since the search for deep snow and steep terrain takes the skier inevitably into avalanche territory, we may as well admit at the outset that deep powder skiing is synonymous with skiing avalanche slopes, or at least potential avalanche slopes.

It therefore behooves the prospective powder hound to learn at least the rudiments of avalanche lore and safety, before blundering blindly into the vast white ocean. I would also point out that you need advance permission or good connections or

*"As the snow begins
to surge higher and higher, it is
important to remember to
breathe through one's nose, so as to
keep from choking
on inhaled snow, or irritating
one's dental work."*

some other legitimate reason than your own pleasure to embark on untracked parts of most mountains, without which you risk losing your season lift ticket if you get caught.

I recommend that anyone seriously interested in the subject read the U.S. Forest Service Publication, **"Snow Avalanches,"** at least those of you who have not yet gone so far into McLuhan as to be unable to focus on the printed word. This booklet does as much as any to expose the nature of snow as a plastic medium, subject to the laws of stress and compression, creep and shear; and furnishes a good general intuition of the physics of snow and its metamorphosis through time, temperature, and load pressure changes, as well as the standard routines of avalanche control and rescue.

For tales of sheer horror, I recommend Colin Fraser's, **The Avalanche Enigma.** This fine $9 volume makes highly interesting reading, but unfortunately, aside from recommending the efficiency of the Parsenn Ski Patrol, does little to enlighten the deep snow enthusiast as to how to make use of his own faculties in coming to terms with the elements.

Indeed, if we were to make the general orientation of both volumes very literally, we would be forced to conclude that deep snow skiing on potential avalanche slopes outside the boundaries of commercial ski areas is sheer lunacy, and a highly questionable one within them.

This general avalanche paranoia also seems to be the prevailing philosophy among most, though thankfully not all, ski area personnel and sign painters.

When the largest commercially advertised powder skiing area in the United States is completely enclosed by fencing festooned with avalanche warning signs, and actively policed for violations and punitive measures duly dispensed, it is perhaps not uncharitable to make certain comparisons with a similarly conceived and managed large California cattle-feeding operation.

It remains for ski area personnel in general to become better informed on the possibilities offered by modern avalanche control methods and equipment, but above all the desirability and even necessity of utilizing such tools due to the advanced state and scope of the art of powder skiing. Yesterday's corniced headwall, awesome couloir, abandoned mine dump, and open alpine cirque are tomorrow's free powder skiing areas. The time has arrived to learn to stabilize such areas instead of forbidding them.

In the meantime, the skier should develop, on his own, some general tactics on skiing deep snow in potential avalanche terrain.

Ski in the trees during a storm. Some of the best snow is to be had while it is snowing, but it is best to stay off open slopes until some time after the weather has cleared. One needs the trees for visibility, since on an open slope in a snowstorm there is no way to tell where you are, how fast you are going, which way is up or down, or whether you are moving at all. Complete vertigo is the result, so unless for some reason that's your trip, stay in the trees until the storm is over.

When the snow has settled enough to think about confronting a wide open slope, approach the slope from the very top if at all possible, rather than entering at an intermediate point part way down.

Test the snow pack by jamming a ski pole down into the snow. This will reveal any crust or slab situation that has developed under or along with a fall of new snow. Ideally, one should know the seasonal history of the snowpack typical of the area, at least in outline form, so as to make an intelligent estimate of what one is about to ski on, in, or through.

Stomp with the skis and/or make a shallow traverse through a small section of the snowpack. This will bring further information as to the underlying strata, and under certain conditions settle a section of the snowpack around you, or occasionally, trigger a slide below you if the snow is highly unstable. Surface sluffs are common under these conditions, and are not necessarily negative indications for overall stability.

If explosives are available, they are the surest means of getting an answer in this situation, and properly used, will either settle and stabilize the snowpack or release it as an avalanche. Regardless of technique employed, the object is to get an answer, one way or the other, if it is possible to get one.

Having thoroughly investigated and tested the

*"Ego trips
are definitely out of place
in the mountains."*

snowpack, re-estimate the overall situation as to snow and terrain and attempt to come to some clear feeling for the degree of danger to which you are submitting yourself. If your intuitions are negative at this point, do not hesitate to ski elsewhere. Ego trips are definitely out of place in the mountains.

Finally, **WAIT** for a few moments to make certain that your activities have not produced some delayed action in the snowpack.

If the situation seems on the whole positive, visualize where the potential slide path might likely be and pick a line down the slope which will utilize such natural safety points as groups of trees or rocks as exist, and have in mind where the exits, if any, are.

Pick a line and stick to it. Ski only in the fall line if possible, keeping your eyes open and your mouth shut.

If you set off an avalanche, it may simply slide away below you, although the more common occurrence is to find that the snow all around you is beginning to move and break up into blocks and you feel it sifting away from beneath your skis like a giant sieve. Under these circumstances, there is very little else to do except ride with the slide, stay upright if possible, and attempt to counteract the sieve action under your skis by making tiny "feather" stepping motions which allow the snow to sift downward while keeping your skis relatively near the surface. If the slide is a small one, you may find that you have simply come to a sudden halt completely encased in concrete up to your waist; but if the slide continues to grow and deepen around you, the best advice seems to be to drop your poles and swim for it—it being the surface.

As the slide comes to a halt, the snow will almost instantly freeze tight, so an effort should be made to free a hand above the surface or protect your face, or both. If in fact you are buried, the most important consideration is to obtain a breathing space, however small, and above all to conserve energy, especially energy of mind, while your companions (don't go into the deep powder boondocks without at least one) thoughtfully begin rescue operations.

On the whole, however, direct and meaningful experience with avalanches seems to be a fairly rare commodity, despite the profusion of horror stories available at every hand, and it seems quite possible for the deep powder skier to live a long and active life without the necessity of undergoing such exotic stimulation.

Above all, an efficient program of snow stabilization with modern tools and explosives, coupled with an educated intuitional sense for the nature and movement of the elements, should open the mountains more fully to one of the more elegant experiences of which man is capable: the Deep and the Steep.

TO: ALL MEMBERS OF THE BLACK AND BLUE SKI CLUB

FROM: MARILYN SMITH (GEORGE'S WIFE()

RE: ALL SKI CLUB CABIN RULES

As the ski season again approaches, and in view of the few minor problems we had
last season. George decided we would issue rules for the cabin this season. (even
though we're not sure Ted and Sue Davidson were divorced ONLY because of thecabin
enough of us were called to testify to convince us that some new rules should be ^
MADE & ENFORCED?

If the rules seem harsh. please remember that after the fire last year. the Cold
County fire marshall DEMANDED certain revisions of our procedures. Also. if you have
any question--please be sure to call me. (most of you know that although George is
Cabin Manager. I am really in charge--he has never been responsible about anything!)

A. RESERVATIONS
1. No member shall arrive without a confirmed reservation, his IBM reservation
card. and club identification card. and the usual Upper arm tattoo of all Balck and Blues
2. We take members first, then guests, then new members who are trying to make
their compulsory trip to the cabin. (If your reservation is confirmed and one of
the "old gang" shows up, you may be asked to leave. After all, sebiority is important.)
3. All reservations shall be confirmed not later tham midnight Friday.
4. Guestfee is $% per night. payable by member to Cabin Manager ('s wife.)
    5.50

B. ROOMING
1. All rooms have 14 bunk beds, and all beds are numbered 1 through 14.
2. Specific beds may be requested by number, bottom bunks are even-numbered.
3. All the men£s dorms are downstairs, girls are up. (No exceptions!)

C. Arrivals
1. All members holding confirmed reservations ahall arrive no later than 10 PM on
Friday. (For those whose reservations are confirmed ■ after 10 PM. and arrive after
the deadline--a late fee of £1 shall be imposed. ($2.40 in American money.)
2. Members should arrive quietly respecting those members already asleep.
3. NO lights shall be turned on FOR ANY REASON after 10 PM. Flashlights are
approved, but they .must be inspect3d and stamped approved by Cabin Manager('s wife.)

D. qWORK DETAILS (This Is Important- READ CAREFULLY.)
1. Each bed number corresponds to a work duty. Before you leave for skiing on
Saturday. you must complete the duty; thave the Cabin Manager('s wife) inspect job
and initial IBM card. You may not reenter cabin wthout initialed IBM card.
2. If your duty is too time consuming to allow Saturday skiing. you must make
arrangements to have IBM card initialed when Cabin Manager('s wife) returns from
skiing--and before her dinner. (remember. you may not leave the cabin until done.)
3. If duty is not satisfactoriely completed member shall re-do work until it
is approved. (If your duty requires skilled labor. you may hire workmen--but the
job must be completed by dinner. If you are assigned re-wiring or plumbing work,
and don£t know how to do it--PLEASE hire help. We all remember last year£s flood.)

B'16!

E. MEALS

1. Cabin shall provide breakfast a ddinner. but no lunch on weekends.
2. All members shall east these meals unless spedial permission is given to
visit another cabin or restaurant. (The IBM reservation card must be punched to
indicate &meal out" or members sahll be be alloed to leave cabin in the evening.)
3. Because of fire regulations. no cookin shall be don in or near premises.
4. Breakfast: 6:00 to 6:15; Dinner 4:00 to 4:10. Members arrivin more than
4 minutes late shall be charged a @late fee" not to exceed $% per three minutex.)
    10.00

F. PRICES
   1. One night lodging: $3.00 member. $7.00 guests
   2. Breakfast: $6.50 members. $11.00 guests
   3. Dinner: $10.00 members. $16.00 guests
   4. WEEKEND SPECIAL: 2 nights. 2 breakfasts. 1 dinner. $ 4.50 ~~$16.00~~ members
$16.00 guests.
   5. Mid week rates available on request from Cabin Manager ('s wife.) Special
rates are offered to old friends. all new members pay regular rates.
   6. Member£s holding the "1,000 nights" card (those who have used the cabin
1,000 nights or more. are entitled to a 88 % discount on all quoted prices.
   7. All fees shall be paid to Cabin Manager('s wife) by cashier's Certified
check immed ately upon arrival. any laTe fees. conduct fines. or othet expenses
incurred during the weekend shall be paid by Certified check before departure.
(Banks are availablel in Frozen. 175 miles west of cabin.) We take traveler£s checks

G. CABIN RULES (NO EXCEPTIONS! except for "OLD GANG")
   1. NO SMOKING in or near premises.
   2. No liquor shall be consumed from glass containers. (all cups must be OK£d)
   3. Windows sall be left open at all timesto profide escape routes in case of
fire. Ropes are coiled near w ndows for the prupose of evacuating upper stories.)
   4. Members sleeping in the part of the cabin destrooyed by fire shall noticē
thatwalls have not been replaced; this shoould facilitate exit.
   5. Card games played for money shall not exceed $5,000 table limit. (Those
wishing to play cards shall report to Manager or Wife for complete imspection--
NO FIREARMS are allowed in the cabin. (Remember Tom and Frank--poor Tom.)
   6. No abusive language. (A list of all forbidden words appears in bathrooms.)
   7. No drugs shall be taken. All pills will be turned in to Cabin Manager('s wife)
for dispensing during weekend.
   8. Domestic quarrels shallnot be aired. (Husbands and wifes are discouraged
from using cabin simultaneously. This has simply not worked out in the past.)

H. APPROVED DRESS CODE
   1. Membersshall not leave bedrooms or bathrooms without adequate covering of
entire boday. (Towels arenot adequage.)
   2. All members shall wear shirts. showes and socks at all times.
   3. Clothoing shall be neat and clean.
   4. Men arw to wear conservative colors and fabrics. Hawaiian shirts. striped
slacks or bell-bottom pants are not acceptable.
   5. Women may wear slacks or modest dresses. Mini-skir£s, see-throggh shirts,
and all other clothing deemed "provocative" by the majority of women (of age 40)
present shall not be acceptable. (Men are not to judge propriety of ladie£s wear.)

I. All discussion and donversations shall concern skiing only. No politics,
religion) peace) ethnic) or other controversial subjects shall be aired publicly.

J. No newspapers. news magaines or other inflammatory literature shall be read.

K. Anhy infraction of the above rules shall result in immediate dismissal and
possible court action against ex-member.

We are looking for ward to another fun-filled. sun-filled ski season with the B & B£

Skiingly yours,

M. Smith. Cabin Manager('s wife.)

TOM IS MEEN.

(SORRY, BUT WE ALL HAVE KIDS!)

Established in 1954 as a permanent place of honor for skiing greats, the National Ski Hall of Fame in Ishpeming, Michigan, also serves as a central collection point for display of trophies, records, and historical data related to skiing.

Four men were named to the Hall of Fame in 1956. Since then a total of 108 men and women in four categories have been named. A special selection procedure took time to evolve between 1954 and 1956 and has been reviewed again several times since. The election of the 108th member, the legendary Snowshoe Thompson *(pictured opposite in non-ski attire)* took place at the 1970 U.S. Ski Ass'n convention.

The program operates in four categories, each carrying equal honor. SKI ATHLETES must be at least 40 years of age at time of selection, but this requirement can be waived on grounds of pre-eminence and skill, and has recently been waived for Holmenkollen winner John Bower and World Cup Winner Nancy Greene, both of whom were still in their twenties when elected.

SKISPORT BUILDERS are those who have contributed to the sport in North America at the divisional, national, and international level, or in combination with competitive careers. The POSTHUMOUS category honors both builders and athletes and combinations. The FOREIGN category includes athletes and builders who have contributed to the sport in North America.

Owned by the USSA, the two-story building of the Hall of Fame and historical museum was built at a cost of more than $50,-000 and was dedicated on February 21, 1954. Burton H. Boyum, one of the leaders in the drive to establish the institution, became the first Hall of Fame curator.

THE NATIONAL SKI HALL OF FAME

IN HONOR OF GREATNESS